SPEECH AND THE HEARING-IMPAIRED CHILD: THEORY AND PRACTICE

Daniel Ling, Ph.D.

Speech and the Hearing-Impaired Child: Theory and Practice

The Alexander Graham Bell Association for the Deaf, Inc.
3417 Volta Place, N.W., Washington, D.C. 20007, U.S.A.

Library of Congress Catalogue Card Number 76-21920
ISBN 0-88200-074-8

*This Book Is Dedicated to the Many
Hearing-Impaired Children Who Extended
My Skills as I Taught Them, and to Parents
Who Want Their Children to Talk.*

Preface

This book is about speech and its acquisition by hearing-impaired children. As such, it is concerned with the form rather than with the content of spoken language—with phonetics and phonology rather than with morphology, syntax, and semantics. It does not, however, ignore language. It concentrates on how to overcome the inadequacies of speech generally associated with deafness so that intelligible spoken expression can be achieved. It provides a framework for the systematic development and evaluation of speech target behaviors and the subskills that underlie them, but it recognizes that more than exercises or drills is required if the child is to learn to talk.

This text deals with basic theoretical issues, though it also provides detailed description of strategies that may be used to evoke and develop specific sound patterns. These strategies indicate how thoughtful readers may—through reference to basic principles—program their work to meet the particular needs of the individual child, whether the child suffers moderate, severe, profound, or total deafness. Strategies such as those proposed are necessary, but not sufficient. Beyond them lies the need for dynamic, creative teaching. Similarly, beyond the theories and principles put forward remains the need for further research.

Daniel Ling
Montreal, 1976

Acknowledgments

My thanks are due to R. G. Leckie and F. J. Iliffe, who painstakingly criticized the first draft of the manuscript, and to my colleagues in the McGill School of Human Communication Disorders, especially D. G. Doehring and K. K. Charan, who commented on the first revision, and M. R. Seitz, who discussed many of the chapters with me before, during, and after their preparation. I am grateful to F. Barry for preparing Figure 3.1, to S. J. Naish for typing the final manuscript, preparing other figures and checking the references, and to L. Tenpenny, who typed the first draft of the last chapters. The book was meticulously edited in its entirety by R. L. Wittusen, and designed and produced under the direction of B. L. Donley. I was encouraged to prepare this text by R. F. P. Cronin, Dean, Faculty of Medicine, McGill University, who kindly arranged for me to take a sabbatical leave to begin the writing of it. I also owe thanks to D. J. Leckie, Principal of the Montreal Oral School for the Deaf, who helped me experiment with various aspects of speech teaching and evaluation, to R. Lach, who worked closely with us, and to the entire School staff for their continued cooperation. My greatest debt is to my wife, A. H. Ling, whose expertise and interest in this work helped to shape both my thinking and my writing.

Table of Contents

List of Figures xii
List of Tables xiii

1 **An Introduction and Overview** 1
Scope and Intention of the Text 1
Speech Teaching and Prevailing Standards 6

2 **Studies Relating to Speech Production Among**
Hearing-Impaired Children 11
Studies of Speech Intelligibility 11
Typical Speech Errors of Hearing-Impaired Children . 12
Speech Development and Hearing Level 16
Summary 17

3 **The Sense Modalities in Speech Reception** 22
Auditory Speech Reception 23
Visual Speech Reception 32
Tactile Speech Reception 36
Summary 39

4 **Multisensory Speech Reception** 45
Hearing and Vision 50
Hearing and Touch 51
Vision and Touch 52
Hearing, Vision, and Touch 53
Phonetic Symbolization Systems 54
Signs and Speech 60
Summary 62

5 **Feedback and Feedforward Mechanisms**
in Speech Production 66
Sensory-Motor Reaction Time 67
Sensory-Motor Control 68
Feedforward 69
Articulatory Targets 69
Summary 71

6 The Sense Modalities in Speech
Production 74
   Orosensory-Motor Patterns 74
   Auditory Feedback 77
   Visual Feedback 79
   Summary 83

7 Levels of Speech Acquisition and
Automaticity 86
   Automaticity 89
   Phonetic Level Development 91
   Phonetic-Phonologic Correspondence 95
   Phonologic Level Development 98
   Summary 102

8 Order or Chaos? 105
   The Literature on Teaching Order 107
   Order and Frequency of Occurrence 110
   The Broad Stages of Speech Acquisition: A Sequential
      Framework 112
   Target Behaviors Within Successive Stages 114
   Summary 129

9 Evaluation 135
   Oral-Peripheral Structures and Function 137
   Phonologic Speech Evaluation 144
   Phonetic Level Evaluation 147
   Other Aspects of Evaluation 157
   Summary 159

10 Teaching Order and Evaluation:
A Synthesis and a Model 173
   A Speech Teaching Model 173
   Summary 183

11 Breath and Voice Control 184
   Mechanisms of Breathing 185
   Mechanisms of Voicing 188
   Summary 193

12 Vocalization and Voice Patterns:
Targets, Subskills, and Teaching
Strategies 195
   Spontaneous Vocalization and Vocalization on
      Demand 196
   Voice Patterns: The Bases of Suprasegmental Structure 199
   Remedial Treatment of Deviant Patterns 211

Voice Patterns in Phonologic Speech 215
Summary 217

13 **Vowels and Diphthongs** 220
Acoustic Properties of Vowels and Their Sensory
Correlates 226
Subskills and Teaching Strategies 230
Remedial Treatment of Deviant Patterns 241
Summary 254

14 **Consonants: Their Acoustic Properties**
and Sensory Correlates 258
Manner, Place, and Voicing 261
Summary 281

15 **Manner Distinctions in Consonant**
Production 286
Teaching Step 1: Target Behaviors, Subskills, and
Teaching Strategies Relating to Front Consonants . 295
Summary 315

16 **Place Distinctions in Consonant**
Production 316
Teaching Step 2: Target Behaviors, Subskills, and
Teaching Strategies Relating to Alveolar and Palatal
Sounds 319
Teaching Step 3: Target Behaviors, Subskills, and
Teaching Strategies Relating to Palatal and Velar
Sounds 339
Summary 353

17 **Voiced-Voiceless Distinctions and the**
Treatment of Deviant Consonant
Patterns 354
Teaching Step 4: Target Behaviors, Subskills, and
Teaching Strategies Relating to Voiced-Voiceless
Distinctions 355
The Treatment of Deviant Consonant Patterns 362
Summary 369

18 **Consonant Blends** 370
Word-Initial Blends 372
Word-Final Blends 377
Medial and Interlexical Blends 381
Summary 386

Index of Subjects 389
Index of Authors 395

List of Figures

Figure

3.1   *An audiogram compared to a shoreline.*   24

3.2   *Spectrogram showing the vowels* [u], [a], *and* [i].   29

4.1   *Suggested mechanisms underlying the simultaneous use of the senses in speech reception.*   55

7.1   *The mechanisms employed in the acquisition of spoken language.* . .   87

8.1   *The* [u]-*like effect that results from lip-rounding a central vowel* .   117

10.1   *A seven-stage model for speech acquisition.*   174–175

10.2   *Relationship of target behaviors and subskills to the speech acquisition model.*   177

11.1   *Positions assumed by the vocal cords*   191

13.1   *Spectrograms illustrating voicing, whispering, and breathy voicing of the vowel [ɛ].*   221

13.2   *Spectrograms of vowels with similar* F_1 *frequencies.*   227

13.3   *Spectrograms showing multiple faults of prolongation, neutralization, and nasalization*   253

16.1   *A strategy for the progressive generalization of consonants to all vowel contexts.*   318

List of Tables

Table

1.A   *International Phonetic Alphabet symbols representing speech sounds and modifiers.* 7

4.A   *The types of speech features available through each sense modality* . . 47

8.A   *Teaching order for consonants.* 121

8.B   *Framework for determining the comparative effects of adjacency.* . . . 129

9.A   *Summary of oral-peripheral examination.* 143

9.B   *Summary of phonologic level speech evaluation.* 160

9.C   *Summary of phonetic level speech evaluation.* 163

13.A   *Summary of speech organ adjustments and formant frequency values of the English vowels.* 225

14.A   *Consonants classified according to manner, place, and voicing.* . . . 259

14.B   *The frequency range of variant and invariant acoustic cues in relation to manner and place of production* 275

TO THE READER: To avoid unnecessary formality in style the pronoun "we" has been used throughout this text to refer to the writer. Its use is intended as an indirect acknowledgment of long collaboration with many colleagues who have helped to shape, but cannot be held responsible for, my views. The person who works (or plays) with the child to promote speech is referred to throughout as the "teacher," "she," or "her," although the "teacher" may indeed be of either sex, the child's father or mother, a speech pathologist, an audiologist, or some other person. The child is referred to as such, or by the masculine pronouns "he," or "his," simply in order to distinguish between teacher and child. We apologize if the reader's sensibilities are offended by these somewhat sexist conventions.

/1/

An Introduction and Overview

Scope and Intention of the Text

The purpose of this book is to examine the problems underlying the acquisition of speech by children with various degrees of hearing impairment and to suggest an approach through which increasingly effective speech communication skills may be established. Speech communication skills have long been recognized as being important to the hearing-impaired person who seeks to function independently as a member of society at large—even by those who have primarily advocated the use of signs and fingerspelling (de l'Epée, 1784; Storrs, 1882; Mindel and Vernon, 1971). Speech continues to be encouraged whether hearing-impaired children are taught within the framework of an auditory-oral approach or by means of total communication. Regardless of allegiance to either of these prevailing educational philosophies, the reader should, therefore, find this text of value.

The needs of two groups have been borne in mind: those of the student/teacher/clinician/informed parent who requires a rationale and an organization of material from which to structure a sound educational approach to speech development, and those of the student/researcher who needs to know what relevant work has been done and what type of further work would yield new and substantial information. While certain aspects of speech communication and speech development of hearing-impaired children have been carefully studied and are well documented, other aspects have been barely explored or completely neglected. Accordingly, in order to treat the subject matter coherently, we have had to theorize on the basis of indirect evidence where data is insubstantial and also draw upon informed opinion as well as clinical and teaching experience. The alert reader should have no problem in

1

differentiating statements of fact, opinion, and theory. In providing references we have attempted to indicate where the reader may seek a more detailed treatment of a topic, which workers have made original contributions, and what recent work is relevant. Readers interested in more extensive bibliographies may thus employ the reference material provided as the basis for scanning the Science Citation Index or initiating the search services available through most university libraries.

The history of teaching hearing-impaired children to talk spans several centuries (Hodgson, 1953; Bender, 1960; DiCarlo, 1964); and, as our examination of the literature will show, approaches to speech teaching have been more frequently haphazard and pragmatic than systematic and rational. Over time, many strategies of teaching speech have been proposed. Some have been adopted and have become part of the traditional repertoire of skills used by teachers of the deaf, others have been ignored or abandoned (often for no apparent reason), and many have been adhered to despite their incompatibility with present-day knowledge. This situation led DiCarlo (1964, p. 111) to observe that no theory or model had yet emerged to provide hearing-impaired children with a clear route to better levels of speech acquisition. This text responds to the challenge implicit in DiCarlo's observation, for we have constructed, tested, and herein described an approach centered on a speech acquisition model which integrates much of the traditional body of expertise on speech teaching with emerging knowledge in phonetics, audiology, speech science, psychology, and other related disciplines.

The model we have proposed depicts speech acquisition as a developmental process which occurs in seven broad, sequential stages. Each stage is considered as requiring the achievement of a number of specific speech production target behaviors, some of which may be simultaneously rather than sequentially developed. Underlying these target behaviors is a range of subskills, the mastery of which the child may attain through the use of whatever sense modality is most appropriate for him. Thus, what we have proposed is not a speech development curriculum but, rather, a structured framework for the prescription of an optimal speech development program for individual children, whatever their age, degree of hearing impairment, or educational background.

One needs more than a model in order to work effectively. Beyond the specification of stages, definition of target behaviors, and description of subskills is the need for the person working with the child to be able to evaluate the child's performance and, on the basis of such evaluation, choose and employ effective teaching strategies to foster further speech development. A new approach to speech evaluation procedures which closely accords with the framework afforded by our model is therefore described. This approach to evaluation requires relatively simple auditory judgments within the capabilities of most normally hearing listeners. To ensure objectivity in evaluation, collaboration of the teacher with an additional specialist, such as a speech therapist, is advised. Through the use of the procedures described, the child's immediate needs (and hence the teacher's immediate goals) can be specified and the child's progress through the various stages charted in detail.

The choice and use of the most appropriate teaching strategies for a given child require sound knowledge of the potential of the senses in speech reception and the sensory-motor mechanisms underlying feedforward and feedback control of speech production. Sensory potential and sensory-motor mechanisms have therefore been discussed prior to evaluation procedures and teaching strategies in this text, because evaluation must include measures of sensory-motor integrity and because the teaching strategies required for a given child will depend on his sensory-motor capabilities. For example, the term *hearing-impaired* is applied to a range of children which includes both the hard-of-hearing and the totally deaf child. Speech evaluation procedures and teaching strategies involving audition would be appropriate for the one, but procedures or strategies involving primarily touch or vision would be required for the other.

The book is primarily concerned with speech rather than language. It is assumed that the child's vocabulary and his knowledge of the lexical, morphological, syntactic, and semantic rules which are essential to meaningful speech communication will be developed in parallel with his progressive acquisition of speech as recommended in this text. Indeed, the model proposed is congruent with what is currently known in the area of developmental psycholinguistics. Accordingly, we describe evaluation procedures and teaching strategies at only two levels: the phonetic and the phonologic. At the phonetic level we are concerned with the child's capacity to produce the required sound patterns. At the phonologic level we are concerned with the systematic and meaningful use of these sound patterns without reference to their grammatical content. The distinction here drawn between speech and language is widely recognized as a convenient fiction (Abercrombie, 1965).

There are two prerequisites for the development of speech communication skills in hearing-impaired children: effective teaching and adequate experience. In this text we propose that the person principally responsible for speech teaching (phonetic level development) should be either the professional who provides parent guidance (for young infants) or the class teacher (for older children). We also propose that this person should be prepared to ensure that she, others, or both provide the child with adequate opportunity for meaningful (phonologic level) speech communication experience through the appropriate use of his available sense modalities at all times. The child's need for speech experience is not bounded by the walls of a clinic or classroom, nor by the duration of a parent guidance session or the hours of a school day.

We suggest that the time devoted to teaching specific speech skills should be allocated to brief blocks of two or three minutes' duration for each child, four or five times a day, rather than to longer lessons. The phonetic level subskills specified in the second half of this book can best be taught through brief, frequently repeated sessions. This approach provides the child with the necessary repertoire of speech patterns which can be differentiated, if not through hearing, through unambiguous orosensory images and motor codes (see Chapter 6). Such training enables the child to produce speech patterns automatically so that, in phonologic speech, conscious attention can be directed to what he wants to say rather than to how it should be said. In the case of the infant, the mother can be expected to develop many of these subskills through play under guidance from a professional worker. With older children, the teacher can provide the necessary training during the intervals which occur after a child has completed one classwork assignment and needs the teacher's direction to begin another. To keep track of the variety of individual children's specific speech training needs, a range of subskills may be displayed on a wall-chart and each child's progress marked on it.

We suggest that if any additional speech lessons are given by another person (for example, a speech therapist), the teacher should ensure that they are congruent with the goals she has set for the child—goals that she herself would otherwise work to achieve. Such lessons might include the introduction of a new subskill, the revision of subskills already learned to ensure their retention, or the use of target behaviors learned at the phonetic level in phonologic contexts. Through orderly phonetic level development, whether additional lessons coordinated with the teacher's work are provided or not, the need to correct at a phonologic level is minimized. This is important, for phonologic level speech should be mainly communicative speech and, as such, should be accepted so far as possible without corrective intervention.

The approach we recommend demands the utmost use of residual hearing. Indeed, we treat speech acquisition as the basis of auditory training. In the development of each subskill the child is expected, within the limits of his capacity to hear, to be auditorily aware of the sounds he produces, to discriminate between them, and to identify these patterns when produced by others. The order in which speech patterns are developed, as specified in the model we have proposed, ensures the systematic teaching of speech reception skills according to a sequence of increasing complexity and decreasing redundancy. In this respect it is congruent with the model proposed by Sanders (1971). We differ from Sanders in that we do not regard the auditory discrimination of nonverbal and speech sounds to be part of a developmental continuum, but believe that auditory training in the processing of speech requires the use of speech. Recent work has shown that nonverbal sounds are usually processed in the right hemisphere of the brain rather than the left, whereas the reverse is true for speech, and that the characteristics of such sounds are so unlike those of speech that little or no carry-over to speech discrimination can be expected (A. H. Ling, 1975). In order to ensure that optimal use can be made of residual audition, we have specified the range of frequency, intensity, and duration that is characteristic of each of the sounds which we seek to develop. These sounds are treated together with the definition of target behaviors, the description of subskills, and discussion of teaching strategies in the second half of the text.

That speech is more than a system of communication between consenting partners is widely recognized. In addition to the evidence that ability to speak enhances speech reception, there is also evidence that speech codes are normally used in all forms of verbal learning. They are used to rehearse and to organize linguistic material in memory, and they shape our perceptual strategies. It is in this regard that the simultaneous use of manual communication and speech requires careful experimental scrutiny. The question is, essentially, whether speech production and the perceptual and memory processes normally associated with the speech mode are adversely affected if signs and fingerspelling are also employed.

Discussion of conflicting philosophies is not within the scope of this text. However, it is pertinent to note that manual communication is commonly held to be detrimental to the development of speech and spoken language, a view disputed by Mindel and Vernon (1971, pp. 73 *et seq.*). The evidence in this regard is at best equivocal. While, at present, few hearing-impaired children who sign learn to speak well and are able to integrate into regular classes, many orally taught children communicate by speech so effectively that they integrate into the regular school system from an early age (Northcott, 1973). However, it is equally true that many orally taught children speak very poorly and no better than children who also sign (Montgomery, 1966). Of course, the presence or absence of interactions between manual methods and speech acquisition could be demonstrated experimentally by teaching comparable groups of children to the limits of their auditory-oral potential in both oral programs and total communication programs. It is hoped that this text will stimulate such research.

Nevertheless, individual differences are such that one approach is not likely to be successful with all children. Indeed, it has been shown that a substantial proportion of children fail to acquire any effective communication skills, whether taught manually, orally, or by total communication (Klopping, 1972). No doubt fewer would fail if the most appropriate method for a particular child could be determined through early and ongoing evaluation and if teaching programs were substantially improved. Both the evaluation procedures and the speech teaching strategies suggested in this text should be helpful in these regards.

It has been assumed that the reader will come to this text with at least an elementary knowledge of educational principles, audition, hearing impairment, speech development, linguistics, and phonetics. The reader should thus be able to use the IPA symbols presented in Table 1.A, which will be employed throughout. These symbols are enclosed in brackets, [a], when used to represent speech sounds without reference to meaning; they are enclosed in slashes, /a/, when they represent phonemes within a meaning system.

Speech Teaching and Prevailing Standards

Recent studies of hearing-impaired children attending special schools for the deaf have indicated that prevailing standards of speech are extremely poor (see Chapter 2). These studies showed that, on the average, only one word in five spoken by children who had been taught speech from infancy through the elementary grades could be identified by listeners unfamiliar wth the speech of hearing-impaired children. Comparison of these results with those obtained in similar studies some 40 years ago suggests that there has been no improvement in standards despite the technological advances which have been made and the knowledge relating to speech which has emerged during this period. Such poor standards of oral achievement are often used by advocates of manual communication to support the point of view that education should be principally, if not entirely, through signs and fingerspelling. The point is not unreasonable, for if a child, on leaving school, has acquired no means of direct communication other than such inefficient speech skills, most aspects of his life will inevitably be impoverished. One must, however, question whether such an inadequate standard of speech is necessarily associated with deafness. The speech achievements of many profoundly and totally deaf children and adults indicate that it is not.

TABLE 1.A

International Phonetic Alphabet symbols
representing speech sounds and modifiers.

Consonants		Vowels	
Symbol	*Key Word*	*Symbol*	*Key Word*
[p]	*p*ea	[u]	wh*o*
[b]	*b*ee	[ʊ]	wo*u*ld
[t]	*t*ea	[o]	kn*o*w
[d]	*d*o	[ɔ]	m*o*re
[k]	*k*ey	[ɑ]	*o*f
[g]	*g*o	[a]	*a*rt
[m]	*m*y	[ʌ]	m*u*st
[n]	*n*o	[ɜ˞]	l*ea*rn
[ŋ]	Li*ng*	[ə]	*a*gain
[h]	*h*op	[ɚ]	moth*er*
[f]	*f*ee	[æ]	*a*nd
[v]	*v*ery	[ɛ]	th*e*n
[θ]	*th*in	[e]	t*a*ke
[ð]	*th*at	[ɪ]	h*i*s
[s]	*s*o	[i]	*ea*se
[z]	*z*oo	**Diphthongs**	
[ʃ]	*sh*e	*Symbol*	*Key Word*
[ʒ]	ca*s*ual	[aɪ]	p*ie*
[tʃ]	*ch*eap	[aʊ]	c*ow*
[dʒ]	*j*eep	[ɔɪ]	t*oy*
[ʍ]	*wh*ey	[eɪ]	pl*ay*
[w]	*w*e	[ɪɚ]	h*ere*
[j]	*y*ou	**Modifiers**	
[r]	*r*ed	[ʰ]	aspirated
[l]	*l*ook	[ₒ]	voiceless
		[⁻]	unreleased
		[.]	syllabic consonant

It is difficult for those responsible for the education of hearing-impaired children to justify the inadequate standards of speech which prevail. It is true that increasing numbers of children who would formerly have attended special schools for the deaf now attend regular schools, having benefited from early use of hearing aids in auditory-oral programs initiated in early infancy; but even among such children, it is unusual to find speech that is not defective (Berg and Fletcher, 1970). It is also true that the characteristics of the population of children attending schools for the deaf have changed over the past 40 years. This is partly due to the trend toward integration of less severely handicapped children into regular classes and partly due to an increase in the actual incidence of defects additional to deafness. For these reasons, a greater proportion of pupils in special schools are more severely hearing-impaired and/or have multiple handicaps than was formerly the case (Schein, 1974). However, while recent studies of speech intelligibility have been undertaken with subjects having comparable hearing loss to that of subjects used in earlier studies, children with handicaps in addition to deafness have been excluded from them. Had such subjects been included in these recent studies, mean standards of speech achievement would no doubt be lower than currently documented.

Generally impoverished speech among hearing-impaired children is, perhaps, less difficult to explain than to justify. Schools for the deaf cannot, by their very nature, provide the hearing-impaired children who attend them with the abundance of normal speech experience that is available to the normally hearing child who is in constant communication with his hearing and talking peers. Even so, the speech of pupils who attend day schools, and who thus have more opportunity for exposure to normal speech patterns, appears to be little, if at all, better than that of residential school pupils (Markides, 1970). Experience alone is clearly not enough. Our observations suggest that the value of exposure to speech increases with the child's acquisition of the fundamental skills underlying both speech perception and speech production. These, for the most part, have to be taught. Reeves (1974) suggests that the widespread problem of poor speech is directly due to inadequate teaching. He states:

> It should be of grave concern to all of us that the decreasing proportion of specially trained teachers, the relatively short careers of many teachers, and their shallow depth of experience are contributing to a situation in which the teaching of speech is a dying art.

Of course, this statement does not imply that blame for the generally poor standards of speech rests solely with the teacher. Some responsibility also lies with personnel at the teacher training level, educational administrators, support staff, and parents. It is, however, evident that widespread failure to acquire useful speech will result if those in direct contact with the child do not consider acquisition of speech skills a worthwhile goal, lack the required teaching techniques, or have inadequate understanding of the many variables which underlie speech development.

The point of view taken in this book is that speech communication is a worthwhile goal and that high standards of speech production can be achieved through informed, systematic, and sustained effort. There is considerable evidence that speech teaching efforts have, in general, rarely merited these three adjectives. *Informed effort*, according to certain writers (DeLand, 1918; Haycock, 1933; Carhart, 1943; John and Howarth, 1965, among others), appears to be a scarce commodity. They suggest that many of the problems in the speech of hearing-impaired children are the direct result of inappropriate teaching. *Systematic effort* appears to be equally rare. In most of the studies discussed in Chapter 2, the authors reported a lack of methodical speech work. Markides (1970), for example, stated that in only one of the four schools from which his deaf subjects were drawn was there any attempt to plan speech work or to keep records of speech progress. In the remaining schools the only speech intervention was incidental correction of communicative speech during play or other lessons. *Sustained effort* is, apparently, also quite unusual. Vorce (1971, 1974) reports surveys which indicate that speech is rarely developed consistently throughout school life. As Heidinger (1972) remarks, this is often the result of placing undue emphasis on academic content areas. She also points out that when speech work is not undertaken by the teacher, but instead is delegated to a clinician-therapist, speech production tends to become less relevant and less functional for the child. Whatever professional help may be available, it is the teacher, it seems, who must ensure that parents receive counseling on speech appropriate to the needs of the child. Ironically, speech is the area of work in which the majority of teachers are reported to feel most inadequate (Dale, 1971).

REFERENCES

Abercrombie, D. *Studies in Phonetics and Linguistics.* London: Oxford University Press, 1965.

Bender, R. E. *The Conquest of Deafness.* Cleveland, Ohio: Press of Western Reserve University, 1960.

Berg, F. S., & Fletcher, S. G. *The Hard of Hearing Child.* New York: Grune and Stratton, 1970.

Carhart, R.   Hearing deficiencies and speech problems. *J. Speech Hear. Disord.*, 8, 247–254, 1943.

Dale, D. M. C.   Social aspects of speech. In L. E. Connor (Ed.), *Speech for the Deaf Child: Knowledge and Use*. Washington, D.C.: A. G. Bell Assoc. for the Deaf, 1971.

DeLand, F.   Give your child the best educational advantages. *Volta Rev.*, 20, 329–333, 1918.

de l'Epée, C. M.   *La véritable manière d'instruire les sourds et muets, confirmée par une longue expérience*. Paris: Nyon l'aîné, 1784.

DiCarlo, L. M.   *The Deaf*. Englewood Cliffs, N.J.: Prentice-Hall, 1964.

Haycock, G. S.   *The Teaching of Speech*. Washington, D.C.: Volta Bureau, 1933.

Heidinger, V. A.   *An exploratory study of procedures for improving temporal features in the speech of deaf children*. Unpublished Ed.D. diss., Columbia University, 1972.

Hodgson, K. W.   *The Deaf and Their Problems*. London: Watts, 1953.

John, J. E. J., & Howarth, J. N.   The effect of time distortions on the intelligibility of deaf children's speech. *Lang. Speech*, 8, 127–134, 1965.

Klopping, H. W. E.   Language understanding of deaf students under three auditory-visual stimulus conditions. *Am. Ann. Deaf*, 117, 389–396, 1972.

Ling, A. H.   Memory for verbal and nonverbal auditory sequences in hearing-impaired and normal-hearing children. *J. Am. Audiol. Soc.*, 1, 37–45, 1975.

Markides, A.   The speech of deaf and partially-hearing children with special reference to factors affecting intelligibility. *Br. J. Disord. Commun.*, 5, 126–140, 1970.

Mindel, E. D., & Vernon, M.   *They Grow in Silence*. Silver Spring, Md.: National Assoc. of the Deaf, 1971.

Montgomery, G. W. G.   The relationship of oral skills to manual communication in profoundly deaf students. *Am. Ann. Deaf*, 111, 557–565, 1966.

Northcott, W. H. (Ed.)   *The Hearing-Impaired Child in a Regular Classroom: Preschool, Elementary, and Secondary Years*. Washington, D.C.: A. G. Bell Assoc. for the Deaf, 1973.

Reeves, J. K.   Editor's comments. *Teach. Deaf*, 72, 49–50, 1974.

Sanders, D. A.   *Aural Rehabilitation*. Englewood Cliffs, N.J.: Prentice-Hall, 1971.

Schein, J. D. (Ed.)   *Education and Rehabilitation of Deaf Persons With Other Disabilities*. New York: Deafness Research and Training Center, New York University School of Education, 1974.

Storrs, R. S.   Articulation in deaf-mute instruction. *Am. Ann. Deaf*, 27, 160–162, 1882.

Vorce, E.   Speech curriculum. In L. E. Connor (Ed.), *Speech for the Deaf Child: Knowledge and Use*. Washington, D.C.: A. G. Bell Assoc. for the Deaf, 1971.

Vorce, E.   *Teaching Speech to Deaf Children*. Washington, D.C.: A. G. Bell Assoc. for the Deaf, 1974.

=/2/=

Studies Relating to Speech Production Among Hearing-Impaired Children

If anything is required to persuade the reader that a radically improved approach to fostering speech acquisition in hearing-impaired children is required, it is a review of the literature. Results of recent studies suggest that overall levels of speech intelligibility are utterly inadequate for oral communication and that typical speech errors of children attending special schools for the deaf today are much the same as they were 40 years ago. Advances in acoustic phonetics, speech science, psychology, hearing aid technology, and other related fields appear to have made no significant impact on standards of speech production. These facts are an implicit indictment of those engaged in, or responsible for, the education of hearing-impaired children. It may be argued that the studies briefly reviewed below are not representative, but there is no direct evidence from published material indicating that such poor standards do not generally prevail.

Studies of Speech Intelligibility

Brannon (1964) worked with 20 children selected from a large day school. They were 12–15 years old, had hearing levels of 75 dB or more, possessed at least normal intelligence, and had no known additional handicaps. He found only 20–25% of the words in their practiced speech intelligible to listeners unfamiliar with hearing-impaired children's diction.

Nober (1967) studied 46 children aged 3–15 years attending a residential school. He found none with hearing loss greater than 80 dB who were able to score at a 3-year level and none with hearing losses ranging from 60 to 80 dB able to score higher than a 4-year level on the Templin-Darley Test of Articulation (Templin and Darley, 1960).

11

Markides (1970) made a similar study of 58 hearing-impaired children who were 7 and 9 years old. They were drawn from both day and residential schools. About 31% of their words were intelligible to their teachers whereas only 19% were intelligible to naive listeners. Phonetic analysis of the children's responses showed that some 56% of their vowels and diphthongs and 72% of their consonants were misarticulated.

Heidinger (1972) studied the speech of 20 children enrolled in a residential school. They were 10–14 years old and had no handicaps other than hearing loss of 85 dB (ISO) or more in the better ear. Her three judges, who were experienced teachers of the deaf and knew what the children were trying to say, rated less than 20% of their words in short sentences as intelligible.

Smith (1972) studied 40 day and residential pupils in the age groups 8–10 and 13–15 years. All had hearing loss greater than 80 dB at 1,000 Hz. Word intelligibility, as assessed by 120 listeners unfamiliar with the speech of hearing-impaired children, ranged from 76% down to 0%, with a mean of 18.7%.

Of course, intelligibility ratings vary not only with the type of judge employed (experienced or naive), but also with the materials used and with the method of analysis. Thus, sentences spoken by hearing-impaired children tend to be more intelligible than words, and sentences which are spoken directly to the listener in a face-to-face situation are more intelligible than sentences which are tape recorded (Hudgins, 1949; Thomas, 1964). Various types of spoken materials and methods of rating have been used in numerous other studies (Kerridge, 1938; Hudgins and Numbers, 1942; Hood, 1966; Goda, 1959; Quigley and Frisina, 1961; Angelocci, 1962; John and Howarth, 1965; Montgomery, 1967; Toback, 1967; Braverman, 1974). All have shown that similarly poor levels of speech achievement among hearing-impaired children are commonplace in our special schools and have been so for many years. Documented exceptions to this picture (e.g., van Uden, 1970) are few.

Typical Speech Errors of Hearing-Impaired Children

The most all-embracing statement made on deviant speech production due to hearing impairment must be attributed to Black (1971, p. 156), who stated that "the speech of deaf children differs from normal speech in all regards." The majority of articles written on speech in the *American Annals of the Deaf* and *The Volta Review* since they were first published (see Fellendorf, 1966, 1973) attest to the validity of Black's view. The faults on which attention has been most frequently focused relate to respiration, phonation, and rate. Although devices which could have been used to define these problems with some precision were available at the beginning of this century (Scripture, 1913), the first objective studies of the speech of hearing-impaired children did not appear until the mid-1930's. Then, in the space of a few years, a rash of research reports appeared. These and later studies will be briefly reviewed below. Further reference to most of this work will be made in later sections.

Respiration, Phonation, and Rate

Among the first scientific studies of respiration and phonation in the speech of hearing-impaired children were those of Hudgins (1934, 1936, 1937, 1946, 1949), Scuri (1935), Rawlings (1935, 1936), Voelker (1935, 1938), and Mason and Bright (1937). These studies indicated that there was in general a lack of coordination between the articulators (tongue, lips, and jaw) and the breath-voice system. The musculature controlling the one group of organs did not usually function in synchrony with those controlling the other. These studies also showed that deaf children expended more breath during speech production than did hearing children, that the range of voice pitch was more restricted among deaf than among hearing children, and that duration of phonation was about three times greater. Specifically, Voelker (1938) found that while the rate of utterance for his normally hearing subjects ranged from 134 to 210 words per minute (wpm), it ranged from 28 to 145 wpm for his deaf children. As Mason and Bright (1937) pointed out, the slow, labored speech of their subjects was not due to the time it took them to formulate ideas, since most of the material spoken was read and even practiced; it was due simply to the fact that the children had not been taught to articulate at a normal rate.

These early findings relating to various aspects of breathing and voice do not appear to have led to the amelioration of the problem through the adaptation of old, or the creation of new, teaching procedures (except perhaps for those children who have benefited from the use of their residual hearing). The same faults continue to be reported in several later studies (Green, 1956; Calvert, 1961; Lindner, 1962; Mártony, 1965; Black, 1971; and Monsen, 1974, among others).

Speech Rhythm

In this context the term *rhythm* is used to describe the complex time-based pattern of speech in which the primary elements are rate, stress, juncture, breath-grouping, and pauses. The importance of rhythm to the intelligibility of speech was recognized by Bell (1916, p. 15), who criticized some of his own early work for lack of insight in this regard.

Although slightly overstating his case, perhaps for good reason, he wrote:

> Ordinary people who know nothing of phonetics or elocution have difficulty in understanding slow speech composed of perfect elementary sounds, while they have no difficulty in comprehending an imperfect gabble if only the accent and rhythm are natural.

Voelker (1935, 1938), Hudgins (1949), and Hudgins and Numbers (1942) all found that rhythmic speech had better-than-average intelligibility. These findings were confirmed in further experimental work by Clarke (1957), John and Howarth (1965), Hood (1966), Hood and Dixon (1969), and Heidinger (1972). However, results relating to speech rhythm should not be interpreted simplistically. Children who produce rhythmic speech also tend to articulate more accurately than those whose speech is labored (Brannon, 1964). In few of the above studies was any attempt made to separate out the effects of articulation and rhythm.

The importance to clear speech of both appropriate rhythm and good articulation has been most clearly demonstrated by Boothroyd, Nickerson, and Stevens (1974). After daily training in the temporal patterning of speech totaling 7-1/2 hours over a six-week period, their group of eight orally trained subjects, aged 9–17 years, all improved with respect to durational aspects of production. However, this improvement did not result in increased intelligibility, which—for the group as a whole—remained at about 20%. Levels of intelligibility improved in three subjects, were not significantly changed in two, and were actually worse in the remaining three. This finding indicates that attempts to impose a normal rhythmic structure on speech characterized by defective articulation have little to recommend them. In our view, it would be more appropriate to reverse the strategy and, from the earliest stages, encourage more normal patterns of rhythm and intonation within which increasingly accurate coarticulation of segments can be incorporated. The essentials of such an approach will be developed in later chapters.

Vowel Production

Defects in vowel production among hearing-impaired children tend to follow certain patterns. Hudgins and Numbers (1942) found that substitution, neutralization, diphthongization, and nasalization of vowels were the most frequent errors. Over 20 years later, Angelocci, Kopp, and Holbrook (1964) reported similar findings. The amplitude of all vowels was weaker among the deaf than among the hearing boys they studied, and vowel production was frequently accompanied by excessive aspiration, nasality, and hoarseness. Only 32% of the vowels uttered by the deaf children could be identified by the 24 students who served as judges. The most frequent errors noted were substitution and neutralization. One vowel tended to sound very much like any other, a finding that indicated very restricted and stereotyped tongue movement. Nober (1967) reported similar types of distortion but a higher proportion (70%) of correct vowel productions. Two possible reasons for the difference between Nober's findings and those of Angelocci *et al.* (1964) may be suggested. Nober used four judges, each of whom was a qualified speech clinician with at least two years of experience in work with deaf children, whereas the judges employed by Angelocci *et al.* were unfamiliar with the speech of hearing-impaired children. Also, Nober's subjects were younger and had had greater opportunity to benefit from amplification.

Two of the most recent studies which provide data on vowel production by deaf children (Markides, 1970; Smith, 1972) have already been mentioned. In brief, their results confirm those obtained in much earlier studies. Of particular importance was Smith's finding (p. 74) that total vowel errors were highly correlated with both total number of consonant errors and prosodic score. This finding indicates the importance of vowel production to intelligibility. In earlier writings on phonetics it was not unusual for consonants to be considered more important than vowels, and written examples such as "J-ck -nd J-ll w-nt -p th- h-ll" were provided to support this view. However, more recent research, much of it from the Haskins Laboratories (e.g., Liberman, Cooper, Shankweiler, and Studdert-Kennedy, 1967; Liberman, 1970), shows that vowels not only differentiate between words in their own right (e.g., *bid, bed, bad*) but also carry information essential to the correct identification of adjacent consonants. Such information, normally contained in formant transitions, was typically absent in the speech of hearing-impaired children studied by Mártony and Franzén (1966).

The evidence from studies of speech of severely hearing-impaired children strongly suggests that the importance of vowel production has not been adequately appreciated by their teachers. Recent work in acoustic and articulatory phonetics, reviewed in subsequent chapters, should provide both the impetus and the guidelines for reorientation toward more adequate teaching strategies.

Articulation of Consonants

The first quantitative study on the articulation of consonants by hearing-impaired children was carried out by Hudgins and Numbers

(1942). Misarticulations were categorized as follows: voiced-voiceless errors; omission or distortion of initial consonants; omission of consonants in blends; omission or distortion of final consonants; nasalization; substitution of one consonant for another; and intrusive voicing between abutting consonants. The most common errors of the more severely hearing-impaired children were those related to voicing, initial consonants, and nasality. Those of the less severely hearing-impaired involved mainly substitutions, blends, and final consonants. Similar results were obtained by Morley (1949) in a spectrographic study and by Nober (1967). Nober noted that the least visible sounds tended to be misarticulated most frequently. Voiced-voiceless errors were numerous. Final consonant errors averaged 83%; medial consonant errors, 69%; and initial consonant errors, 59%. Very few blends were articulated correctly, even by children over 8 years of age. Nober further noted that his subjects produced only 28% of nasal consonants correctly and also that his subjects spoke with excessive nasal resonance, but he did not consider the two types of errors related. Our experience indicates very strongly that they are. This point will be discussed more fully in a later chapter. While otherwise confirming the findings of Hudgins and Numbers (1942), neither Nober (1967) nor Markides (1970) mentioned the prevalence of intrusive voicing; yet this feature was quite marked among the groups studied by Heidinger (1972) and by Smith (1972). Indeed, Smith (p. 73) reported that an added release vowel, generally in word-final position, was the most frequent consonant error.

Speech Development and Hearing Level

Among the many variables affecting speech development, hearing level is perhaps the most important. It is not, therefore, surprising that most of the studies mentioned above show that—other things being equal—the more residual hearing a child has and uses, the more natural his speech is likely to be. This is not to say that a totally deaf child will be unable to produce intelligible speech. If the child has a reasonably intact central nervous system and no marked anatomical or physiological deficits affecting the speech organs, an appropriate training program can provide him with fluent, intelligible speech. To be sure, the program has to include far more structured speech teaching than is required for less severely hearing-impaired children. Some structured speech teaching is, however, necessary for many children classed as hard-of-hearing (a pragmatic grouping, as demonstrated by Huizing (1961), Whetnall and Fry (1971), and Griffiths (1967), among others). In spite of their superior auditory potential, a substantial proportion of such children have consistently failed to develop normal articulation (Hughson, Ciocco, Witting, and Lawrence, 1942; Hudgins and Numbers, 1942; Waldon, 1963; Stewart, 1969). Because hearing level is not the only variable underlying speech development, the extent of specific speech training needed by any particular child cannot be determined solely from an audiogram. Individual needs can only be defined by the teacher in the course of observation, evaluation, and teaching.

Although occasional mention of the benefits of exploiting residual audition has been made for at least two hundred years (see Wedenberg, 1951), few programs can yet claim to make optimal use of residual hearing. In some, the attempt falls short of the goal for technical reasons (Ling, 1971, 1975). In others, the importance of audition has not yet been recognized. It is difficult for some teachers to accept the concept that certain children who may be regarded as "deaf," according to the standard suggested by Davis (1965) for medico-legal purposes (average threshold for the frequencies 500, 1,000, and 2,000 Hz greater than 92 dB ISO), may have educationally useful audition and be able to hear several aspects of speech. Yet this is, in fact, the case (Stark, 1974).

In earlier times, arguments for using residual audition were not as strongly supported by technology and research evidence as they are today. Thus, while Bell (1897)—with his technical background—was able to write forcefully on the need to exploit residual hearing, Haycock (1933) could not be criticized for ignoring audition in his otherwise excellent treatise on the teaching of speech. Books by both Bell (1916) and Haycock (1933) are, quite reasonably, still widely used as texts in many teacher-training centers. More modern texts dealing with the teaching of speech (Ewing and Ewing, 1964; Dale, 1967; Davis and Silverman, 1970; Connor, 1971; Vorce, 1974; Calvert and Silverman, 1975) suggest the wider use of a more natural approach and, like Goldstein (1939), emphasize the need to use whatever residual hearing a child may possess. To accept the premise that one should make the utmost use of hearing is not to reject the use of other sense modalities. Some children, including those who are totally deaf, require structured speech teaching through the use of vision, touch, and kinesthesis.

Summary

Results of representative studies relating to speech production by hearing-impaired children are reviewed. These indicate that technological advances, emerging knowledge in speech science, and contributions from related areas are having little, or no, impact on the speech patterns of many of the children attending our special schools. It may be concluded that teachers do not have or are not using strategies which integrate current knowledge with compatible, traditional procedures.

REFERENCES

Angelocci, A. A.   Some observations on the speech of the deaf. *Volta Rev.*, 64, 403–405, 1962.

Angelocci, A. A., Kopp, G. A., & Holbrook, A.   The vowel formants of deaf and normal-hearing eleven- to fourteen-year-old boys. *J. Speech Hear. Disord.*, 29, 156–170, 1964.

Bell, A. G.   *The Mystic Oral School, An Argument in Its Favor.* Washington, D.C.: Gibson Brothers, 1897.

Bell, A. G.   *The Mechanism of Speech.* New York: Funk and Wagnalls, 1916.

Black, J. W.   Speech pathology for the deaf. In L. E. Connor (Ed.), *Speech for the Deaf Child: Knowledge and Use.* Washington, D.C.: A. G. Bell Assoc. for the Deaf, 1971, pp. 154–169.

Boothroyd, A., Nickerson, R. S., & Stevens, K. N.   *Temporal patterns in the speech of the deaf—A study in remedial training.* S.A.R.P. 15, Northampton, Mass.: Clarke School for the Deaf, 1974.

Brannon, J.   *Visual feedback of glossal motions and its influence upon the speech of deaf children.* Unpublished Ph.D. diss., Northwestern University, 1964.

Braverman, J. H.   *A comparison of oral form discrimination in deaf and hearing children and the relationship of orosensory skill and other factors to speech articulation in deaf talkers.* Unpublished Ph.D. diss., Columbia University, 1974.

Calvert, D. R.   *Some acoustic characteristics of the speech of profoundly deaf individuals.* Unpublished Ph.D. diss., Stanford University, 1961.

Calvert, D. R., & Silverman, S. R.   *Speech and Deafness.* Washington, D.C.: A. G. Bell Assoc. for the Deaf, 1975.

Clarke, B. R.   Use of a group hearing aid by profoundly deaf children. In A. W. G. Ewing (Ed.), *Educational Guidance and the Deaf Child.* Manchester: Manchester University Press, 1957.

Connor, L. E. (Ed.),   *Speech for the Deaf Child: Knowledge and Use.* Washington, D.C.: A. G. Bell Assoc. for the Deaf, 1971.

Dale, D. M. C.   *Deaf Children at Home and at School.* London: London University Press, 1967.

Davis, H.   Guide for the classification and evaluation of hearing handicap in relation to the International Audiometric Zero. *Trans. Am. Acad. Ophthalmol. Otol.*, 6, 419–424, 1965.

Davis, H., & Silverman, S. R. (Eds.)   *Hearing and Deafness.* New York: Holt, Rinehart, and Winston, 1970.

Ewing, A. W. G., & Ewing, E. C.   *Teaching Deaf Children To Talk.* Manchester: Manchester University Press, 1964.

Fellendorf, G. W. (Ed.)   *Bibliography on Deafness.* Washington, D.C.: A. G. Bell Assoc. for the Deaf, 1966.

Fellendorf, G. W. (Ed.)   *Bibliography on Deafness. Supplement 1966–72.* Washington, D.C.: A. G. Bell Assoc. for the Deaf, 1973.

Goda, S.   Language skills of profoundly deaf adolescent children. *J. Speech Hear. Res.*, 2, 369–376, 1959.

Goldstein, M. A.   *The Acoustic Method for the Training of the Deaf and Hard of Hearing Child*. St. Louis: Laryngoscope Press, 1939.

Green, D. S.   *Fundamental frequency characteristics of the speech of profoundly deaf individuals*. Unpublished Ph.D. diss., Purdue University, 1956.

Griffiths, C.   *Conquering Childhood Deafness*. New York: Exposition Press, 1967.

Haycock, G. S.   *The Teaching of Speech*. Washington, D.C.: Volta Bureau, 1933.

Heidinger, V. A.   *An exploratory study of procedures for improving temporal features in the speech of deaf children*. Unpublished Ed.D. diss., Columbia University, 1972.

Hood, R. B.   *Some physical concomitants of the perception of speech rhythm of the deaf*. Unpublished Ph.D. diss., Stanford University, 1966.

Hood, R. B., & Dixon, R. F.   Physical characteristics of speech rhythm of deaf and normal speakers. *J. Commun. Disord.*, 2, 20–28, 1969.

Hudgins, C. V.   A comparative study of the speech coordinations of deaf and normally hearing subjects. *J. Genet. Psychol.*, 44, 3–48, 1934.

Hudgins, C. V.   A study of respiration and speech. *Volta Rev.*, 38, 341–343, passim., 1936.

Hudgins, C. V.   Voice production and breath control in the speech of the deaf. *Am. Ann. Deaf*, 82, 338–363, 1937.

Hudgins, C. V.   Speech breathing and speech intelligibility. *Volta Rev.*, 48, 642–644, 1946.

Hudgins, C. V.   A method of appraising the speech of the deaf. *Volta Rev.*, 51, 597–601, passim., 1949.

Hudgins, C. V., & Numbers, F. C.   An investigation of the intelligibility of the speech of the deaf. *Genet. Psychol. Monogr.*, 25, 289–392, 1942.

Hughson, W., Ciocco, A., Witting, E. G., & Lawrence, P. S.   Studies of pupils of the Pennsylvania School for the Deaf. III. An analysis of speech characteristics in deafened children with observations on training methods. *Child Dev.*, 13, 131–158, 1942.

Huizing, H. C.   Audition—its basic skills in early childhood. *Proc. 2nd Int. Course in Paedo-Audiology*, Groningen University, 1961, pp. 51–60.

John, J. E. J., & Howarth, J. N.   The effect of time distortions on the intelligibility of deaf children's speech. *Lang. Speech*, 8, 127–134, 1965.

Kerridge, P. M. T.   Hearing and speech in deaf children. *J. Laryngol. Otol.*, 53, 46–68, 1938.

Liberman, A. M.   The grammars of speech and language. *Cogn. Psychol.*, 1, 301–323, 1970.

Liberman, A. M., Cooper, F. S., Shankweiler, D. P., & Studdert-Kennedy, M.   Perception of the speech code. *Psychol. Rev.*, 74, 431–461, 1967.

Lindner, G.   Ueber den zeitlichen Verlauf der Sprechweise bei Gerhoerlosen. *Folia Phoniatr.*, 14, 67–76, 1962.

Ling, D.   Conventional hearing aids: An overview. *Volta Rev.*, 73, 343–352, passim., 1971.

Ling, D.   Recent developments affecting the education of hearing-impaired children. *Public Health Rev.*, 4, 117–152, 1975.

Markides, A.   The speech of deaf and partially-hearing children with special reference to factors affecting intelligibility. *Br. J. Disord. Commun.*, 5, 126–140, 1970.

Mártony, J.   *Studies on the speech of the deaf—I*. STL-QPSR 2/65. Stockholm: R. Inst. Technol., 1965.

Mártony, J., & Franzén, O.   *Formant transitions and phoneme lengths as constituents of speech naturalness*. STL-QPSR 1/66. Stockholm: R. Inst. Technol., 1966.

Mason, M. K., & Bright, M.   Tempo in rhythmic speech education. *Am. Ann. Deaf*, 82, 385–401, 1937.

Monsen, R. B.   Durational aspects of vowel production in the speech of deaf children. *J. Speech Hear. Res.*, 17, 386–398, 1974.

Montgomery, G. W. G.   Analysis of pure-tone audiometric responses in relation to speech development in the profoundly deaf. *J. Acoust. Soc. Am.*, 41, 53–59, 1967.

Morley, D. E.   *An analysis by means of sound spectrograph of intelligibility variations of consonant sounds spoken by deaf persons*. Unpublished Ph.D. diss., University of Michigan, 1949.

Nober, E. H.   Articulation of the deaf. *Except. Child.*, 33, 611–621, 1967.

Quigley, S. P., & Frisina, D. R.   Institutionalization and psychoeducational development of deaf children. *C.E.C. Res. Monogr.*, No. 3, 1961.

Rawlings, C. G.   A comparative study of the movements of breathing muscles in speech and quiet breathing of deaf and normal subjects. *Am. Ann. Deaf*, 80, 147–156, 1935.

Rawlings, C. G.   A comparative study of the movements of breathing muscles in speech and quiet breathing of deaf and normal subjects. *Am. Ann. Deaf*, 81, 136–150, 1936.

Scripture, E. W.   The voices of the deaf. *Volta Rev.*, 15, 77–80, passim., 1913.

Scuri, D.   Respirazione e fonazione nei sordomuti. *Rassegna di sordomuti e fonetica biologica*, 14, 82–113, 1935.

Smith, C. R.   *Residual hearing and speech production in deaf children*. Unpublished Ph.D. diss., City University of New York, 1972.

Stark, R. E. (Ed.)   *Sensory Capabilities of Hearing-Impaired Children*. Baltimore, Md.: University Park Press, 1974.

Stewart, R. B.   The speech of children with high frequency losses of hearing. *Sound*, 3, 40–43, 1969.

Templin, M. C., & Darley, F. L.   *The Templin-Darley Tests of Articulation*. Iowa City: Bureau of Educational Research, State University of Iowa, 1960.

Thomas, W. G.   Intelligibility of the speech of deaf children. *Proc. Int. Congr. on Educ. of the Deaf*. Washington, D.C.: U.S. Govt. Printing Office, 1964, pp. 245–261.

Toback, C.   *Speech intelligibility of congenitally deaf children as related to intelligence and language ability*. Unpublished Ph.D. diss., New York University, 1967.

van Uden, A.   New realizations in the light of the pure oral method. *Volta Rev.*, 72, 524–537, 1970.

Voelker, C. H.   A preliminary strobophotoscopic study of the speech of the deaf. *Am. Ann. Deaf*, 80, 243–259, 1935.

Voelker, C. H.   An experimental study of the comparative rate of utterance of deaf and normal hearing speakers. *Am. Ann. Deaf*, 83, 274–284, 1938.

Vorce, E.   *Teaching Speech to Deaf Children*. Washington, D.C.: A. G. Bell Assoc. for the Deaf, 1974.

Waldon, E. F.   *A study of the spoken and written language of children with impaired hearing*. Unpublished Ph.D. diss., Ohio State University, 1963.

Wedenberg, E.   Auditory training of deaf and hard of hearing children. *Acta Otolaryngol. Suppl.*, 94, 1951.

Whetnall, E., & Fry, D. B.   *The Deaf Child*. Springfield, Ill.: Thomas, 1971.

/3/

The Sense Modalities
in Speech Reception

In order to learn how to speak, the hearing-impaired child must, in some way, receive the speech patterns on which his own production can be modeled. In addition—or as alternatives—to residual hearing, there are three sense modalities available: vision, touch, and kinesthesis. Each can be made to serve a somewhat different function in speech reception and speech production. In none has the range of possibilities and limitations for speech acquisition been fully explored.

Hearing is particularly sensitive to temporal events within the frequency range 80–8,000 Hz, while vision—though relatively poor as a temporal sense—excels in providing spatial information. Touch, which is maximally sensitive in the frequency range 200–800 Hz, is not quite as effective as the ear in dealing with time, or as the eye in dealing with space, but it outstrips the ear as a spatial sense and the eye as a temporal sense (Geldard, 1970; Montagu, 1971). Kinesthesis, which provides information on orientation of one's body and its parts in space, plays a limited role in speech reception but assumes considerable importance in speech production (Gammon, Smith, Daniloff, and Kim, 1971). As this chapter is primarily concerned with speech reception, kinesthesis will receive no further consideration at this point. Our immediate concern will be with auditory, visual, and tactile input.

Of the available senses, residual audition must be regarded as potentially the most important because it is the only one directly capable of appreciating the primary characteristics of communicative speech, which are acoustic. Both other exteroceptive senses, vision and touch, may be regarded as surrogates capable of responding only to the secondary characteristics of speech: the visible movements associated with sound production and the tangible correlates of speech such as the breath stream and vibration. Vision, like hearing, is a distance sense, which gives it some advantages over touch, for the distance within which touch can operate is normally restricted. However, speech sounds can be transformed to vibrations by means of electronic aids (e.g., hearing aid coupled to a vibrator) and presented to the skin, thus converting touch into a distance sense.

In this chapter, we shall briefly discuss what is known about each of these modalities and the nature of the input cues they can provide. In following chapters we shall discuss the simultaneous use of more than one sense modality in speech reception and the role of the senses in speech production.

Auditory Speech Reception

The severity of speech problems tends to vary with hearing level, as shown by many of the studies mentioned in Chapter 2. The speech of the child with little or no residual hearing is generally much poorer than that of the hard-of-hearing child. The vast majority of children with normal hearing acquire speech and language free of functional disorders, some in spite of developmental or environmental problems that might be expected to interfere drastically with verbal learning (Powers, 1971; Subcommittee on Human Communication and Its Disorders, 1969). These facts attest to the importance of hearing and explain why the use of residual audition was singled out for specific mention in Chapter 2. Audition will continue to receive emphasis throughout this text, as it is known that relatively few hearing-impaired children are totally deaf (Watson, 1961; Ling, 1964a; Elliott, 1967; Boothroyd, 1970).

The Audiogram

The audiogram is currently our most useful, single predictor of auditory speech reception ability. However, predictions made simply on the basis of an audiogram are prone to considerable error (Sher and Owens, 1974). Since such predictions may result in self-fulfilling prophecies disadvantageous to the child, it is worthwhile to examine the nature of the information provided by the audiogram and its relation to speech reception.

Not all pure-tone audiograms are reliable. Children's audiograms tend, for a variety of reasons, to vary from one audiometric test to another (Ling and Naish, 1975). Further, sound has three aspects—intensity, frequency, and duration—whereas the audiogram is a two-dimensional plot of intensity by frequency. It provides no information on how well (or badly) a child may be able to process the time relationships which are so important to speech intelligibility. This has to be determined in the course of teaching. Also, the audiogram provides only a threshold measure, whereas hearing-impaired listeners generally require speech amplified to 20–30 dB above threshold (Gengel and Foust, 1975). The audiogram provides no information on the quality of audition present at these levels. It merely indicates the dividing line between hearing and not hearing, much as the shoreline in Figure 3.1 divides land from water. From this figure it is impossible to deduce the water's depth, warmth, or its suitability for drinking or swimming. Similarly, from an

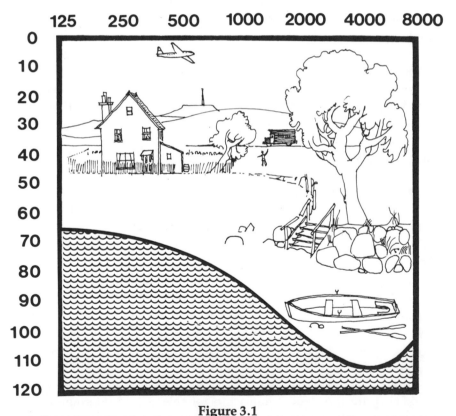

Figure 3.1

An audiogram in which the threshold is compared to a shoreline. The contour of the shoreline tells nothing about the quality of water; similarly, the threshold curve yields no information about the quality of hearing present at suprathreshold levels.

audiogram having the same "shoreline" configuration, one cannot deduce a child's ability to distinguish one frequency from another, to track formant transitions, or to judge one sound as louder or quieter than another. Nor does an audiogram indicate a child's level of tolerance for amplified sound. For these (and yet other) reasons, it is possible for several children with identical pure-tone audiograms to differ greatly in ability to use residual hearing and to discriminate speech.

The audiogram represents the child's thresholds to steady-state pure tones, but speech is made up of complex and rapidly changing acoustic events. Recent work (Abbs and Sussmann, 1971; Cooper, 1974; Cooper and Blumstein, 1974) suggests that ability to process speech may involve auditory detection mechanisms which respond only to transitional, multidimensional stimuli. Eimas (1974) suggests that such mechanisms may account for ability to discriminate between certain speech sounds from early infancy. The presence and integrity of mechanisms which respond only to rapidly changing, multidimensional sounds cannot, obviously, be measured through the use of steady-state pure-tone audiometry.

What has so far been said in no way questions the value of the audiogram as a tool in medical diagnosis. In this regard it may contribute essential audiologic information (see Katz, 1972). Nor do we question its usefulness in indicating the approximate frequency range over which a child's responses to sound are present and the minimal level at which the sounds of speech must be presented in order for them to be audible. Audibility is a necessary, though insufficient, condition for speech reception.

Not all responses to sound necessarily indicate the presence of audition. Some responses, particularly those to low-frequency tones, may result from tactile sensation (Nober, 1964; Boothroyd and Cawkwell, 1970) which may or may not be useful for certain aspects of speech discrimination (Erber, 1972a). Failure to respond within the upper frequency and intensity range of the audiometer does not necessarily mean that the child has no hearing for these frequencies. It may be that the child's threshold is just beyond the limits of the audiometer. If this is so, then tones at these frequencies would be audible when the child is tested wearing a hearing aid.

Even assuming that an audiogram shows hearing at levels sufficient for auditory speech processing, there is still more to hearing than meets the ear. Performance in auditory perceptual tasks depends strongly on context (Miller, Heise, and Lichten, 1951), upon the frequency with which words occur (Rosenzweig and Postman, 1958), upon a subject's awareness of the class of stimuli with which he must deal (Garner, 1966), and on his ability to resolve complex sound patterns.

Motor Speech Ability and Auditory Skills

It seems reasonable to assume that the more familiar a child is with the various aspects of speech as a speaker, the more likely he is to be able to make use of his residual hearing for speech as a listener. This notion is not without support (Ladefoged, 1967). Clearly the processes involved in both listening and speaking have much in common (Hirsh, 1973).

To illustrate the intricate nature of the relationship between speech perception and speech production, we shall briefly explore the model proposed for normally hearing listeners by Liberman, Cooper, Shankweiler, and Studdert-Kennedy (1967). This model has wide-ranging implications for the development of speech and speech reception among hearing-impaired children. Underlying the model is the observation that if each phoneme were represented by a specific sound, the limited temporal resolving power of the ear would not permit speech to be received as such. If speech were a series of discrete acoustic events, it would, at the normal rate, "merge into an unanalyzable buzz" (p. 432). Speech can be perceived at normal rates because phonemes are *encoded*. They do not follow each other like separate beads on a string, but are produced and perceived as parallel events.

The encoding of speech sounds, one in parallel with another, results from their coarticulation (Liberman, 1970). Thus, in the syllable [tu], both the [t] and the [u] are influenced by each other and together form a unit of syllabic size. The same is true of [t] and [i] in the syllable [ti]. If one contrasts the two syllables in a whisper, the two allophones of [t] will be heard as two distinctly different acoustic signals. The [t] in each has become encoded. Adequate encoding is, of course, made more difficult for hearing-impaired children by those who attempt to teach the production of consonants in isolation.

An encoded message must be decoded if the phonemes used are to be identified. It has been suggested by Liberman, Cooper, Shankweiler, and Studdert-Kennedy (1968) that this decoding process can only be achieved by means of auditory input (p. 128). They also suggest that what we hear requires an intermediate decoding which involves some form of association with the articulatory process. In other words, other people's speech appears to be mediated in some way through reference to one's own speech system.

The implications of this model may appear to cast gloom on the efforts of the teacher faced with a severely or totally deaf child, but Liberman *et al.* (1967) point out that linguistic units of syllabic or word size are relatively invariant and hence are not encoded in the acoustic signal to the same extent as phonemes. This is because they contain most of the transitional components which appear to be so important in speech reception and may therefore be perceived holistically. Liberman *et al.* nevertheless reject the notion of the whole-pattern perception. They consider it uneconomical and inelegant. They point out that in pattern recognition, instead of dealing with 40 or so phonemes, one would be dealing with hundreds of syllables or thousands of words and speaker variants. However, there is evidence that the human being is capable of pattern production and pattern recognition on this scale (Massaro, 1972). Hearing-impaired children who are unable to identify certain phonemes may have to develop perceptual strategies based mainly on such pattern recognition. Their recovery of the phonetic structure of a message would then require synthesis based on knowledge of both the articulatory patterns involved and the prosodic, phonologic, morphologic, and syntactic rules by which speech is structured. Such analysis by synthesis is an everyday exercise for the lipreader. More detail on current models of speech reception, including that proposed by Liberman *et al.* (1967), are presented and discussed in a book edited by Wathen-Dunn (1967).

It should be further emphasized that competence in speech production appears to be advantageous as a basis for the reception of running speech, and that the use of audition is not passive. Learning involves active exploration, a "tuning" not only of hearing, but also of all the senses (J. J. Gibson, 1966). The child does not just hear, he listens. He does not just see, he looks. He does not just touch, he feels. Thus, the extent to which the hearing-impaired child learns to listen does not depend only on the degree of his hearing loss. The opportunities provided for him to develop speech, the encouragement he receives to learn through audition, and the amount of meaningful auditory experience he receives all interact with hearing level to determine how attuned the child will be to using his residual audition.

Acoustic Cues

The acoustic cues available in speech derive lawfully from the source (breath and voice) and signal (vocal tract) characteristics of the speaker (Fant, 1960). As the size of the larynx and the length and shape of the vocal tract differ from speaker to speaker, so, too, do the acoustic properties of the speech signal (Stevens and House, 1961). Accordingly, the listener has, by some means, to equate widely differing acoustic cues with the same speech sound. Such a normalization process (Ladefoged and Broadbent, 1957) is required if, say, the vowel [a] is to be recognized as such whether spoken by a man, a woman, or a child.

Suprasegmental Aspects: The suprasegmental aspects of speech within a breath group—intonation, stress, rhythm, and disjuncture— are carried mainly by the voiced components of speech. These are the frequency of the fundamental (F_0) and its harmonics, which are determined by the rate of vibration of the vocal cords; the relative intensity of the syllable, determined by subglottal pressure, by laryngeal adjustment, and by the resonances of the vocal tract; and duration (Lieberman, 1967). Since voicing information is normally present below 300 Hz, the suprasegmental features should be audible to most hearing-impaired children, including those with only low-frequency residue, if appropriate amplification is provided (Ling, 1964b).

Vowel Sounds: Vowel sounds are produced when the harmonics of the voice are selectively filtered by the vocal tract. When the vocal cords vibrate at, say, a fundamental frequency (F_0) of 125 Hz, harmonics at multiples of this frequency are also present. Thus, acoustic energy will also occur at 250, 375, 500, 625 Hz, and so on across the range of hearing. These harmonics would become weaker and weaker with increasing frequency if it were not for the vocal tract through which this energy has to pass. There, as the tongue and lips assume particular positions, cavities and apertures of certain proportions are formed which filter and resonate the sound to produce the peaks of energy (formants) which characterize each vowel.

In the spectrogram shown in Figure 3.2, the three vowels [u], [a], and [i] spoken by the writer show the harmonics generated by the larynx and the formants generated as a result of the filtering and resonance in the vocal tract. The horizontal axis represents the duration of the sounds; the vertical axis, their frequency; and the shading, their intensity. The harmonics are seen as parallel lines across the spectrogram. The darker harmonics—those that have the greatest intensity—are the formants. Note that the formants of each vowel are in quite different frequency regions.

The frequencies of the formants may be predicted by three factors: the degree of constriction created by the height of the tongue; the distance from the larynx at which this constriction occurs; and the amount of lip-rounding, lip-protrusion, or lip-spreading present (Stevens and

House, 1955). The approximate frequencies of the first (lower) two formants (F_1 and F_2) of the high-back, lip-rounded vowel [u] for the writer, a male, are about 270 and 800 Hz. For a female speaker they would typically be somewhat higher, about 380 and 900 Hz. For young children the values would probably be somewhat higher still (Peterson, 1951).

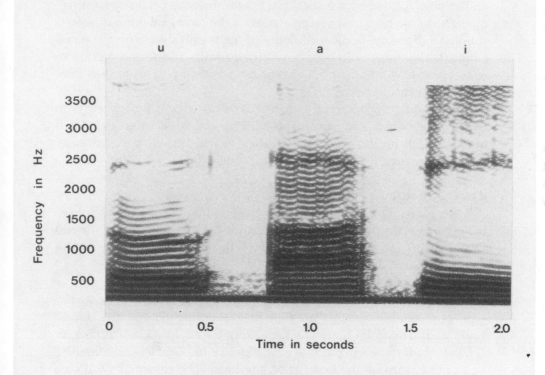

Figure 3.2

Spectrogram showing the vowels [u], [a], and [i] spoken by the writer. The horizontal axis represents time (in this case about 2 secs.) and the vertical axis, frequency. Intensity is shown by shading. The dark areas are the high-energy vowel formants, which are made up of parallel dark lines, the resonated harmonics generated by the larynx.

Thus, while F_2 of the vowel [i] is about 2,500 Hz for the writer, it would be nearer 3,000 Hz for most young children. These examples indicate the frequency range of hearing (270–3,000 Hz) that has to be present if the first two formants of all vowels are to be audible to a hearing-impaired child. In general, perception of F_1 and F_2 is sufficient for the recognition of vowels (Delattre, Liberman, Cooper, and Gerstman, 1952).

Consonant Sounds: Consonant sounds are produced with more constriction of the vocal tract than vowels. The consonants formed with the least constriction are the semivowels [w] and [j], and those with the most, the stop/plosives, which require complete closure of certain articulators. In general, the source-filter effect operates in the production of consonants much as it does in the production of vowels: the apertures and cavities formed by the vocal tract determine the peak resonant frequencies of the harmonics associated with the laryngeal tone (in voiced sounds) and the aperiodic turbulence of the breath stream (in unvoiced sounds). The range of frequency required for the auditory reception of consonants is from about 250 Hz for the nasals [m, n, ŋ] to well over 4,000 Hz for fricatives such as [s].

In subsequent chapters, the principal acoustic cues associated with each of the vowels and consonants will be discussed in greater detail together with results of various studies in which their perception by hearing-impaired listeners has been investigated.

Amplification for Speech

Attempts to augment auditory speech reception may be considered as belonging to two categories: those concerned with conventional (linear) amplification and those in which some forms of frequency transposing amplifiers have been used.

Conventional Hearing Aids: Conventional hearing aids have undergone considerable change since they first came into general use 30 to 40 years ago. Their development has been traced in detail by Berger (1970a). Modern hearing aids are small, have reasonably good fidelity, and can be worn on the body or on the head. The amount by which a hearing aid amplifies sound is termed its *gain*. It is measured in decibels. Hearing aids do not provide the same amount of gain at different frequencies, so gain is usually defined as the average amount of amplification present for the three frequencies 500, 1,000, and 2,000 Hz. The *frequency range* of wearable hearing aids is quite restricted and is usually less than the frequency range represented on an audiogram. Each hearing aid is limited in its *maximum output*. This level is reached when an increase in level of the input signal no longer results in an increase in the level of output. To select appropriate hearing aids for the child (and two aids, one for each ear, should normally be worn), their performance in respect to each of these three parameters (gain, frequency range, and maximum output) must be considered, as must their inherent distortions, their cost, and the type, cost, and efficiency of the batteries. These and other factors relating to the selection of aids are discussed by various specialists in the handbook edited by Katz (1972). Hearing aid design and the principles underlying the use of amplification for speech development have been treated in considerable detail by Ling (1971, 1975). With the provision of appropriate conventional amplification, some hearing-impaired children can hear and discriminate all that is said. Few can hear all aspects of speech, but most can effectively supplement what they hear by using additional visual or tactile cues.

Frequency Transposing Aids: Frequency transposing aids are devices by means of which high-frequency sounds, inaudible to certain hearing-impaired children wearing conventional aids, are translated into audible, low-frequency sounds. The best known of these was designed by Johansson (1966). Evaluation of this and of several other such devices has been reported by Ling (1968, 1972). In general, these studies indicate that the forms of frequency transposition attempted to date have little, if any, advantage over conventional amplification. It is true that some children can make distinctions such as [s] versus [ʃ] with frequency transposition (Guttman, Levitt, and Bellefleur, 1970), but it has also been shown that this may be possible with similar children using conventional amplification (Ling, 1969). In the latter case, the distinction is made on the basis of audible [ʃ] versus inaudible [s]. Such discriminations are trivial in relation to the total requirements of auditory speech reception. Indeed, one of the fundamental problems in transposition is that by utilizing low-frequency hearing for the reception of cues that normally occur in the high-frequency range, one may mask or detract from the reception of low-frequency, suprasegmental, and vowel cues which are equally important in speech. One robs Peter to pay Paul. The one attempt made to avoid this problem, by relaying natural low-frequency cues to one ear and transposed high-frequency sounds to the other, was a failure (Ling and Maretic, 1971). While work to devise and evaluate new forms of frequency transposition continues, insights gained from work to date suggest that the limitations imposed on auditory speech reception by severe hearing impairment will prevent frequency transposing devices from ever being more than limited teaching aids. Except for specific purposes, they are poor rivals to conventional hearing aids.

Visual Speech Reception

Visual speech reception is a complex task. To speechread, the child has to watch the speaker's face; observe the movements of the lips, jaw, and—as far as possible—the tongue; and deduce from the transient shapes what the speaker has said. Vision has been utilized as a substitute for audition among the hearing-impaired not because it is an effective alternative, but because it has been the only other distance sense available. Since there is known to be an unusually high incidence of visual problems among hearing-impaired children (Stockwell, 1952; Suchman, 1967), periodic tests and correction of faulty vision are essential. Even minor visual defects are known to affect speechreading performance (Hardick, Oyer, and Irion, 1970).

Suprasegmental Features and Their Visual Correlates

Sight does little to aid the discrimination of the suprasegmental (prosodic) features of speech. There is no visual pattern corresponding to the intensity with which words, syllables, and phonemes in a sentence are spoken. The pitch of a speaker's voice and the intonation pattern used are equally invisible. The duration of phonemes, syllables, words, phrases, and pauses cannot be determined with precision since the features which mark their boundaries are frequently inaccessible to the eye. Thus, the closing of the lips may signal an /m/ or a pause; the neutral opening of the lips, a vowel or a break in vocalization for breath; and an apparent prolongation of a particular shape, stress on a particular phoneme or a consonant blend made with a part of the tongue which cannot be seen. Although a considerable number of studies have been concerned with the speechreading of phonemes, syllables, words, and phrases, little attention has been paid to the visual reception of suprasegmental features (O'Neill and Oyer, 1961; Berger, 1972).

The Visibility of Vowels

The lip patterns associated with vowel sounds appear to provide the clearest of the many ambiguous cues in speechreading. Vowel sounds in English are each associated with a certain amount of lip-spreading as in [i] or lip-rounding as in [u], although the amount depends on the speaker's characteristic mode of production, on whether speech is accompanied by a smile, on what other sounds precede or follow the vowel, on the speed of speaking, and so on. Experimental studies (Berger, 1970b; Smith, 1972) indicate that there are more correct identifications than errors among all but the central vowels and that most errors involve adjacent vowels (for example, [ɪ] for [i]; [o] for [ɔ]; [ʊ] for [u], etc.). While lip-spreading and lip-rounding bear a direct relationship to the tongue position in the vowels of English, tongue position is usually masked by the lips and teeth in normal speech. Thus, while the tongue is normally placed toward the back of the mouth in the production of [u] and toward the front of the mouth for the vowel [i], neither tongue placement is visible. Young hearing-impaired children who rely mainly on visual cues and who have not been taught or have not deduced the tongue positions which correspond with lip configurations therefore tend to produce these vowels incorrectly, often with appropriate lip shaping, but with the tongue in a neutral position (Ling and Bennett, 1974–75). It has been demonstrated in an electromyographic study of two young deaf adults by Huntington, Harris, Shankweiler, and Sholes (1968) that incorrect tongue placement for speech sounds which are not visible may become habitual.

The Visibility of Consonants

The visual patterns associated with consonant sounds range from being visible but ambiguous to being completely invisible. The ambiguity arises mainly because several speech sounds such as [p], [b], and [m] are homophenous—i.e., look alike on the lips. Nitchie (1930), one of the pioneer teachers of speechreading, considered some 40% of speech sounds to be homophenous, a proportion substantially confirmed by later experimental studies (Heider and Heider, 1940; Woodward and Barber, 1960; Fisher, 1968; Erber, 1972b). Some ambiguity of consonants is also due to the coarticulation of adjacent sounds. The extent of lip-spreading and lip-rounding required for vowels which precede and follow a consonant influences lip configurations, an effect associated with speaking rate. Thus, in the words *two* and *tea*, the phoneme /t/ has quite different visual characteristics. Similarly, an adjacent consonant can influence the articulation and hence the visual pattern of a phoneme. For example, the /n/ in the phrase *on a bike* and the /n/ in *on the bike* differ considerably. In the latter phrase, the /n/ is usually produced interdentally in anticipation of the following consonant.

With regard to visibility, velar sounds such as [k], [g], and [ŋ] are usually obscured by the lips if the adjacent vowel involves lip-rounding (e.g., *cook*) or by the teeth if the lips are spread (e.g., *key*). Nor can formation of these sounds be inferred from jaw movements. In velar sounds jaw movements are much less marked than in alveolar sounds such as [t], [d], and [n] (Kent and Moll, 1972).

In spite of the poverty of information on speech provided by the visual modality, the speechreader with good linguistic skills and a knowledge of the verbal context in which the message is embedded may be able to complete the partial pattern he receives in the same way that a sophisticated reader can usually understand a partly obliterated document on a familiar subject. The speechreader is helped by the speaker's facial expression, body posture, and situational cues (Sanders, 1971). The most helpful additional cues are, of course, those derived from residual audition (I. R. Ewing, 1944).

Visual Cue Systems

Visual cue systems designed to aid the child in both speech reception and speech production take a variety of forms. They differ from visual symbolization systems in a very important and fundamental way. Symbol systems (discussed in Chapter 4) involve the unique association of a particular symbol with a particular sound and may be used as a means of communication, whereas cue systems provide the child with information that indicates underlying features of certain speech sounds such as nasality or voicing. Cue systems are primarily used as an aid to teaching speech and are discarded when they have served their purpose in this regard.

One traditional visual cue is the placement of a finger on the nose to indicate nasality, or on the chest to indicate voicing. New (1940, 1942) has also described the use of a color key, in which unvoiced sounds are represented by blue, voiced sounds by red, and nasals by brown. She first used colored strips to differentiate between the [p], [b], and [m] in speech and speechreading and found that a child thus taught could then generalize, for example, to the sounds [t], [d], and [n]. Charts in which letters were similarly classified by color were also constructed to aid in pronunciation of written material. Of course, this procedure would not be necessary for children with adequate residual hearing for auditory discrimination of voiced, unvoiced, and nasal sounds. It might, in fact, detract from the spontaneous production of these sounds.

Cued speech, a formal system in which particular hand positions and hand configurations are used to supplement speechreading, has recently been proposed by Cornett (1967). Evaluation of the system suggests that it may have some advantages for children who have failed to succeed following a traditional lipreading approach (Ling and Clarke, 1975), but that the visual burden imposed by such hand cues may distract attention from auditory cues (Clarke and Ling, 1976).

Signals directly derived from the acoustic properties of the spoken message are used in a further visual cueing aid to speechreading developed by Upton (1968). The process involves the use of eyeglasses in which lights on the periphery of the lens are used to signal the presence of such features as nasality, voicing, plosion, and friction. This sytem is presently being modified and evaluated. It has recently been used with hearing-impaired children, but with negative results (Mártony, 1974).

The Speechreading Task

In order to understand the fleeting succession of inconstant shapes associated with running speech, the child must engage in active visual search, utilize whatever peripheral cues accompany the message, and draw heavily upon past experience and training. To encourage the development of such skills, the teacher must refrain from making exaggerated lip movements and avoid the teaching of isolated words and speech sounds. Either process may satisfy an immediate (and possibly trivial) teaching goal, but only at the risk of the child's adopting inappropriate strategies that will impede later speech communication.

It seems plausible that the development of speech would positively influence speechreading ability. The child with reasonable articulation skills should be in a better position than poorer speakers to appreciate the significance of movements associated with the speech of others, since reference to his own articulatory processes is likely to help him to divine the intention of the speaker. Indeed, a positive correlation between speech production ability and speechreading ability (not necessarily causal) has been reported by Myklebust (1960).

Speechreading seems destined to remain the dominant visual method of speech reception even though—with or without cues, and with or without articulatory ability on the part of the observer—one cannot obtain from it the totality of information required for perceiving all aspects of speech. Speechreading fails at the suprasegmental level, and it remains doubtful whether the perceptual and memory processes associated with vision—a predominantly spatial sense—will permit the adequate temporal resolution and integration of supplementary visual cues. Alternative visual transforms of speech such as the spectrogram are hard to read at any speed and impossible at a normal speaking rate (Liberman *et al.*, 1968). We conclude that the greatest gains in visual speech reception are likely to be made by developing cue systems that supplement rather than compete with speechreading—cue systems that utilize another sense modality such as touch.

Tactile Speech Reception

Teaching Strategies Using Direct Touch

For several centuries, teachers have attempted to convey information on their speech by encouraging their pupils to use the sense of touch. Thus, Green (1783, p.142) reported that Braidwood encouraged his children to see *and to feel* the movements and effects of his speech. The Abbé de l'Epée (1784, p.165) stated that he worked "avec le doigt de mon disciple toujours dans ma bouche" (with my pupil's finger always in my mouth). Requiring the child occasionally to feel the movements of the tongue was also intrinsic to the method employed by Arrowsmith (1819). Apparently, this form of tactile input (no pun intended) lapsed for well over a century, for there are no accounts of its use known to the writer until it was again reported by Zaliouk (1954). Its effectiveness for teaching certain vowel sounds, to be discussed in a later chapter, has recently been demonstrated by Ling and Bennett (1974–75).

Story (1917) advocated that the child should be allowed to touch the teacher's face and larynx but warned against the teacher touching the child's. His point was that the drive to speak should come from the child, not be imposed by the teacher. The use of touch to clarify the teacher's pronunciation by feeling both vibration and breath stream was also suggested by Haycock (1933).

Joiner (1936, p.26–27) recommended training the child's tactile sense for speech reception during his first year in school through exercises such as recognizing objects by touch alone and identifying the pitch of musical instruments through vibration. K. Alcorn (1938) reported that she constantly "saturated" each child with vibration and that, prior to allowing the child to speak, she ensured that he was familiar with the tactile model of the teacher's voice. This speech familiarization period—involving both vibration and lipreading, Alcorn stated—usually lasted some three to four months from admission to school and was a necessary first step in the child's "long, tedious journey towards speech." S. Alcorn is better known for her vibratory-tactile "Tadoma Method" (Alcorn, 1945), which has been universally used in the education of children who are both deaf and blind. In this method, the child places both hands on the speaker's face so that the thumbs rest on the lips, index fingers on the nose, little fingers on the throat, and the remaining fingers on the cheeks. Thus, both touch and kinesthesis are involved since the fingers also bend with the movement of the speaker's lips and jaw. In the application of the Tadoma Method to hearing-impaired children, it was customary to exclude simultaneous visual input by blindfolding the child (Gruver, 1955) in order to permit him to attend more readily to the haptic touch patterns. Under these conditions, difficult sounds such as [i], [ʃ], [s], and [k] were reported to be imitated with comparative ease.

Goldstein (1939) devoted a section of his book to the use of touch, but texts by more recent writers have not discussed in any detail the merits of having the child touch the speaker's face as a means of improving speech reception. The procedure is, however, commonly to be observed in current practice and is demonstrated in many of the films on speech teaching produced by the John Tracy Clinic in 1971.

Direct touch is a much more difficult avenue for teaching than is either audition or vision. It is a close—as opposed to a distance—sense and it may carry personal-social hazards that are unacceptable to the teacher, the child, or both. As shown by studies in the field of proxemics (Hall, 1963), care has to be taken not to invade another's personal space. If the relationship between the child and teacher is as happy and healthy as it should be, touch can, of course, provide more than just a means of communication about the speech learning process. Such contact may, in this case, be beneficial to the child.

Although certain studies (Rosenstein, 1957; Schiff and Dytell, 1972) indicate that deaf children may have better-than-average tactile sensitivity on the hands and fingers, there appears to have been very little experimental work on the precise nature of the tactile cues afforded the child by having him touch the speaker, place his fingers on a resonator such as a balloon or a drum, or feel the breath stream. Touching the speaker's face or chest can clearly afford some information about voice: its presence or absence, its relative duration, its intensity, and—if the fingers are correctly placed on the face—its pitch. Indeed, Zaliouk (1960) used the localization of resonance in the facial bone structure during production of [m] as his primary method of treating falsetto voice and of establishing optimal speaking register. The method entails certain assumptions, including that of the speaker's constant vocal effort (House, 1959). However, while a given pitch of voice will cause vibration to appear maximally at one point of the speaker's body or face, the vibration itself affords little or no pitch cue. Changes in the frequency of vibration must be quite large before they can be discriminated by touch (Goff, 1967). Thus, an intonation pattern cannot be perceived if vibrations are derived directly from voice and presented to the skin.

The Tangibility of Vowels

The vowels can be felt either by using a resonator or by placing the hands on the face. Either way, they are extremely difficult to differentiate by touch alone. Vowels with the greatest degree of constriction (the high-back and high-front vowels [u] and [i]) generate more vibration in the bones of the facial structure than do the more open vowels. The type of vowel therefore interacts with voice intensity: a great deal more vocal effort is required to produce a particular level of vibration with [a] than with [i]. Of course, vibration plus kinesthetic information derived from jaw and lip movement can permit differentiation of the vowels, but information on the intensity of voice is unstable if different vowels are used. The breath stream associated with the vowels [i] and [u] is directed through relatively narrow apertures and, as a result, can be more readily felt than the breath stream associated with central vowels, which is more widely dispersed. Wetting the fingers enhances their sensitivity to the breath stream and to the relative sensations of coolness associated with the close vowels [i] and [u].

The Tangibility of Consonants

The consonants [m, n, ŋ] are readily felt as vibration on the bridge of the nose. However, facial vibration seems to be relatively weak for other types of consonants and yields fewer cues than feeling the breath stream. Feeling the breath stream can afford certain manner and voicing cues. Thus, the sudden onset of the plosives [p, b, t, d, k, g] can be felt, as can the relatively greater airflow associated with those plosives which are unvoiced and aspirated [p, t, k]. The turbulent breath stream associated with all fricatives is also tangible to the fingertips, as are the different direction and spread of the breath stream characteristic of [s] and [ʃ]. The relatively cooler sensation experienced with [s] is due to the breath stream's being more narrowly funneled than for the [ʃ]. The affricates, [tʃ] and [dʒ] share properties of the breath stream common to both the plosives and the fricatives. In talking to the child close to the ear without a hearing aid, as in the *ad concham* method employed by Wedenberg (1951), the teacher provides the child with tactile, breath stream cues on the ear and surrounding surfaces in addition to the auditory pattern.

Aids to Tactile Speech Reception

The tactile sense can be made to serve as a distance modality by the use of electronic aids. Effectiveness of this procedure, however, is subject to the vital consideration that the skin senses can, in fact, decode the speech signal if it is electronically transformed for presentation by means of a vibrotactile device or by electrical stimulation. The devices so far created for transforming speech for tactile presentation have provided relatively simple displays. These include a single vibrator which is driven by a hearing aid or a comparable amplifier (Gault, 1925–26; Boothroyd, 1972; Neate, 1972; Erber and Cramer, 1974) and speech analyzing devices in which different frequency regions of the speech spectrum are sampled and relayed to each of the several vibrators (Gault, 1929–30; Pickett, 1963; Woldring, 1968; and Kringlebotn, 1968, among others). None of these devices has yielded the type of transform which will allow adequate reception of speech by touch alone. One of the problems is illustrated by the type of device developed by Ling and Sofin (1975) which, with a single vibrator, can signal the presence of fricatives. Many more vibrators and a much more complex circuitry would be required to provide information as to which of the several fricatives is spoken. Similarly, with the device designed by Willemain and Lee (1971) only one aspect of speech, pitch contour, was provided. A more complex array would be necessary to display detailed, segmental information; and Kirman (1973), in an excellent analysis of the problems inherent in presenting tactual transforms of speech perception, does, indeed, suggest that a much more complex spacio-temporal display might feasibly provide sufficient information for the adequate reception of speech by touch alone. The development and application of such a device remain to be explored.

Finally, it should be emphasized that the tactile devices which have been explored to date do yield information which can supplement visual speech reception. It is to the consideration of such multisensory speech reception that we turn in the next chapter.

Summary

The characteristics of sense modalities and their use in speech reception by hearing-impaired children are discussed, and associated research studies—some concerned with sensory aids—are reviewed.

Because audition is the only sense capable of appreciating all aspects of speech—the suprasegmental features, vowels, and consonants—it is emphasized that whatever residual hearing a child may possess should be exploited. Reservations about the audiogram as a predictor of speech reception are expressed.

The type of information provided by speechreading indicates that the eye is a poor substitute for the ear. It is shown that the possibilities and limitations of the other senses in relation to speech reception among hearing-impaired children have not yet been fully explored and that very little is known about the possible contributions of touch.

Attention is drawn to the facilitating relationship that exists between speech production ability and speech reception in any modality. The active use of the sense modalities in speech reception is stressed: we listen, look, and feel; we do not simply hear, see, and touch.

REFERENCES

Abbs, J. H., & Sussmann, H. M.　Neurophysiological feature detectors and speech perception: A discussion of theoretical implications. *J. Speech Hear. Res.*, 14, 23–36, 1971.

Alcorn, K.　Speech developed through vibration. *Volta Rev.*, 40, 633–637, 1938.

Alcorn, S.　Development of the Tadoma Method for the deaf-blind. *Except. Child.*, 11, 117–119, 1945.

Arrowsmith, J. P.　*The Art of Instructing the Infant Deaf and Dumb*. London: Taylor and Hessey, 1819.

Berger, K. W.　*The Hearing Aid: Its Operation and Development*. Detroit, Mich.: National Hearing Aid Society, 1970a.

Berger, K. W.　Vowel confusions in speechreading. *Ohio J. Speech Hear.*, 5, 123–128, 1970b.

Berger, K. W.　*Speechreading: Principles and Methods*. Baltimore, Md.: National Educational Press, 1972.

Boothroyd, A.　*Distribution of hearing levels in the student population of the Clarke School for the Deaf*. S.A.R.P. 3, Northampton, Mass.: Clarke School for the Deaf, 1970.

Boothroyd, A.　Some comments on the use of classroom amplification equipment with children having sensitivity to high intensity low frequency sound only. *Proc. Int. Congr. on Educ. of the Deaf*, Vol. 1. Stockholm: Sveriges Lärarförbund, 1972, pp. 58–60.

Boothroyd, A., & Cawkwell, S.　Vibrotactile thresholds in pure tone audiometry. *Acta Otolaryngol.*, 69, 381–387, 1970.

Clarke, B. R., & Ling, D.　The effects of cued speech: A follow-up study. *Volta Rev.*, 78, 23–34, 1976.

Cooper, W. E.　Adaptation of phonetic feature analyzers for place of articulation. *J. Acoust. Soc. Am.*, 56, 617–627, 1974.

Cooper, W. E., & Blumstein, S. E.　A "labial" feature analyzer in speech perception. *Percept. Psychophys.*, 15, 591–600, 1974.

Cornett, R. O.　Cued speech. *Am. Ann. Deaf*, 112, 3–13, 1967.

Delattre, P., Liberman, A. M., Cooper, F. S., & Gerstman, L. J.　An experimental study of the acoustic determinants of vowel color; observations on one- and two-formant vowels synthesized from spectrographic patterns. *Word*, 8, 195–210, 1952.

de l'Epée, C. M.　*La véritable manière d'instruire les sourds et muets, confirmée par une longue expérience*. Paris: Nyon l'aîné, 1784.

Eimas, P.　Auditory and linguistic processing of cues for place of articulation by infants. *Percept. Psychophys.*, 16, 513–521, 1974.

Elliott, L. L.　Descriptive analysis of audiometric and psychometric scores of students at a school for the deaf. *J. Speech Hear. Res.*, 10, 21–40, 1967.

Erber, N. P. Speech-envelope cues as an acoustic aid to lipreading for profoundly deaf children. *J. Acoust. Soc. Am.*, 51, 1224–1227, 1972a.

Erber, N. P. Auditory, visual and auditory-visual recognition of consonants by children with normal and impaired hearing. *J. Speech Hear. Res.*, 15, 413–422, 1972b.

Erber, N. P., & Cramer, K. D. Vibrotactile recognition of sentences. *Am. Ann. Deaf*, 119, 716–720, 1974.

Ewing, I. R. *Lipreading and Hearing Aids*. Manchester: Manchester University Press, 1944.

Fant, G. *Acoustic Theory of Speech Production With Calculations Based on X-Ray Studies of Russian Articulations*. The Hague: Mouton, 1960.

Fisher, C. G. Confusions among visually perceived consonants. *J. Speech Hear. Res.*, 11, 796–804, 1968.

Gammon, S. A., Smith, P. J., Daniloff, R. G., & Kim, C. W. Articulation and stress/juncture production under oral anaesthetization and masking. *J. Speech Hear. Res.*, 14, 271–282, 1971.

Garner, W. R. To perceive is to know. *Am. Psychol.*, 21, 11–19, 1966.

Gault, R. H. Progress in experiments on identification of speech by touch. *J. Abnorm. Soc. Psychol.*, 20, 118–127, 1925–26.

Gault, R. H. On the effect of simultaneous tactual-visual stimulation in relation to the interpretation of speech. *J. Abnorm. Soc. Psychol.*, 24, 498–517, 1929–30.

Geldard, F. A. Vision, audition and beyond. *Contrib. Sens. Physiol.*, 4, 1–17, 1970.

Gengel, R. W., & Foust, K. O. Some implications of listening levels for speech reception by sensorineural hearing-impaired children. *Lang., Speech Hear. Serv. in Sch.*, 6, 14–20, 1975.

Gibson, J. J. *The Senses Considered as Perceptual Systems*. Boston: Houghton Mifflin, 1966.

Goff, G. D. Differential discrimination of frequency of cutaneous mechanical vibration. *J. Exp. Psychol.*, 74, 294–299, 1967.

Goldstein, M. A. *The Acoustic Method for the Training of the Deaf and Hard of Hearing Child*. St. Louis: Laryngoscope Press, 1939.

Green, F. *Vox Oculis Subjecta*. London: Benjamin White, 1783.

Gruver, M. H. The Tadoma Method. *Volta Rev.*, 57, 17–19, 1955.

Guttman, N., Levitt, H., & Bellefleur, P. A. Articulatory training of the deaf using low-frequency surrogate fricatives. *J. Speech Hear. Res.*, 13, 19–29, 1970.

Hall, E. T. A system for the notation of proxemic behavior. *Am. Anthropol.*, 65, 1003–1026, 1963.

Hardick, E. J., Oyer, H. J., & Irion, P. E. Lipreading performance as related to measurements of vision. *J. Speech Hear. Res.*, 13, 92–100, 1970.

Haycock, G. S. *The Teaching of Speech*. Washington, D.C.: Volta Bureau, 1933.

Heider, F., & Heider, G. M. An experimental investigation of lipreading. *Psychol. Monogr.*, 52, 124–133, 1940.

Hirsh, I. J. Third Annual Fairey Lecture: Acoustical bases of speech perception. *J. Sound & Vib.*, 27, 111–122, 1973.

House, A. S. A note on optimal vocal frequency. *J. Speech Hear. Res.*, 2, 55–60, 1959.

Huntington, D. A., Harris, K. S., Shankweiler, D., & Sholes, G. N. Some observations on monosyllable production by deaf speakers and dysarthric speakers. *Am. Ann. Deaf*, 113, 134–146, 1968.

Johansson, B.   The use of the transposer for the management of the deaf child. *J. Int. Audiol.*, 5, 362–372, 1966.

Joiner, E.   *Graded Lessons in Speech*. Morganton, N.C.: North Carolina School for the Deaf, 1936.

Katz, J. (Ed.)   *Handbook of Clinical Audiology*. Baltimore, Md.: Williams and Wilkins, 1972.

Kent, R. D., & Moll, K. L.   Cinefluorographic analyses of selected lingual consonants. *J. Speech Hear. Res.*, 15, 453–473, 1972.

Kirman, J. H.   Tactile communication of speech: A review and an analysis. *Psychol. Bull.*, 80, 54–74, 1973.

Kringlebotn, M.   Experiments with some visual and vibrotactile aids for the deaf. *Am. Ann. Deaf*, 113, 311–317, 1968.

Ladefoged, P.   *Three Areas of Experimental Phonetics*. London: Oxford University Press, 1967.

Ladefoged, P., & Broadbent, D. E.   Information conveyed by vowels. *J. Acoust. Soc. Am.*, 29, 98–104, 1957.

Liberman, A. M.   The grammars of speech and language. *Cogn. Psychol.*, 1, 301–323, 1970.

Liberman, A. M., Cooper, F. S., Shankweiler, D. P., & Studdert-Kennedy, M. Perception of the speech code. *Psychol. Rev.*, 74, 431–461, 1967.

Liberman, A. M., Cooper, F. S., Shankweiler, D. P., & Studdert-Kennedy, M.   Why are speech spectrograms hard to read? *Am. Ann. Deaf*, 113, 127–133, 1968.

Lieberman, P.   *Intonation, Perception and Language*. Cambridge, Mass.: M.I.T. Press, 1967.

Ling, D.   An auditory approach to the education of deaf children. *Audecibel*, 13, 96–101, 1964a.

Ling, D.   Implications of hearing aid amplification below 300 cps. *Volta Rev.*, 66, 723–729, 1964b.

Ling, D.   Three experiments on frequency transposition. *Am. Ann. Deaf*, 113, 283–294, 1968.

Ling, D.   Speech discrimination by profoundly deaf children using linear and coding amplifiers. *IEEE Trans. Audio Electroacoust.*, AU-17, 298–303, 1969.

Ling, D.   Conventional hearing aids: An overview. *Volta Rev.*, 73, 343–352, passim, 1971.

Ling, D.   Auditory discrimination of speech transposed by a sample-and-hold process. In G. Fant (Ed.), *Speech Communication Ability and Profound Deafness*. Washington, D.C.: A. G. Bell Assoc. for the Deaf, 1972.

Ling, D.   Amplification for speech. In D. R. Calvert and S. R. Silverman, *Speech and Deafness*. Washington, D.C.: A. G. Bell Assoc. for the Deaf, 1975.

Ling, D., & Bennett, C. W.   Training severely hearing-impaired children in vowel imitation. *Hum. Commun.*, 3, 5–18, 1974–75.

Ling, D., & Clarke, B. R.   Cued speech: An evaluative study. *Am. Ann. Deaf*, 120, 480–488, 1975.

Ling, D., & Maretic, H.   Frequency transposition in the teaching of speech to deaf children. *J. Speech Hear. Res.*, 14, 37–46, 1971.

Ling, D., & Naish, S. J.   Threshold variations in repeated audiograms. *Volta Rev.*, 77, 97–104, 1975.

Ling, D., & Sofin, B.   Discrimination of fricatives by hearing-impaired children using a vibrotactile cue. *Br. J. Audiol.*, 9, 14–18, 1975.

Mártony, J.   *Some experiments with electronic speechreading aids*. STL-QPSR 2-3, 34–56, Stockholm: R. Inst. Technol., 1974.

Massaro, D. W.   Preperceptual images, processing time, and perceptual units in auditory perception. *Psychol. Rev.*, 79, 124–145, 1972.

Miller, G. A., Heise, G. A., & Lichten, W.   The intelligibility of speech as a function of the context of the test materials. *J. Exp. Psychol.*, 41, 329–335, 1951.

Montagu, A.   *Touching: The Human Significance of the Skin*. New York: Harper and Row, 1971.

Myklebust, H. R.   *The Psychology of Deafness*. New York: Grune and Stratton, 1960.

Neate, D. M.   The use of tactile vibration in the teaching of speech to severely and profoundly deaf children. *Teach. Deaf*, 70, 137–146, 1972.

New, M. C.   Speech for the young deaf child. *Volta Rev.*, 42, 592–599, 1940.

New, M. C.   Color in speech teaching. *Volta Rev.*, 44, 133–138, passim., 1942.

Nitchie, E. B.   *Lip-Reading Principles and Practice*. New York: F. Stokes & Co., 1930.

Nober, E. H.   Pseudoauditory bone-conduction thresholds. *J. Speech Hear. Disord.*, 29, 469–476, 1964.

O'Neill, J. J., & Oyer, H. J.   *Visual Communication for the Hard of Hearing*. Englewood Cliffs, N.J.: Prentice-Hall, 1961.

Peterson, G. E.   Vocal gestures. *Bell Labs. Record*, 29, 500–503, 1951.

Pickett, J. M.   Tactual communication of speech sounds to the deaf: Comparison with lipreading. *J. Speech Hear. Disord.*, 28, 315–330, 1963.

Powers, M. H.   Functional disorders of articulation—symptomatology and etiology. In L. E. Travis (Ed.), *Handbook of Speech Pathology*. New York: Appleton-Century-Crofts, 1971.

Rosenstein, J.   Tactile perception of rhythmic patterns by normal, blind, deaf and aphasic children. *Am. Ann. Deaf*, 102, 399–403, 1957.

Rosenzweig, M. R., & Postman, L.   Frequency of usage and the perception of words. *Science*, 127, 263–266, 1958.

Sanders, D. A.   *Aural Rehabilitation*. Englewood Cliffs, N.J.: Prentice-Hall, 1971.

Schiff, W., & Dytell, R. S.   Deaf and hearing children's performance on a tactual perception battery. *Percept. Mot. Skills*, 35, 683–706, 1972.

Sher, A. E., & Owens, E.   Consonant confusions associated with hearing loss above 2,000 Hz. *J. Speech Hear. Res.*, 17, 669–681, 1974.

Smith, C. R.   *Residual hearing and speech production in deaf children*. Unpublished Ph.D. diss., City University of New York, 1972.

Stevens, K. N., & House, A. S.   Development of a quantitative description of vowel articulation. *J. Acoust. Soc. Am.*, 27, 484–493, 1955.

Stevens, K. N., & House, A. S.   An acoustical theory of vowel production and some of its implications. *J. Speech Hear. Res.*, 4, 303–320, 1961.

Stockwell, E.   Visual defects in the deaf child. *A.M.A. Arch. Ophthalmol.*, 48, 428–432, 1952.

Story, A. J.   Talks to young teachers of speech: The development of voice for speaking. *Volta Rev.*, 19, 68–70, 1917.

Subcommittee on Human Communication and Its Disorders. *Human Communication and Its Disorders: An Overview*. National Institute of Neurological Diseases and Stroke, N.I.H., Bethesda, Md.: U.S. Dept. Health, Educ. & Welfare, 1969.

Suchman, R. G.   Visual impairment among deaf children. *Arch. Ophthalmol.*, 77, 18–21, 1967.

Upton, H. W.   Wearable eyeglass speechreading aid. *Am. Ann. Deaf*, 113, 222–229, 1968.

Wathen-Dunn, W. (Ed.)   *Models for the Perception of Speech and Visual Form*. Cambridge, Mass.: M.I.T. Press, 1967.

Watson, T. J.   The use of residual hearing in the education of deaf children. *Volta Rev.*, 63, 328–334, passim., 1961.

Wedenberg, E.   Auditory training of deaf and hard of hearing children. *Acta Otolaryngol. Suppl.*, 94, 1951.

Willemain, T. R., & Lee, F. F.   Tactile pitch feedback for deaf speakers. *Volta Rev.*, 73, 541–553, 1971.

Woldring, S.   Breathing patterns during the speech of deaf children. *Ann. New York Acad. Sci.*, 155, 206–207, 1968.

Woodward, M. F., & Barber, C. G.   Phoneme perception in lipreading. *J. Speech Hear. Res.*, 3, 213–222, 1960.

Zaliouk, A.   A visual-tactile system of phonetical symbolization. *J. Speech Hear. Disord.*, 19, 190–207, 1954.

Zaliouk, A.   Falsetto voice in deaf children. *Curr. Probl. Phoniatr. Logop.*, 1, 217–226, 1960.

/4/

Multisensory Speech Reception

The extent to which simultaneous use can be made of two or more sense modalities in speech reception has not yet been fully explored. Most of the work on multisensory speech reception to date has been concerned with speechreading as a supplement to residual audition, and a considerable body of evidence has been amassed which shows that speech reception in communication is enhanced when vision and audition are both employed. Much less work has been done on the use of touch to supplement residual hearing, vision, or both. Still less study has been made of the means by which multisensory speech reception can be most effectively taught or of the carry-over into everyday communication which can be expected from specific training procedures. In this chapter we shall examine the possible ways in which the tactual and visual correlates of speech may together serve as alternatives to audition or be used to supplement residual hearing. We shall then review what is known about speech reception through the simultaneous use of two or more sense modalities, indicate areas in which more work is required, and discuss multimodal teaching strategies in current use.

In the context of speech teaching, we are concerned with the child's reception of speech patterns at two levels: the phonetic level, which demands the child's reception of particular features of sounds which we require him to produce; and the phonologic level, which demands his recognition of speech patterns and their meanings. The strategies we may employ or expect the child to employ during speech acquisition are not necessarily appropriate to communicative speech. In fact, adherence to strategies used at the learning stage may seriously impede progress toward skilled performance. For example, the teacher may legiti-

45

mately provide supplementary visual or tactile cues during training to indicate the nature of the acoustic features which differentiate one sound from another. However, continued provision of such cues may well focus the child's attention on feature structure, obviate his need to employ residual audition, and detract from his acquisition of skill in utilizing linguistic and semantic cues available from the prevailing context. An analogous situation occurs in reading. In the early stages, attention to letter-sound correspondence may be important. In later stages such attention would detract from ability to read for meaning (Smith, 1971).

In the absence of evidence to the contrary, let us assume that simultaneous cues from hearing, touch, and vision can be integrated by the child in a manner which provides him with information on the features of speech which differentiate one sound pattern from another. Then let us examine what tactile and visual correlates of speech features are available in training (where direct touch can be used and optimal use of amplification can be made), and in everyday communication (where direct touch is not feasible and conditions often exclude full use of residual hearing). Table 4.A indicates the range of possibilities. This table, based on data discussed in the previous chapter, shows the extent to which the various speech features may be received through each and all sense modalities.

Reference to Table 4.A indicates that in the complete absence of audition, information on voice features is particularly difficult to transmit except in training situations, since touch provides more information on voice features than does vision. There are vibratory correlates of vocal duration and vocal intensity, but only through feeling the point of maximum vibration on the head or body of the speaker can the child derive information on voice pitch (F_0). Vision offers correlates of neither vocal intensity nor F_0, and only ambiguous information on vocal duration. However, in vowel production, the position of the lips, jaw, and sometimes the tongue can be seen but cannot be deduced from corresponding vibration.

The type of information afforded by vision and by direct touch in relation to vowels is quite similar, but since the speech organs are partially obscured by the use of direct touch, their simultaneous use would be precluded. In consonant reception, vibratory and visual cues together would yield partial information on all three features: manner, place, and voicing. In training situations, when the teacher's objective is to develop the production of particular speech features, it would seem reasonable for her to emphasize the use of touch if it affords the most information on the feature to be taught. The use of touch may also provide

TABLE 4.A

The types of speech features available (A), partly available (P), or unavailable (–) in speech reception through each sense modality.*

Sense Modality	Voice Features		Vowel Features			Consonant Features		
	Duration	Intensity	F$_0$	F$_1$	F$_2$	Manner	Place	Voicing
Audition:								
up to 750 Hz	A	A	A	A	–	P	–	P
up to 1,500 Hz	A	A	A	A	P	A	P	A
up to 3,000 Hz	A	A	A	A	A	A	A	A
Touch:								
Vibration	A	A	–	–		P	–	P
Direct touch	A	P	P	Tactile Correlates		A	P	P
Vision:								
Speechreading	P	–	–	Visual Correlates		–	P	–

*N.B. Audition is assumed if the characteristic frequencies of given features fall mainly within the specified range of hearing. Vibratory correlates shown are those which may be obtained from either feeling a resonator or wearing a bone-conduction receiver driven by a hearing aid. The tactile correlates depicted for direct touch (fingers on the face of the speaker) have not been substantiated by research. The lip, jaw, and tongue movements associated with vowel production are not considered to yield complete and unambiguous visual or tactile correlates of sounds and should hence be considered as providing only partial information on vowel features.

vibratory cues for the totally deaf child both to supplement speechreading in training and to augment the child's experience of speech at other times. The data in Table 4.A suggest that the appropriate use of direct touch in training may provide the child with sufficient cues to develop production of speech containing all eight of the features specified. However, Table 4.A also indicates the need for sensory aids which extend the supplementary use of touch in the reception of features within and, beyond the training situation. The further development of tactile aids is suggested on the grounds that for the totally deaf child, vision is already a heavily burdened sense modality.

Further reference to Table 4.A indicates the extent to which children with various amounts of residual hearing might be expected to receive the various features of speech as presented through audition alone or through audition supplemented by vision, touch, or both. It is clear that when residual audition alone is used, certain of the eight speech features will not be available except to those whose range of hearing extends up to 3,000 Hz. For those with the most limited audition, speechreading can complement residual hearing in such a way that at least partial information on each of the eight speech features is available. This being the case, one must question whether anything would be gained from adding tactile cues for children with useful residual hearing. At best, such cues would parallel those already available through audition and vision. It may be argued that duplication of information for most features might lead the child to ignore one of the other available channels. If this were so, and if audition were ignored, then information on F_0 would be lost. On the other hand, the redundancy afforded might provide the child with cues which would be useful when receiving speech under difficult conditions.

In training and in carefully controlled communication situations, optimal use of residual hearing and vision can be ensured. However, in many real-life situations, even those children with a wide range of hearing are expected to receive speech at a distance or in background noise that renders audition impossible. Similarly, visual conditions are not uniformly ideal. Skills which permit the child to function optimally through the use of a remaining channel (vision under conditions of noise, audition in dark) are therefore highly desirable. One doubts, however, that vibratory cues would be a useful supplement to vision at a distance or under conditions of noise because vibratory stimuli decrease in intensity with distance, as does sound; and vibrations are also caused by background noise with the result that speech stimuli are masked or otherwise confounded.

The conditions under which research on multisensory speech reception has been undertaken rarely reflect the range of those conditions encountered in everyday life. Similarly, the speech reception strategies we encourage the child to adopt in training may not be the most propitious for him in other situations. Until more research has been carried out on multisensory speech reception, we can but hazard an informed guess as to the effects of our teaching procedures; for multimodal presentation poses many unanswered questions. For example:

• If either vision or touch supplements residual audition in certain ways, can they detract from the use of audition in others?

• What is the exact nature of the cues that touch can add to audition, to vision, or to both?

• Are the cues that one sense modality provides on its own unchanged when they are presented along with cues in another modality, or does some form of sensory inhibition or enhancement operate to reduce or to radically change them?

• If we find that the simultaneous use of two modalities enhances phoneme reception in nonsense syllables or words, can we assume that similar enhancement will occur in running speech?

• The characteristics of short-term memory associated with each of the three input modalities are known to differ:
  What effects do such differences cause in multimodal presentation?

• We know that hearing-impaired children have difficulty in generalizing from skills acquired through training on specific tasks:
  Does the simultaneous use of two or three modalities in teaching encourage the child to adopt strategies for the perception and memory of speech that are inappropriate to, and detract from, performance in communication situations when the same number of modalities cannot be used?

• Does the use of a visual phonetic symbolization system provide the child with a frame of reference that truly assists in speech reception at a phonemic level, and if so, does such a frame of reference assist or inhibit speech reception at a word, sentence, or suprasentential level?

• Does the concurrent use of signs detract from speech reception?

There are dozens more questions that one might ask. None of the answers is available at the present time. Sufficient experimental work has not yet been done.

Hearing and Vision

It is our everyday experience that under less than optimal acoustic conditions, we can enhance speech reception by watching the speaker. That such is generally the case with normally hearing subjects has been confirmed in experiments by O'Neill (1954) and by Sumby and Pollack (1954), among others. The extent to which sentence reception is enhanced by the simultaneous use of audition and vision among adult hearing-impaired listeners was demonstrated somewhat earlier by I. R. Ewing (1944). Using 92 listeners who suffered hearing impairment after the acquisition of language, she demonstrated the relative contributions of audition and vision under four conditions. With unaided hearing and no speechreading, subjects achieved mean scores of 21%; with unaided hearing and speechreading, their mean scores improved to 64%; with aided hearing, but no speechreading, mean scores were also 64%; and with both aided hearing and speechreading, mean scores of 90% were obtained. No analysis to determine the specific cues contributing to such gains was made.

Hutton (1959) presented multiple-choice word lists to 25 hearing-impaired adults under conditions similar to those described in the preceding paragraph. He also found that audition and vision together yielded better scores than vision or audition alone. Bisensory scores (83%) were considerably less than the sum of the separate auditory (68%) and visual (38%) scores. Analysis of vowels and consonants identified under each condition indicated that audition played a much larger role than vision in the bisensory reception of vowels, and that the differentiation of certain consonants such as [b] and [v] was better under the auditory-visual condition than under the auditory condition alone. The reason why bisensory scores were not equal to the sum of the visual and auditory scores was that information on some of the features of speech was conveyed in parallel by both audition and vision. The reason why bisensory scores were nevertheless superior to scores obtained by vision and audition alone was that certain cues available through one sense, but not the other, could still be perceived when both sense modalities were used simultaneously. These and other similar findings have been confirmed and extended by Erber (1972), who worked with both normally hearing and hearing-impaired children.

The above studies suggest that the case for auditory-visual speech reception is relatively strong. However, this case may be accepted only with certain reservations. In most studies, nonsense syllables and words rather than running speech were used, and in most studies the nonsense syllables were constructed with the vowel [a]. This vowel provides much better cues on place of consonant production than do others. While visual identification of five places of consonant production (bilabial to velar) may be possible with [a] (Binnie, Montgomery, and Jackson, 1974), this is not the case for consonants in other vowel contexts (Birtles, 1970). Even if consonant reception in running speech were superior among hearing-impaired children when both hearing and vision are used, it does not follow that all other aspects of speech would be similarly enhanced. Indeed, in view of the poor vowel and rhythm structure typical of the speech of hearing-impaired children (see Chapter 2), this seems unlikely.

The extent to which full use of either modality can be developed when an auditory-visual or visual-auditory approach is used is also open to question. So far, the evidence is indirect, but in numerous studies (see below) we have found that children taught exclusively through a multisensory approach generally make less than optimal use of residual audition. Significant and often dramatic improvement in their auditory speech reception usually occurs in experimental work in which audition alone is employed and speechreading is suppressed. Thus, Ling (1968) reported improvement in word reception through practice in the auditory modality alone. Doehring and Ling (1971) found similar gains for vowels; Aston (1972), for the manner of production and voicing of consonants; Bennett (1973), for the voice onset time of consonants; and A. H. Ling (1975, 1976), for sequences of digits and words. These studies suggest that in order to develop ability to perceive many of the acoustic cues that are required for adequate auditory-visual speech reception, prior and parallel training in speech reception through audition alone should be provided. Specific training exclusively through audition has been advocated by many educators including Pollack (1970).

Hearing and Touch

Well designed studies of the use of touch as a supplement to residual audition have not yet been reported. Research in the field has been mainly concerned with tactile sensation as a means of augmenting speechreading. Nevertheless, amplification systems which incorporate a vibratory output (Schulte, 1972) are currently used in many schools for the deaf. Comparisons of hearing and touch with respect to temporal gap detection have been made by Boothroyd (1973), and potential problems in using vibratory signals in classroom communication have been indicated in observations made by Erber and Zeiser (1974). Their work confirmed that ambient noise tends to distort the temporal patterning of the teacher's speech.

Vision and Touch
No experimental work has been published which describes either the quantity or the types of additional cues added to speechreading by having the child touch the speaker's face. Quantitative improvements in speechreading have been reported for hearing-impaired subjects using a single vibrator output from an amplifier (Gault, 1926; Boothroyd, 1972; Neate, 1972). However, no systematic qualitative studies of the cues which result in such improvement have been reported. Gault's (1926) work with adults suggested that suprasegmental information conveyed by touch (rhythm, relative intensity, duration, and number of syllables) was of particular help in discriminating between sentences and that touch also assisted in the discrimination of vowels (possibly again due to relative intensity and duration). Gault found that words differing by one consonant feature (*chair-share, pluck-plug*, and *grease-crease*) could not be differentiated, either by vision or touch separately, or by vision and touch together. Gault's equipment was later used by Carhart (1935) to study responses of hearing-impaired children. Results essentially confirmed those obtained with adults.

Pickett (1963) and Suzuki, Kagami, and Takahashi (1968) trained children with devices having 10 vibratory outputs. Both devices transposed energy from specific bands in the speech frequencies to drive low-frequency vibrators. Pickett (1963) ascribed most of the enhancement of speechreading noted in his study to the additional information provided on relative duration and to better discrimination of the number of syllables in words. High-frequency consonant sounds such as [s] and [t] could also be differentiated by some of his subjects with speechreading supplemented by touch. The addition of touch did not appear to detract from speechreading ability. In the study reported by Suzuki *et al.* (1968), speechreading of neither vowels in words nor vowels in isolation was improved by the additional use of touch. However, certain homophenous words (*patto, manto, batto*) were discriminated significantly better when vision was aided by touch. The investigators concluded that the vibratory stimulus they provided supplied gross features of spectrum, time, and amplitude. The use of a tactile vocoder employing 23 channels was more recently reported by Englemann and Rosov (1975). It permitted the discrimination of certain words and phrases by touch alone and conveyed voice features in addition to information on vowels and consonants. Its use as an aid to speechreading has not yet been fully explored.

Although certain advantages appear to accrue from the use of tactile aids which employ several vibratory outputs, it is clear that the devices so far developed have not helped speechreaders to learn to differentiate optimally between consonants. Since cues on place of production are visible, perhaps more success would be achieved if tactile devices were designed to supplement speechreading by providing information specifically relating to cues on voicing and manner of production. A beginning in this direction has been made by Ling and Sofin (1975), who used a single vibrator to signal fricatives. However, signaling other manners of production becomes increasingly complicated electronically, particularly if the objective is to do this by means of a portable tactile device. Further, the limits of a child's capacity to integrate such cues into his perceptual system have not yet been explored.

Hearing, Vision, and Touch

Handel and Buffardi (1968) have studied the perception of complete patterns partly presented in one modality and partly in another. The paired modalities were auditory-visual, auditory-tactile, and visual-tactile. Auditory-tactile pairing was less effective than auditory-visual or visual-tactile pairing for the 54 normally hearing subjects employed. The question of whether speech presented by all three senses simultaneously leads to ignoring the third modality in the face of a more efficient pairing of two modalities remains to be resolved (Loveless, Brebner, and Hamilton, 1970).

The selective attention given to available sense modalities by hearing-impaired subjects requires much more study, particularly among children. Age-related variables and possible visual processing problems, for example, have not been adequately considered, although Piaget (1969) and Abravanel (1972), among others, have observed that the relative amount of attention paid to each sense varies from one age group to another; and Myklebust and Brutten (1953) have found that visual perceptual problems tend to be more frequent among hearing-impaired children than among those with normal hearing. Present theories of selective and simultaneous attention have been discussed by Moray (1970), Broadbent (1974, pp. 31–41), and Norman and Bobrow (1975). These authors consider the possible mechanisms involved in receiving information simultaneously in more than one modality, in switching attention from one channel to another, and in using only one sense to attend to two simultaneous inputs. On the basis of their work we may speculate as to the nature of the mechanism involved in multisensory speech reception.

Probable Mechanisms Underlying Multimodal Processing

Some of the probable mechanisms underlying the simultaneous use of the sense modalities in the reception of speech are illustrated in Figure 4.1. This figure depicts the inputs from each sense as being subject to short-term storage and analysis in which the component cues are actively scanned and weighed for relevant information content prior to selection for summation. The selection of cues for summation is determined by various context criteria such as the child's knowledge of phonetic, phonologic, and higher-level linguistic rules—including those derived from speech production—and the nature of the receptive task. Some cues will be processed serially, others in parallel. The use of the senses and the processes involved while the sensory images are in short-term store are thus determined by direct reference to the long-term store. In the restricted task of the type frequently used in research studies, one might require discrimination of suprasegmental information. In this case, the child's attention may be exclusively directed toward cues derived from residual audition or touch. Similarly, if the task were to involve identification of place of articulation, attention could be paid to visual cues alone. Obviously, in real life the choices are much more complex.

The extent to which children can use audition will vary according to the extent and type of hearing impairment present. Thus, a variable resistance is shown between the auditory sense and the short-term storage. For the very deaf child, resistance is maximum and there are few, if any, cues available; whereas for hard-of-hearing children, resistance may assume a minimal value and cues for the auditory modality can receive the main or exclusive weighting in most speech reception tasks. Interactions between the long-term and short-term stores may proceed while new, incoming information is also being received, coded, and, perhaps, rehearsed. We know relatively little about multisensory inputs and the mechanisms depicted in Figure 4.1. Nevertheless, we know that inputs and mechanisms of the sort discussed have to be studied if we are to understand multisensory processing of speech. We shall refer back to short-term and long-term memory processes as depicted in Figure 4.1 as we go on to discuss phonetic symbolization systems and signs, for the way we code visual symbols is certainly quite different from the way we process sounds.

Phonetic Symbolization Systems

It has become traditional in teaching speech to hearing-impaired children to use visual phonetic symbolization systems. These differ from

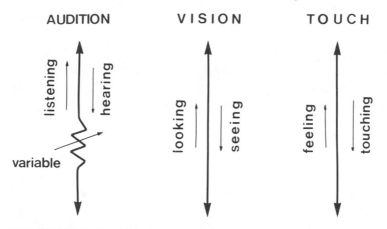

AUDITION   VISION   TOUCH

listening   hearing   looking   seeing   feeling   touching

variable

SHORT-TERM STORAGE, ANALYSIS AND SYNTHESIS

Scanning→Weighing → Summation ——→Pattern Extraction

LONG-TERM MEMORY STORE

Expectations based on past experience. Knowledge

of speech production and other linguistic rules.

Semantic context. Direction of attention.

Association.

Figure 4.1

*Suggested mechanisms underlying simultaneous use of the senses in speech re-
ception. Two-way arrows indicate active search by the senses as well as passive
reception and interaction between short-term storage and long-term memory
store. The variable indicates that the quantity and type of information sought and
provided by audition will depend on hearing level.*

cueing systems such as those described in Chapter 3 in that particular finger configurations, letters, pictures, or visual forms are used to represent individual phonemes rather than common features such as nasality or voicing. Orthographic systems have been most favored. Silverman (1954), in reviewing issues then current in the oral education of hearing-impaired children, questioned *what* system of orthography should be generally adopted rather than *whether* a symbolization system should be used at all. Silverman and Lane (1970, p. 409) concluded that "a functional system of visual phonetic aids is essential" in the development of speech, and Magner (1971, p. 251) likewise held that "a phonetic system of orthography must be established and followed through the [speech teaching] program." We do not entirely agree with these views.

In our work, we have found visual symbolization systems to be unnecessary for most hearing-impaired children. Children with useful residual hearing have adequate sensory-motor capacity to develop speech without their use (see Chapters 5 and 7). Valuable time, which could be employed to advantage in developing auditory-oral skills in very young children, can easily be wasted by attempting to teach by such means. In general, we believe that phonetic symbolization systems can impede rather than assist progress in the acquisition of spoken language. This view is substantiated in the discussion which follows.

Fingerspelling

Fingerspelling was employed by Bonet (1620) as an adjunct to speech production and speechreading. It is used in a similar fashion today, both in Russia (Gerankina, 1964) and in the USA, where it is known as the Rochester Method (Castle, 1974). As a means of aiding specific speech sound production, fingerspelling has as much (or as little) to recommend it as does the written form.

Writing

The written form was the basis of the speech teaching method devised by Wallis (1698). The development of reading and writing skills as a basis for later speech has its advocates to the present day. Few, perhaps, are as extreme as Meyer (1938), who did not begin to teach speech until the child had received 95 lessons in reading and writing. Arguments against the use of writing have been mainly based on the lack of correspondence between pronunciation and the way words are spelled. In English, particularly, such correspondence is poor, although it could be improved by the use of an orthographic system such as the Initial Teaching Alphabet (Pitman, 1962). As a result, speech based on the prior teaching of the usual written form tends to be bizarre. The writer once asked a child thus taught, who was apparently doing nothing, why she was not working. She replied /aməθɪnəkɪnəgə/ (I'm thinking). The case is extreme, but it illustrates the point.

There are many other objections to making speech parasitic on the written form. Few children are developmentally ready to read and write before 4 or 5 years of age, by which time many speech and language skills should already have been established. Acquisition of reading and writing skills at an earlier stage can, of course, be forced, but the going is slow and the written vocabulary and language that can be taught in a given time is much less than could be learned over a comparable span of time a year or two later (Hart, 1975). If reading and writing skills are taught first, then the optimal period of learning oral language (Whetnall and Fry, 1971) is being wasted. If speech is taught concurrently with reading and writing, then the simultaneous acquisition of four major types of skills (speech, language, reading, and writing) is demanded. This approach would have an enormous burden even for the older, intelligent pupils taught by Wallis (1698). For the average hearing-impaired infant, such demands fly in the face of reason. We speculate that such early overload is one of the main reasons why so few hearing-impaired children exposed to this approach develop good speech, language, and educational skills, and why they rarely read for pleasure at a later stage.

These objections are not new. For example, Sicard (1800, p. 9), reasoning similarly, adopted an approach to speech and language teaching using only pictures and conversation ("On parle aux oreilles de l'entendant, on parle aux yeux du sourd-muet."). Only after oral language had been established did he use the written form as a guide to pronunciation. With older children and using French as a language, this was a reasonable procedure. The written and spoken forms of French have a better correspondence than do those of English. Similar objections to using writing at an early age, before oral language has developed, were also expressed by Garrett (1908) and by Story (1915).

One attempt to compare children taught with and without early exposure to written forms has been recorded. Jones (1914) reported that children learned new words more quickly and pronounced them more accurately when the words were taught orally from syllable drills than when vocabulary and pronunciation were developed from writing. Nevertheless, the practice of demanding reading and writing from the earliest stages of schooling, well before speech and language have been developed, is still frequently to be observed.

The Northampton Charts: The Northampton Charts, developed by Worcester (1915), are lists of letters arranged to represent sounds according to the manner in which they are commonly pronounced in various words. They have undergone several revisions (Clarke School for the Deaf, 1971) but, in underlying principle, remain unchanged. They are, in short, a symbolization system based on the written form. They are in widespread use with hearing-impaired children as an aid in the development of spoken language. Detailed examples of their application were provided by Monro (1919, 1920). According to Worcester (1915), they were designed so that "spoken language and written language would become in a fundamental sense, the same." This, she believed, would lead the child to "think in speech as far as he thought in words."

Recent experimental work by Conrad (1964, 1970, 1972) and by Chovan and McGettigan (1971) does not support Worcester's point of view, but rather suggests that learning spoken language by relating it to a written form is likely to affect normal memory and perceptual processes adversely. As indicated in Figure 4.1, if sensory input is to enter short-term storage, it has to be identified through reference to the long-term store. This implies that the information extracted from sensory images has to be held in short-term memory in a coded form. We speculate that the type of coding the child develops will be determined by the type of information to which the child's attention is directed and will have far-reaching effects on his verbal learning. If a visual system is used as the basis of speech and language acquisition, then the memory codes developed will reflect this influence. The codes developed will be quite different from the auditory/articulatory codes we normally use (see Wickelgren, 1969). This in itself might not be a serious matter, but as Conrad (1971) has shown, visual coding can interfere with the comprehension of written language. On similar grounds, it appears likely that speech fluency would also be adversely affected since the encoded visual component would represent an unnecessary dimension causing short-term memory load and interference in the planning of an utterance (see Chapters 5 and 7). These problems, together with inevitable neglect of suprasegmental aspects of speech production occasioned by attention to phonemic symbols, are common to all visual symbolization systems.

The Northampton Charts were severely criticized by Utley and Walker (1942). They demonstrated that the charts covered the pronunciation rules for only 24 percent of the words commonly used by 6-year-old children. However, the alternative they offered, the Thorndike diacritical markings, is open to all the other objections raised in connection with early language learning through association with visual symbols. The objections raised do not, of course, apply to the use of orthographic systems with children who have acquired most of the rules of language or with children whose suprasegmental speech patterns are so well established that visual attention to pronunciation will not detract from breath-grouping, speech rhythm, and voice quality.

Other Phonetic Symbolization Systems

Other phonetic symbolization systems used include those of Bell (1872), Van Praagh (1884), and Zaliouk (1954). The Visible Speech system developed by A. M. Bell and described by A. G. Bell (1872) was used in the Clarke School under Bell's supervision prior to the introduction of the Northampton Charts. According to Numbers (1974, p.28), the visible speech symbols were discarded as a speech teaching aid because the children began to use them for communication by writing the symbols in the air and because they delayed the children's voluntary use of speech.

Van Praagh (1884), in order to ensure that his pupils were familiar with the pronunciation of specific sounds, assigned each phoneme a key word and represented each key word pictorially. Thus, [t] was represented by a cup being filled by a teapot, and so on. The system is mentioned here because it is a particularly apt example of a system which demanded mediation in short-term memory by means of unrelated imagery—in this case, irrelevant vocabulary items. It would be hard to design a more efficient system to impede coarticulation and automaticity in the production of running speech.

Zaliouk (1954) developed a dynamic system of phonetic symbolization in which the fingers are used to indicate the most salient visual and tactile components of each sound. Thus, for [p] the index finger is placed vertically in front of the closed lips so that the explosive emission of breath can be felt on lip-opening. For [b] the fingers are placed laterally across the closed lips so that vibration from voice, the mandibular movement, and the breath stream on opening are felt. For [u] the index finger is inserted into the mouth through the rounded lips. Movements from consonant to vowel to succeeding consonant are intended to facilitate coarticulation. The main problems with this method are the development of an abnormal coding system which is reflected in the child's dependency on the symbols, the limitation of speaking rate, and detraction from the suprasegmental aspects of speech.

Should Phonetic Symbol Systems Be Discarded?   In view of the problems associated with systems of phonetic symbolization, one has to query why they were ever invented and why their use has persisted. Their invention was certainly due to the assumption that without them, insufficient cues were available to the child for the development of speech. This assumption now has to be questioned. When these symbol systems were developed, the means of utilizing residual audition were not available. Now that hearing aids and residual hearing can be used, the situation has changed. For many, perhaps for the majority, residual hearing can provide more appropriate exteroceptive and proprioceptive information than any visual symbolization system. Thus, the continued use of phonetic symbolization systems as a means of teaching speech to children who have substantial residual hearing is, we believe, an example of professional inertia, involving the adherence to a practice incompatible with emerging knowledge.

What of the use of phonetic symbolization systems with totally and near-totally deaf children? We have seen that these systems have many disadvantages. Are they really necessary for such children? If not, what are the possible alternatives? Again, we must remind ourselves that these systems were devised on the assumption that sufficient cues for learning and maintaining speech would not otherwise be available. This assumption must be challenged on the grounds that the act of speech itself generates a considerable array of sensory-motor information, which may be sufficient to support speech learning and maintenance. While extra visual, tactile, and kinesthetic cues may initially be required to help the child differentiate sounds in speech production, their persistent use and incorporation into a system of symbols, each of which parallels the sensory-motor information generated by particular speech sounds, may be superfluous. This question is pursued in greater depth in the next few chapters.

Signs and Speech

Discussion of the relative merits of communication by signs and by speech is outside the scope of this book. In the present context we shall therefore comment only on the possible effects of signing on speech development. There has been no direct research bearing on the matter, and—as stated in Chapter 1—the evidence as to whether teaching by sign detracts from speech development is at best equivocal.

In view of the vastly different nature of the two modes of communication, it appears highly unlikely that a child learning signs and speech can attend to both simultaneously. If the child is totally deaf and no tactile cues are provided, then he must observe both the lips and the hands and be capable of processing both modes—which involve different coding processes—at one and the same time in short-term memory. One suspects that certain persons with well established skills in both speech-reading and signing might be able to keep pace with the task if rate of presentation were favorable, but that it would be beyond the capability of a child whose performance in either mode was yet unskilled. One would also suspect that attention would be given to sign rather than to speechreading among partially skilled children if only one mode could be received since, of the two modes, sign offers more direct cues as to meaning. These views would be relatively simple to verify or refute experimentally. If tactile (vibratory) cues were added for the totally deaf child, one would postulate that attention to speech would be strengthened; but this hypothesis also requires testing.

Children with useful residual hearing would have much more complete (auditory-visual) information available to them than would totally deaf children, and for them there might be even stronger conflict between synchronous signs and speech. Alternatively, depending on the child's hearing level and past experience, signs might be less well attended to than speech. Whatever the case, one still has the problem of two widely different modes competing for simultaneous attention and memory capacity. In the absence of research, we speculate that if a total communication approach were adopted, serial—rather than parallel—presentation of speech and sign would be advisable at least in the early stages of acquisition.

Serial presentation of sign and speech also poses certain problems. The child's experience of speech may be limited if too long a time is devoted to developing the use of signs. His reliance on speech may also be weakened if it is assumed that speech cannot be understood except when sign is used to elucidate its meaning. Reinforcement of the child's attempts to speak may also be reduced by the ready reinforcement of his attempts to sign. Further, the two distinctly different memory and perceptual strategies required for sign and speech may conflict even if developed serially. We need much more evidence before we can be sure that those taught by both speech and sign can learn to speak as well as those taught by speech alone, or can learn to sign as well as those taught by sign alone. Comparison of similar groups measured during the acquisition stages and toward the limits of their capacity under the various conditions would permit inferences to be drawn in this regard. Such studies, which the speech evaluation procedures and teaching strategies suggested in this text should encourage, could be expected to yield valuable information on multisensory speech reception. They should also help oral teachers speedily identify those children who cannot, for whatever reason, learn to communicate by speech so that full opportunity can be provided for them to learn through manual communication from an early age.

Summary

Knowledge and problems relating to the various possible combinations of senses in multimodal speech reception are reviewed, the probable mechanisms underlying multisensory speech reception by hearing-impaired children are presented, and phonetic symbolization systems as a means of teaching speech are discussed. Possible interactions between signs and speech are also briefly outlined.

We show that multisensory reception of speech has often been superior to unisensory reception, but that there is some indirect evidence to suggest that children taught by auditory-visual methods may need prior and parallel training in auditory speech reception in order to achieve optimal performance. We also indicate that little is known about many areas of multisensory speech reception and that hearing impairment is likely to affect developmental patterns of selective attention, short-term memory, and long-term memory. We conclude that visual symbolization systems have no proven value as speech teaching aids and that for children with useful residual hearing they may be disadvantageous. Examination of the mechanisms involved suggests that their use is incompatible with the natural development of spoken language.

We suggest that if a total communication approach were used, signs and speech might be more propitiously presented separately rather than in parallel. We point out that evidence as to whether the concurrent use of speech and signs impedes the development of one or the other remains equivocal, but that hypotheses relating to the question may be tested experimentally. We conclude that in our future teaching and research we must focus much more strongly on acquiring fuller knowledge of sensory, memory, and perceptual systems in multimodal speech reception and on developing the means whereby this knowledge can be used more systematically and effectively.

REFERENCES
Abravanel, E.   How children combine vision and touch when perceiving the shape of objects. *Percept. Psychophys.*, 12, 171–175, 1972.

Aston, C. H.   Hearing-impaired children's discrimination of filtered speech. *J. Audit. Res.*, 12, 162–167, 1972.

Bell, A. G.   Visible speech as a means of communicating articulation to deaf-mutes. *Am. Ann. Deaf*, 17, 1–21, 1872.

Bennett, C. W.   *Discrimination of stop consonants by severely hearing-impaired children*. Unpublished Ph.D. diss., McGill University, 1973.

Binnie, C. A., Montgomery, A. A., & Jackson, P. L.   Auditory and visual contributions to the perception of consonants. *J. Speech Hear. Res.*, 17, 619–630, 1974.

Birtles, G. J.   *Auditory and visual speech discrimination by hearing-impaired children*. Unpublished M.Sc. thesis, McGill University, 1970.

Bonet, J. P.   *Reduccion de las letras y arte para ensenar a hablar los mudos*. Madrid: Francisco Abarca de Anguls, 1620.

Boothroyd, A.   Sensory aids research project—Clarke School for the Deaf. In G. Fant (Ed.), *Speech Communication Ability and Profound Deafness*. Washington, D.C.: A. G. Bell Assoc. for the Deaf, 1972.

Boothroyd, A.   *Detection of temporal gaps by deaf and hearing subjects*. S.A.R.P. #12. Northampton, Mass.: Clarke School for the Deaf, 1973.

Broadbent, D. E.   Division of function and integration of behavior. In F. O. Schmitt and F. G. Worden (Eds.), *The Neurosciences. Third Study Program*. Cambridge, Mass.: M.I.T. Press, 1974, pp. 31–41.

Carhart, R.   A method of using the Gault-Teletactor to teach speech rhythms. *Am. Ann. Deaf*, 80, 260–263, 1935.

Castle, D.   The Rochester Method. *J. Acad. Rehab. Audiol.*, 7, 12–17, 1974.

Chovan, W. I., & McGettigan, J. F.   The effects of vocal mediating responses on visual motor tasks with deaf and hearing children. *Except. Child.*, 37, 435–440, 1971.

Clarke School for the Deaf.   *Speech Development*. Northampton, Mass.: Clarke School for the Deaf Curriculum Series, 1971.

Conrad, R.   Acoustic confusions in immediate memory. *Br. J. Psychol.*, 55, 75–84, 1964.

Conrad, R.   Short-term memory processes in the deaf. *Br. J. Psychol.*, 61, 179–195, 1970.

Conrad, R.   The effect of vocalizing on comprehension in the profoundly deaf. *Br. J. Psychol.*, 62, 147–150, 1971.

Conrad, R.   The developmental role of vocalizing in short-term memory. *J. Verbal Learn. Verbal Behav.*, 11, 521–533, 1972.

Doehring, D. G., & Ling, D.   Programmed instruction of hearing-impaired children in the auditory discrimination of vowels. *J. Speech Hear. Res.*, 14, 746–754, 1971.

Englemann, S., & Rosov, R.   Tactual hearing experiment with deaf and hearing subjects. *J. Except. Child.*, 41, 243–253, 1975.

Erber, N. P.   Auditory, visual and auditory-visual recognition of consonants by children with normal and impaired hearing. *J. Speech Hear. Res.*, 15, 413–422, 1972.

Erber, N. P., & Zeiser, M. L.   Classroom observation under conditions of simulated profound deafness. *Volta Rev.*, 76, 352–360, 1974.

Ewing, I. R.   *Lipreading and Hearing Aids*. Manchester: Manchester University Press, 1944.

Garrett, M. S.   Helps and hindrances in acquiring speech and language at the natural age. *Volta Rev.*, 10, 274–276, 1908.

Gault, R. H.   Touch as a substitute for hearing in the interpretation and control of speech. *Arch. Otolaryngol.*, 3, 121–135, 1926.

Gerankina, A. G.   The dactyl form of speech and its mastery. *Voprosy Defektologii*. Moscow: Lenin Pedagogical Institute, 1964, pp. 179–197.

Handel, S., & Buffardi, L.   Pattern perception: Integrating information presented in two modalities. *Science*, 162, 1026–1028, 1968.

Hart, B. O.   Learning to read begins at birth. *Volta Rev.*, 77, 168–172, 1975.

Hutton, C.   Combining auditory and visual stimuli in aural rehabilitation. *Volta Rev.*, 61, 316–319, 1959.

Jones, E. P.   Details of work in beginning class from February to June, 1913. *Volta Rev.*, 16, 110–114, 1914.

Ling, A. H.   Memory for verbal and nonverbal auditory sequences in hearing-impaired and normal-hearing children. *J. Am. Audiol. Soc.*, 1, 37–45, 1975.

Ling, A. H.   The training of auditory memory in hearing-impaired children: Some problems of generalization. *J. Am. Audiol. Soc.*, 1, 150–157, 1976.

Ling, D.   Three experiments on frequency transposition. *Am. Ann. Deaf*, 113, 283–294, 1968.

Ling, D., & Sofin, B.   Discrimination of fricatives by hearing-impaired children using a vibrotactile cue. *Br. J. Audiol.*, 9, 14–18, 1975.

Loveless, N. E., Brebner, J., & Hamilton, P.   Bisensory presentation of information. *Psychol. Bull.*, 73, 161–199, 1970.

Magner, M. E.   Techniques of teaching. In L. E. Connor (Ed.), *Speech for the Deaf Child: Knowledge and Use*. Washington, D.C.: A. G. Bell Assoc. for the Deaf, 1971.

Meyer, M. F.   What retards speech teaching to the deaf? *Am. Ann. Deaf*, 83, 153–168, 1938.

Monro, S. J.   Phonetics and word study: A plan for pronunciation and speech drill. *Volta Rev.*, 21, 213–216, passim, 1919.

Monro, S. J.   Phonetics and word study: A plan for pronunciation and speech drill. *Volta Rev.*, 22, 15–18, passim, 1920.

Moray, N.   *Attention: Selective Processes in Vision and Hearing*. New York: Academic Press, 1970.

Myklebust, H. R., & Brutten, M.   A study of the visual perception of deaf children. *Acta Otolaryngol. Suppl.* 105, 1953.

Neate, D. M.   The use of tactile vibration in the teaching of speech to severely and profoundly deaf children. *Teach. Deaf*, 70, 137–146, 1972.

Norman, D. A., & Bobrow, D. G.   On data-limited and resource-limited processes. *Cogn. Psychol.*, 7, 44–64, 1975.

Numbers, M. E.   *My Words Fell on Deaf Ears*. Washington, D.C.: A. G. Bell Assoc. for the Deaf, 1974.

O'Neill, J. J.   Contributions of the visual components of oral symbols to speech comprehension. *J. Speech Hear. Disord.*, 19, 429–439, 1954.

Piaget, J. *The Mechanisms of Perception*. London: Routledge and Kegan Paul, 1969.

Pickett, J. M. Tactual communication of speech sounds to the deaf: Comparison with lipreading. *J. Speech Hear. Disord.*, 28, 315–330, 1963.

Pitman, J. Teaching the deaf. *Teach. Deaf*, 60, 311–316, 1962.

Pollack, D. *Educational Audiology for the Limited Hearing Infant*. Springfield, Ill.: Thomas, 1970.

Schulte, K. Fonator system: Speech stimulation and speech feedback by technically amplified one-channel vibrations. In G. Fant (Ed.), *Speech Communication Ability and Profound Deafness*. Washington, D.C.: A. G. Bell Assoc. for the Deaf, 1972.

Sicard, R. A. C. *Cours d'instruction d'un sourd-muet de naissance, pour servir à l'éducation des sourds-muets*. Paris: Le Clere, 1800.

Silverman, S. R. Teaching speech to the deaf—the issues. *Volta Rev.*, 56, 385–389, passim, 1954.

Silverman, S. R., & Lane, H. S. Deaf children. In H. Davis and S. R. Silverman (Eds.), *Hearing and Deafness*. (3rd ed.) New York: Holt, Rinehart and Winston, 1970.

Smith, F. *Understanding Reading*. New York: Holt, Rinehart and Winston, 1971.

Story, A. J. Some practical points. *Volta Rev.*, 17, 155–158, 1915.

Sumby, W. H., & Pollack, I. Visual contribution to speech intelligibility in noise. *J. Acoust. Soc. Am.*, 26, 212–215, 1954.

Suzuki, H., Kagami, R., & Takahashi, T. Tactphone as an aid for the deaf. *Proc. 6th Int. Congr. Acoust.*, Tokyo, 1968.

Utley, J., & Walker, N. F. Are the Northampton Charts outmoded? *Volta Rev.*, 44, 485–490, 1942.

Van Praagh, W. *Lessons for the Instruction of Deaf and Dumb Children*. London: Truebner, 1884.

Wallis, J. A letter to Mr. Thomas Beverly, September 30, 1698, concerning his method of instructing persons deaf and dumb. First published in *Philosophical Transactions*, Oxford, October 1698. (A. G. Bell Assoc. for the Deaf Access #RB150.W1).

Whetnall, E., & Fry, D. B. *The Deaf Child*. Springfield, Ill.: Thomas, 1971.

Wickelgren, W. A. Auditory or articulatory coding in verbal short-term memory. *Psychol. Rev.*, 76, 232–235, 1969.

Worcester, A. E. Pronunciation at sight. *Volta Rev.*, 17, 85–93, 1915.

Zaliouk, A. A visual-tactile system of phonetical symbolization. *J. Speech Hear. Disord.*, 19, 190–207, 1954.

/5/

Feedback and Feedforward Mechanisms in Speech Production

Feedback may be considered as being intrinsic or extrinsic to an organism (Annett, 1969). The child receives *intrinsic feedback* about his speech when his available senses inform him, either consciously or unconsciously, about the position of his speech organs and the consequences of moving them. Thus, he might hear what he has said or obtain somesthetic information about his breathing, phonation, or articulation from the sensory receptors present in the various organs employed in speech. *Extrinsic feedback* is provided when something or someone other than the child provides him with information on his speech production. The something might be a mirror, a feather moving in response to breath flow, or an oscillographic pattern provided by a visual aid. The somebody might be his teacher or his parent whose response indicates comprehension of his utterance or who informs him as to the acceptability of his pronunciation. Vegeley (1964) found that the deaf children she studied tended to rely much more on extrinsic than on intrinsic feedback. The extent to which a child relies on one form of feedback rather than another will depend on the acuity of his auditory, visual, tactual, and kinesthetic senses, on the integrity of his perceptual mechanisms, and on the way in which he is trained to use them.

Present-day knowledge of the role of the senses in speech production is piecemeal. Accordingly, current theory and practice are somewhat speculative (MacNeilage, 1972). Until quite recently speech production was considered to be a closed loop system: one in which, by constant monitoring through the senses, we control the serial timing of speech and the immediate adjustment of the articulators as they assume one target position and move to the next (Fairbanks, 1954). This view, derived from Wiener (1948), is no longer tenable. In normal speech, some

10 to 15 phonemes may be produced in a second, and many phonemes have durations of 50 milliseconds (msec.) or less (Liberman, Cooper, Shankweiler, and Studdert-Kennedy, 1967). Immediate control would therefore require a sensory-motor system in which neural and mechanical response time approximates zero. When we hear the sounds we produce, they certainly appear to parallel the orosensory information we receive from the articulators; but this is not to say that we have immediate perception or moment-by-moment control of articulation. In fact, we do not; our sensory-motor control of speech is rather sluggish. It takes about 70 msec. longer to identify a stop consonant than to produce it (McNeill and Repp, 1973) and much longer to identify a mispronunciation, reorganize, and initiate a correction. Massaro (1972) suggests that a lag of about 250 msec. is involved in the auditory-perceptual processing of speech.

Sensory-Motor Reaction Time

Ladefoged (1960) studied response time in motor speech by measuring the speed at which subjects could initiate internal intercostal activity for speech production following an auditory stimulus (neural response time) and the time it took for this activity to result in the increased subglottal pressure required for speech (mechanical response time). Neural response time ranged from 140 to 320 msec. Mechanical response time was consistently found to be about 48 msec. Similarly, raising the velum was estimated by Bjork (1961) to take up to 120 msec. Like results were obtained in an extensive series of studies by Kozhevnikov and Chistovich (1965/1966), who confirmed that response times associated with different parts of the speech mechanism were not identical. Work in this area continues. For example, Netsall and Daniel (1974) recently showed that neural response time for the lips (orbicularis oris) was about 140 msec. and mechanical response time, 60 msec.

Neural response times in relation to voluntary initiation of movement are generally somewhat greater than those measured for movements initiated by reflex mechanisms. This is because different neural networks are involved. The neural response times mentioned above may therefore be rather longer than those operating in normal speech production. Nevertheless, since reflex behaviors associated with learned movement commonly involve latencies of 70 to 100 msec. (Evarts, 1973), the notion that moment-by-moment control can operate in consonant production—except possibly in long-duration fricatives—is insupportable.

Though Kozhevnikov and Chistovich (1965/1966) considered ongoing correction of most phonemes by means of immediate feedback to be impossible, they suggested that some ongoing sensory control of the more slowly changing components of speech—the suprasegmental features of loudness, pitch, stress, and rate—might occur. However, Elliott and Niemoeller (1970) found that listeners required about 500 msec. to match the fundamental (F_0) of their voices to a target frequency. In running speech such fine target matching for F_0 is not demanded. Nevertheless, neural and mechanical response times required to achieve suprasegmental targets in running speech appear to be too great to support the notion of moment-by-moment control.

Sensory-Motor Control

Findings such as those reported above indicate that sensory monitoring of running speech is carried out to determine not whether the necessary movements of the speech mechanism *are being* made, but whether they *have been* made. In other words, the order of activity in producing speech appears to be, first, feedforward—or planning prior to production; next, the completion of an utterance in which the successive components are already practiced to an automatic level; and finally, feedback—the verification that production has satisfied intention. In these respects, speech appears to have much in common with the performance of any other motor task involving a series of skilled movements (Miller, Galanter, and Pribram, 1960; MacKay, 1966; Hardy, 1972).

Corollary Discharge Theory

Currently available evidence on the neural mechanisms underlying control of skilled movements supports a corollary discharge theory (Evarts, 1971). This theory suggests that feedforward is characterized by a simultaneous efferent discharge both to the motor system, which will effect the desired system of movements, and to the associated sensory system. Only if there is a mismatch between the sensory patterns derived from the movements executed and the sensory patterns forecast by feedforward does conscious feedback occur. When the movements are carried out as planned, the one discharge may be said to cancel out the other at a reflex level, which allows conscious attention to be focused on other tasks. The feedback loops involved at the reflex level are, of course, created in the course of learning speech and underlie automaticity in speech production. If speech is not practiced by the hearing-impaired child until speech sound sequences are produced automatically, then the normal feedforward and feedback mechanisms cannot operate and conscious attention will not be free for higher-level tasks.

Feedforward

Feedforward was envisaged (though not labeled as such) by Stetson (1951) as the organization of skilled speech movements involving units of at least syllabic length. It was, however, Lashley (1951) who formulated the theoretical groundwork for later studies on the feedforward mechanisms underlying speech production involving units of even greater complexity. That planning of speech sequences normally occurs while the speaker is still producing those previously planned (Osgood, 1963) indicates how necessary it is for the motor acts involved to be at an automatic level. Where sufficient levels of automaticity are not reached, breakdown in either the feedforward or the production mechanisms, or both, inevitably occurs (Goldman-Eisler, 1961; Ohala, 1970; Butterworth, 1975).

The nature of feedforward mechanisms is not amenable to direct measurement, but the extent of feedforward normally involved in the ordering of an utterance can be inferred from slips of the tongue and from the structure of spoonerisms (Boomer and Laver, 1968; MacKay, 1970; Fromkin, 1971, 1973). Misplacement of words in a sentence such as, "If the baby turns pink, the bathwater is too hot for your elbow," is evidence of a breakdown in planning speech structures of at least sentence length. Similar breakdowns in feedforward efficiency are illustrated by word or phoneme reversals, omissions, and replacements. Many of these (as the reader has no doubt discovered personally) can be amusing or embarrassing. Such breakdowns can occur in the earliest stages of formulating the linguistic structure, in the selection of the appropriate words to use, or in the transmission of the neuromuscular commands to the speech organs. They tend to increase as a function of rate (MacKay, 1971) and most commonly involve the substitution of one phoneme target for another.

Articulatory Targets

There has been a great deal of discussion in recent years on the nature of targets in speech. Targets may be considered as being the units of speech which are encoded in memory and which we employ in feedforward to structure an utterance. They may be primarily acoustic or articulatory images. Most workers (Lindblom, 1963; Haggard and Mattingly, 1968; Nooteboom, 1970; and Hamlet, 1973, among others) consider the smallest meaningful acoustic target to be the phoneme, although Wickelgren (1969) has suggested that since phonemes vary in relation to context, targets may, in fact, be context-sensitive allophones. There is no question that normal speech assumes context sensitivity, but this may be expected to result from both neural and mechanical constraints inherent in the speech mechanism which cause overlapping in time (MacNeilage, 1970).

Articulatory targets may be considered to be the particular positions and movements required of each articulator in the formation of a phoneme. Thus, an elevated velum, tongue-grooving, and vocal cord vibration are all articulatory targets for [z]. However, exact articulatory targets—while crucial for [s] and [z]—are difficult to specify for certain other phonemes. The tongue target for [k], for example, is dorsal contact with the palate; but such contact can be made at several points, the actual one being determined by the vowel which precedes or follows it. Indeed, different muscles may be used to produce the same consonant in different vowel contexts (Harris, 1971). Such being the case, the teacher should not persist in teaching a consonant in only one vowel environment, for this will tend to inhibit the child's development of adequate feedforward and feedback processes. Similarly, targets involving the velum are hard to specify, largely because movement of the velum is sluggish. Thus, in moving to and from its lowered position for nasal consonants, the velum has to begin its movement during the preceding vowel and leave its target position during the production of the nasal consonant in readiness for the next non-nasal sound (Kent, Carney, and Severeid, 1974). Such anticipatory coarticulation effects, though varying from one consonant to another, may range over several phonemes. They are the rule rather than the exception in speech (Daniloff and Moll, 1968) and serve to stress the importance of feedforward mechanisms.

Vowel targets are less difficult to specify than are consonant targets. Teaching ideal targets for all vowels is mandatory, for the consonant-to-vowel and vowel-to-consonant transitions carry much of the essential information in speech. However, in running speech, ideal vowel targets are rarely reached, probably because of inertial constraints. Thus, the faster the speech, the less likely it is that target positions will be fully attained (Lindblom, 1963). Nevertheless, the extent and direction of undershoot in the production of vowels in normal speech are systematic and hence cause the listener no problem. Two jointly operating mechanisms underlie the achievement of vowel targets: the position of the tongue in the mouth and the extent of jaw-opening (Lindblom and Sundberg, 1971). If vowels are taught through visual means using an abnormally wide-open mouth, then the tongue has to be arched in a deviant manner to compensate and thus to reach the appropriate acoustic target. This again leads to inappropriate feedforward and feedback mechanisms which can profoundly affect both intelligibility and speech rhythm. Those of us with normal hearing can adjust the tongue to produce the required sound even if the shape of the mouth is changed grossly by the introduction of an artificial palate (Hamlet, 1973), but the hearing-impaired child who has to rely entirely or mainly on somesthesis has no such recourse. It is therefore essential that appropriate articulatory gestures be taught in the first place, for it is from these rather than from hearing that the deaf child derives the sensory control of his speech. (See Chapter 7.)

Summary

Neurological and mechanical constraints operate to prevent us from using feedback to exercise moment-by-moment control over speech production. We therefore suggest that feedback can do no more than allow us to determine whether production has satisfied intention. We also suggest that preplanning of speech sequences (feedforward) should receive more emphasis than hitherto in our speech teaching programs and that automaticity in achieving articulatory targets is essential to the development of feedforward mechanisms and sensory control.

REFERENCES

Annett, J. *Feedback and Human Behaviour.* Harmondsworth, Middx.: Penguin, 1969.

Bjork, L. Velopharyngeal function in connected speech. *Acta Radiol. Suppl.* 202, 1961.

Boomer, D. S., & Laver, J. D. M. Slips of the tongue. *Br. J. Disord. Commun.*, 3, 2–12, 1968.

Butterworth, B. Hesitation and semantic planning in speech. *J. Psycholinguist. Res.*, 4, 75–87, 1975.

Daniloff, R. G., & Moll, K. L. Coarticulation of lip rounding. *J. Speech Hear. Res.*, 11, 707–721, 1968.

Elliott, L. L., & Niemoeller, A. F. The role of hearing in controlling voice fundamental frequency. *Int. Audiol.*, 9, 47–52, 1970.

Evarts, E. V. Feedback and corollory discharge: A merging of the concepts. *Neurosci. Res. Prog. Bull.*, 9, 86–112, 1971.

Evarts, E. V. Motor cortex reflexes associated with learned movement. *Science*, 179, 501–503, 1973.

Fairbanks, G. Systematic research in experimental phonetics: 1. A theory of the speech mechanism as a servosystem. *J. Speech Hear. Disord.*, 19, 133–139, 1954.

Fromkin, V. A. The non-anomalous nature of anomalous utterances. *Language*, 47, 27–52, 1971.

Fromkin, V. A.   Slips of the tongue. *Sci. Am.*, 229 (6), 110–117, 1973.

Goldman-Eisler, F.   Hesitation and information in speech. In C. Cherry (Ed.), *Information Theory*. Washington, D.C.: Butterworths, 1961.

Haggard, M. P., & Mattingly, I. G.   A simple program for synthesizing British English. *IEEE Trans. Audio Electroacoust.*, AU-16, 95–99, 1968.

Hamlet, S. L.   Speech adaptation to dental appliances: Theoretical considerations. *J. Baltimore Coll. Dental Surgery*, 28, 52–63, 1973.

Hardy, W. G.   Feedback and feedforward in language acquisition. *Acta Symbolica*, 3, 70–82, 1972.

Harris, K. S.   *Action of the extrinsic musculature in the control of tongue position.* Haskins Labs. SR-25/26, 87–96, 1971.

Kent, R. D., Carney, P. J., & Severeid, L. R.   Velar movement and timing: Evaluation of a model for binary control. *J. Speech Hear. Res.*, 17, 470–488, 1974.

Kozhevnikov, V. A., & Chistovich, L. A.   [*Speech: Articulation and Perception*] Transl.: Washington, D.C.: U.S. Dept. of Commerce, Joint Publications Research Service, 1966. (Originally published 1965.)

Ladefoged, P.   The regulation of sub-glottal pressure. *Folia Phoniatr.*, 12, 169–175, 1960.

Lashley, K. S.   The problem of serial order in behavior. In L. A. Jeffress (Ed.), *Cerebral Mechanisms in Behavior*. New York: Wiley, 1951.

Liberman, A. M., Cooper, F. S., Shankweiler, D. P., & Studdert-Kennedy, M.   Perception of the speech code. *Psychol. Rev.*, 74, 431–461, 1967.

Lindblom, B. E. F.   Spectrographic study of vowel reduction. *J. Acoust. Soc. Am.*, 35, 1773–1781, 1963.

Lindblom, B. E. F., & Sundberg, J. E. F.   Acoustical consequences of lip, tongue, jaw and larynx movement. *J. Acoust. Soc. Am.*, 50, 1166–1179, 1971.

MacKay, D. G.   Spoonerisms: The structure of errors in the serial order of speech. *Neuropsychol.*, 8, 323–350, 1970.

MacKay, D. G.   Stress pre-entry in motor systems. *Am. J. Psychol.*, 84, 35–51, 1971.

MacKay, D. M.   Cerebral organization and the conscious control of action. In J. C. Eccles (Ed.), *Brain and Conscious Experience*. New York: Springer-Verlag, 1966, pp. 422–445.

MacNeilage, P. F.   Motor control of serial ordering of speech. *Psychol. Rev.*, 77, 182–196, 1970.

MacNeilage, P. F.   Speech physiology. In J. H. Gilbert (Ed.), *Speech and Cortical Functioning*. New York: Academic Press, 1972.

Massaro, D. W.   Preperceptual images, processing time, and perceptual units in auditory perception. *Psychol. Rev.*, 79, 124–145, 1972.

McNeill, D., & Repp, B.   Internal processes in speech perception. *J. Acoust. Soc. Am.*, 53, 1320–1326, 1973.

Miller, G. A., Galanter, E., & Pribram, K. H.   *Plans and the Structure of Behavior.* New York: Henry Holt, 1960.

Netsall, R., & Daniel, B.   Neural and mechanical response time for speech production. *J. Speech Hear. Res.*, 17, 608–618, 1974.

Nooteboom, S. G.   *The target theory of speech production.* IPO Annual Progress Rep., 5, 51–55, 1970.

Ohala, J. J. *Aspects of the control and production of speech*. UCLA Working Papers in Phonetics, #15, 1970.

Osgood, C. E. On understanding and creating sentences. *Am. Psychol.*, 18, 735–751, 1963.

Stetson, R. H. *Motor Phonetics, A Study of Speech Movements in Action*. Amsterdam: North Holland Publishing Co., 1951.

Vegely, C. Monitoring of monosyllabic words by deaf children. In *Proc. Int. Congr. Educ. Deaf*. Washington, D.C.: U.S. Govt. Printing Office, 1964, pp. 735–744.

Wickelgren, W. A. Context-sensitive coding in speech recognition, articulation and development. In K. N. Leibovic (Ed.), *Information Processing in the Nervous System*. New York: Springer-Verlag, 1969, pp. 85–95.

Wiener, N. *Cybernetics; or, Control and Communication in the Animal and the Machine*. New York: Wiley, 1948.

/6/

The Sense Modalities
in Speech Production

The proprioceptive use of our senses in speech production differs in many ways from their exteroceptive use in speech reception. Audition of our own speech involves reception of both air- and bone-conducted elements; and what we hear parallels the orosensory-motor patterns, both tactile and kinesthetic, which are associated with movements in the vocal tract. Vision is not normally used proprioceptively in speech production and can be used to only a limited extent in teaching hearing-impaired children to talk. In this chapter, we emphasize the importance of orosensory information. Indeed, we reason that the development of well differentiated orosensory-motor patterns should be the teacher's prime concern in fostering a hearing-impaired child's speech production skills. For the totally deaf child, there is no alternative since audition is simply not available and vision—for reasons already discussed—provides too little information. For the child with useful residual hearing, well developed orosensory-motor patterns which underlie automaticity in speech production serve to provide a frame of reference which facilitates auditory or multisensory speech reception.

Orosensory-Motor Patterns

Orosensory information is provided by touch and kinesthesis through neural receptors present in the chest, throat, mandibula joints, tongue, palate, velum, and lips. Their density of distribution varies from one site to another. Thus, there are many more receptors and greater sensitivity at the front of the mouth—in the lips, tongue, and palate—than in the back of the mouth and the velum (Ringel and Ewanowski, 1965; Grossman and Hattis, 1967). These differences in sensitivity can be employed to advantage in teaching speech. In the production

74

of stops, for example, the child can more readily generalize from [p] at the lips to [t] at the tongue blade than to [k] at the tongue dorsum. The tip of the tongue is about twice as sensitive as the dorsum (Pleasonton, 1970), which may be the reason that front consonants are more common than back consonants in most languages.

The mouth can identify the shape, size, and geometry of objects placed in the mouth without the child's even seeing them, an ability shared by the fingers (J. J. Gibson, 1966). The oral perception of shapes (oral stereognosis) has received a considerable amount of attention. Performance is known to improve with the maturation of the child, and poorer-than-average ability to identify geometrically different forms is known to be associated with speech defects (Ringel, 1970). Manually taught hearing-impaired children do less well at oral stereognosis than orally taught hearing-impaired children or children with normal hearing (Bishop, Ringel, and House, 1972). This indicates that failure to develop and to use speech may lead to deficits in the use of orosensory mechanisms and suggests that hearing-impaired children who begin speech acquisition late in life will face more physiological difficulty than those who begin at an early age.

Both tactile and kinesthetic sensations allow us to discriminate objects orally—to feel a cavity in a tooth and to introspect about certain tongue positions. We do not, however, have detailed knowledge on the exact function of the variety of sensory receptors in the mouth. It is likely that some receptors provide both tactile and kinesthetic sensation. The quality of this sensation differs according to whether it is actively *obtained* through oral exploration or whether it is *imposed* (Gibson, 1966). The sensation due to active exploration is much more vivid. Thus, the teacher's manipulation of the child's tongue is less likely to result in a satisfactory placement than the child's discovery of the required articulatory posture by active search. The child's finger, as Arrowsmith (1819) found, is likely to be more effective than the spatula.

Sensory-Motor Patterns

Active search is particularly appropriate to the mouth since the vocal mechanisms involved in speech production have both sensory and motor components. Both efferent and afferent neural patterns are involved. These patterns, once acquired, are strongly resistant to distortion even when there is deprivation of auditory feedback. Indeed, an established motor command system can function fairly well even in the absence of both auditory and oral sensation (McCroskey, 1958; Gammon, Smith, Daniloff, and Kim, 1971; Putnam and Ringel, 1972; Hutchinson and Putnam, 1974). Habitual motor feedforward mechanisms seem to be adequate on their own for the production of speech except possibly for the articulation of fricatives and affricates. These become distorted when the sensory pathways are anesthetized, although Harris (1973) quotes some preliminary work by Borden which suggests that some such presumed sensory effects of oral anesthesia may be due to artifacts causing partial motor paralysis. Whatever the case, it is clear that motor speech skills, once established, require little if any exteroceptive feedback to be maintained.

Motor Codes: Speech production, like other motor skills such as riding a bicycle, can be performed while our conscious attention is focused on another task. We attend, by and large, to where we are going rather than to how we sit, balance, and steer a bicycle, and to what we are saying rather than to how we say it. Because our motor acts are not normally under conscious control, memory codes which preserve motor activity tend to be quite different from the visual and auditory imagery that preserve other aspects of our experience (Posner, 1973). For one thing, once a motor skill has become automatic (swimming, skating, talking), it remains permanently with us unless we suffer physical insult to the brain or to related peripheral mechanisms. For another, we have very little ability to use the memory codes which preserve these skills to introspect about the processes involved.

Conscious Awareness: It has always been assumed that hearing-impaired children need to acquire more conscious awareness than normally hearing children of the processes associated with the production of speech, and in the earliest stages of speech acquisition this may be so. However, conscious awareness of skilled movements is unnecessary. Attempts to gain conscious awareness of motor processes may also inhibit their acquisition and adversely affect their performance. As Haycock (1933) points out, if we were to think about how we run upstairs, we should most likely trip and fall down. Such observations suggest that we may justifiably seek to provide awareness of speech organ postures underlying acquisition of certain simple speech targets but should not encourage conscious awareness beyond this preliminary stage. In fact, we can never make the child aware of all the necessary physiological adjustments which underlie speech. Neurological studies show that adjustments of the intercostal muscles essential to adequate speech production are due to reflexive action of the gamma loop system (Matthews, 1964), as are fine adjustments of the larynx (Wyke, 1967) and of the jaw (Abbs, 1971). We can control these reflexes, once they are established, no better than we can control the defensive eye blink. To seek extensive conscious control is incompatible with our quest for the automaticity necessary for fluent serial ordering and coarticulation in speech and for the availability of the child's conscious attention for the higher-order functions in speech communication. Conscious control of some speech organs in conjunction with reflex control of others cannot but result in the lack of coordination observed by Scuri (1935) and since confirmed by other workers (see Chapter 2).

The velum is poorly endowed with sensory receptors and is inaccessible to vision during speech. Hence, it is difficult to modify its movement consciously. Attempts have been made to provide ongoing visual feedback of velar movement (Moller, Path, Werth, and Christiansen, 1973), but with little success. Shelton, Knox, Elbert, and Johnson (1970) trained subjects to raise and lower the velum by means of exercises, but there was no carry-over into everyday speech. This work indicates that if we are to deal effectively with the ubiquitous nasality of hearing-impaired children, we should concentrate not so much on sensory awareness of velar movement as on the formation, through actual speech production, of reflex motor codes. The means by which this can be achieved will be discussed in a later section on nasality. The reason for suggesting concentration on developing adequate motor codes involving the velum is not simply that sensory control is difficult. The pharyngeal walls are also involved in velopharyngeal closure (Fritzell, 1969), and coordination of their movement with that of the velum is essential. To work at modifying the function of the velum outside the context of speech is to invite enhancement of speech resonance faults associated with pharyngeal wall tension, a problem long known to be common in the speech of hearing-impaired children (Bell, 1916, pp. 19–21).

Auditory Feedback

Proprioceptive use of audition differs from exteroceptive use of audition in that, in the former, the sound of one's own speech may be received both by air and by bone conduction. Whether or not a child is able to hear his own voice by bone conduction may be quite important to his speech development. The extent of bone-conducted speech reception by the speaker depends on its intensity, the frequency of its component features, and, of course, the speaker's hearing level. In order to study the effects of eliminating audition as a means of feedback in speech production among normally hearing subjects, both the air-conducted and bone-conducted components have to be masked by the presence of high-level noise.

Work of this type has recently been reviewed by Siegel and Pick (1974), who themselves found their adult speakers able to cope quite well without hearing themselves talk. This finding is not surprising in view of general experience with adults and children with well established speech patterns who suddenly lose all hearing. It is usually some months or even some years before abnormalities of speech become manifest. Similarly, complete absence of auditory feedback has no immediate or drastic effect on the performance of an accomplished pianist (Gates and Bradshaw, 1974). Among adults with well established skills, feedforward and production mechanisms have become automatic and auditory feedback is therefore no longer essential. We know that Beethoven wrote some of his most outstanding works after he became deaf.

With children who are learning to speak the case is quite different. For them, partial or complete lack of hearing means that other forms of intrinsic or extrinsic feedback must be used as supplements or alternatives to audition in order to build the feedforward and production skills involved in speech.

The exact role usually played by auditory feedback in the normal acquisition of speech is not known. Observation indicates that it is particularly important in the early stages in that it allows the child to develop the same speech characteristics as those around him (Van Riper and Irwin, 1958). However, there is no experimental evidence in regard to how much auditory self-monitoring the normally hearing child does, whether it is a continuous or an intermittent function, or whether some aspects of speech require more attention to auditory feedback than others. In the absence of such evidence the safest thing is to give the hearing-impaired child as much opportunity as possible to develop auditory feedback skills. The constant use of audition for proprioceptive feedback may or may not be necessary; its complete absence must be disadvantageous.

Several experiments have been undertaken using delayed side-tone (delayed speech feedback) with normally hearing subjects (Soderberg, 1968). This approach to the study of auditory feedback in hearing-impaired children was adopted by DiCarlo (1960), who showed that the speech of hearing-impaired children who had had auditory training was more disturbed by delayed feedback than was the speech of those who had been taught without hearing aids. In other words, results indicated that subjects had become able to tell through proprioceptive audition when their production satisfied their intention.

Visual Feedback

The most obvious form of visual feedback is that provided by a mirror. While it can be used in teaching situations, it cannot be employed by the child in everyday communication. On this account, its constant use in teaching must be questioned. Bell (1916, p. 75) considered that familiarity with speech through the use of a mirror leads to a perception of muscular feeling of the positions assumed by the vocal organs. However, Haycock (1933, p. 123) strongly counseled that the mirror should not be used except in the correction of faults or in time of difficulty and warned against making a necessity of it. The writer has rarely found it necessary to use a mirror, for most children appear to be able to imitate movements they can see, including mouth and visible tongue movements, without requiring visual feedback. This capability seems to be present in children from only a few months of age (Piaget, 1962), although the mechanisms by which such skill is achieved have not been studied.

Other extrinsic forms of visual feedback of speech may include the listener's reactions to what is said; the visualization of some aspects of speech by means of a simple device such as a feather, a piece of paper, or a toy windmill to indicate the nature of breath stream movement; or complex electronic devices which provide visual displays of some sort.

The Listener's Reactions

Cues provided by the listener's reactions are important since they are continuously available both in teaching periods and during everyday communication. Children are very sensitive to this form of feedback, often more so than is the teacher or parent who provides it. The types of visual cues provided by the listener may include any or all of the visual, nonverbal signals that are popularly assumed by the term "Body English"—eye movement, facial reactions, body posture, and so on—and whatever the child is able to speechread of the listener's verbal response. If the verbal and nonverbal cues are not consistent with each other—if the lips say "yes" and the body says "no"—then the child may be quite confused by the visual feedback he receives.

Simple Visual Aids

Cues provided by objects such as a piece of paper, a flame, a fragment of cotton, or anything else that moves in response to breath stream may be useful in demonstrating how well certain aspects of the child's speech match those of the teacher. The cues thus observed may as read-ily be provided by touch, but vision offers an alternative approach and hence a certain amount of variety. The use of such devices is inherently restricted to those sounds characterized by a fairly strong breath stream (lip-rounded vowels, fricatives, and plosives). Provision of such cues is not without danger. The amount of breath stream required for vowels can easily be exaggerated; excessive intraoral pressure may be encour-aged for plosives; and incorrect adjustment of the articulatory organs for fricatives can result.

Incorrect articulation of fricatives may occur because the required tur-bulence for fricative sounds stems from two associated variables: the breath stream and the aperture through which it has to pass (Fant, 1960). Thus, if the breath stream is stronger than that normally required for the production of a fricative, the size of the aperture required to pro-duce turbulence is also greater. Having learned to produce a fricative in isolation with a breath stream powerful enough to move a simple visual device, the child may also have learned to adjust his articulatory organs so that the aperture is too large to produce the required turbulence with the amount of breath used in running speech. This is the type of prob-lem that occurs when any sound is taught in isolation, and it often ac-counts for the child's apparent failure to generalize skills from articula-tion lessons to communicative speech.

Complex Visual Aids

Devices which transform the acoustic or articulatory patterns of the child's speech so that they become visible are both complex and vari-ous. Several are described by Pickett (1971) and in *Sensory Training Aids for the Hearing-Impaired*, edited by Levitt and Nye (1971). Typically such devices provide oscillographic displays or drive a meter to indicate voice pitch or some other specific speech feature. Yet others, such as the Bell Telephone Visible Speech Translator, provide real-time (immedi-ate) spectrographic displays (Stark, 1972). Visual displays which allow the child to practice various aspects of speech by interacting with a com-puter have also been reported (Boothroyd, Archambault, Adams, and Storm, 1974).

The energy that has been devoted to the creation of visual speech teaching aids for hearing-impaired children probably equals that spent by alchemists in their efforts to transform base metals into gold and by early physicists in their pursuit of perpetual motion: efforts to improve speech substantially through the use of visual feedback devices promise no greater success. The reasons for doubt are various: visual displays provide less information than alternative forms of feedback; there are restrictions imposed on speech processing by the characteristics of vision (Liberman, Cooper, Shankweiler, and Studdert-Kennedy, 1968); there are problems inherent in isolating one aspect of speech for attention; and many such devices are designed and used to provide only moment-by-moment information on production and thus accord with an outdated notion of the feedback process. Even devices with storage capacity can display only limited information and may encourage the production of a particular feature to the detriment of others. The production of a feature may be important, but its interaction with other aspects of speech is more so. Teaching a feature in isolation may be warranted if it is carried out at the appropriate time during the speech development of the child. For example, attention to nasality or to the voiced-voiceless distinction in plosives is trivial, if not misplaced, when a child cannot produce voice and vowels satisfactorily. Similarly, attending to vowels while ignoring the voice patterns with which they must interact is equally unhelpful. When voice pitch increases, the length of the vocal tract decreases and the position of the tongue must also be changed to compensate for this effect if the vowel is to have a natural quality. The machine does not recognize this, and, accordingly, such training—unless carried out under the guidance of a skilled teacher—may do more harm than good.

We have already seen that physiological response time has two types of components, neural and mechanical. These operate whether we use visual transforms of the acoustic energy in speech or visual transforms derived from articulatory movements. Feedback by these means can only improve speech if the transforms are used by the child to determine whether production has satisfied the intention previously fed forward. The neural and mechanical constraints of speech production introduce too great a delay to permit the immediate monitoring and ongoing adjustment of the articulators. This is probably why Brannon (1964) obtained negative results from training with a visual display of glossal (tongue) movement, and it is one of the reasons why any other attempt to teach by using moment-by-moment visual transforms of articulation is also likely to fail.

Visual Reinforcement

Speech training lends itself particularly well to behavior modification procedures, and visual reinforcement may play a powerful role in shaping desired speech behaviors. Visual reinforcement presented as a consequence of the child's producing the required response differs from visual feedback in that it need bear no relationship to the articulatory process. Indeed, anything that is interesting to the child may be used as a reinforcement: a smile, a star to be stuck on a chart, or something that is dispensed or displayed by some complex piece of electronic gadgetry. Teachers concerned with the speech of hearing-impaired children should have a thorough knowledge of operant conditioning procedures (Skinner, 1957) and their application to speech training (Sloane and MacAulay, 1968; Mowrer, 1973).

We have provided visual reinforcement for voicing by using a voice-operated relay (VOR) in conjunction with a tape recorder. This equipment was arranged so that when the teacher or the child used voice, the spools to which we had attached an array of toy animals automatically began to revolve. Similarly, we had used VORs to operate an electric train; and, to foil the child who learned to make it work by banging on the table, as well as to extend our flexibility, we added electronic circuitry to make the train go forward for [i], stop for [a], and reverse direction for [u]. All this we found unnecessarily complex and somewhat unreliable because appropriate vowel formants for children are rather higher than those for teachers, and adjustments had to be made for each child.

After a considerable amount of experience (and frustration) with complex devices, we realized that the teacher's ear is a better analyzer than any equipment we or anyone else could build, so we simply had her push the appropriate switches under the carpet or under the table when the child produced the desired utterance. This procedure was foolproof and simple. Furthermore, it allowed us to give different visual reinforcement for the same sort of task and thus avoid boredom for the child.

When a child of 2 years or older discovered that voicing would make the reels of the tape recorder revolve or a train move, we obtained a great deal of spontaneous voicing—for the first few sessions. Then, when we wanted to shape vowels using the voicing obtained, we found that these toys had lost their appeal. With a greater variety of hand-switched toys—lights that waver, frogs that jump, birds that move wings, windmills that turn—we were able to maintain attention (in operant terms, to keep the child under stimulus control) for the necessary learning period. With slightly older children, tokens may work equally as well (Bennett, 1974). The reactions and interest of others are, of course, essential ingredients of reinforcement, particularly in early infancy (Dodd, 1972). We should never lose sight of the social nature of speech or the development of the child as a social being.

Visual reinforcement is, of course, preferable to tangible reinforcement such as food, which distracts from or prevents the type of behavior we seek to elicit. Because the severely hearing-impaired child tends to use vision rather than audition to scan his environment (Myklebust, 1960), vision appears to be a particularly appropriate reinforcement modality. Visual feedback devices often do not possess reinforcing properties; and even if they do, the child may rapidly lose interest in them through repeated exposure. The use of vision for feedback may also deprive the child of its use for instrumental or social reinforcement, which may be more important, for more adequate feedback on speech is available through the orosensory system.

Summary

The senses may be used proprioceptively, i.e., to provide information arising from within the organism, or exteroceptively, i.e., to receive input from the environment. The various ways in which they are used (and may be exploited) in the acquisition of speech are discussed. The evidence reviewed indicates that the child's development of well differentiated orosensory-motor patterns is of prime importance since, once the motor speech command system is well established, speech can be produced in the absence of sensory feedback. Procedures traditionally and recently employed in teaching hearing-impaired children through visual means—including electronic visual aids—are critically examined, and possible visual reinforcement procedures are described.

REFERENCES

Abbs, J. H. *The influence of the gamma motor system on jaw movement during speech.* Unpublished Ph.D. diss., University of Wisconsin, 1971.

Arrowsmith, J. P. *The Art of Instructing the Infant Deaf and Dumb.* London: Taylor and Hessey, 1819.

Bell, A. G. *The Mechanism of Speech.* New York: Funk and Wagnalls, 1916.

Bennett, C. W. Articulation training of two hearing-impaired girls. *J. Appl. Behav. Anal.*, 7, 439–445, 1974.

Bishop, M. E., Ringel, R. L., & House, A. S. Orosensory perception in the deaf. *Volta Rev.*, 74, 289–298, 1972.

Boothroyd, A., Archambault, P., Adams, R. E., & Storm, R. D. *Use of a computer based system of speech analysis and display in a remedial speech program for deaf children.* S.A.R.P. #14. Northampton, Mass.: Clarke School for the Deaf, 1974.

Brannon, J. B. *Visual feedback of glossal motions and its influence on the speech of deaf children.* Unpublished Ph.D. diss., Northwestern University, 1964.

DiCarlo, L. M. The effect of hearing one's own voice among children with impaired hearing. In A. Ewing (Ed.), *The Modern Educational Treatment of Deafness.* Manchester: Manchester University Press, 1960.

Dodd, B. J.   Effects of social and vocal stimulation on infant babbling. *Dev. Psychol.*, 7, 80–83, 1972.

Fant, G.   *Acoustic Theory of Speech Production, with Calculations Based on X-Ray Studies of Russian Articulations*. The Hague: Mouton, 1960.

Fritzell, B.   The velopharyngeal muscles in speech: An electromyographic and cineradiographic study. *Acta Oto-Laryngol. Suppl.*, 250, 1969.

Gammon, S. A., Smith, P. J., Daniloff, R. G., & Kim, C. W.   Articulation and stress/juncture production under oral anesthetization and masking. *J. Speech Hear. Res.*, 14, 271–282, 1971.

Gates, A., & Bradshaw, J. L.   Effects of auditory feedback on a musical performance task. *Percept. Psychophys.*, 16, 105–109, 1974.

Gibson, J. J.   *The Senses Considered as Perceptual Systems*. Boston: Houghton Mifflin, 1966.

Grossman, R. C., & Hattis, B. F.   Oral mucosal sensory innervation and sensory experience: A review. In J. F. Bosma (Ed.), *Symposium on Oral Sensation and Perception*. Springfield, Ill.: Thomas, 1967.

Harris, K. S.   The physiological substrate of speaking. In W. D. Wolfe and D. J. Goulding (Eds.), *Articulation and Learning*. Springfield, Ill.: Thomas, 1973.

Haycock, G. S.   *The Teaching of Speech*. Washington, D.C.: Volta Bureau, 1933.

Hutchinson, J. M., & Putnam, A. H. B.   Aerodynamic aspect of sensory deprived speech. *J. Acoust. Soc. Am.*, 56, 1612–1617, 1974.

Levitt, H., & Nye, P. W. (Eds.)   *Sensory Training Aids for the Hearing Impaired*. Washington, D.C.: National Academy of Engineering, 1971.

Liberman, A. M., Cooper, F. S., Shankweiler, D. P., & Studdert-Kennedy, M.   Why are speech spectrograms hard to read? *Am. Ann. Deaf*, 113, 127–133, 1968.

Matthews, P. B. C.   Muscle spindles and their motor control. *Physiol. Rev.*, 44, 219–288, 1964.

McCroskey, R. L.   *Some effects of anesthetizing the articulators under conditions of normal and delayed side tone*. Project NM 001 104 500, Report #65. Pensacola, Florida: U.S. Naval School of Aviation Medicine, 1958.

Moller, K. T., Path, M., Werth, L. J., & Christiansen, R. L.   The modification of velar movement. *J. Speech Hear. Disord.*, 38, 323–334, 1973.

Mowrer, D. E.   A behavioristic approach to modification of articulation. In W. D. Wolfe and D. J. Goulding (Eds.), *Articulation and Learning*. Springfield, Ill.: Thomas, 1973.

Myklebust, H. R.   *The Psychology of Deafness*. New York: Grune and Stratton, 1960.

Piaget, J.   *Play, Dreams and Imitation in Childhood*. London: Heinemann, 1962.

Pickett, J. M.   Speech science research and speech communication for the deaf. In L. E. Connor (Ed.), *Speech for the Deaf Child: Knowledge and Use*. Washington, D.C.: A. G. Bell Assoc. for the Deaf, 1971.

Pleasonton, A. K.   Sensitivity of the tongue to electrical stimulation. *J. Speech Hear. Res.*, 13, 635–644, 1970.

Posner, M. I.   *Cognition: An Introduction*. Glenview, Ill.: Scott Foresman, 1973.

Putnam, A. H. B., & Ringel, R. L.   Some observations of articulation during labial sensory deprivation. *J. Speech Hear. Res.*, 15, 529–542, 1972.

Ringel, R. L.   Oral sensation and perception: A selective review. *ASHA Report* #5, 188–206, 1970.

Ringel, R. L., & Ewanowski, S. J.   Oral perception: I. Two-point discrimination. *J. Speech Hear. Res.*, 8, 389–398, 1965.

Scuri, D.   Respirazione e fonazione nei sordomuti. *Rassegna di sordomuti e fonetica biologica*, 14, 82–113, 1935.

Shelton, R. L., Knox, A. W., Elbert, M., & Johnson, T. S.   Palate awareness and nonspeech voluntary palate movement. In J. F. Bosma (Ed.), *Second Symposium on Oral Sensation and Perception.* Springfield, Ill.: Thomas, 1970.

Siegel, G. M., & Pick, H. L.   Auditory feedback in the regulation of voice. *J. Acoust. Soc. Am.*, 56, 1618–1624, 1974.

Skinner, B. F.   *Verbal Behavior.* New York: Appleton-Century-Crofts, 1957.

Sloane, H. N., & MacAulay, B. D.   *Operant Procedures in Remedial Speech and Language Training.* New York: Houghton Mifflin, 1968.

Soderberg, G. A.   Delayed auditory feedback and stuttering. *J. Speech Hear. Disord.*, 33, 260–267, 1968.

Stark, R. E.   Some features of the vocalizations of young deaf children. In J. F. Bosma (Ed.), *Third Symposium on Oral Sensation and Perception: The Mouth of the Infant.* Springfield, Ill.: Thomas, 1972.

Van Riper, C., & Irwin, J.   *Voice and Articulation.* Englewood Cliffs, N.J.: Prentice-Hall, 1958.

Wyke, B.   Recent advances in the neurology of phonation: Phonatory reflex mechanisms in the larynx. *Br. J. Disord. Commun.*, 2, 2–14, 1967.

/7/

Levels of
Speech Acquisition
and Automaticity

Auditory feedback may not be required for the maintenance of speech, but some forms of both proprioception and exteroception are essential for its acquisition. The child must have the type of information which will allow him to (1) differentiate between the sounds he makes, (2) derive meaning from the sounds that others make, and (3) be aware of the extent to which his own speech corresponds with that of others. Hearing-impaired children tend to have problems in each of these areas. In this chapter we shall, therefore, describe in some detail the phonetic and phonologic mechanisms involved and discuss strategies that can be adopted to promote the child's acquisition of spoken language. We specify five distinct mechanisms as being prerequisite to the development of spoken language. These five mechanisms, each of which involves numerous subskills and abilities, are depicted in Figure 7.1. They are arranged to indicate the two levels of acquisition mentioned above.

The Phonetic Level

The first two mechanisms—**(a)** and **(b)**—shown in Figure 7.1 are at a phonetic level. Thus, **(a)** involves the production of vocalizations (suprasegmental features, vowels, and consonants) that are differentiated through proprioception of specific orosensory-motor patterns, and **(b)** represents the parallel differentiation of these patterns through proprioceptive audition. The treatment of these two mechanisms as phonetic level activities accords with the classification used by Fry (1968), who points out that a child may produce and differentiate between sounds that are not meaningful. Only when speech sounds are incorporated into a meaningful system which corresponds with the phonology of the community do they become phonemes.

The third mechanism **(c)** is an essential intermediate stage between the phonetic and phonologic levels. It represents the child's increasing awareness of, and search for, correspondence between his own speech patterns and those of others. Whereas the child's awareness of his own patterns demands proprioception, this and subsequent levels of processing demand active exteroception (cf. J. J. Gibson, 1966). It is at this level that hearing, which is used both proprioceptively and exteroceptively, provides the greatest advantage, since the correspondences sought are most simply achieved in that modality.

The Phonologic Level

Mechanism **(d)** involves the child's increasing awareness of meaning in the speech of others and his evolving comprehension of their speech

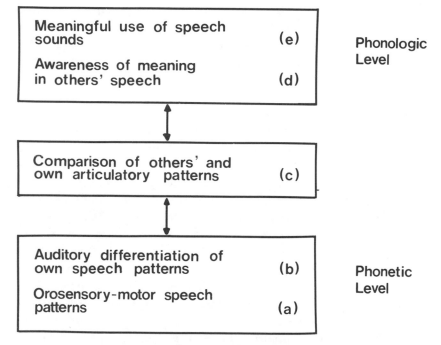

Figure 7.1

The mechanisms employed in the acquisition of spoken language by a normally hearing child. The child's comparison of his own and others' articulatory patterns **(c)** *is represented as a mediation mechanism between the phonetic* **(a + b)** *and phonologic* **(d + e)** *levels. Phonologic development evolves with the acquisition of vocabulary and linguistic rules.*

patterns. These provide the essential foundations for mechanism **(e)**: the increasing incorporation by the child of his own (previously non-meaningful) articulations into his phonologic (meaningful) system. The phonetic—**(a)** and **(b)**—and phonologic—**(d)** and **(e)**—mechanisms may be viewed as having reciprocal functions: as one develops, so does the other, each leading to a successively greater range of sounds and to the child's increasingly accurate differentiation of the available information in speech (E. J. Gibson, 1969).

In general, the development of sounds at a phonetic level precedes their use at a phonological level (Fry, 1966). This is not to say that the order in which a child acquires sounds phonetically is necessarily the same as that in which he establishes their phonologic use. Before they begin to speak, normally hearing children babble most, if not all, of the sounds they will use; but the order in which the sounds appear in babble is usually quite different from the order in which they become incorporated into meaningful speech (Winitz, 1969). This is an important point, for in teaching speech to hearing-impaired children we may wish to ensure the early use of a frequently occurring phoneme, but we may first need to develop its production from one that occurs much less often. We shall discuss this more fully in later chapters.

Phonetic-to-Phonologic Transition

Even among normally hearing children, the transition from the purely phonetic level to the phonologic and higher levels of spoken language is not achieved quickly. The rate varies from child to child. Many factors, several of which will be discussed in later chapters, may account for such differences in rate. The order in which speech patterns take on phonologic and linguistic significance is fairly predictable. First, the prosodic features and vowels are used to carry meaning (Lewis, 1951), and then the correct pronunciation of consonants emerges, the sequence being similar from one child to the next (Templin, 1957). Details on normal and deviant phonologic development are provided by McCarthy (1954), Menyuk (1968), Winitz (1969), Compton (1970), and Sheets (1971), among others.

In teaching hearing-impaired children, it is essential for us to know not only what phonemes a child uses in his phonology, but what speech sounds are present in his phonetic repertoire. Different types of evaluative procedures are therefore required to measure performance at each level. At most stages of speech acquisition the teacher's task will be twofold: developing speech patterns in the child's phonetic repertoire to an automatic level and, concurrently, promoting the transition of already well developed patterns into meaningful use. In general, a child's phonetic performance may be expected to exceed his phonologic capability since some sounds present in his phonetic repertoire will not have reached the level of automaticity required for easy transition from one level to the next.

Fostering the production of speech patterns by the child and encouraging their eventual assimilation into his phonologic system is the essence of speech teaching. The most fundamental aspect of the process is optimal use of the child's proprioceptive and exteroceptive senses, of which hearing is the most important. We may use the senses for speech development in two ways: to afford experience and to provide training. For children who have adequate residual hearing, a rich experience of speech may be all that is required for the acquisition of spoken language. Through such experience they may spontaneously develop each of the mechanisms described above. On the other hand, children with little or no residual hearing will, in addition to rich experience, require specific training, the amount and type depending largely on hearing level. The primary objective in the development of speech skills is the promotion of their automatic use so that conscious attention to articulation does not interfere with the higher-level activities required for fluent spoken language.

Automaticity

The foundations for automatic speech production are acquired by normally hearing children through babble. Before sounds are used phonologically (within a meaning system), they are used phonetically. Hearing-impaired children also need to develop a phonetic repertoire as a basis for phonologic development. Training hearing-impaired children toward automaticity through phonetic (non-meaningful) speech development may greatly speed the process of acquisition and also reduce the need for correction at the phonologic level, when emphasis should be on communication rather than on the mechanisms of production. Practice at the phonetic level will not, of course, be sufficient for the development of automaticity. Following the development of a phonetic level repertoire, the child, whether normally hearing or hearing-impaired, requires a vast experience in the use of meaningful spoken language before sounds are automatically produced.

Speech patterns should be rehearsed until it takes conscious attention to produce them inaccurately. Essentially, this means that accuracy of production is not an adequate criterion of success even at a phonetic level. A skill may be accurately performed, yet continue to require the child's conscious attention. Repeated performance beyond the stage when accuracy is attained is required before automaticity is achieved and conscious attention is no longer essential. This is true of any skill, whether it relates to a process such as reading (LaBerge and Samuels, 1974) or to coordinated motor movements such as those involved in speech (Keele, 1968). Response latency is normally used to determine the extent to which a skill has become automatic. It is well established that in verbal as in other tasks, latency decreases well after accuracy has been achieved (Millward, 1964).

Attention to latency is as important as concern with accuracy. In other words, we cannot be satisfied when a hearing-impaired child is able to produce a pitch change of a certain interval, a vowel with falling or rising intonation, or certain consonants in syllables or words. He must also be able to do these things with ease, and do them in various contexts at the rate required in normal speech. For example, vowels may be produced accurately in isolation, but they must also be rehearsed in syllabic contexts until target positions and transitions are achieved speedily and without attention. Before we can expect a child to use vowels correctly in fluent speech, he should be able to produce strings of syllables such as [bibibibi] correctly at a rate of at least three syllables per second while concentrating on a picture-sorting task. Similarly, we must be prepared to have the child practice consonants so that syllables released with any plosive can be repeated at rates of better than three per second. These rates are still below the averages found in studies of diadochokinesis (repetition) in young children with normal hearing (Blomquist, 1950), and faster rates should be attempted as the child's speech improves. Syllables in which the consonant involves fine adjustment of the tongue (e.g., [s, ʃ]) cannot usually be repeated quite as fast as those in which simple closure is involved (e.g., [p, t, k]). Very few hearing-impaired children have been trained to the level of automaticity required for performance at normal diadochokinetic rates, and hence the poor rhythm and lack of accuracy noted in the studies reviewed in Chapter 2 are not surprising.

Automaticity is of particular importance to us in teaching speech to hearing-impaired children for several reasons. First, we must expect even longer neural and mechanical response times to operate in the early stages of speech teaching than were discussed in Chapter 5. This being the case, we cannot expect efficient feedforward and feedback mechanisms to be learned if we are satisfied with accuracy rather than with automaticity. Conversely, we cannot expect to establish automaticity if we teach in such a way that feedback of the type which focuses attention on production is employed beyond the point when accuracy has been achieved. Thus, a visual display might help a child to obtain a correct sound, but it could impede the automatic production of the sound if continued attention to the visual display were demanded. Second, we cannot expect speech to function as an adequate means of expression if we train only to an accuracy level. Attention can only be fully available for higher-level tasks if speech patterns are automatic. For this reason, production of most sound patterns at an automatic level is required before the child can transfer speech skills acquired in training and in everyday experience to new situations. Third, because longer-than-normal latencies are involved in the production of sounds which are not automatic, distortions of timing can be readily introduced and can become habitual if sounds are taught only in a meaningful (phoneme, word, or sentence) context.

Phonetic Level Development
Figure 7.1, Mechanisms (a) and (b)

It has been shown that phonetic level vocalization and speech sound production are generally present among hearing-impaired children during early infancy and on admission to special school (Sykes, 1940; Carr, 1955; Lenneberg, 1967; Mavilya, 1969; Lach, Ling, Ling, and Ship, 1970; Manolson, 1972). However, such vocalization and speech sound production is usually limited in quantity and abnormal in quality, though in some cases—for example, those reported by Carr (1955)—certain patterns may be well differentiated. Well differentiated speech patterns at the phonetic level are common among hearing-impaired children who have sufficient unaided residual audition for proprioception. However, many such children are not sufficiently aware of others' speech to perceive the correspondence between their own patterns and those of the community and, hence, do not develop speech at a phonologic level.

The obvious strategy in such cases is, first, to provide appropriate amplification; next, to utilize residual hearing to reinforce those patterns present and to encourage new patterns to emerge; and, finally, as these patterns become automatic, to foster their use in meaningful expression. Too early attention to teaching specific sounds tends to result in the destruction of natural voice patterns (Story, 1915; Ewing and Ewing, 1964). Further, if specific sounds are taught in words before they are produced accurately and with ease, they tend to persist in the child's phonology in an inaccurate form. As Winitz (1973) points out, once wrong responses have become thoroughly established at the phonologic level, they have semantic, lexical, and morphemic associations that make them harder to change than responses at the phonetic level.

The Phonetic Repertoire

Systematic babble as a first step in teaching speech to hearing-impaired children has long had its advocates. Holder (1669, p. 155) had his pupils babble syllables until they were accurately and easily produced. Much later, Kinsey (1883), who was aware of the observations made by Taine (1877) on the value of babble, devised a full course of syllabic exercises. They were remarkably comprehensive and modern in concept. The exercises included CV (consonant-vowel), VC, VCV, and CVC syllables. All consonants were systematically combined with all vowels and, with the exception of certain continuants, consonants were never developed in isolation.

For many years, teaching speech to hearing-impaired children involved systematic, daily drills so that speech production at a phonetic level became an automatic process. Thus, Dyer (1914), while advocating that speech should be developed in young children through natural play and communication in which mothers were involved, recognized that daily speech drills were also essential. Buell (1914), too, pointed out that normal speech sequences are pre-planned and automatic. She also recommended drills that rendered them so.

The most systematic drill system to be developed in the USA was that of Avondino (1918, 1919). Her methods were adopted by many teachers including Eccleston (1928) and Goldstein (1939). She began with prolonged vowels and would not permit a new drill to be initiated until the preceding one had become fluent. She recognized that spaced practice yielded superior results to massed practice, and that correction by means of nonsense syllables yielded better results than correction by means of words—something rediscovered and confirmed much later in work with normally hearing children (Scott and Milisen, 1954; Carter and Buck, 1958). A similar system has also been advocated by the writer (Ling, 1963). This system proposes babbling as a means of building both orosensory-motor patterns and their parallel differentiation by proprioceptive audition. It will be fully discussed in later chapters.

The first of two evaluative studies on the effects of vocal drills of the type recommended by Avondino (1918, 1919) was carried out by A. G. Bell and reported by Yale (1927). Over a three-year period, pupils at the Clarke School for the Deaf were given extensive oral exercises ("vocal gymnastics," Bell called them) before any attempt at communicative speech was made. Except for Bell's vocal training the children were taught only by writing. Yale (1927) reported that results were "far in advance of anything attained previously." They led to good voice (one totally deaf girl was able to sing more than an octave in tune), as well as to good speech sound production. The whole program was evidently given up because the teachers were no longer willing to tolerate the imposition of a delay in the child's use of spontaneous speech. It would have been useful if Bell had tested the value of an imposed silence outside training. It seems likely that fostering phonologic growth in addition to phonetic development would have yielded superior results. The view that phonetic and phonologic development should proceed in parallel has long been held (Lewin, 1927; Magner, 1971, p.250).

The second evaluative study of a babbling approach was undertaken and reported by Shaffer (1942). It was a well designed experiment involving two comparable groups, a nine-month training period, objective testing methods, and statistical analysis of results. At the end of the training period, children taught speech by means of sounds in syllable drills were greatly superior to the group taught speech by means of sounds in words. They correctly produced about twice the range of sounds in spontaneous speech and were able to recognize a greater proportion of the words they were able to say than the group taught by means of sounds in words. This finding clearly accords with the motor theory of speech perception discussed in Chapter 3.

Although babbling was once very much in evidence as a teaching method, it seems to have largely disappeared as an everyday practice, and it is unusual to see mention of it in the current literature. Certainly, one sees mention of "formal teaching," but such teaching is usually at the phonologic level, which involves either obtaining a sound from the child and immediately putting it into a word or a sentence or initially teaching it in a meaningful context. For reasons already given, we consider this to be poor practice. If a child has need of formal speech teaching, then he also has need of specific training at the phonetic level to develop well differentiated orosensory-motor patterns and—if adequate hearing is present—parallel differentiation of sounds by auditory proprioception.

Auditory Proprioception

Not all children are so fortunate as to have adequate residual audition for the differentiation of all speech patterns at the phonetic level. The extent to which aided hearing can provide proprioceptive information (in parallel with orosensory-motor patterns) will clearly depend on the degree and type of hearing impairment. With no hearing for high frequencies but good hearing for low frequencies, a child may be expected to develop in a natural way whatever sound patterns are audible and discriminable. Since the majority of hearing-impaired children have low-frequency residual audition, most can hear and discriminate between voice patterns varying in duration, loudness, and pitch. Such patterns, if the child is encouraged to produce them and is given adequate reinforcement, should become part of his phonology, differentiable through both orosensory-motor experience and auditory proprioception. If sufficient residual low-frequency hearing is present, then F_1 of the vowels produced by the child will similarly be differentiable, as will many voiced consonants with primarily low-frequency energy, such as [m, n, w, b]. The need to ensure the proprioceptive audibility of these aspects of speech led us to design and use hearing aids with extended low-frequency response (Ling, 1965).

What of the sounds which cannot be heard by the child with only low-frequency audition? Many such sounds will normally be produced by the child as he is encouraged to vocalize those that are audible to him. If these inaudible sounds are adequately reinforced when they occur "by accident," as it were, then the child will differentiate them through the specific orosensory-motor patterns associated with their production. Of course, not all sounds will be produced "by accident," and many will have to be taught.

With the totally deaf child, all sounds may have to be taught, i.e., established at the phonetic level through differentiation involving only the orosensory-motor patterns his speech creates. There is presently no apparent way that any other form of proprioceptive feedback can be satisfactorily substituted for a completely nonfunctioning auditory sense. If sensory aids which provide pattern perception by way of the skin could be developed, the story might be different; but such aids are only just beginning to be produced. Although some promising engineering approaches were discussed and demonstrated at the International Congress on Education of the Deaf in Tokyo (August 1975), the most sophisticated devices constructed to date provide only a limited range of patterns. Further, children's ability to process complex vibratory patterns remains to be tested. We cannot assume that because a pattern is provided it can be perceived. Though tactile cues on intensity and time may be perceived with fair accuracy, discrimination of frequency in the speech range appears to be extremely limited (Goff, 1967; Franzén and Nordmark, 1975); and the frequency dimension in a complex device would have to be represented spatially on the skin. With only proprioception of orosensory-motor patterns available, the acquisition of speech thus remains a difficult task for the totally deaf child. It can, nevertheless, be achieved if the teacher is fully aware of the nature of the problem. Training may then be organized in such a way that the child's target productions are unambiguously specified, systematically developed from antecedent behaviors, and specifically reinforced.

Phonetic-Phonologic Correspondence
Figure 7.1, Mechanism (c)

The awareness of others' speech patterns and the extent to which they correspond with those of the child involves exteroception. The normally hearing child becomes aware of his own and others' speech principally through audition. It is through this awareness that sounds within the child's phonetic repertoire become incorporated into his phonology. Children who are hearing-impaired suffer their greatest disadvantage at this level. They are capable of producing sounds phonetically, but only to the extent that sounds are auditorily, tactually, or visually discriminable are the children able to match their own (proprioceptive) and others' (exteroceptive) speech patterns. Since audition is the sense that permits the most satisfactory matching, the most successful strategy for the teacher is to utilize to the full whatever residual hearing is present. Audition, even when it is quite restricted, can provide cues on many more aspects of speech than can either touch or vision; and it can provide them not only in training situations but also in the course of communicative experience.

Auditory Speech Awareness

In the initial stages, when amplification is first provided, speech patterns which are audible to the child are not necessarily differentiable. Before a child can discriminate various patterns, one from another, he must be familiar with them, and auditory familiarization through both training and experience will usually be a necessary preliminary to the child's awareness of correspondence between his own and others' speech patterns. If the training of residual hearing for the purpose of providing such awareness is the goal, then the means become relatively clear: the child must be encouraged to produce speech patterns and to differentiate them, so far as possible, through hearing; and the teacher must primarily use speech patterns as stimuli. Awareness of correspondence between proprioceptive and exteroceptive speech patterns cannot be fostered by discrimination training using nonverbal stimuli such as bells, drums, and whistles. Such a nonverbal approach to early auditory training, which is traditional, is still widely advocated (Pollack, 1970; Sanders, 1971). Of course, knowledge of environmental sounds is important to the child. However, little or no amelioration of speech discrimination can be expected to result from training with such stimuli because the acoustic characteristics of speech and of non-speech stimuli are very different, because they are processed in different hemispheres of the brain, and because the perceptual and memory strategies appropriate for one type of sound are inappropriate for the other. These points are discussed more fully by A. H. Ling (1971, 1974).

Tactile Speech Awareness

More cues on speech are available through touch than through vision. Strategies involving touch are, however, limited to a teaching situation unless a portable device which provides tactile information is worn. Such a device (already discussed) is not recommended for children who have useful residual hearing, but it may be beneficial to totally or near-totally deaf children. In view of the limitations inherent in devices which offer only a single vibrator (and only this type is currently portable), the teacher cannot rely on such aids alone to foster the profoundly deaf child's awareness of correspondence between his own and others' speech. The use of such a device must be supplemented by the teacher through strategies which compensate for the tactile aid's deficiencies—strategies which encourage the child to use vision to supplement touch.

Tactile cues of the type described by Zaliouk (1954) are both appropriate and helpful in teaching situations, though their use as a symbol system should be questioned (see Chapter 4). They can help foster awareness of correspondence between the child's own and others' speech patterns and, when provided as cues, may help to promote a varied and well differentiated phonetic repertoire. For the child with no useful hearing, touch can—in a teaching situation—be used to provide information on all aspects of speech: suprasegmental features, vowels, and consonants.

Visual Speech Awareness

As the development of an extensive phonetic repertoire proceeds, the child will become visually aware of certain aspects of correspondence between his own and others' speech without specific visual training. The patterns of speech he receives through vision will be more and more easily interpreted as his phonetic repertoire is extended since he requires orosensory-motor patterns to serve as a reference for the discrimination of visually received patterns. However, complete awareness of correspondence between his own and others' speech cannot be expected of a child who is trained only through vision. Direct vision provides too meager and ambiguous a range of cues for adequate speech reception in the early stages of acquisition. It is particularly weak in conveying information on suprasegmental aspects of speech, it does not provide any information on F_1/F_2 relationships, and it offers but a partial range of cues on place of production for consonants. Its weaknesses as an avenue for everyday speech experience suggest that in communicative speech, the most appropriate use of vision is as a supplement to other modalities. For example, vision can supply cues that are not available through limited residual audition, and it may complement the cues available from a vibrator driven by a hearing aid. Only when a child's phonetic repertoire is well developed and he can refer to extensive speech and language experience can the meager visual information afforded by speechreading be meaningful. The information in visual speech reception lies not so much in what is seen but in what the child knows he must look for.

To reduce the ambiguity inherent in speechreading, Cornett (1967) proposed the use of "Cued Speech," a revised hand-mouth system. In this system, certain hand positions and hand configurations are used to distinguish between speech sounds that look alike on the lips. The strength of the system is that no hand position or configuration uniquely specifies a phoneme; hence, continuous, simultaneous attention to the lips of the speaker is demanded. There is some evidence that both cued and uncued speech reception improves through the use of the system. One disadvantage is that it does not incorporate cues on suprasegmental structure, although the skilled sender may indicate word stress. The system has not yet been adequately evaluated with children who are totally or near-totally deaf but have no other handicaps. This is to be deplored since, theoretically, it could help such children to become more fully aware of certain patterns of correspondence between others' speech and their own. Cued Speech would appear to be unnecessary for children with useful residual hearing since audition can supply more adequate information than can any visual cueing system. Indeed, as suggested in Chapter 3, the extra visual load added to an already heavily burdened sense modality might detract from such a child's optimal use of residual hearing. Both the possibilities and limitations of Cued Speech as a communication aid merit substantially more investigation.

Other visual cueing systems which may be used to increase awareness of the correspondence between the child's speech patterns and those of people with whom he communicates include those of Zaliouk (1954), Ewing and Ewing (1964), and Schulte (1972). All differ from

Cued Speech in that hand position, configuration, and movement in these systems may uniquely specify particular phonemes and indicate particular articulatory features relating to them. Thus, the position of the fingers in Zaliouk's system and the configuration of the hand or hands in the Ewings' and in Schulte's systems are intended to be analogous to speech organ positions. The speed and direction of movement of the hand(s) are intended to show the characteristic manner of consonant release. In practice, these systems are too cumbersome to be used in the course of communication. They are more appropriate to speech teaching situations for which they were primarily designed. Knowledge of these systems provides the teacher with a battery of alternative strategies by which she may develop the child's phonetic level repertoire.

There are, in short, various ways in which an ingenious teacher can provide visual cues on speech or visual reinforcement in training situations. The required grouping of sounds and their duration, intensity, and frequency can all be signaled by appropriate gestures with hand or even with eyebrow. The finger can be as effective an indicator of pitch or loudness as the oscilloscope. Tongue positions and movements for vowels can be demonstrated by means of models, hand analogies, or pictures, as can the manner, place, and voicing of consonants. The extent and variety of visual cues which the teacher can use to indicate correspondence between her speech and the child's are limited only by the extent of the imagination. We should not allow deference to technology to blind us to the possibilities of the teacher as a source of effective visual cues.

Phonologic Level Development
Figure 7.1, Mechanisms (d) and (e)
Deriving Meaning from Speech

At the phonologic level the child is concerned with both deriving meaning from the speech of others and using his own speech in a meaningful way. In the normal course of events, meaning is initially derived from the situations in which speech occurs. Particularly in the early stages of speech acquisition, mothers talk to their children mainly about things that are part of the children's "here and now" experience, and they tend to provide situational cues in parallel with speech (Ling and Ling, 1974). There are many situations that are routine and repetitive in the young child's life. These include activities associated with handling, toilet, dressing, feeding, outings, and play. It is within the structure provided by such situations that a child normally arrives at the meaning of others' speech—at the association between sound patterns and the objects and activities to which they refer. In early work with young hearing-impaired children, many similar everyday situations can be used to provide the framework and repetition within which the meaning intended by the speaker can become clear. The more severely hearing-impaired the child is, the more carefully structured the teaching situation must be if he is to derive meaning from it, and the more careful the teacher must be to exploit the child's senses in such a way that the sounds she makes are optimally perceptible and meaningful.

Meaningful Articulation

As the child develops a varied, well differentiated phonetic repertoire, he will, through appropriate ongoing training and experience, come to an awareness of the correspondence between his own speech patterns and those of others and learn that speech is used in a meaningful way. The child's use of breath-grouped vocalizations to attract attention, to indicate needs, and to express pleasure or displeasure is the first step toward phonologic development. He must be given the opportunity to see that the use of such patterns can elicit responses from those around him. As training at a phonetic level proceeds and as phonologic experience of speech is gained, the child can be expected to refine his vocalizations and to increase the range of sounds they contain. If necessary, his attention may be called to the correspondence of a phonologic pattern with one that is present in his phonetic repertoire, but on no account should such a procedure be allowed to interrupt his use of speech for communication. Constant interruption too readily causes a child's reluctance to speak (Anon., 1935).

Speech Correction

There are, in our view, few reasons for incidental speech teaching at a phonologic level. If speech patterns are practiced phonetically toward a level of automaticity—and to this end they should be systematically practiced for a few minutes several times each day—then the transition of these patterns to the child's phonology should require relatively little of the teacher's attention. If the child has problems using particular speech patterns at the phonologic level, it is usually because they have not been practiced in a sufficient variety of phonetic contexts, or because their correspondence with the adult's phonology is not apparent to the child. There is little one can do in the middle of a lesson concerned with something other than speech to remedy these problems.

Teachers should distinguish between speech teaching and speech correction. The more concerned a teacher is with the former, the less need there will be to undertake the latter. Speech patterns taught at a phonetic level do not need to be taught again at a phonologic level, but their correct usage in the broader and more demanding context of meaningful speech may need to be encouraged. The process involved is one of refinement rather than correction, with attention being given to the use of appropriate suprasegmental patterns—including timing—and to the transfer of phonetic level patterns into the child's evolving phonology. Suprasegmental patterns are important in communicative speech because they convey information on intention in parallel and in harmony with segmental structures. Development at a phonologic level should be encouraged, so far as possible, with meaningful material outside communicative speech. However, some modeling, expansion, and repetition of communicative speech patterns are inevitably required in order to ensure optimal performance. Unclear and inadequate speech will persist if the teacher does not consistently expect the child to employ established phonetic level patterns in his phonology. Thus, while seeking improvement of communicative speech is reasonable, teaching new speech patterns during communication is not.

Sporadic, incidental correction also has its limitations. If the speech of hearing-impaired children in a class is as poor as that reported in the studies reviewed in Chapter 2, then sporadic, incidental correction would lead to little amelioration. Moreover, the children could easily become confused because they would see no reason why a particular pattern they produce should receive disapproval at one time and not at another. A child may also infer approval from the teacher's failure to correct a poorly produced pattern. Such inferred approval provides reinforcement for inadequate speech. Teaching speech incidentally in class also tends to hold up the lesson for other children. Good class management demands the attention of all members of the class to the task at hand. Helping the child incorporate an already acquired phonetic pattern into his phonology should—like teaching the pattern in the first place—be an activity for the individual and his teacher.

Once the child has started to use speech linguistically, numerous errors of production will occur. Errors of language—i.e., inadequately derived phonemic, morphemic, lexical, and syntactic rules—must be differentiated from errors of speech—i.e., inadequately produced suprasegmental features, vowels, and consonants. It is in communicative speech that the child's deficiencies in coarticulation become evident since it is in running discourse that suprasegmental and segmental aspects of speech interact most strongly. Development of appropriate coarticulation—not simply within words, but between all elements of a sentence—cannot be expected unless the allophones required are part of the child's phonetic repertoire and have been used phonologically. Deficiencies in coarticulation are therefore best remedied by practice at phonetic and phonologic levels. Techniques appropriate to teaching at a phonologic level have been effectively described by Ewing and Ewing (1964) and by Vorce (1974); and the essential conditions for the development of spoken language have been clearly summarized by both Di-Carlo (1960) and Miller (1960). The reader should be aware that many writers either do not recognize or frequently confuse the levels described in this chapter and the mechanisms which underlie them.

Speech and Communication

There are usually two reasons why one sets out to acquire a skill: to obtain intrinsic pleasure from its mastery, and to enjoy its utility. Learning to ride a bicycle is fun. It is also useful for getting around. The desire to get around helps us overcome the knocks and provides the impetus we must sustain in learning to ride. So it should be with speech. The skilled teacher will avoid allowing the child to sustain too many setbacks and difficulties by carefully grading and systematically teaching the subskills involved and, at the same time, will provide the impetus toward mastery through the creation of situations in which the child can use the skills he has acquired in communication. Neither speech nor language is an end unto itself. It is simply the means by which we achieve effective communication of our thoughts and feelings. Thus, once differentiated sound patterns have become established in the child's phonetic repertoire, every attempt should be made to give them communicative significance. This can be achieved more readily by the association and use of sounds within meaningful linguistic units than by the association of sounds with symbols. Symbols can merely label orosensory-motor patterns in the phonetic repertoire, once they are acquired. We do not, therefore, require them for acquisition. If meaningful use is made of orosensory-motor patterns when they have been established, then the linguistic and communicative associations which can be made with the sounds will be sufficient to maintain them.

In determining the appropriate strategies for teaching the child to talk, one must bear in mind not only the child's sensory capacities and levels of achievement but also his age, interests, and needs. Our concern with speech should not lead us to ignore other aspects of the child's development. Conversely, we must not be so concerned with other aspects of development that we pay too little heed to speech, for a child who is not taught to communicate effectively by speech will be deprived of an extremely useful tool and an enormous fund of common human experience.

Summary

Two levels of speech production are delineated: the phonetic and the phonologic. At the phonetic level, speech patterns may be differentiated by the listener and by the child, but they are not linguistically organized. At the phonologic level, speech patterns become part of a linguistic system. We propose that sound patterns must be developed at a phonetic level before they can be used phonologically, and that practice toward automaticity at a phonetic level is necessary (though not sufficient) for a fluently produced phonology. The literature relating to automaticity and phonetic level work with hearing-impaired children is reviewed, and the mechanisms by which phonetic skills may be assimilated into the child's phonology are described and discussed.

REFERENCES

Anonymous.   Demonstration of how NOT to teach speech. *Volta Rev.*, 37, 585 & 617, 1935.

Avondino, J.   The babbling method. *Volta Rev.*, 20, 667–671, passim, 1918.

Avondino, J.   The babbling method. *Volta Rev.*, 21, 67–71, passim, 1919.

Blomquist, B. L.   Diadochokinetic movement of nine-, ten-, and eleven-year-old children. *J. Speech Hear. Disord.*, 15, 159–164, 1950.

Buell, E. M.   Easy and natural speech. *Am. Ann. Deaf*, 59, 379–386, passim, 1914.

Carr, J.   The use of spontaneous speech. *Volta Rev.*, 57, 20–21, 1955.

Carter, E. T., & Buck, M.   Prognostic testing for functional articulation disorders among children in the first grade. *J. Speech Hear. Disord.*, 23, 124–133, 1958.

Compton, A. J.   Generative studies of children's phonological disorders. *J. Speech Hear. Disord.*, 35, 315–339, 1970.

Cornett, R. O.   Cued speech. *Am. Ann. Deaf*, 112, 3–13, 1967.

DiCarlo, L. M.   Speech and communication for the deaf. *Volta Rev.*, 62, 317–319, 1960.

Dyer, H. L.   Need a deaf child's speech be expressionless? *Volta Rev.*, 16, 85–87, 1914.

Eccleston, M. M.   How we learn speech in the beginning. *Volta Rev.*, 30, 279–280, 1928.

Ewing, A. W. G., & Ewing, E. C.   *Teaching Deaf Children To Talk*. Manchester: Manchester University Press, 1964.

Franzén, O., & Nordmark, J.   Vibrotactile frequency discrimination. *Percept. Psychophys.*, 17, 480–484, 1975.

Fry, D. B.   The development of the phonological system in the normal and the deaf child. In F. Smith & G. A. Miller (Eds.), *The Genesis of Language*. Cambridge, Mass.: M.I.T. Press, 1966.

Fry, D. B.   The phonemic system in children's speech. *Br. J. Disord. Commun.*, 3, 13–19, 1968.

Gibson, E. J.   *Principles of Perceptual Learning and Development*. New York: Appleton-Century-Crofts, 1969.

Gibson, J. J.   *The Senses Considered as Perceptual Systems*. Boston: Houghton Mifflin, 1966.

Goff, G. D.   Differential discrimination of frequency of cutaneous mechanical vibration. *J. Exp. Psychol.*, 74, 294–299, 1967.

Goldstein, M. A.   *The Acoustic Method for the Training of the Deaf and Hard of Hearing Child*. St. Louis: Laryngoscope Press, 1939.

Holder, W.   *Elements of Speech*. London: J. Martyn, 1669.

Keele, S. W.   Movement control in skilled motor performance. *Psychol. Bull.*, 70, 387–403, 1968.

Kinsey, A.   *A Full Course of Exercises in Articulation for Deaf Children*. London: W. H. Allen, 1883.

LaBerge, D., & Samuels, S. J.   Toward a theory of automatic information processing in reading. *Cogn. Psychol.*, 6, 293–323, 1974.

Lach, R., Ling, D., Ling, A. H., & Ship, N.   Early speech development in deaf infants. *Am. Ann. Deaf*, 115, 522–526, 1970.

Lenneberg, E. H.   *Biological Foundations of Language*. New York: Wiley, 1967.

Lewin, L. M.   The speech habit. *Volta Rev.*, 29, 242–244, 1927.

Lewis, M. M.   *Infant Speech*. London: Routledge & Kegan Paul, 1951.

Ling. A. H.   Dichotic listening in hearing-impaired children. *J. Speech Hear. Res.*, 14, 793–803, 1971.

Ling, A. H.   Sequential processing in hearing-impaired children. In C. Griffiths (Ed.), *Auditory Techniques*. Springfield, Ill.: Thomas, 1974, pp. 97–106.

Ling, D.   The use of hearing and the teaching of speech. *Teach. Deaf*, 61, 59–68, 1963.

Ling, D.   Low frequency amplification. *Acta Oto-Laryngol. Suppl.*, 206, 232–237, 1965.

Ling, D., & Ling, A. H.   Communication development in the first three years of life. *J. Speech Hear. Res.*, 17, 146–159, 1974.

Magner, M. E.   Techniques of teaching. In L. E. Connor (Ed.), *Speech for the Deaf Child: Knowledge and Use*. Washington, D.C.: A. G. Bell Assoc. for the Deaf, 1971, pp. 245–264.

Manolson, A.   Comparative study of intonation patterns in normal hearing and hearing-impaired children. In A. Rigault & R. Charbonneau (Eds.), *Proc. 7th Int. Congr. Phonetic Sciences*. The Hague: Mouton, 1972, pp. 962–965.

Mavilya, M. P.   *Spontaneous vocalization and babbling in hearing-impaired infants*. Unpublished Ed.D. diss., Teachers College, Columbia University, 1969.

McCarthy, D.   Language development in children. In L. Carmichael (Ed.), *Manual of Child Psychology*. New York: Wiley, 1954.

Menyuk, P.   The role of distinctive features in children's acquisition of phonology. *J. Speech Hear. Res.*, 11, 138–146, 1968.

Miller, J.   Speech and the preschool child. *Volta Rev.*, 62, 315–317, 1960.

Millward, R.   Latency in a modified paired-associate learning experiment. *J. Verbal Learn. Verbal Behav.*, 3, 309–316, 1964.

Pollack, D.   *Educational Audiology for the Limited Hearing Infant*. Springfield, Ill.: Thomas, 1970.

Sanders, D. A.   *Aural Rehabilitation*. Englewood Cliffs, N.J.: Prentice-Hall, 1971.

Schulte, K.   Phonemetransmitting manual system (PSM). In G. Fant (Ed.), *Speech Communication Ability and Profound Deafness*. Washington, D.C.: A. G. Bell Assoc. for the Deaf, 1972, pp. 255–260.

Scott, D. A., & Milisen, R. L.   The effectiveness of combined visual-auditory stimulation in improving articulation. *J. Speech Hear. Disord. Monogr. Suppl.*, 4, 51–56, 1954.

Shaffer, C. M.   The kinesthetic method of speech development and speech-reading. *Am. Ann. Deaf*, 87, 421–442, 1942.

Sheets, B. V.   The development of speech. In L. E. Connor (Ed.), *Speech for the Deaf Child: Knowledge and Use*. Washington, D.C.: A. G. Bell Assoc. for the Deaf, 1971.

Story, A. J.   *Speech-Reading and Speech for the Deaf*. Stoke-On-Trent: Hill and Ainsworth, 1915.

Sykes, J. L.   A study of the spontaneous vocalizations of young deaf children. *Psychol. Monogr.*, 52, 104–123, 1940.

Taine, M.   The acquisition of language by children. *Mind*, 2, 252–259, 1877.

Templin, M. C.   *Certain Language Skills in Children*. Institute of Child Welfare Monogr. Series No. 26. Minneapolis: University of Minneapolis Press, 1957.

Vorce, E.   *Teaching Speech to Deaf Children*. Washington, D.C.: A. G. Bell Assoc. for the Deaf, 1974.

Winitz, H.   *Articulatory Acquisition and Behavior*. New York: Appleton-Century-Crofts, 1969.

Winitz, H.   Articulatory acquisition: Some behavioral considerations. In W. D. Wolfe & D. J. Goulding (Eds.), *Articulation and Learning*. Springfield, Ill.: Thomas, 1973.

Yale, C. A.   Dr. Bell's early experiments in giving speech to the deaf. *Volta Rev.*, 29, 293–295, 1927.

Zaliouk, A.   A visual-tactile system of phonetical symbolization. *J. Speech Hear. Disord.*, 19, 190–207, 1954.

/8/

Order
or
Chaos?

The global, long-term goal in teaching speech is to ensure that the child acquires spoken language which conforms closely to the phonologic and linguistic patterns of the community at large. With certain hearing-impaired children this goal can be achieved simply and naturally by talking with them clearly enough and often enough over an adequate period of time within the context of everyday activities. With other hearing-impaired children, certainly the majority of those whose auditory handicap is severe, such an approach would be unlikely to succeed. The more severely hearing-impaired the child, the more likely he is to require a structured program of training in specific speech production skills in order to learn to talk.

The order in which speech skills are developed is fundamental to the provision of a structured program. Such order is a critical issue for three reasons: first, attempts to develop particular speech skills before the necessary antecedent behaviors have been established result in a wasteful expenditure of time; second, because incorrect production is fostered unless adequate foundations have been laid, premature endeavors to teach particular skills may result in the development of habitual faults; and third, repeated failure to achieve targets which are set beyond the child's immediate range of ability frustrate both the child and the teacher and may lead to their having negative attitudes toward speech. Given this perspective it is evident that orderly intervention requires that we (a) specify what behaviors constitute antecedents for the adequate development of particular targets within each broad stage of speech acquisition, and (b) define what criteria should be employed to measure these prerequisite behaviors so that we may determine when the child has an adequate base for the development of further skills. In this chapter we shall discuss the first of these problems: namely, the question of orderly progression. We shall turn to the second of these problems, the selection of criteria to monitor development, in the next chapter.

Speech is an activity that employs many organs which serve other functions. We need the lungs for breathing, the jaw for chewing, the tongue and laryngeal structures for swallowing, and so on. If these organs function normally for such purposes, the likelihood is that they can also function normally for speech. Indeed, we may need to develop certain aspects of speech from antecedent, non-speech behaviors. For example, we may teach control of breath through making the child aware of respiration; the approximation of the vocal cords, through exertion; the elevation of the velum, through yawning; and tongue tip positioning, through sucking. Unless such activities are carried out in a logical sequence, however, progress cannot be made. In other words, the foundations of the speech skills we seek to learn are to be found in previously developed behaviors. These behaviors may be either verbal, such as other speech patterns, or nonverbal, such as the vegetative behaviors mentioned above.

This is not to say that we regard the acquisition of speech as an entirely sequential or hierarchical process. There appears to be a series of broad stages of speech acquisition that call for sequential development. For example, vowels cannot be shaped before vocalization has been established, and consonants cannot be satisfactorily taught before a range of vowels can be produced. However, there also appears to be no reason why certain speech patterns—such as consonants differing in manner of production—should not be developed concurrently rather than successively. Indeed, concurrent teaching of certain skills may be advisable if their acquisition is founded on the same prerequisite behaviors and if they have little else in common.

Few writers in the field have given careful consideration to the principles underlying an orderly approach to speech development. Hence, guidelines for the teacher seeking to structure her approach have tended to be grossly inadequate. In general, workers have failed (a) to provide a cogent rationale to support their suggestions relating to the order of teaching speech patterns, (b) to specify what antecedent behaviors are required for the acquisition of any given skill or how well established these behaviors should be, and (c) to recognize that there are two aspects of order which underlie any attempt at systematic teaching of speech: the sequence in which broad classes of sounds (vocalization, nonsegmental patterns, vowels, and consonants) should be developed, and the organization required for teaching specific target behaviors within each of these broad classes. In general, the trend has been to concentrate unduly on segmental elements, mainly consonants.

After reviewing the literature relating to the sequential teaching of speech skills, we shall present a more comprehensive framework for orderly intervention than has previously been suggested. The rationale provided to support our recommendations, will be somewhat speculative since there has been little research in the area. While we seek to proselytize teachers to an orderly approach—and suggest that the notions expressed in this chapter will be helpful in this regard—we also stress that our views on order should be accepted but tentatively in view of the need for further study of the topic.

The Literature on Teaching Order

There is a remarkable lack of accord in the literature relating to the order in which sound patterns should be taught to hearing-impaired children. Opinions on the topic are often vague. Few writers provide a rationale for their views; but among those who do, the rationale may not logically support the position taken. A similar statement was made by Love (1896), who reviewed the literature on order in speech teaching up to the end of the last century. Some well-regarded writers such as Story (1909a, 1915) and Joiner (1946, 1948) put forward notions that are self-contradictory. Story, for example, who espoused a natural approach, quite rightly advocated teaching sounds in syllables but suggested that consonants should be taught prior to vowels. Joiner (1946) provided a detailed framework for graded lessons in speech, beginning with voiceless front consonants and back vowels, and suggested the need for systematic development to all other elements; yet she stated two years later that one could "plunge immediately into the intricacies of combining elements, of accenting syllables, of phrasing, and remembering phonetic markings and at the same time thinking of speech" (Joiner, 1948).

The Traditional Approach to Teaching Order

Teaching voiceless consonants first in combination with back vowels may be regarded as the traditional approach (Arnold, 1881; White, 1884; Haycock, 1933; Yale, 1938; Joiner, 1946). The procedure, according to White, was adopted to prevent the development of intrusive voicing at a later stage. However, there has long been evidence that the procedure does not achieve this objective (see Hudgins, 1937). Using back vowels during the initial stages of consonant teaching has some merit, but the procedure is not without potential dangers. The back vowels have the lowest formant frequencies, and hence they may be audible to children whose residual hearing extends up to or just beyond 1,000 Hz. Not only may these formants be audible, but so may many of the consonant-to-vowel transitions, particularly those associated with labial and alveolar consonants that are voiced. Not surprisingly, Gay (1970) demonstrated that auditory discrimination of consonants associated with back and central vowels tended to be more accurate than that associated with front vowels under low-pass filtering conditions. The danger of first teaching consonants in combination with back vowels is that the procedure may encourage habitual tongue retraction, a common fault among hearing-impaired speakers (Story, 1909b). This can be avoided if front vowels are also developed prior to specific consonant teaching. Then, once a consonant is produced with a back vowel, its production can be immediately generalized through association with central and front vowels, a technique that ensures appropriate allophonic variance.

Haycock (1933, p. 111) also recommended the traditional (voiceless consonant/back vowel) order. His rationale for the approach was based on the relative organic facility in the production of the sounds and on their visibility. Careful consideration indicates that this rationale is unsound. The [s] and [tʃ], which were included among his first group of seven sounds to be taught, are organically among the most difficult since they involve finer adjustment and placement of the tongue than is demanded by stops, which call for simple closure of the vocal tract. Furthermore, several of the unvoiced consonants are not visually discriminable (Woodward and Barber, 1960). Haycock did not, however, consider it necessary to adhere rigidly to the traditional order and recommended departure from it if flexibility were justified by the pupil's intelligence, articulatory control, or sensory awareness.

Yale (1938, p. 34) suggested that teaching unvoiced consonants as a first step allows the child to learn, at one and the same time, elements that do not too closely resemble each other in formation. The idea that those consonants developed first should contrast strongly in the orosensory-motor patterns they yield is supported in this text. However, Yale's notion that unvoiced consonants yield the greatest contrast is demonstrably wrong. The inclusion of voiced sounds provides a much better set for orosensory-motor differentiation, and voiced items within such a set also have the advantage of being more audible and hence more discriminable to the child with useful residual hearing (Ling and Maretic, 1971). The possibilities offered not only by residual hearing but also by vision and exteroceptive touch must also be taken into account in initial consonant teaching based on contrast.

While contrast is important in the teaching of speech, strategies which serve to highlight similarities in the production of sounds are equally so. Thus, sounds which are analogous in place of production may be derived one from the other. For example, [g] may be developed from [ŋ], which has similar tongue target features. Wright (1926) suggested teaching nasal sounds first so that stops with analogous place of production could be derived from them. Such strategies have a valid place in present-day work. While we disagree with the priority that Wright assigned to the nasal sounds (see later sections of this chapter), we fully agree with the view that any sound having articulatory features in common with those of the target sound—manner of production, place of production, or voicing—may advantageously be used to facilitate target acquisition.

The traditional approach was largely based on the assumption that all consonants can be taught in isolation. Certain continuants such as [m, n, l, s] can be so produced, but stops and, indeed, most other consonants can only be taught effectively as part of a syllable. Attempts to teach consonants by themselves, particularly at an early stage of speech acquisition, not only lead to poor coarticulation in running speech, but also detract from the development of adequate suprasegmental structure (Numbers, 1942). Teaching sounds in isolation was a procedure derived from the "posture and glide" view of speech in which segments were envisaged as separate postures of the vocal organs joined one to another by glides. The concept has probably taken a long time to die because tongue postures are typically shown in textbooks and because it is simple to think of phonemes as succeeding one another like letters on a printed page (Abercrombie, 1965). The temptation to regard tongue postures as static rather than as dynamic targets must be resisted, as must seduction by analogy with the written form. Otherwise, speech teaching will result in faulty production, which in turn will require breaking of bad habits before one can establish new and more appropriate patterns. We cannot afford to teach in such a way that results of earlier work have to be undone before progress can be made.

Orderly teaching demands that training result in the cumulative acquisition of subskills, each subskill providing some immediate gain compatible with later achievement. The traditional approach was not designed to yield cumulative gains. Nor was it formulated with reference to the previous acquisition of behaviors which can serve as a basis for speech development. It is incompatible with the optimal use of the senses in speech reception; and it does not accord with current knowledge of the processes involved in speech production. On these grounds, one must reject the traditional approach.

Order and Frequency of Occurrence

An appealing, but impractical, alternative to the traditional approach was proposed by Steinberg (1929), who suggested that the order in which speech patterns are taught should reflect their frequency of occurrence in everyday communication. He suggested that those syllables which are used most frequently in everyday speech should be taught first and those which are seldom employed, left until later. Steinberg's insistence that the syllables rather than the isolated speech sounds are the basic units of speech production represented an advance, but in application his system fails because some of the most frequently occurring syllables in phonologic speech involve sounds which are among the most difficult for hearing-impaired children to produce at a phonetic level (Ling, 1963). These include syllables released with [k] and [s] and syllables arrested with [z] and [ŋ]. In essence, Steinberg failed to realize that certain previously acquired speech behaviors either facilitate or are prerequisite to the adequate production of such patterns. Further, while one should set out to teach consonants in syllables as soon as a variety of vowels can be produced, it is more parsimonious to teach each of the 25 consonants with available vowels—and thus develop the child's ability to generalize—than to teach hundreds of syllables as separate units. We personally found this to be so in a study relating to the teaching of syllables to hearing-impaired children (Ling, 1963) for which we analyzed the 500 words that Burroughs (1957) recorded as being those most frequently used by preschool children in England. Our analysis showed that 15% of the 500 words in this sample were initiated by one of 16 CV (consonant-vowel) syllables, that 38% were terminated by 24 different VC syllables, and that more than 400 of the words contained syllables which occurred only once. Our findings were that more than 300 syllables had to be acquired before half of the words could be produced intelligibly.

Voelker (1935) derived a sound count for individual phonemes from a series of radio announcements and suggested that his findings should be used as guidelines for arriving at an effective order for teaching speech sounds to hearing-impaired children. He confounded initial and final sounds, many of which (e.g., stops and liquids) are—according to their position in the word—produced quite differently and have different frequencies of occurrence. For example, an initial /b/ differs from a final, unreleased /b/ and occurs much more frequently. While words beginning with /b/ are common, words ending in /b/ are relatively rare (Ling, 1963). Even if Voelker's sound count had been carried out more effectively, his suggestion that phoneme frequency could provide guidelines for an effective teaching order would be open to question. While the frequency of occurrence of a particular sound might influence the extent to which it is reinforced phonologically, there appears to be no relationship between frequency of phonologic occurrence and relative ease of phonetic level acquisition. Indeed, the most comprehensive sound count undertaken to date, that completed by Denes (1963), shows that most of the load in speech is borne by alveolar consonants, and these are notoriously more difficult for the hearing-impaired child to acquire than are labial or labiodental consonants (see Chapter 2).

In short, we reject the notion that frequency of occurrence either of syllables (Steinberg, 1929) or of speech sounds (Voelker, 1935) can serve as the basis for an effective order in teaching speech to hearing-impaired children. Neither order gives adequate emphasis to the speech skills that have to be established before one can reasonably begin to teach consonants. Nor does either order reflect the relative difficulty that hearing-impaired children may experience in producing or perceiving speech patterns.

A Natural Order of Speech Sound Acquisition

In a study of 48 five-year-old children at the time of their admission to a special program for the deaf, Carr (1953, 1955) discovered that most were able to produce a wide range of (phonetic level) speech sounds in their spontaneous utterances. She suggested that these sounds, rather than the predetermined set of patterns taught by proponents of the traditional approach, should be used as the basis of phonologic speech development. Carr's suggestion was prompted, at least in part, by her observation of the results of the traditional approach, which, she held, did little to ameliorate and much to cause the poor voice quality and deviant articulation typical of hearing-impaired children. Carr's view was that the use of naturally acquired patterns would be likely to yield speech of superior quality. Carr recognized that not all hearing-impaired children produce a wide range of naturally acquired speech patterns. She suggested that in cases where sound production is limited in quality, the child's repertoire of sounds should be developed through adherence to the natural order of acquisition as determined by Irwin and his colleagues with normally hearing children (Irwin and Chen, 1946; Irwin, 1947a, 1947b).

We agree with Carr (1953, 1955) that whatever sounds are present in a hearing-impaired child's phonetic repertoire should be used for the development of the child's phonology. However, we question whether Irwin's data, without adaptation, could usefully provide guidelines on teaching order. The adaptation we suggest is to utilize the trends in normal acquisition only from the point when repetitive babble begins. This is usually from the age of about 6 or 7 months, when the child has established voice control and has a variety of vowel patterns in his vocal repertoire (Irwin, 1948; Murai, 1960). Then the front sounds and, later, the back sounds consistently appear. At this stage, nasal, semivowel, and stop consonants are initially dominant. They precede fricatives, which in turn precede affricates. We make these adaptations because, first, the data on very early speech development from Irwin's studies and those of Nakazima (1962) do not agree and, second, the sounds produced by infants in the very early months of life may reflect uncontrolled cortical and neuromuscular activity rather than coordinated articulatory movement (Lenneberg, 1967). Anyone concerned with the problem of order in acquisition must be concerned with the discontinuity between sounds produced earlier and later in the first year of life (Kaplan and Kaplan, 1971). We suggest that by discarding Irwin's data on the first six months of life we may avoid the problem of discontinuity and be left with the types of guidelines that are appropriate for systematic speech development in hearing-impaired children who are 7 months of age or older at the onset of training. In short, with the above reservations, we tentatively support Carr's viewpoints.

The Broad Stages of Speech Acquisition:
A Sequential Framework

In the introduction to this chapter, we indicated that there are certain hierarchies inherent in the subskills involved in speech production and that two types of order need to be defined: that pertaining to the sequence in which broad classes of sound should be developed, and that pertaining to a schedule for teaching target behaviors within each of these broad classes. In this section we shall discuss the first type of order: that concerning the broad stages of speech acquisition.

In the natural order of speech acquisition varied patterns of vocalization precede the production of specific vowels, which in turn precedes the production of consonants. There is some overlap (Chen and Irwin, 1946), but there are certain constraints inherent in the speech process that govern the extent to which broad classes may be developed in parallel. First, the duration of an utterance and the number of segments within it are limited by the breath available to produce the required pressures for speech. Second, adequate control of duration, intensity, and pitch of voicing appears to be dependent on experience gained through early vocalization. Such vocalization, involving nonspecific vowel-like sounds, permits the independent control of voice patterns and tongue movement essential to subsequent achievement of specific vowel targets within a desired suprasegmental structure. Hearing-impaired children who are taught to produce specific vowels prior to achieving flexible voice patterns tend to develop interdependent rather than independent laryngeal and articulatory adjustments.

Consonants, for the most part, are sounds that do not exist in isolation. Rather, they serve to arrest or to release syllables with a vowel nucleus (McDonald, 1964). Since the vowel largely determines the allophonic form of the consonant, vowels must, in the main, be acquired prior to consonants. The view that consonants are most meaningfully considered in the context of the vowels that precede or follow them and that consonants are to a great extent "carried" by the vocal stream was expressed by Dudley (1940). It receives current acceptance following work by Öhman (1966) and by Mermelstein (1973).

The range of consonants in speech is tremendously varied, and at least two broad stages of consonant acquisition may be identified: that involving the production of simple consonants in initial, medial (intervocalic), and final position in syllables or words; and that involving the production of consonant blends. Such a division is in accordance with the data available on the development of consonant blends in normally hearing children (Hawkins, 1973.)

Essentially, then, there appear to be five broad, mainly sequential stages through which children must—and normally do—pass as they develop speech production skills. The patterns produced in each of the five stages may be described as: (1) undifferentiated vocalization; (2) nonsegmental voice patterns varied in duration, intensity, and pitch; (3) a range of distinctly different vowel sounds; (4) simple consonants releasing, modifying, or arresting syllables; and (5) consonant blends. These patterns may or may not have initial communicative significance depending on whether they are produced at a phonetic level (simply as sounds) or a phonologic level (within a meaningful system). The skills acquired have both hierarchical and cumulative importance since, at each stage, the acquisition of control over production serves to supply the foundations for adequate development in the next and subsequent stages. It appears feasible to divide certain of the broad stages specified above into smaller sequential units for the purpose of teaching, and this we propose to do in a later section.

In operational terms, we suggest that the first step in training a hearing-impaired child should be to determine what sound patterns, if any, he has in his phonetic repertoire. Then, much as Carr (1953, 1955) suggests, we should work toward extending this repertoire at both the phonetic and phonologic levels. The principle underlying this suggested use of existing patterns has long been established in pedagogy: the individual should proceed from the known to the unknown. We suggest, however, that unless the child can vocalize on demand and can produce a wide range of voice patterns and a variety of vowels, we should not seek to initiate or extend his consonant repertoire. Rather, we should ensure prior mastery of the various stages specified above, since the patterns that are established in the earlier stages—and their proprioceptive correlates—provide the breath grouping, the suprasegmental stream, and the sensory-motor capacities on which successful consonant articulation must ultimately rest. For the hearing-impaired child with no naturally acquired speech patterns, we suggest that there is no feasible alternative but to promote sequential acquisition as outlined in the preceding paragraphs, first promoting the production of abundant vocalization.

The notion that one should not attempt to teach specific vowels or consonants to a hearing-impaired child before he is able to vocalize abundantly, with variety, and on demand is not new. Watson (1809), Farrar (1901), Muyskens (1938), Hudgins (1946), and DiCarlo (1960), among many others, have emphasized that no attempt should be made to teach specific sounds until a variety of pleasant vocal patterns is habitually used for communication and in vocal play. This is not to say that one waits passively for the child to attain what Ewing and Ewing (1964), among others, term "speech readiness." Early vocalization and breath-grouped patterns can be systematically encouraged. Should an attempt to teach a specific sound interfere with the quality of these carrier patterns, then further attempts should be postponed. The orosensory-motor patterns we seek to establish do not exist in the production of isolated segments.

Target Behaviors Within Successive Stages

In order to implement a systematic speech development program for hearing-impaired children, one must not only define the broad sequential stages of acquisition, but also specify what target behaviors must be achieved within each of them. Further, one must decide whether the various targets at a given stage require sequential teaching because they constitute prerequisite behaviors for the achievement of other targets in that stage, or whether certain such target behaviors may be developed concurrently. These are the problems that will concern us in this section. We shall discuss in turn each of the broad stages specified in the previous section except the first, which we omit not because it is unimportant but because only one type of behavior—namely, vocalization—is called for at that stage.

Order of Nonsegmental Patterns

Although methods of obtaining voice and of modifying its pitch, loudness, and duration are discussed in the literature, we know of no discussion relating to the order in which control of these patterns should be established. In normally hearing infants younger than 6 months of age, vocalization is varied in intensity, frequency, and duration from the beginning, and the three aspects tend to be correlated with one another (Sheppard and Lane, 1968). The likelihood is that similar variability will occur with hearing-impaired children at the onset of training, whatever the age, unless patterns have already become differentiated through proprioceptive audition. Subglottal pressure will change during sounds of long duration before voice control is established. Accordingly, required patterns of pitch and loudness can be selectively reinforced if adequate duration of vocalization is first obtained. Pitch is by far the most difficult aspect of voice to modify in the absence of hearing because cues on pitch are not easily conveyed by either vision or touch (see Chapter 8). Whether pitch should receive attention before loudness is questionable. We suggest not: intensity control is easier for the child to obtain, and establishing the concepts of "loud" and "quiet" first may help prevent confusion of "loud" with "high" and "quiet" with "low." However, the opposite view could reasonably be taken. The main point is that difficulties in differentiating between these two aspects of voice may be avoided if taught sequentially.

Since voice patterns cannot be selectively reinforced until vocalization can be freely elicited, primary emphasis should be given to obtaining an abundance of vocalization regardless of its characteristics. (Operant principles applicable to the development of vocalization are discussed by Skinner (1957), Baer, Wolf, and Risley (1968), and Winitz (1969, pp. 29–49), among others.) When vocalization is established, duration, loudness, and pitch may successively be brought under control. The strategies the teacher may employ to achieve such control will be discussed in later chapters.

The use of vocalization should be encouraged not only as the first step in training, but also as the earliest form of speech communication. As training proceeds, the number of vocalizations per breath should be increased and brought under control. The specific use of voice patterns to give suprasegmental structure to phonetic, phonologic, and linguistic level utterances must also be fostered. The teacher's continued attention to suprasegmental structure is required at each stage of spoken language development. Thus, vowels and, later, various syllables, words, and sentences should be produced using the variety of voice patterns acquired at this stage.

Order of Vowel Development

Hearing-impaired children have persistent problems relating to vowel production (see Chapter 2). The high-front vowel [i] in particular is notoriously difficult for severely hearing-impaired children unless it is taught through touch. The tongue placement required is among the least visible and its acoustic properties are among the least audible of those for all vowels (Oyer and Doudna, 1959). It is not particularly hard to teach through touch since tongue placement can be felt quite simply with the fingertip. Workers such as Braidwood (see Green, 1783) and the Abbé de l'Epée (1784), who taught vowels prior to consonants, developed [i] at an early stage by this technique. Bell (1916, p. 107) taught [i] as the first vowel, if necessary having the child feel the tongue's position, so that the child learned from the beginning to think of speech as an activity primarily carried out at the front of the mouth. He stressed that once sounds were habitually produced too far back in the mouth and tongue retraction became established, faults were extremely hard to correct. Brehm (1922) similarly counseled that [i] should be taught early, but on the grounds that if it were not, then neutral or central tongue placement for vowels would become habitual.

As Zaliouk (1954) points out, a wide range of vowels, including an [u]-like vowel, can be produced with neutral or central tongue placement because lip-rounding alone can produce a sufficient lowering of all formants. This is shown spectrographically in Figure 8.1. The effect shown was produced by keeping the tongue in a neutral position and simply rounding the lips. Careful analysis of the back vowels of many hearing-impaired children indicates that they are, indeed, often produced in this fashion. The variety in the range of vowels produced by very young infants results in the same way from changes in lip configuration and jaw movement, rather than from modification in the shape of the tongue, which is relatively immobile during early vocalization (Lieberman, Harris, Wolff, and Russell, 1971).

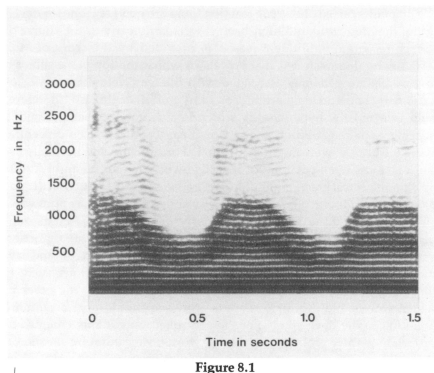

Figure 8.1

The [u]-*like effect, seen as troughs in the spectrogram, resulting from lip-rounding a vowel produced with central tongue placement, as in* [a].

Brehm and Zaliouk showed considerable insight, for there is physiological evidence that quite different muscle patterns are involved in the production of the central vowels and in production of those such as [i] and [u] which require greater tongue height. For example, posterior genioglossal contraction is required for [i], and contraction of the styloglossus with the genioglossus serving as an antagonist is required for [u]. These muscles are not primarily involved in the production of central vowels (MacNeilage and Sholes, 1964). There is, certainly, a danger that nonuse of these muscles may become habitual if [i] is not developed at an early stage and if lip-rounding is permitted to substitute for tongue placement in [u]. Many normal speakers obtain adequate lip-rounding and lip-protrusion for [u] by moving only the lower lip (Harris, Gay, Sholes, and Lieberman, 1969). Their predominant use of the tongue serves as a good model. This is not to say that [i] and [u] should be taught first, but rather to suggest that the child should not be allowed to develop the concept that vowel production involves only central or near-central tongue placement.

The points raised above suggest that there are good reasons for developing the high-front and high-back vowels fairly early in the course of speech teaching. Additional reason is provided by the work of Moll (1962), who demonstrated that vowels in which the tongue assumes a low profile are generally associated with the least velopharyngeal closure. Early and adequate production of [i] and [u] could also, therefore, help to avoid the hypernasality which is commonly observed among hearing-impaired children and to which early concentration on central and mid-back vowels might contribute. Further, the jaw normally assumes a more open position for central vowels than for [u] and [i], thus optimizing vocal tract configurations for adequate production (Lindblom and Sundberg, 1971). Undue early concentration on central vowels, particularly if the orientation is mainly visual, tends to lead to exaggerated jaw movement. This in turn results in both tongue retraction and the destruction of the natural synergy between tongue and jaw which is required for fluent coarticulation. Considerations such as these suggest that while one should be concerned about the order in which vowels and diphthongs are taught, one should give even more attention to the development of the controlled tongue movements appropriate to their production. In other words, we cannot be satisfied if the child produces vowels that are acoustically acceptable unless they are also produced with appropriate adjustments of the tongue, lips, and jaw. Even beyond this, the phonetic quality of each must be independent of voice pitch, duration, and intensity.

Our primary concern in promoting adequate vowel production in hearing-impaired children is the development of tongue control. Because movements of the lips and jaw are visible, they pose little problem providing that any temptation to exaggerate is resisted by the teacher and discouraged in the child. The tongue adjustments required in the early stages are neither particularly delicate nor numerous. They may be arrived at by creating a high or low tongue profile at the front, in the middle, or toward the back of the mouth. Since these adjustments are relative to the spatial characteristics of the tongue and mouth, we suggest that they can best be learned if the child can contrast the orosensory-motor patterns associated with tongue positions or movements that are widely diverse. Through such contrast we may expect the child to conceptualize the dimensions within which the tongue must operate and to establish reference points for further development. As a first step, therefore, we recommend concurrent attention to production of a high-front [i], a low-central [a], and a high-back [u]. To these we may quickly add a low-back [ɔ] and a low-front [ɛ]. Maintenance of the tongue in these positions while the duration, intensity, and pitch of voice is varied will ensure the control and coordination of breath flow, voice, and upper articulators, prerequisites to further development.

Not only should the child be able to maintain the tongue in the five basic positions specified above, but he should also be able to move his tongue rapidly and accurately from one of these positions to another. In doing so he will produce a range of sounds which approximate the English diphthongs [aɪ, aʊ, ɔɪ, and eɪ]. The purpose here is not simply to teach the diphthongs, but to ensure that adjustment and positioning of the tongue—rather than lip and jaw configurations—are central to the child's concept of vowel production. Since movement of the tongue in both [aɪ] and [aʊ] is readily felt, the vowels [i] and [u] may be developed through reference to these diphthongs rather than vice versa. Some children can produce a sustained [i] or [u] more readily if these are developed through the diphthongs [aɪ] and [aʊ] rather than through a direct approach. With others, the reverse is true. The best strategy to use is the one that works for the individual child. Either way, if adequate antecedent behaviors have been established and if the teaching strategy is appropriate, the required tongue movement should be obtained in less than a minute.

Production of the remaining vowels and diphthongs, which involves finer and finer orosensory-motor differentiation, may be regarded as the next step of this suggested sequence. Concurrently with training at each step, production must involve adequate breath patterns and systematic variation of voice pitch, intensity, and duration to ensure independence of laryngeal and articulatory function. The final stages of vowel teaching can only be achieved when consonants are employed, for vowel and diphthong targets are inevitably influenced by the consonant context, speed of production, and other such factors. With this particular approach to the teaching of vowels, certain consonants can be expected to develop spontaneously, providing that skills—as they are acquired—are employed for the purpose of communication. No approach should ever be so rigid as to preclude spontaneous development, to limit the child's opportunity to communicate by speech, or to detract from his urge to do so.

Children with useful residual hearing for both proprioception and exteroception, even if it is limited to frequencies below 1,000 Hz, may be expected to complete this stage of training quickly. For them, the structure involved should advance speech reception as well as speech production skills, for, as Paget (1930, p. 125) remarked, vowel discrimination involves "listening to indications of the position and gestures of the organs of articulation." For those who can receive only part of the acoustic information, or even none of it, the sequence still permits the systematic development of orosensory-motor skills.

Order of Consonant Development

The order of consonant development suggested here is shown in Table 8.A. It is based on consideration of several factors previously discussed: the relative ease with which consonants may be assimilated into well established, breath-grouped voice and vowel patterns; the relative salience of the sensory cues by means of which the consonants may be differentiated; the extent to which the consonants share features in common; and their relative organic difficulty. The arrangement proposed represents the order that requires least compromise to satisfy each of these four considerations. We have arranged the consonants in four groups or successive teaching steps. Sounds within each group differ mainly in their manner of production, and they are therefore highly differentiable. In order to exploit the contrasts they afford, they should be taught concurrently. Production skills mastered at each step provide a basis of features from which sounds in the next step can be derived. The arrangement closely accords with the model for the development of phoneme contrasts proposed by Jakobson and Halle (1956), as illustrated for the acquisition of English by Winitz (1969, p. 91). In arriving at this arrangement, we have chosen to classify consonants by manner, place, and voicing rather than by the more complex distinctive-feature systems proposed, for example, by Jakobson, Fant, and Halle (1963), by Wickelgren (1966), or by Chomsky and Halle (1968). These systems classify sounds in terms that are too abstract for clinical or educational application (Walsh, 1974). They relate poorly to the physiological characteristics of speech production (Fant, 1967; Lieberman, 1970), and the extent to which they relate to speech reception depends on the type and extent of hearing impairment (Ling and Maretic, 1971; Walden, 1971).

The sounds in the first step shown in Table 8.A can readily be incorporated into the existing vocal stream since they modify in relatively simple ways the breath, voice, and vowel patterns established at previous stages. Sounds in the second and third steps differ from those taught in the first only in place of production. Voicing differences may be developed as training proceeds, but they are not specifically treated until the fourth and final step. This arrangement yields an order in which contrast is emphasized within each step and similarity is exploited in moving from one step to the next.

Initial and final (unreleased) stops are treated separately because they

TABLE 8.A

Teaching order for consonants. Sounds contrasting in manner of production are taught concurrently at each step. Sounds sharing manner of production are taught sequentially, according to place of production (front, mid, back). Voicing contrasts within cognate pairs are not specifically taught until Step 4. The development of plosives as voiced sounds and of unreleased stops and fricatives as unvoiced sounds is recommended in Steps 1 through 3 (see text). However, the child's production of either member of a cognate pair is initially acceptable since our primary concern is not with voicing.

Concurrent Manner Contrasts

Sequential Teaching Steps	Plosives	Unreleased Stops	Nasals	Semi-vowels	Liquids	Fricatives	Affricates
Step 1	[b] or [p]	[b̄] or [p̄]	[m]	[w] or [ʍ]*		[h] & [f, θ] or [v, ð]	
Step 2	[d] or [t]	[d̄] or [t̄]	[n]	[j]	[l]	[ʃ, s] or [ʒ, z]	
Step 3	[g] or [k]	[ḡ] or [k̄]	[ŋ]		[r]		[tʃ] or [dʒ]
Step 4	[b, d, g] versus [p, t, k]	[b̄, d̄, ḡ] versus [p̄, t̄, k̄]		[w] versus [ʍ]*		[f, θ, ʃ, s] versus [v, ð, ʒ, z]	[tʃ] versus [dʒ]

*The development of [ʍ] is essential only if it is used phonologically in the child's community.

do not fulfill the same function in speech and because they differ physiologically. Lip-closing gestures in [p] and [p̄], for example, are quite distinct (Harris, Lysaught, and Schvey, 1965). Intrusive bursts and intrusive voicing may be avoided by teaching unreleased stops as a distinctly separate group of sounds, particularly if the unvoiced members are developed first. Under no circumstances should they be confused by introducing orthography before they are established phonetically and phonologically. Table 8.A is for the teacher, not for the child beginning to speak.

The arrangement proposed broadly reflects the organic difficulty of the consonants. Most sounds included in Step 1 do not involve the tongue. As one proceeds through to Step 4, increasingly complex tongue adjustments are required. Sensory salience is also reflected in this arrangement. For example, the sounds toward the top of Table 8.A would be most likely to provide auditory cues to the severely hearing-impaired child since the formant transitions of these sounds tend to be lower in frequency than those of other sounds. This has been shown for initial stops (Halle, Hughes, and Radley, 1957), for unreleased stops (Andrésen, 1960), for nasals (Liberman, Delattre, Cooper, and Gerstman, 1954), for semivowels and liquids (Lisker, 1957), and for fricatives (Delattre, Liberman, and Cooper, 1964). Visual cues are likewise more salient for consonants toward the top of Table 8.A, as are orosensory cues, since sensitivity decreases toward the back of the mouth and tongue (see Chapter 6).

With the possible exception of certain nasals and fricatives, all consonants should be taught in the context of units of at least syllabic size, practiced toward automaticity at a phonetic level, and—as the result of appropriate encouragement—used by the child shortly thereafter in communicative speech. Under these circumstances spontaneous development of certain sounds may be expected to occur. Indeed, children whose vocal skills have been adequately developed through previous training with voice patterns and vowels usually produce several sounds in Step 1 without specific training. Teaching particular sounds in a given step does not have to wait on the acquisition of all sounds at a previous step. Such rigidity is not required. It is usually best, however, for sounds sharing the same manner of production to be taught in the sequence shown. Thus, if the child has acquired [b] but not [m], one can reasonably move to teaching [d], using analogy with [b] to provide the appropriate set for stop production.

Manner of production is given primary importance in the arrangement suggested. This is because manner distinctions carry the heaviest information load in speech (Denes, 1963; Peters, 1963). They are also made largely on the basis of duration (Grimm, 1966; Scharf, 1971). Even finer durational differences are used to discriminate between certain fricatives (Miller and Nicely, 1955) and between voiced and voiceless sounds (Lisker and Abramson, 1964). Initial experience with manner differentiation should, therefore, provide some preparation for development of skills relating to place and voicing.

Place of production is presented in Table 8.A as being second in importance to manner and of greater importance than voicing. This is because place of production is more crucial to speech intelligibility than voicing (if you do not believe it, try whispering), and also because voicing distinctions of the type that can be taught in syllables have limited applicability in phonologic and syntactic level speech production. In running speech, except in word-initial stops, the main cue to voicing is not vocal cord vibration but is duration of the preceding segment.

The contribution of vowel duration to the identification of consonants has long been recognized. House and Fairbanks (1953) found that the duration of vowels preceding voiceless fricatives was greater than that of vowels preceding voiceless stops, and that duration was increasingly greater for vowels preceding nasals and voiced stops. Vowels preceding voiced fricatives tended to be longer than those preceding other sounds. These results were confirmed and extended by Raphael (1972). Denes (1955) showed that when the fricative [s] following a vowel was reduced in duration but changed in no other way, it was perceived as [z]. Teachers with inadequate training in phonetics and those seduced by the written form often fail to realize that in normal speech, vocal cord vibration is frequently absent in the final consonant of a word such as *rise*; and they hence waste a great deal of time "correcting" pronunciation by insisting on the child's producing /z/. All that is required is an /s/ which has substantially less duration than the preceding diphthong. This does not produce the word *rice*. The final consonant in *rice* is relatively longer than that in *rise*, and the two words are never perceptually confused on this account. The reader may verify this by whispering the two words (or any other pair of words where the final /s/ and /z/ are contrastive). In whispered speech the vocal cords are not vibrating, yet the two words are heard as being distinctly different.

Greater lip and tongue pressures and faster rates of closure are normally associated with voiceless members of cognate pairs such as [p-b] and [t-d]. It has been suggested that these differences could result from the more forceful movements of the articulators needed to counteract the greater aerodynamic flow imposed by an open glottal condition

(Chen, 1970). However, the consonant-vowel duration differences noted by House and Fairbanks (1953) are greater than the 30 msec. or so required simply to counteract greater aerodynamic flow (Lisker, 1974); and in certain languages (e.g., German), differences in vowel-consonant duration are not as marked as they are in English. These differences must therefore be primarily of linguistic rather than of mechanical origin. The production of such differences in the speech of hearing-impaired children clearly cannot be fostered unless manner and place of production are first practiced to an automatic level so that attention is available for timing and is not occupied by problems in correctly placing the articulators.

The signaling of voicing contrasts in succeeding consonants by means of duration is a function not restricted to vowels. The duration of nasal consonants preceding voiced stops is generally greater than that of nasals preceding unvoiced stops (Dorman, Raphael, Freeman, and Tobin, 1974). These effects occur whether the sounds are in a word-final position or not. Voiced-voiceless contrasts in a medial position are also signaled by durational cues, but presence or absence of vocal cord vibration may also be used to differentiate words such as *betting* and *bedding*. Only in the initial position are voiced-voiceless contrasts signaled mainly by presence or absence of vocal cord vibration. In word-initial voiced plosives the onset of vocal cord vibration approximately coincides with the release of breath (burst), whereas in unvoiced plosives the burst precedes the onset of vocal cord vibration by about 30 to 40 msec. (Lisker and Abramson, 1967). The gap between burst and vocal cord vibration is known as voice onset time (VOT). VOTs vary from one consonant to another so that a VOT for [p] is usually different from that for either [t] or [k]. These differences are highly consistent (Zlatin, 1974).

Hearing-impaired children tend to make many rhythm and voicing errors. One reason they do so seems to be that they lack the coordination of the various parts of the speech apparatus. It would therefore seem logical to use the following sequence in developing timing aspects in the speech of hearing-impaired children: first, to concentrate on obtaining automatic-level control in relation to such gross temporal differences as those required for the production of suprasegmental features; second, to give attention to the automatic achievement of vowel targets and their durational control; third, to develop automaticity in relation to manner and place of consonant production; and fourth, to encourage the durational aspects of vowel-consonant interaction which principally signal voicing. Only after these skills have been achieved need we be concerned with correct production in relation to VOT.

Intrusive voicing is one of the principal speech problems among hearing-impaired children. One aspect of this problem is voicing lead (Stark, 1968). This occurs when vocal cord vibration precedes burst. This fault may be worsened by the teaching of [b] as a sound analogous and subsequent to [m]. Early concentration on the production of [b] in isolated syllables also aggravates this problem because the vocal cords can be set in motion well before the lips have to be parted to release the intraoral pressure. The mouth cavity, being large and flexible in the production of [b], can accommodate a considerable volume of breath and thus permit long-duration voicing leads. With [d] and with [g] there is less oral volume available to accommodate voicing lead and hence less possibility of its occurring. If we therefore postpone close attention to VOT until place targets have been established, then the correct VOT targets can be derived from whichever plosives yield the most natural patterns. Normally, these will be the alveolar [d] and the velar [g] which are made closest to the larynx.

Although we rate the voiced-voiceless distinction as the least critical of the three features distinguishing consonants, we do not suggest that it is unimportant. While we do not attempt to teach differentiation of cognate pairs until Step 4, we seek to lay the foundations for such development from the earliest stages of consonant teaching. For this and other reasons given below, we advocate that the production of voiceless rather than voiced fricatives be encouraged in the early stages of consonant acquisition. First, the characteristic turbulence of fricatives is enhanced by voicelessness. (Less breath stream normally results from voiced sounds because the adducted vocal cords impede aerodynamic flow.) On this account voiceless fricatives are generally easier for the child to acquire than are their voiced cognates. Second, voiceless as compared with voiced fricatives contrast more strongly with the predominantly voiced sounds of different manner which we strive to develop concurrently in the same teaching steps. Third, reduction in the duration of a voiceless fricative is often sufficient to lead to its perception as the voiced cognate, but never vice versa. Fourth, the adduction and abduction of the vocal cords required to produce vowels alternated with unvoiced fricatives tend to stabilize the voice within an acceptable range in the chest register (see Chapter 11). Fifth, the adequate production of voiceless fricatives demands complete velopharyngeal closure, a fact that may be used to advantage in combatting any tendency toward hypernasality (see Chapter 14). The foundations for teaching voiceless fricatives in Step 1, it should be noted, lie in the previously acquired skill of whispering a range of vowels and diphthongs.

Order of Consonant Blend Development

Blends, sometimes called clusters, may be regarded as compound elements, each comprised of two or more single consonants. Adequate production of simple consonants is therefore a prerequisite for their acquisition. This is not to say that the elements within a blend are unchanged in the blending process. Through mutual assimilation, they may form a distinctly different unit. Thus, /t/ as in *tap* and /r/ as in *rap*, when combined in the word *trap*, yield an initial blend which has an affricate quality approximating [tʃ]. The /t/ is no longer the simple stop and the /r/ is no longer voiced. Children taught simple elements by reference to orthographic symbols are thus at a disadvantage when they come to blend production, as is the teacher who has prior allegiance to the written form. Not surprisingly, blends tend to be planned at the feedforward stage as single units, as evidenced by slips of the tongue (Fromkin, 1973). Their production and perception as single units (Claxton, 1974) must be borne in mind when we teach.

A thorough understanding of assimilation is essential in teaching speech. Assimilation is discussed insightfully by Heffner (1960), by Abercrombie (1967), and by Haggard (1974), among others. An example of its utility is provided by the word *orchard*. This was originally two words: *ort* (from Latin *hortus*) and *yard* (Abercrombie, 1967). The final unreleased /t/ followed by the initial /j/, in rapid speech, yielded /tʃ/ and led to the currently accepted pronunciation of the two words as one, in which the element /tʃ/ is the medial consonant. The principle of developing compound consonants such as [tʃ] and [dʒ] from similarly juxtaposed syllables may be used to advantage in developing speech in hearing-impaired children.

Blends may occur in any position within words: initially, medially, and finally. They may also occur between words. Blends occurring medially within words are subject to assimilation to much the same extent as blends that occur between words (interlexical blends). They are therefore treated in this text as one entity: namely, medial-lexical blends. Word-initial blends share few characteristics with blends occurring in medial or final positions. Similarly, word-final blends have little in common with medial-lexical blends. Systematic and detailed orders for teaching only word-initial and word-final blends are given below. In the interests of space we provide but a bare framework within which medial-lexical blends may be systematically developed.

Word-Initial Blends: The most appropriate order for the teaching of initial blends appears to be that based on organic difficulty and extent of coarticulation. Thus, blends which demand the use of two organs (tongue and lips) in the sequential production of two sounds will be organically simpler than those involving only one organ (the tongue) and its simultaneous adjustment. Using this rationale, initial blends may be assigned to five categories:

Type 1: *Two-organ sequentially formulated blends.* These include [sm] and [sp]. The completion of [s] is required before the second element can be formulated. (The unvoiced stops in blends are not aspirated.)

Type 2: *One-organ sequentially formulated blends.* These include [sn], [st], and [θr]. The completion of the first element is again required before the second can be formulated.

Type 3: *Two-organ simultaneously formulated blends.* These include [pl], [br], and [fl]. The second element must be formulated prior to completion of the first. It is with this type of blend that intrusive burst or intrusive voicing will occur unless the principle of coformulation of the two elements is observed.

Type 4: *One-organ simultaneously formulated blends.* These include [tr], [ʃr], and [gl]. The second element must be partially formulated prior to completion of the first. It is with this type of blend that the elements involved are most radically changed. If the first is unvoiced, so too is the second. Thus, the [r] becomes [t̩r] and the [l] becomes [kl̩]. If the first element is a stop, then it tends to assume affricative qualities in the blend. Intrusive burst and intrusive voicing tend to occur in blends beginning with stops if the consonants involved have been taught in isolation or if unreleased stops have not been adequately developed. (Unvoiced stops releasing such blends are not aspirated.)

Type 5: *Complex blends.* These include three elements such as in [skr], [str], and [spr]. Type 2 and Type 4 blends are combined in [skr]; [spr] combines Type 1 and Type 3 blends. Mastery of these cannot be expected until Type 1–4 blends have been acquired and practiced to a level of automaticity.

Word-Final Blends: The ordering of final blends may again be determined by reference to organic difficulty. The greatest parsimony in training can, however, be achieved if the manner of production of the two elements is also considered. Five types of final blend may thus be distinguished:

Type 1: *Continuant-continuant blends.* These blends include [lz], [ns], and [sl̩]. They are the simplest of the final blends because neither of the two elements involved is ever radically changed by its proximity to the other. The two elements, developed separately, may simply be juxtaposed.

Type 2: *Continuant-stop blends.* These include [ld], [st], and [nt]. The first element is a continuant, and the second cannot be formulated until the first is completed. Whether the second element is released is not critical to the pronunciation of the word in isolation. If the word is followed by another beginning with a vowel,the second element is normally used to release the vowel.

Type 3: *Stop-continuant blends.* These include [ts], [gz], [kl̩], and [tn̩]. The first element, the stop, is in all cases unreleased. Thus, blends of this type cannot be acquired until final stops have been mastered. The syllabic [l̩] occurs in words like *bottle* and usually assumes the dark form of the consonant.

Type 4: *Stop-stop blends.* These include [kt] and [pt]. This is the most difficult form of final blend. The first element always arrests the breath flow, which is released through the second element. These blends, in which [t] is the second element, provide the only example where a [t] in isolation is essential to adequate production.

Type 5: *Complex blends.* These include [lmz] and [sps]. They are derived from various combinations of other word-final blends. Their development depends on the mastery of the simpler blends.

Medial-Lexical Blends: Most of the rules governing the pronunciation of medial-lexical blends may be derived from observation of the assimilation process. For example, the word *income* contains a blend and may be pronounced /ɪnkʌm/. More usually, it is pronounced /ɪŋkʌm/, due to assimilation resulting in a shift of place for the nasal element. Medial-lexical blends include many more combinations of sounds than either of the other groups considered above. This is because any element can combine with any other element in the successive syllables of running speech, whereas there are rigid constraints relating to the order in which phonemes can follow each other in syllables forming English words (see Harms, 1968). In our view, the ordering of all possible medial-lexical blends is unnecessary provided, first, that the child's acquisition of speech has been fostered in accordance with the sequence proposed in this chapter and, second, that the teacher is aware of the way in which assimilation normally changes the characteristics of adjacent consonants.

Rather than attempting to describe the rules of adjacency for learning by rote, we propose that the reader should enter rules in each of the 36 cells in Table 8.B, which provides an appropriate skeleton for such study. This table is arranged so that the mutual influence of abutting consonants can be systematically considered. To derive the rules to com-

TABLE 8.B

*Framework for determining the comparative effects of adjacency
in relation to the manner, place, and voicing of abutting consonants.*

Word-Final	Word-Initial					
	Stops	Nasals	Semi-vowels	Liquids	Fricatives	Affricates
Stops	1	2	3	4	5	6
Nasals	7	8	9	10	11	12
Semivowels	13	14	15	16	17	18
Liquids	19	20	21	22	23	24
Fricatives	25	26	27	28	29	30
Affricates	31	32	33	34	35	36

plete Cell 1, for example, the reader should first list words with final and initial stops and then say them together, listening for effects of adjacency. Words with final stops might include *big*, *hat*, and *sit*; and words with initial stops, *top*, *down*, and *gun*. What adjacency effect is noted for the homorganic pairs /g-g/ and /t-d/ as in "a big gun" and "please sit down"? Does the effect differ when one of the adjacent stops is voiced and the other is voiceless? What happens when the adjacent stops do not share the same place of production? What happens when the two stops differ in regard to both place and voicing? The task is enormous, but certain rules soon become apparent. For those unprepared to undertake the task, the important rules will be mentioned in a later section on the teaching of blends.

Summary

In this chapter we examine the principles underlying the orderly acquisition of speech skills and propose that a sequential approach to their teaching is essential because the acquisition of any given sound pattern can be shown to demand the presence of previously acquired behaviors. In other words, order is of critical importance when antecedent patterns must be established before new skills can be learned; whereas patterns that are founded on the same prerequisite behaviors but have little else in common can be developed concurrently. Our review of the literature indicates that earlier workers have not provided cogent arguments to support their suggestions relating to order. In general, they have failed either to identify the range of behaviors which are prerequisite to the speedy and accurate acquisition of specific sound patterns or to consider the effects that their suggested order of teaching would have on subsequent speech development.

We have approached the problem by discussing the order in which one should introduce five broadly different classes of speech patterns— undifferentiated vocalization, nonsegmental voice patterns, vowels and diphthongs, consonants, and consonant blends. We conclude that, in the order listed, they represent five mainly sequential, but partly overlapping, stages of acquisition. Finally, we discuss the various speech target behaviors which must be developed within each of these broad stages and suggest how they might best be ordered to ensure their cumulative acquisition. We provide specific guidelines for those seeking to structure their approach to teaching speech and present an extensive rationale to support our suggestions which, in the absence of research, we recognize as being somewhat speculative.

REFERENCES

Abercrombie, D.   *Studies in Phonetics and Linguistics.* London: Oxford University Press, 1965.

Abercrombie, D.   *Elements of General Phonetics.* Chicago: Aldine Publishing Co., 1967.

Andrésen, B. S.   On the perception of unreleased voiceless plosives in English. *Lang. Speech*, 3, 109–119, 1960.

Arnold, T.   *A Method of Teaching the Deaf and Dumb Speech, Lip-Reading, and Language.* London: Smith, Elder & Co., 1881.

Baer, D. M., Wolf, M. M., & Risley, T. R.   Some current dimensions of applied behavior analysis. *J. Appl. Behav. Anal.*, 1, 91–97, 1968.

Bell, A. G.   *The Mechanism of Speech.* New York: Funk and Wagnalls, 1916.

Brehm, F. E.   Speech correction. *Am. Ann. Deaf*, 67, 361–370, 1922.

Burroughs, G. E. R.   *A Study of the Vocabulary of Young Children.* (University of Birmingham Educational Monograph) London: Oliver and Boyd, 1957.

Carr, J.   An investigation of the spontaneous speech sounds of five-year-old deaf-born children. *J. Speech Hear. Disord.*, 18, 22–29, 1953.

Carr, J.   The use of spontaneous speech. *Volta Rev.*, 57, 20–21, 1955.

Chen, H. P., & Irwin, O. C.   Infant speech vowel and consonant types. *J. Speech Disord.*, 11, 27–29, 1946.

Chen, M.   Vowel length variation as a function of the voicing of the consonant environment. *Phonetica*, 22, 129–159, 1970.

Chomsky, N., & Halle, M.   *The Sound Pattern of English.* New York: Harper and Row, 1968.

Claxton, G. L.   Initial consonant groups function as units in word production. *Lang. Speech*, 17, 271–277, 1974.

Delattre, P. C., Liberman, A. M., & Cooper, F. S.   Formant transitions and loci as acoustic correlates of place of articulation in American fricatives. *Studia Linguistica*, 18, 104–121, 1964.

de l'Epée, C. M.   La véritable manière d'instruire les sourds et muets confirmée par une longue expérience. Paris: Nyon l'aîné, 1784.

Denes, P. B.   Effect of duration on the perception of voicing. *J. Acoust. Soc. Am.*, 27, 761–764, 1955.

Denes, P. B.   On the statistics of spoken English. *J. Acoust. Soc. Am.*, 35, 892–904, 1963.

DiCarlo, L. M.   Speech and communication for the deaf. *Volta Rev.*, 62, 317–319, 1960.

Dorman, M. F., Raphael, L. J., Freeman, F., & Tobin, C.   *Vowel and nasal durations as perceptual cues to voicing in word final stop consonants.* Haskins Labs. SR37/38, 263–270, 1974.

Dudley, H.   The carrier nature of speech. *Bell Syst. Tech. J.*, 19, 495–515, 1940.

Ewing, A. W. G., & Ewing, E. C.   *Teaching Deaf Children To Talk.* Washington, D.C.: Volta Bureau, 1964.

Fant, G.   Auditory patterns of speech. In W. Wathen-Dunn (Ed.), *Models for the Perception of Speech and Visual Form: Proceedings of a Symposium.* Cambridge, Mass.: M.I.T. Press, 1967, pp. 44–120.

Farrar, A.   *Arnold on the Education of the Deaf.* London: (College of Teachers of the Deaf) Simpkin, Marshall & Co., 1901.

Fromkin, V. A. (Ed.)   *Speech Errors as Linguistic Evidence.* The Hague: Mouton, 1973.

Gay, T.   Effects of filtering and vowel environment on consonant perception. *J. Acoust. Soc. Am.*, 48, 993–998, 1970.

Green, F.   *Vox Oculis Subjecta.* London: Benjamin White, 1783.

Grimm, W. A.   Perception of segments of English-spoken consonant-vowel syllables. *J. Acoust. Soc. Am.*, 40, 1454–1461, 1966.

Haggard, M. P.   The perception of speech. In S. E. Gerber (Ed.), *Introductory Hearing Science.* Philadelphia: Saunders, 1974.

Halle, M., Hughes, G. W., & Radley, J-P. A.   Acoustic properties of stop consonants. *J. Acoust. Soc. Am.*, 29, 107–116, 1957.

Harms, R. T.   *Introduction to Phonological Theory.* Englewood Cliffs, N.J.: Prentice-Hall, 1968.

Harris, K. S., Gay, T., Sholes, G. N., & Lieberman, P.   *Some stress effects on electromyographic measures of consonant articulation.* Haskins Labs. SR13/14, 1969.

Harris, K. S., Lysaught, G. F., & Schvey, M. M.   Some aspects of the production of oral and nasal labial stops. *Lang. Speech*, 8, 135–147, 1965.

Hawkins, S.   Temporal coordination of consonants in the speech of children: Preliminary data. *J. Phonetics*, 1, 181–217, 1973.

Haycock, G. S.   *The Teaching of Speech.* Washington, D.C.: Volta Bureau, 1933.

Heffner, R. M. S.   *General Phonetics.* Madison: University of Wisconsin Press, 1960.

House, A. S., & Fairbanks, G.   The influence of consonant environment upon the secondary acoustical characteristics of vowels. *J. Acoust. Soc. Am.*, 25, 105–113, 1953.

Hudgins, C. V.   Voice production and breath control in the speech of the deaf. *Am. Ann. Deaf*, 82, 338–363, 1937.

Hudgins, C. V.   Speech breathing and speech intelligibility. *Volta Rev.*, 48, 642–644, 1946.

Irwin, O. C.   Development of speech during infancy: Curve of phonemic frequencies. *J. Exp. Psychol.*, 37, 187–193, 1947a.

Irwin, O. C.   Infant speech: Consonantal sounds according to place of articulation. *J. Speech Disord.*, 12, 397–401, 1947b.

Irwin, O. C.   Infant speech: Development of vowel sounds. *J. Speech Hear. Disord.*, 13, 31–34, 1948.

Irwin, O. C., & Chen, H. P.   Development of speech during infancy: Curve of phonemic types. *J. Exp. Psychol.*, 36, 431–436, 1946.

Jakobson, R., Fant, C. G. M., & Halle, M.   *Preliminaries to Speech Analysis*. Cambridge, Mass.: M.I.T. Press, 1963.

Jakobson, R., & Halle, M.   *Fundamentals of Language*. The Hague: Mouton, 1956.

Joiner, E.   *Graded Lessons in Speech*. Danville, Kentucky: Kentucky School for the Deaf, 1946.

Joiner, E.   Our speech teaching heritage. *Volta Rev.*, 50, 417–422, 1948.

Kaplan, E.L., & Kaplan, G.   The prelinguistic child. In J. Eliot (Ed.), *Human Development and Cognitive Processes*. New York: Holt, Rinehart and Winston, 1971.

Lenneberg, E. H.   *Biological Foundations of Language*. New York: Wiley, 1967.

Liberman, A. M., Delattre, P. C., Cooper, F. S., & Gerstman, L. J.   The role of consonant-vowel transitions in the perception of the stop and nasal consonants. *Psychol. Monogr.*, 68, 1–13, 1954.

Lieberman, P.   Primate vocalizations and human linguistic ability. *J. Acoust. Soc. Am.*, 44, 1574–1584, 1968.

Lieberman, P.   Toward a unified phonetic theory. *Linguistic Inquiry*, 1, 307–322, 1970.

Lieberman, P., Harris, K. S., Wolff, P., & Russell, L. H.   Newborn infant cry and nonhuman primate vocalization. *J. Speech Hear. Res.*, 14, 718–727, 1971.

Lindblom, B. E. F., & Sundberg, J. E. F.   Acoustical consequences of lip, tongue, jaw and larynx movement. *J. Acoust. Soc. Am.*, 50, 1166–1179, 1971.

Ling, D.   The use of hearing and the teaching of speech. *Teach. Deaf*, 61, 59–68, 1963.

Ling, D., & Maretic, H.   Frequency transposition in the teaching of speech to deaf children. *J. Speech Hear. Res.*, 14, 37–46, 1971.

Lisker, L.   Minimal cues for separating /w, r, l, y/ in intervocal position. *Word*, 13, 256–267, 1957.

Lisker, L.   *On "explaining" vowel duration variation*. Haskins Labs. SR37/38, 225–232, 1974.

Lisker, L., & Abramson, A. S.   A cross-language study of voicing in initial stops: Acoustical measurements. *Word*, 20, 384–422, 1964.

Lisker, L., & Abramson, A. S.   Some effects of context on voice onset time in English stops. *Lang. Speech*, 10, 1–28, 1967.

Love, J. K.   *Deaf Mutism: A Clinical and Pathological Study*. Glasgow: James MacLehose & Sons, 1896.

MacNeilage, P. F., & Sholes, G. N.   An electromyographic study of the tongue during vowel production. *J. Speech Hear. Res.*, 7, 209–232, 1964.

McDonald, E. T.   *Articulatory Testing and Treatment: A Sensory-Motor Approach*. Pittsburgh, Pa.: Stanwix House, 1964.

Mermelstein, P.   Articulatory model for the study of speech production. *J. Acoust. Soc. Am.*, 53, 1070–1082, 1973.

Miller, G. A., & Nicely, P. E.   An analysis of perceptual confusions among some English consonants. *J. Acoust. Soc. Am.*, 27, 338–352, 1955.

Moll, K. L.   Velopharyngeal closure on vowels. *J. Speech Hear. Res.*, 5, 30–37, 1962.

Murai, J-I.   Speech development of infants. Analysis of speech sounds by sona-graph. *Psychologia*, 3, 27–35, 1960.

Muyskens, J. H.   The building and maintenance of clear speech for the deaf. *Volta Rev.*, 40, 655–657, 1938.

Nakazima, S.   A comparative study of the speech development of Japanese and American English in childhood. (1) A comparison of the developments of voices at the prelinguistic period. *Studia Phonologica*, 2, 27–46, 1962.

Numbers, M. E.   The place of elements teaching in speech development. *Volta Rev.*, 44, 261–265, 1942.

Öhman, S. E. G.   Coarticulation in VCV utterances: Spectrographic measurements. *J. Acoust. Soc. Am.*, 39, 151–168, 1966.

Oyer, H. J., & Doudna, M.   Structural analysis of word responses made by hard of hearing subjects on a discrimination test. *A.M.A. Arch. Otolaryngol.*, 70, 357–364, 1959.

Paget, R.   *Human Speech*. London: K. Paul, Trench, Trubner & Co., 1930.

Peters, R. W.   Dimensions of perception for consonants. *J. Acoust. Soc. Am.*, 35, 1985–1989, 1963.

Raphael, L. J.   Preceding vowel duration as a cue to the perception of the voicing characteristic of word-final consonants in American English. *J. Acoust. Soc. Am.*, 51, 1296–1303, 1972.

Scharf, D. J.   Perceptual parameters of consonant sounds. *Lang. Speech*, 14, 169–177, 1971.

Sheppard, W. C., & Lane, H. L.   Development of the prosodic features of infant vocalizing. *J. Speech Hear. Res.*, 11, 94–108, 1968.

Skinner, B. F.   *Verbal Behavior*. New York: Appleton-Century-Crofts, 1957.

Stark, R. E.   *Voicing in initial stop-consonants produced by hearing-impaired children*. (Annual Report, Neurocommunications Lab.) Baltimore, Md.: Johns Hopkins University School of Medicine, 1968, pp. 174–210.

Steinberg, J. C.   The teaching of speech. *Volta Rev.*, 31, 408–409, 1929.

Story, A. J.   The importance of the consonants in speech and speech-reading. *Volta Rev.*, 11, 479–488, 1909a.

Story, A. J.   The speaking mouth. *Volta Rev.*, 11, 13–19, 1909b.

Story, A. J.   *Speech-Reading and Speech for the Deaf*. Stoke-on-Trent: Hill and Ainsworth, 1915.

Voelker, C. H.   A sound count for the oral curriculum. *Volta Rev.*, 37, 155–156, 1935.

Walden, B. E.   *Dimensions of consonant perception in normal hearing and hearing-impaired listeners*. Unpublished Ph.D. diss., Purdue University, 1971.

Walsh, H.   On certain practical inadequacies of distinctive feature systems. *J. Speech Hear. Disord.*, 39, 32–43, 1974.

Watson, J.   *Instruction of the Deaf and Dumb*. London: Darton and Harvey, 1809.

White, H. W.   *The Education of the Deaf and Dumb on the Pure Oral System*. London: W. H. Allen, 1884.

Wickelgren, W. A.   Distinctive features and errors in short-term memory for

English consonants. *J. Acoust. Soc. Am.*, 39, 388–398, 1966.

Winitz, H.   *Articulatory Acquisition and Behavior*. New York: Appleton-Century-Crofts, 1969.

Woodward, M. F., & Barber, C. G.   Phoneme perception in lipreading. *J. Speech Hear. Res.*, 3, 213–222, 1960.

Wright, J. D.   Some homely suggestions in speech teaching. *Volta Rev.*, 28, 614–616, 1926.

Yale, C. A.   *Formation and Development of Elementary English Sounds*. Northampton, Mass.: Clarke School for the Deaf, 1938.

Zaliouk, A.   A visual-tactile system of phonetical symbolization. *J. Speech Hear. Disord.*, 19, 190–207, 1954.

Zlatin, M. A.   Voicing contrast: Perceptual and productive voice onset time characteristics of adults. *J. Acoust. Soc. Am.*, 56, 981–994, 1974.

/9/

Evaluation

To teach speech effectively, one must know what spoken language skills, if any, the child has already acquired and what characteristics of the child and his environment may present problems that could adversely affect his speech development. This information can be obtained only through systematic evaluation. Because such evaluation has many facets, it calls for coordinated effort by a team of specialists. As a rule, it also involves observation and assessment as training proceeds. It therefore demands that the teacher be able to contribute in areas other than speech. For example, hearing levels or conditions of apparent autism or hyperactivity may be difficult to confirm except through the teacher's ongoing appraisal of the child in the course of treatment. Much as others can seek the teacher's assistance in their evaluation of the child, she should also be able to turn to others for help in those aspects for which she is primarily responsible. We consider these to be: (1) the oral-peripheral examination of the child's speech organ structure and function, (2) the analysis of his phonologic level speech, and (3) the assessment of his phonetic level skills. Procedures which may be followed in each of these areas of evaluation are therefore treated extensively in this chapter. Such areas as audiological, psychological, social, educational, and medical evaluation, for which the teacher is not primarily responsible, are covered in less depth.

Few children when first diagnosed as hearing-impaired have skills in spoken language; but for those who have acquired communicative speech, either before or after training, measures of speech production status and growth are essential. One needs such measures both to provide specific guidelines for remedial work and to serve as a base line against which results of training can be compared. With Glaser (1963) we consider that effective work demands criterion-referenced testing: teaching toward the achievement of sequentially ordered test items. We also agree with Mager (1962) that unless one can identify the behaviors one seeks to establish and then demonstrate that the child is achieving successive mastery of them, one cannot show that one is teaching anything at all. These points of view, which call for teaching programs specifically prescribed for individual children and emphasize accountability, are in accord with those of many modern workers concerned with the treatment of various types of spoken language defect (Johnston and Harris, 1968; Mowrer, 1969; Girardeau and Spradlin, 1970; Lahey, 1973; Turton, 1973; MacDonald and Blott, 1974).

There are many articulation tests on the market. These include the Deep Test of Articulation (McDonald, 1964), the Templin-Darley Test of Articulation (Templin and Darley, 1969), the Photo Articulation Test (Pendergast, Dickey, Selmar, and Soder, 1969), the Test of Articulation (Goldman and Fristoe, 1969), and the Fisher-Logemann Test of Articulation Competence (Fisher and Logemann, 1971). They may be used in the speech evaluation of hearing-impaired children but are neither necessary nor sufficient for our purpose. Pictures of comparable quality to those used in these tests are in plentiful supply and may be selected so that the child can be tested with materials that closely reflect his everyday experience and that call for familiar language. Although standard tests are generally designed to stimulate the use of sounds in initial, medial, and final positions, they do not present opportunity to check if consonants can be produced in all vowel contexts. Tests other than that devised by McDonald (1964) are not systematically structured to test abutting consonants, and those aimed to stimulate only single-word responses do not provide sufficient occasion for assessment of coarticulation skills and for appraisal of suprasegmental structure.

There has been remarkably little discussion of speech evaluation procedures in the literature relating to hearing-impaired children. Most has been quite limited in scope, and apart from a suggestion that the phonograph should be used for recording and assessing progress in speech (Taylor, 1914), publications relating to evaluation are relatively recent. Haycock (1933) appeared to take it for granted that the teacher would at all times be familiar with the extent of the child's speech skills. Ewing and Ewing (1964, pp. 57-81) treated evaluation of speech only at the phonologic level. Indeed, most tests or testing procedures proposed (Barrett, 1947; Bjuggren, 1954; Farman, 1954; Larr and Stockwell, 1959) show concern mainly or only with intelligibility of meaningful material (see also Chapter 2).

Tests of intelligibility involving meaningful material have questionable validity as measures of speech skill unless language acquisition is quite advanced. In the early stages of acquisition, spontaneous speech—or speech elicited from pictures—tends to contain distortions which reflect the child's syntactic or morphological incompetence rather than his inability to produce adequate speech patterns. Awareness of this problem has led to the judging of speech intelligibility from standard samples read by the child (viz., Voelker, 1938; Farman, 1954; Clarke School for the Deaf, 1971). Results of such tests, however, depend on the child's reading skill and on the extent to which orthography has been associated with sounds in the course of speech training. They are not, therefore, straight tests of intelligibility, and the results they provide do not reliably indicate how well a child will be understood, say, when shopping in an unfamiliar store.

Even if a valid measure of intelligibility could be designed, we would have to question its diagnostic value in a speech training program (see Vorce, 1974, pp. 97-102). In speech development, the teacher is concerned not with comparison of one child or group of children with another, but with the type of evaluation that gives focus to her work as a teacher. Economy demands that the measures we use for this purpose are simple to administer, reliable, quick and easy to score even without the help of judges, and structured to reveal not general deficits but particular faults for which specific step-by-step remedial work can be planned.

The order in which the teacher should carry out the three evaluation tasks for which we consider her primarily responsible is unimportant; but no evaluation should be attempted until a pleasant relationship between the teacher and child has been established. This may take only minutes, but with certain children it may take days. The time taken to establish this relationship is not necessarily lost. Deficits in oral-peripheral structures or function may become apparent or be suspected as a result of observations made when the child uses speech in an unstructured play situation. Further, the communication patterns typically used by the child must be recognized as such before one can set out to record a representative sample of speech for linguistic-phonologic analysis. Similarly, having prior experience of the child's speech may guide the teacher in testing phonetic level skills.

Oral-Peripheral Structures and Function

There are few absolute physical requirements for speech production. The movements necessary for adequate speech production vary from one speaker to another in relation to the size and shape of the oral structures, which differ no less than do faces, chins, or noses (Haycock, 1933, p. 124). Accordingly, individual differences and even certain deficiencies in peripheral structure and function do not necessarily prevent speech acquisition. Some deficiencies may, however, call for specific intervention: a structural deficiency may require treatment by surgery or prosthesis; inadequate function of an organ may call for remedial exercises or specific training to develop compensatory mechanisms (McDonald, 1964, pp. 66-67). Individual needs in this regard may complicate the already difficult task of teaching hearing-impaired children to talk. If these needs go unidentified, they may result in unnecessary failure. Evaluation must, therefore, include an oral-peripheral examination.

The prevalence of oral-peripheral disorders among hearing-impaired children is not known. Nor is there data which indicate whether a given disorder of a certain severity may have a more adverse effect on speech development in hearing-impaired than in normally hearing children. Our own observations indicate that about 5% of hearing-impaired children have some abnormality of the oral-peripheral structures that may impede the acquisition of speech, and that the speech organ adjustments required to compensate for structural problems are often harder for hearing-impaired children to make than for their normally hearing peers. In order for the teacher to be able to recognize the variations of structure that fall within a normal range (i.e., a range which permits all speech patterns to be produced) and to identify significant anomalies, she requires considerable experience. Such experience must be gained through examination of hearing children with both normal and deviant speech. Other specialists, such as orthodontists and otolaryngologists, may be called upon to provide the teacher with opportunity to observe the effects of deviant structures in normally hearing children and to collaborate when defects are suspected in those who are hearing-impaired.

The oral-peripheral examination should be carried out systematically to ensure that nothing of importance is missed. We recommend the order in which the various aspects of the examination are described in this chapter. The procedures we suggest for the examination are essentially those proposed by Johnson, Darley, and Spriestersbach (1963), but modifications have been introduced to take account of more recent work and to indicate how one may make the required observations with hearing-impaired children who have little or no linguistic skill. Defects that are amenable to medical treatment have been specified so that the teacher can initiate appropriate referral procedures. Strate-

gies that may be adopted to treat certain defects which respond to remedial exercises are mentioned below. They are more extensively treated
in the second half of this book.

Facial Structure

Observations made in the course of playing with the child permit the
identification of problems associated with facial structure. Nasal ob-
struction is relatively easy to identify. It results in persistent mouth-
breathing, causes difficulty in the production of the nasal consonants,
and adversely affects the resonance of all voiced sounds. If nasal ob-
struction is a problem, the child should be referred for medical/surgical
treatment. The overall shape of the nose is unimportant, but a collapsed
nasal arch may indicate a cleft palate. The two are often associated.

Facial asymmetry is not necessarily of diagnostic significance. However, muscular weakness on one side of the face, which can best be seen
when the child smiles, may indicate neurological impairment affecting
lip and tongue control. Lip asymmetry may be associated with cleft palate (Spriestersbach and Sherman, 1968).

Lip Movement

Lip movement may not occur in an unstructured play situation if the
child has no speech. The four lip functions required in speech (round-
ing-protrusion, spreading, breath retention, and repeated closure) can,
nevertheless, be tested through structured play and imitation. Mase
(1946) found lip-rounding with mouth closed to be more difficult for
subjects with articulation disorders than for normal controls. Difficulty
in lip-rounding-protrusion may be observed in structured play by having the child blow an object or a flame. A smile obtained by amusing,
cajoling, or tickling is adequate evidence of lip-spreading ability. A
game in which Ping-Pong balls, for example, are blown off the hand
with a [pə] when they are brought momentarily into range can verify
breath coordination, labial breath retention, and muscle tonus. Blowing
at one after another can demonstrate ability to effect repeated closure.
Speech problems affecting only the lips are rare. In most cases where lip
abnormalities are observed, anomalies of the tongue and palate are also
present (Johnson *et al.*, 1963).

The Jaw and Teeth

The jaw and its relationship with the position of the dental arch are
particularly important for the production of sounds such as [s] and [z].
Slight compensatory tongue movement can usually permit the facile

pronunciation of other sounds when the teeth alone are abnormally positioned (neutrocclusion); but when the mandible is distal in relation to the maxillae (distocclusion) or protruded in relation to the maxillae (mésiocclusion), difficulty with other sounds may also occur. To produce most fricatives when severe malocclusion is present may require quite bizarre adjustments of the jaw and tongue movement (West, Ansberry, and Carr, 1957, p. 186; Harvold, 1970). Defective hearing and orofacial anomaly are often associated (e.g., in children with Treacher-Collins syndrome), and hearing-impaired children requiring orthodontic treatment are not uncommon. For those with gross dentofacial defects, restorative surgery (Warren, 1970) may be feasible. The loss of deciduous teeth may also affect the production of fricatives even among normally hearing children (Bankson and Byrne, 1962). Among hearing-impaired children whose production targets are articulatory rather than acoustic, the effect on fricatives of losing (or growing) teeth may be considerably more marked. There are no clear relationships between structural abnormality and articulatory competence because the wide range of compensatory adjustments which can be made by certain children cannot so readily be made by others. Therefore, one can accurately predict not that particular speech defects *will* occur as a result of a specific structural abnormality, but only that they *may*. If malocclusion is observed in the course of the oral-peripheral examination, the teacher should consult with the parents and (if they decide on treatment) with the orthodontist. However, she has no alternative but to work as best she can to establish articulatory targets that compensate for the anomaly as it exists. One cannot wait until orthodontic or surgical treatment has been carried out before teaching speech.

Orthodontists prefer to deal with neutrocclusions when the child is of elementary school age—after the permanent teeth have grown in and before the preadolescent growth spurt begins. Orthodontic treatment results in gradual amelioration of the problem, over a period of months or even years, so articulatory targets previously learned have to be modified. The extent to which the teacher has to help the child make these modifications can be determined by ongoing phonetic and phonologic evaluation. If the malocclusions are sufficiently severe to call for surgery, the problem is exacerbated. Not only may it be more difficult to teach compensatory adjustments, but surgery might not be undertaken until the child is well into his teens. Since the effects of surgery may be drastic and sudden, many of the previously acquired articulatory targets may immediately become inappropriate. Following surgery a wide range of new articulatory targets and subskills may have to be developed. Oral-peripheral examination, phonetic level evaluation, and phonologic analysis will be essential to guide the teacher in her work in such an eventuality.

The Tongue

The tongue is the most important of the structures involved in speech. Tongue sensitivity can be tested directly in older subjects (Telage and Fucci, 1973) but must be inferred through observation in young children. Tongue size can be assessed most simply by having the child protrude the tongue either in imitation or in the act of licking a lollipop or, better, a depressor which has been dipped in chocolate syrup. Also, licking dabs of syrup or glucose placed on the corners of the mouth, first moving the tongue from one side and then from the other, can provide information on tongue mobility. One should be particularly alert to weakness. If there is a unilateral paralysis (as there may be in children with hearing impairment associated with cerebral palsy), the tongue will deviate from the center to the affected side on protrusion, and difficulty may be experienced in side-to-side or up-down movement. Chocolate or other syrup is also useful for another reason. To enjoy it, the child has to swallow, and in doing so he provides the examiner with the opportunity to see if there is abnormal tongue movement on swallowing. Tongue-tie (an overly short or thick frenum) as a cause of speech problems is rare, but if present it may lead to abnormal swallowing habits and to open bite malocclusion through tongue thrust. Its surgical correction is simple (Horton, Crawford, Adamson, and Ashbell, 1969).

Diadochokinetic Rate: In classic oral-peripheral examinations, the integrity of tongue movement is also assessed through measures of diadochokinetic (repetition) rate. With hearing-impaired children who cannot speak, such a measure cannot be undertaken because the sounds that are generally used, such as [pʌ], [tʌ], and [kʌ] may not be in the child's phonetic repertoire. No good alternative measure of lip and tongue control is available. It may be possible, nevertheless, to obtain indication of ability to repeat some lip and tongue movements rapidly through imitation. Inability to do so cannot, however, be considered as being important until the child has been trained to articulate the sounds in question. Tests of tongue function which do not require speech sound production lack face validity; but other measures, such as maintaining the tongue tip behind the upper incisors for five seconds, may be useful indicators of problems affecting control (Shelton, Arndt, Kreuger, and Huffman, 1966). Even simple measures such as this may be difficult to carry out with very young children.

The Hard Palate

A cleft palate is not likely to be present if the child has demonstrated that he can retain sufficient breath behind the lips to blow an object or flame with [pə̥]. Nevertheless, one should look for signs of a submucous cleft, such as a notch at the juncture of the hard and soft palate, fistulae, a collapsed nasal arch, or shortening of the anterior-posterior dimension of the palate (Warren, 1970). An abnormally high palatal vault does not necessarily cause speech problems, but difficulty with the velar sounds [k], [g], and [ŋ] may result if the tongue cannot accommodate to palate height. This is often the case with hearing-impaired children who have high palates and in whom restricted tongue movement has been allowed to become habitual.

The Soft Palate

Adequate soft palate function resulting in velopharyngeal closure is essential to non-nasal speech. It may be assumed if an object or flame can be blown out with [pə̥]. If there is difficulty with this task, with blowing out the cheeks, or with inflating a balloon, then there may be a soft palate problem. The size and length of the velum may be difficult to assess simply by observation because, together with the uvula, it can change in relation to pitch of voice. For this reason, hearing-impaired children who have developed falsetto voices often produce nasal speech. The uvula should occupy a midline position and be intact and mobile. A bifid uvula is often associated with a cleft palate condition. Immobility may suggest a paresis (partial paralysis), possibly of congenital origin (Worster-Drought, 1954). Velopharyngeal closure also depends in part on posterior and lateral pharyngeal wall function. This may be tested with the gag reflex. Removal of adenoid tissue can result in nasal escape of air (Greene, 1957a). Among hearing-impaired children who have developed articulatory targets, but who are unable to hear fricatives, it is not unusual to find sufficient reduction of oral breath stream to prevent the adequate production of these sounds following adenoidectomy. The absence of fricatives together with a nasal murmur in vowels is a strong indication of velopharyngeal problems (Peterson, 1975). In most cases brief training or retraining is all that is required following adenoidectomy. Relatively new surgical techniques show promise in the promotion or restoration of soft palate function in cases of severe disorder (Warren, 1970).

The Larynx

The integrity of the larynx can usually be judged from incidental voicing during the examination. Problems detected in this manner should be investigated thoroughly. Huskiness in the production of vowels may indicate nodules on the vocal cords. These may be caused by excess tension, abnormal pitch, or habitual hard glottal attack (Greene, 1957b, p. 82). Breathy quality in speech of hearing-impaired children is usually due to inadequate use of voice, which results in poor tonic condition of the laryngeal musculature. The child's voice in play is likely to be a better guide to laryngeal quality than his voice in speech, unless the speech is naturally acquired or produced without conscious effort.

Summary of Results

Results of the oral-peripheral examination should be summarized in writing and filed with the child's permanent records. A summary form which may be used for this purpose is presented as Table 9.A.

TABLE 9.A

Summary of oral-peripheral examination. Items specified are to be checked (✔)
if normal and described if abnormal either in structure or in function.

Name:_____Age: _____ Date: _____

Facial structure ( )_____

Lips ( )_____

Jaw ( )_____

Teeth ( )_____

Tongue ( )_____

Hard palate ( )_____

Soft palate ( )_____

Larynx ( )_____

Evaluation carried out by:_____

Phonologic Speech Evaluation

Introduction

If the teacher's purpose is to teach the child to communicate by speech—i.e., to use speech as a vehicle for linguistic expression—she must develop and evaluate speech in a linguistic context. Further, she must simultaneously develop and evaluate language in its spoken form. Teachers of hearing-impaired children are often heard to remark, "His speech is poor, but he has good language." When this remark is made it generally indicates that language has been principally developed and tested through the written form. This approach, described by Woodward (1975), may develop literacy but, if taken to the extreme, may impede the development of speech communication. The written form is normally parasitic on speech, not vice versa. Children taught by an approach which emphasizes written language may be "oral" in the sense that they do not know how to sign. They may not be oral in the sense that they are able to communicate efficiently, accurately, and with ease through speech. We believe that, while written expression is important, spoken language skills are more so and must be developed first.

The evaluation of speech in a linguistic context and of language in its spoken form poses several problems. Many of the basic morphological and syntactic markers which have to be present if language is "good" cannot be produced by a child whose speech is "poor." On the other hand, the child with "good" speech but "poor" language may show patterns of error similar to those of the child with "poor" speech because he has not learned the appropriate linguistic rules. In other words, the absence of specific markers in a sample of spoken language may indicate that the child does not know the linguistic rules, that he does not know how to produce the required speech patterns, or, alternatively, that he knows neither. On this account, phonologic analysis by itself can never be regarded as an adequate measure of speech skill. Measures of both linguistic content and simple speech pattern production (phonetic level skills) are also required. There are further weaknesses inherent in phonologic level testing. In any given sample of speech, however representative the utterances recorded may be, certain sound patterns may not occur. Others may occur only in word-final or word-initial positions, and some consonants may be used only in the context of particular vowels. The child's ability to use these patterns in other samples or in other contexts cannot be assumed.

We propose that the teacher should use the same sample of spoken language for both linguistic and phonologic analyses. This saves time and allows one to relate how the child speaks to what he says. A sample of some 50 representative utterances provides an adequate corpus for linguistic assessment (Lee, 1974; Tyack and Gottsleben, 1974) and a sufficiently large, though not exhaustive, sample for phonologic analysis. While screening tests such as those devised for hearing-impaired children by Owrid (1960) and for normally hearing children by Lee (1970) provide a broad description of spoken language skills and, hence, general guidelines for remedial work, analysis of sampled utterances provides data from which more specific steps in training can be derived. We therefore recommend that phonologic evaluation for purposes of teaching be principally based on analysis of communicative speech. At the teacher's discretion, such analysis may be supplemented by a specific test of morphology (Berko, 1958).

Phonologic Speech Sampling

Samples of 50 representative utterances (breath-grouped sound patterns whatever their length, complexity, or grammatical structure) should be obtained for phonologic analysis at the beginning of the school year, again in February or March, and immediately before school closes in the summer. Such spacing allows the teacher to devise, carry out, and evaluate her teaching program in accordance with each child's needs, which—if teaching is effective—should change significantly from one analysis to the next.

There is little likelihood that all variables in a sampling situation can be controlled. What interests and stimulates a child on one occasion may not do so on another (Lee, 1974). As the child's language develops, his length of utterance will also increase. While vocalization and single words might predominate at one stage, complex sentences will do so at another. The only thing that has to be standard about the sampling situation is that the child is performing optimally. Thus, it is reasonable to elicit single-word responses if single words represent the child's level of phonologic development. It would, however, be unreasonable to limit the sample to single words if the child were capable of producing sentences. Only through analysis of an adequate sample of running speech can the suprasegmental and coarticulatory aspects of production be satisfactorily assessed.

Recording the Sample: Whatever means of eliciting spoken language samples are employed, accuracy and objectivity of analysis demand that they be clearly recorded. A good-quality tape recorder is therefore essential, as are relatively good recording conditions. In less-than-ideal acoustic conditions, reverberation and background noise may be reduced relative to the child's speech level if the gain of the tape recorder is turned low and the microphone is kept away from sources of noise and vibration and within a short distance of the child's mouth. To achieve such conditions, Weir (1966) used a radio microphone pinned to the child's clothing. A good signal-to-noise ratio can, however, usually be obtained with more conventional equipment.

Analytic Procedures

The 50 representative utterances selected for analysis should first be played back for the purpose of rating breath control, voice patterns, speed, phrasing, and so on. Control of voice intensity, which cannot always be rated accurately from a tape, should be assessed in the course of obtaining the sample. Nonsegmental items should simply be classified as normal, faulty, or absent.

Segmental analysis need only involve noting what English phonemes are present and correctly used. Our aim is simply to determine the extent to which particular sounds have become incorporated in the child's phonology. We do not require an exhaustive and time-consuming transcription of all utterances. There is no evidence to suggest that a sound which is distorted is any more (or less) difficult to teach than one which is omitted or one for which another has been substituted. Only through additional testing at a phonetic level (see below) can we determine the reason for the absence or inconsistent use of particular sounds in the child's phonology. The segmental analysis, therefore, requires only categorical judgments as to whether or not such or such a phoneme (or phoneme cluster) is being acceptably produced.

Collaboration in the Analysis: Because the person who is teaching the child is familiar with his speech, an additional person who has had training in phonetics and does not know the child's speech should assist in the process of sampling and analysis. Only those utterances they agree are representative should be selected for analysis, and only those sounds they agree are being acceptably produced should be credited to the child. Such collaboration helps to avoid the three main types of rating error described by Guilford (1954): the tendency to be too hard or too easy (a) in all ratings, (b) in rating a particular child, or (c) in rating particular items. The proportion of utterances that are agreed to be completely intelligible may be noted. Intelligibility should be judged only on the first hearing by listeners unfamiliar with the context in which the sample is obtained.

Summary of Results

The results of the phonologic analysis can most appropriately be summarized as shown in Appendix A of this chapter. Such a tabulation of results provides both an overview of the child's current phonologic status and the information required for planning speech development work at the phonologic level. The form may also serve as part of the child's cumulative record. Comparison of summaries obtained on two or more evaluations should indicate in what way the child's phonologic speech profile has changed in the course of training. Most items on the summary form presented as Appendix A are self-explanatory, and the rationale for their inclusion may be derived from the material presented in this and previous chapters. The reader will note that the teacher is not expected to differentiate between sounds within intelligible and unintelligible utterances or to note patterns of phoneme substitution—procedures followed by West and Weber (1973) and Oller and Kelly (1974), respectively. These procedures demand judgments that relate to the speaker's intention and that are therefore very difficult to make—and to defend—in the early stages of phonologic development.

Phonetic Level Evaluation

Introduction

Before sound patterns can be incorporated accurately and fluently into a child's phonology, they must be present in his phonetic repertoire. Phonetic level evaluation is therefore required to determine the extent to which particular sound patterns are present, the stage at which the child can differentiate one motor speech pattern from another, and the rate at which sounds can be repeated and alternated. It is doubtful whether every major subskill involved in speech production has yet been isolated. This, however, need not deter us. What we seek is the definition of certain speech subskills known to be essential and, again, categorical judgments as to whether or not they are present in the child's phonetic repertoire. If the subskills tested are not present, then our task is clear: we must teach them.

Phonetic level evaluation is not an alternative to phonologic level evaluation but, rather, a necessary supplement to it. Our long-term goal is for the child's phonology to conform to that of the community. Only when all patterns are used reliably and correctly in the course of communicative speech can we consider our task complete. A child may, for example, use /k/ phonologically in most but not all initial, medial, and final positions. Phonetic level testing may indicate that the child has trouble in producing this sound in the context of certain vowels, that the sound cannot be repeated rapidly in particular vowel contexts, or that it cannot be fluently alternated with certain other consonants. Thus, even if /k/ production were apparently perfect in a phonological sample, we should still test its production in various contexts at a phonetic level simply because we cannot be certain that the phonologic sample is sufficiently representative.

Testing at both phonologic and phonetic levels may also yield other insights. For example, a child may not be using a particular pattern phonologically; yet evaluation may reveal that the sound is present in the child's phonetic repertoire, can be produced accurately in repeated syllables at rates greater than three per second, and can be acceptably alternated with other sounds. In this case we have clear indication that the child's problem is with phonetic-to-phonologic transfer. He may not be aware of the phonemic structure required or he may not use the sound phonologically because no demands are made that he should. Whatever the reason for the discrepancy, testing at both levels can demonstrate precisely where the solution to the problem must be sought.

In most cases, failure to use a sound phonologically when it is present in the child's phonetic repertoire is due to the fact that the sound has not been established at a sufficiently automatic level. Testing the rate at which the sound can be repeated in syllables and alternated with other sounds reveals this problem most efficiently. We have often made dramatic improvements in phonologic production by working toward automaticity only at a phonetic level.

Of course, it is not uncommon—particularly in the early stages of speech acquisition—to find that a child is unable to produce particular sound patterns either phonologically or phonetically. Alternatively, we may find that a child at the beginning of training can only produce a particular sound pattern when he is provided with a model to imitate. Either way, we have a clear base line from which to begin our teaching.

Imitation in Phonetic Level Evaluation

As demonstrated by Baer and Sherman (1964), imitation skills can be developed through providing appropriate reinforcement, and imitation of non-speech behavior can usually be expected to generalize to imitation of speech. Until speech patterns can be imitated or otherwise produced on demand, it is difficult to measure the extent to which the child can control his speech production or to determine whether orosensory-motor differentiation of a pattern has been achieved. Imitation skills should therefore be developed as soon as possible—if necessary, from non-speech behaviors—so that they may be used to advantage in both teaching and in phonetic level evaluation.

Imitation clearly involves the child's being able to perceive the pattern we seek to elicit. As shown in previous chapters, this may not be a straightforward matter. We cannot, for example, reasonably expect the child to imitate an intonation pattern that he is not able to hear, see, or feel; and we should hesitate to conclude that he cannot differentiate, say, [k] and [g] if he can only see their production. The availability of sensory information must therefore be taken into account and, where necessary, additional auditory, visual, or tactile cues provided.

As might be expected, there are often marked differences between responses obtained on phonologic (spontaneous) level tests and those obtained on phonetic (imitative) level tests. Snow and Milisen (1954), Carter and Buck (1958), Siegel, Winitz, and Conkey (1963), Smith and Ainsworth (1967), Kresheck and Socolofsky (1972), DiSimoni (1975), and Winitz and Bellerose (1975) all found more sounds present and correctly produced when the adult form was provided for normally hearing children to imitate than when speech was elicited without such a model. Among hearing-impaired children, the differences also tend to favor responses obtained through imitation as compared with responses obtained through naming or discussion of meaningful material. Differences in speech production among hearing-impaired children relating even to the level of complexity of meaningful material were reported by Prutting (1970).

Phonetic Level Sampling in the Very Young

Phonetic level production involving orosensory-motor differentiation and, perhaps, auditory proprioceptive differentiation may be developed in hearing-impaired infants during their first year or two of life. Indeed, one of the main objectives of parent-infant programs should be to develop and extend the child's range of vocalization and babble. In early infancy, the child's ability to produce sounds may precede his ability to imitate them. Evaluation of phonetic skills by means of imitation may not, therefore, be feasible with the very young. Sampling, analysis, and recording procedures such as those described for phonologic level evaluation should thus be adopted with children who have not developed adequate imitation skills. Tape recordings of 50 representative vocal respirations should be made so that sound patterns employed can be identified and their frequency of occurrence entered on the child's file. Such samples should be obtained over intervals no greater than three months, for it is important to note not only the sounds which have been acquired but also the extent and speed of the child's speech pattern acquisition. Patterns that are present in two or more samples of 50 representative vocalizations may be tentatively regarded as being acquired. The word "tentatively" is used deliberately. The fact that a pattern is used consistently does not necessarily indicate that the child can differentiate it from other, similar patterns.

Speech patterns that are present in a young child's vocalizations indicate what aspects of production need to be reinforced, what antecedent behaviors should be shaped or developed to obtain new patterns, or—if undesirable traits are noted—what behaviors should be discouraged. If the young child's speech pattern acquisition does not change systematically (rather than randomly) from one phonetic sampling to the next, or if acquisition of new patterns is extremely slow, then all aspects of the approach should be questioned. We do not subscribe to the notion that a young child in the early stages of speech acquisition may reach a plateau. If the skills one is seeking to teach are systematically developed, progress should be consistent and evident.

Phonetic Level Speech Sampling in Older Children

As soon as the child is able to imitate speech, imitation should be used as the principal means of eliciting patterns at the phonetic level. For the sake of simplicity, we suggest that patterns should be classified according to whether they are produced consistently, inconsistently, or not at all. Reinforcement for items correctly produced will help to keep the child attending to the task. The summary of the phonetic level analysis presented in this Chapter as Appendix B may be used as a guide to the order in which the presence or absence of sound patterns may be verified.

Since the primary purpose of phonetic level assessment is to provide the teacher with clearly defined teaching goals in each area of speech production, we assume that the teacher alone can and should undertake the phonetic level evaluation procedure. Indeed, if she is expected to make day-to-day decisions on what to teach as the child makes progress, the evaluation task should not be beyond her. In spite of these remarks, we are aware that some teachers have not acquired sufficient confidence in their judgments to be happy unless their decisions are confirmed by more experienced personnel. Alternatively, supervisory staff may not consider that the teacher's analysis provides objective evidence of the child's speech abilities. For these reasons, high-quality tape recordings of each formal evaluation are recommended. They also enable the teacher to appraise her own efforts realistically through comparison of the several evaluations made in the course of a school year.

Formal phonetic level evaluation should be undertaken over intervals. not exceeding three months. It is not a long procedure since the entire test need not be administered at each stage of speech acquisition. In the early stages, for instance, it is not necessary to test for ability to produce sounds at diadochokinetic rates of three to four syllables per second or to alternate one sound pattern with another if the child cannot produce the required sounds in a single syllable. In the later stages of acquisition the reverse is true: one need not test single-syllable production if the child can repeat and alternate syllabic patterns containing the sound in question. If the teacher is familiar with the child's speech, and hence with what tasks he is likely to accomplish (and she should be if she is teaching subskills systematically day by day), then the evaluation can be completed in 20 minutes. The comprehensive information yielded on the child's needs and progress is an extremely fruitful return for the investment of so little time. The teacher should not feel that formal evaluation duplicates her ongoing, everyday assessment which is carried out as she teaches. It does not. Everyday tests indicate how well the child has learned what he has been taught; formal evaluation, in addition to providing a broader perspective, shows how well he has retained it.

Nonsegmental Analysis: The first step in the nonsegmental analysis is to determine the extent to which the child has acquired control over vocalization. *Spontaneous vocalization* must be abundant if it is to serve as an adequate basis for further development. In active play the child must vocalize on at least 12 occasions during a three-minute period if he is stimulated by the teacher. He must also be able to produce *vocalization on demand*—i.e., vocalization whenever it is required. Otherwise, training or testing cannot be managed efficiently.

Control of vocal duration must be established before further training can be undertaken. The child should be able to produce a sustained vocalization for at least three seconds, a series of brief vocalizations (i.e., sounds lasting one-half second or less), and a stream of up to four vocalizations containing sounds varied in temporal pattern.

Control of vocal intensity can be considered to be present if the child can produce sounds of three-second duration in a *loud* voice, a *quiet* voice, and a *whisper*, as well as a series of several syllables varying in intensity. Voice intensity should not fluctuate unduly during the production of sounds at any given level. If fluctuation is present, sufficient control has not been established for the child to begin to vary pitch without confusing "high" with "loud" and "low" with "quiet"—a common problem.

Pitch control may be considered as being acquired if the child can make sounds which differ by at least eight semitones from "low" to "high" without significantly changing his voice level, i.e., vocal intensity, when doing so; and if he can vary his voice both continuously and discretely within this range (high-mid-low and low-mid-high).

For the purpose of testing nonsegmental aspects in the early stages of acquisition, any vowel within the child's vocal repertoire may be accepted. At later stages, the child should be expected to be able to vary duration, intensity, and pitch of voice when producing particular vowels, syllables, words, or phrases.

Segmental Analysis: In rating segmental production we must seek to determine four things: whether the child is capable of differentiated speech sound production to the extent required; whether patterns can be reliably repeated; whether they can be alternated with other patterns at an acceptable rate; and whether segments can be varied in duration, intensity, and pitch.

Vowels and diphthongs should be elicited one after another in the order depicted in Appendix B. Each vowel should be initiated by whatever consonant the child can produce. The reason for using a consonant— preferably a stop such as [b]—to release the vowel is that the transition provides acoustic cues as to the normalcy of the target position assumed by the tongue. The tongue can assume quite deviant positions in the formation of an isolated vowel, yet the vowel may sound acceptable. (An extreme, but convincing, example is to say [i] with the tip of the tongue protruding from the side of the mouth.) When a consonant is added, any deviant positioning will be detected because the consonant-to-vowel transition will be anomalous. Vowels used in the pronunciation of words vary from region to region and from speaker to speaker. Most vowels employed by most speakers are represented in Appendix B; but if there are local variants of these vowels, they should be used both to train and to test the child.

To pass the test, the child should be able to sustain the target vowel for at least three seconds without its changing in phonetic quality, to produce each vowel or diphthong in syllables repeated loudly, quietly, and in a whisper at a rate of at least three per second; to alternate any two target vowels developed in the same teaching step; and to vary the pitch of voice over a range of at least eight semitones while maintaining the vowel's phonetic quality. Spaces are provided on the evaluation sheet (see Appendix B) to record, in relation to each vowel and diphthong, whether the child can succeed in these tasks consistently, inconsistently (i.e., occasionally), or not at all.

There are advantages in testing the vowels and the diphthongs in the order in which they are taught. First, because the child will probably succeed more frequently with those sounds developed first, he will be more consistently reinforced and hence more likely to maintain attention to the task. Second, the production of vowels in Steps 3 and 4 is not required before one can proceed to train and test differentiated production of consonants. Thus, if the child's attention span is short, one can cover a greater variety of items in the evaluation at one sitting by initially testing Steps 1 and 2. One may return to testing vowels in Steps 3 and 4, which are developed concurrently with consonants, either later in the initial session or at a later date.

The purpose of having the child sustain a vowel for a three-second period is to ensure that he has established tongue, jaw, and lip targets for the sound. The purpose of repeating the vowel in syllables initiated with [b] is to verify that the tongue can be maintained in the appropriate target position when lips and jaw positions are repeatedly changed. Such demands on the child prevent the development of tongue neutralization—as in [bɪə] for [bɪ]—which is a common fault in the speech of hearing-impaired children. The reason for requiring alternation of vowels is not simply that vowels in syllables are normally alternated in running speech, but that the child must learn to move tongue, lips, and jaw toward various target positions with considerable speed and accuracy in order to establish the motor codes which underlie effective coarticulation. Consistently accurate speech sound production is dependent on adequate development of motor sequencing abilities (Gallagher and Shriner, 1975). We demand that the child be able to produce each vowel as voice pitch is varied over a range of at least eight semitones for two reasons: first, this ensures the independence of laryngeal and articulatory mechanisms; second, it demands a sufficient level of automaticity in vowel production to permit attention to be given to voice pitch or, conversely, sufficient automaticity in the control of pitch to allow attention to be directed toward maintaining the phonetic quality of the vowel. Such skill is basic to normal speech production where intonation is used to signal syntactic or semantic structure.

Simple consonants must be tested in the context of various vowels to ensure that the appropriate range of coordinated speech organ gestures has been developed and that adequate groundwork for basic coarticulation has been laid. Of course, fewer vowels are used in testing than in teaching. In the first step (see Appendix B), we employ mainly [u], [a], and [i]. Correct production of consonants with these three vowels (or their local variants) is assumed to be sufficient evidence of competence in consonant production. In practice, we have found this to be so. If a child can produce a particular consonant with only two of the three vowels, however, this consonant is likely to be unsatisfactorily produced with several other vowels as well. More in-depth testing is then required to determine the full extent of the problem and to formulate immediate remedial teaching goals. Not all simple consonants occur frequently in the context of these three vowels, however, and it is important for the child to produce consonants with both short vowels and diphthongs. In later steps we therefore employ a wider variety of contexts.

We expect the child to be able to produce all target consonants in single syllables and in syllables repeated at the rate of at least three items per second. This test ensures that the child not only can make the appropriate sounds, but can do so at the rate required in normal speech production. Ability to produce the consonants in single syllables may be assumed if the child can succeed in the repetition task. It therefore saves time to test first with repeated syllables and then to test for the consonant in single syllables only if he fails in the repetition task.

The teacher should take care to ensure that her judgments of accuracy are consistent. When an observer listens to a great number of repetitions of the same sound, perceptual shifts may occur which can lead to the classification of distortions as acceptable (Shelton, Johnson, and Arndt, 1974). This may be avoided by demanding not more than six repetitions at a time for any one sound. Following the testing of other sounds, the teacher may return to the evaluation of those for which there was initial doubt of phonetic quality. There is often an advantage in looking away from the child's face in order to use only audition when carrying out a speech evaluation. Subtle acoustic distortions may be missed if the teacher attends too closely to the visual aspects of production. For example, in a repeated [bi], she may not detect nasal escape; or in a syllable containing [u], she may accept the lipread form and fail to detect that the child's tongue position is faulty.

In testing simple consonant production we also require that the child be able to alternate consonants in syllables with others taught in the same or previous steps. Such a requirement ensures that the child has developed feedforward processes and coarticulation skills fundamental to the adequate use of the target consonant in running speech. In testing we are concerned with the alternation of a few crucially important syllable pairs. For example, in Step 1 the alternation of [ba-ma], first as a single unit, then as a unit repeated up to six times, tests the child's differentiation of patterns that are visually similar; the alternation of [fi-mi] tests the child's speedy and accurate control of velopharyngeal valving, which cannot be assumed from the repetition of either syllable alone; and the alternation of [θu-bu] calls for rapid exchange of lips and tongue in occluding the breath stream. More complex alternations are called for as the test proceeds. All require sufficient breath control to maintain intraoral pressure for the duration of the increasingly complex sequences of sounds.

Inclusion of the nonsegmental aspects of speech production is essential at each stage of development. Hence, we also require that the child be able to reproduce simple consonants in loud, quiet, and whispered syllables and to vary the pitch of syllables over a range of at least eight semitones.

The simple consonants, as listed in Appendix B, are shown mainly in initial (prevocalic) positions. Those that are presented as final (postvocalic) consonants—such as [ŋ] and the unreleased stops—are exceptions. Where consonants can be used in initial, medial, or final positions, they should also be tested in each of these positions. They should not be scored as "produced consistently" unless they can be made prevocalically, intervocalically, and postvocalically. Opportunity to test production in intervocalic position is afforded when the child repeats a syllable. Thus, [mi] repeated with continuous voicing contains the sequence [imi], and [ʃa] when repeated similarly contains [aʃa]. Since final [r] may be regarded as a vowel modification in [ɝ] and [ɚ] , only its production in initial and medial positions should be insisted upon during evaluation of simple consonants taught in Step 3.

To conserve both space and testing time, cognate pairs are treated as single items in the evaluation of consonants in Step 4. We are here concerned with whether voiced-voiceless consonants in the initial position can be produced with different voice onset time and whether voiced-voiceless consonants in the final position can be produced with appropriate modification of the duration of the vowel.

Word-initial blends are tested in much the same way as simple consonants. In Appendix B we have organized them in sets of three so that each blend is tested simultaneously in the context of all three vowels. There is little reason to alternate word-initial blends in English since they seldom occur as alternated items in running speech. The repetition of sets is sufficient to ensure adequate automaticity for their use in communication.

Word-final blends are tested with only one vowel although they should be taught with several. Some final blends do not follow certain vowels in English, and most occur as a result of inflection. Since the inflected forms of English require /s/, /z/, /t/, or /d/, blends ending in these sounds are among the most commonly encountered. Although most English blends formed with two sounds have been specified in Steps 1 through 4, no attempt has been made to list all possible final blends containing three or more sounds. The dozen sounds listed in Step 5 as complex final blends were simply selected as being representative for the purpose of testing. Other complex blends may be derived through applying the rules of inflection or by referring to the phonetic lexicon prepared by Rockey (1973). Those children who understand the morphologic rules of English may be expected to have mastered some of the final blends tested. Conversely, those children who have been taught to use final blends have an established sound system which may serve as a basis for the development of morphology. The nature of particular word-final blends may be changed by repeating them in syllables. For example, [ɪlm] can become [mɪl] if repeated without pause between syllables. Indeed, the reverse of this process is a strategy that one may use in teaching blends of any type.

Summary of Observations and Teaching Goals

At the end of the summary of the phonetic level analysis (see Appendix B) we have provided space for making observations and for listing immediate teaching goals. Observations should relate to general characteristics which affect a variety of target behaviors. For example, voice quality may not be natural even though the child has control over vocal duration, intensity, and voice pitch. This would be the case if there were abnormal tension affecting the pharynx. To foster a more natural voice quality, relaxation during speech would be a general goal. Similarly, there might be overall hypernasality, which would indicate the need to work toward correcting velopharyngeal targets by establishing and then contrasting nasal and non-nasal sounds. Alternatively, one might find weakness of tongue control principally affecting, say, the alveolar consonants. To remedy this the teacher might provide special exercises or give priority to work on specific alveolar targets. Such observations can thus help the teacher determine the general direction required for her teaching work.

Specific teaching goals should relate to general observations, as suggested above, and to the development of four or five specific phonetic level target behaviors selected from among those that the child should acquire first in accordance with the sequence already discussed. As soon as the selected target behaviors have been established, four or five more specific phonetic level goals should be set on the basis of further evaluation.

Other Aspects of Evaluation

As stated at the outset, evaluation of a child requires a team effort. Many aspects of evaluation carried out by other specialists should also concern the speech teacher, and full reports from other specialists should therefore be available to her. The aspects having most direct bearing on the child's speech development would usually be audiological status, visual capacity, physical and psychological condition, and social-cultural circumstances. We shall briefly comment upon each of these aspects as it relates to speech acquisition.

The audiological status of the child is determined by his hearing levels and by the extent to which his residual hearing can be aided. Clinical evaluations of hearing level in children (see Northern and Downs, 1974) are not always reliable, and the teacher should be alert to possible discrepancies between the findings of the audiologist and the child's responses during speech training. This is particularly important since it is known that, for various reasons, children's responses may vary considerably from one hearing test to another (Ling and Naish, 1975). Further, hearing aid characteristics may change drastically over time (Zink, 1972). Hence, even if the aid appears to be working, the teacher cannot be sure that the child is hearing speech optimally unless she checks the child's ability to detect speech at the beginning of each training session.

For the teacher to listen to or to otherwise test merely the hearing aid is not enough. She must make a rapid check on the functioning of the child's complete auditory system, which begins at the microphone of the hearing aid and ends at the child's cerebral cortex. This can be done in a few seconds by having the child clap hands when he hears the sounds [u], [a], [i], [ʃ], and [s] (see Ling, 1975). These sounds, which sample points across the whole range of speech frequencies, should be spoken by the teacher within the distance over which the child can normally hear them. If the child does not respond as well as usual, then the teacher will be aware that her work on speech cannot be carried out as effectively as it should be through the use of residual audition. A full audiological evaluation of both hearing and hearing aids should be carried out at least annually. Even so, a truly adequate profile of the child's residual hearing will not emerge until the child has begun to use audition in the acquisition of speech.

Speechreading demands optimal use of visual capacity. If corrective lenses are required, the teacher should know if a 20/20 level of vision may be expected. Poor hand-eye coordination may indicate that the child has had abnormally restricted experience for which visual-motor training is required (Kirshner, 1972). It may also indicate a central nervous system disorder which may affect speech acquisition. Habitual failure to make eye contact, together with repetitive motor behaviors (e.g., rocking), may signify autism (Myklebust, 1954).

Deviations of physical development are not likely to prevent the acquisition of speech unless they affect the speech organs. Several health problems may, however, slow the rate of acquisition (FitzSimons, 1958). Conditions such as respiratory infections, lassitude arising from nutritional deficiency, and sleep deprivation may lead to such problems as drive reduction, short attention span, frequent illness, and absence. Great care should be taken to observe the child's gross motor coordination. Gross motor dysfunction, evidenced by a poor gait or by uncoordinated movements, indicates the possibility of organic disorders which may affect the control of motor speech movements.

Intelligence does not appear to be as important in speech acquisition as it is in many other aspects of education. Poor speech (as distinct from language) skills are not generally found to be related to intelligence in normally hearing children unless the children are severely mentally retarded (Winitz, 1969, p. 143). The same probably holds true for hearing-impaired children. For this reason, and also because there are many difficulties inherent in assessing the intellectual capacities of hearing-impaired children (Levine, 1974; Gerweck and Ysseldyke, 1975), the teacher should avoid relating speech skills, or her expectations in speech acquisition, to estimates of intelligence.

Emotional disturbance is known to affect speech development adversely, but research in this area with hearing-impaired children has been limited (Myklebust, 1960). In recent years, emotional disorders among hearing-impaired children have been largely attributed to ineffective oral teaching (Schlesinger and Meadow, 1970), although ineffective communication by any means can result in emotional problems. Emotional disorders are likely to occur if diagnosis and treatment are delayed, if speech development is not speedily and effectively fostered in oral programs, if the child finds his educational environment abrasive, or if home conditions are not conducive to the child's overall growth.

Social and cultural factors play an important role in speech development. The teacher who ignores them may therefore find that progress does not reflect the effort expended. In order to develop normal spoken language, the child must have both effective speech training and adequate experience of normal speech patterns through speech communication with normally hearing adults and peers. The quality of parent-child interaction is particularly important (Goss, 1970; John, 1963; Ling and Ling, 1974). Although some studies have shown that articulatory competence among normally hearing children is related to socio-economic status (see Winitz, 1969, pp. 143–147, for a review), the differences in competence tend to be trivial. Cultural and ethnic background may be more important since this affects parental attitudes toward a handicap (Zola, 1966) and may involve the use of a second language in the home. In this respect the child of deaf parents who communicate principally by sign has much in common with the child of immigrant parents. There are great differences between first-language and second-language learning (Lambert, 1972; Jakobovits and Gordon, 1974), and the hearing-impaired child is at a disadvantage if speech in the language that will be used in his schooling is not mastered as the first and dominant means of communication at home.

Summary

In order to work effectively, the teacher—as a member of a team—should be involved in the evaluation of each child. We propose that she should be primarily concerned with three aspects of such evaluation: the oral-peripheral examination, phonologic speech analysis, and assessment of phonetic level skills. We suggest procedures for carrying out these aspects of evaluation, for summarizing the data obtained, and for using this information to formulate general and specific teaching goals. In addition, we comment upon how the evaluations of various other specialists might relate to the child's acquisition of speech.

APPENDIX A
TABLE 9.B
Summary of Phonologic Level Speech Evaluation

Name: _____ Age: _____ Date: _____

1. Stimuli used to elicit sample (toys, pictures, conversation).

   Specify material or topic: _____

2. Mean number of syllables/utterance _____ . Mean number of sylla-

   bles/sec. _____ .

3. **NONSEGMENTAL ASPECTS** Normal ( )   Faulty ( )

   Breath control _____ Intensity control _____ Pitch control _____

   Intonation _____ Duration of vowels _____

   Duration of consonants _____ Phrasing _____ Stress _____

4. **SEGMENTAL ASPECTS** Indicate if sound is produced consistently
   (✔), inconsistently (+), or not at all (–).

a. **Vowels and diphthongs**

   u _____ ʊ _____ o _____ ɔ _____ ɑ _____ a _____ ʌ _____

   ɝ _____ ə _____ ɚ _____ æ _____ ɛ _____ e _____ ɪ _____

   i _____ aɪ _____ aʊ _____ ɔɪ _____ eɪ _____ Other _____

b. **Simple consonants**

   Plosives: b _____ d _____ g _____ p _____ t _____ k _____

   Unreleased stops: p̄ _____ t̄ _____ k̄ _____ b̄ _____ d̄ _____ ḡ _____

   Nasals: m _____ n _____ ŋ _____

   Semivowels: w _____ j _____ ʍ _____

   Liquids: l _____ r _____

   Fricatives: h _____ f _____ θ _____ ʃ _____ s _____ v _____

   ð _____ ʒ _____ z _____

   Affricates: tʃ _____ dʒ _____

c. **Word-initial blends**

   Two-organ sequential: sm _____ sp _____ sw _____

Single-organ sequential: sk _____ sl _____ sn _____ st _____

θr _____

Two-organ coformulated: bl _____ br _____ fl _____ fr _____

kw _____ pl _____ pr _____ tw _____

Single-organ coformulated: dr _____ gl _____ gr _____ kl _____

kr _____ ʃr _____ tr _____

Complex: skr _____ skw _____ spr _____ str _____

d. **Word-final blends**

Continuant-continuant: fs _____ lm _____ ln _____ lz _____

mz _____ ns _____ nz _____ ŋz _____

sl̩ _____ θs _____ sn̩ _____ vz _____

Continuant-stop: ft _____ ld _____ lp _____ lt _____ mp _____

nd _____ nt _____ ŋk _____ sk _____

sp _____ vd _____ zd _____

Stop-continuant: bl̩ _____ bz _____ dl̩ _____ dz _____ gl̩ _____

gz _____ kl̩ _____ ks _____ pl̩ _____ ps _____

tl̩ _____ tn̩ _____ ts _____

Stop-stop: kt _____ pt _____ gd _____ bd _____

Complex: fts _____ kts _____ bl̩z _____ mpl̩ _____ ndz _____

nts _____ ŋkl̩ _____ pl̩z _____ skt _____ tn̩d _____

spt _____ tn̩z _____ ntʃ _____

5. **LINGUISTIC STRUCTURE** Check if present.

Single words _____ Two-word phrases _____

Noun and verb phrases _____ Kernel sentences _____

Compound sentences _____ Complex sentences

6. **INTELLIGIBILITY**

Number of complete utterances _____ and number of words _____
agreed to be intelligible.

7. COMMON FAULTS

Nasality _____ Intrusive voicing _____ Other _____

8. IMMEDIATE TEACHING GOALS as determined from above:

_____

_____

_____

_____

_____

_____

Evaluation carried out by:

_____

_____

_____

APPENDIX B
TABLE 9.C
Summary of Phonetic Level Speech Evaluation

Name: _____ Age: ____ Date: _____

NONSEGMENTAL ASPECTS
Indicate whether produced consistently (✔), inconsistently (+), or not at all (−).

(a) Vocalization: spontaneous _____ on demand _____

(b) Vocal duration: sustained _____ brief _____ varied _____

(c) Vocal intensity: loud _____ quiet _____ whisper _____

   varied _____

(d) Vocal pitch: low _____ mid _____ high _____

   continuously   varied _____   discretely

   varied _____

VOWELS AND DIPHTHONGS
Release with [b] and indicate whether the sound can be produced consistently (✔), inconsistently (+), or not at all (−). When the target can be sustained at loud, quiet, and whispered levels in *single* syllables, check under S. When sound can be *repeated* at a rate of at least three per second, check under R. When it can be *alternated* accurately with any other at a rate of at least three per second, check under A. When it can be produced with controlled *pitch* variation over a range of eight semitones, check under P.

If most sounds in Steps 1 and 2 are checked as being consistent, proceed to evaluation of simple consonants.

                S R A P   S R A P   S R A P   S R A P   S R A P

Step 1. [a] _ _ _ _   [i] _ _ _ _   [u] _ _ _ _   [aʊ] _ _ _ _   [aɪ] _ _ _ _

                S R A P   S R A P   S R A P   S R A P   S R A P

Step 2. [ɔ] _ _ _ _   [ɔɪ] _ _ _ _   [ε] _ _ _ _   [ʊ] _ _ _ _   [ɪ] _ _ _ _

	S R A P	S R A P		S R A P	S R A P
Step 3.	[æ] _ _ _ _	[ʌ] _ _ _ _	[ɑ] or [ɒ] _ _ _ _	[o] _ _ _ _

	S R A P
[e] or [eɪ]	_ _ _ _

	S R A P	S R A P	S R A P
Step 4.	[ɝ] _ _ _ _	[ə] _ _ _ _	[ɚ] _ _ _ _

SIMPLE CONSONANTS

Indicate whether sounds are produced consistently (✔), inconsistently (+), or not at all (−) in the syllables specified below. Mark each according to whether the sound is produced correctly:
S: in a *single* syllable;
R: in syllables *repeated* at least three times per second;

	S R		S R		S R		S R	
Step 1.	[ba] _ _		[pa] _ _		[wa] _ _		[ʍa] _ _	
	[bi] _ _	or	[pi] _ _		[wi] _ _	or	[ʍi] _ _	
	[bu] _ _		[pu] _ _		[wu] _ _		[ʍu] _ _	
	S R		S R		S R		S R	
	[fa] _ _		[va] _ _		[θa] _ _		[ða] _ _	
	[fi] _ _	or	[vi] _ _		[θi] _ _	or	[ði] _ _	
	[fu] _ _		[vu] _ _		[θu] _ _		[ðu] _ _	
	S R		S R		S R		S R	
	[ha] _ _		[ma] _ _		[æp̄] _ _		[æb̄] _ _	
	[hi] _ _		[mi] _ _		[ɪp̄] _ _	or	[ɪb̄] _ _	
	[hu] _ _		[mu] _ _		[ʌp̄] _ _		[ʌb̄] _ _	

	S R		S R		S R
Can alternate [ba-ma] _ _		[fi-mi] _ _		and [θu-bu] _ _	

Can produce syllables in this step in a loud voice _____
quiet voice _____ whisper _____ .
Can vary pitch of voice over range of at least eight semitones when repeating these syllables _____.

	S R		S R		S R		S R
Step 2.	[da] __		[ta] __		[ʃa] __		[ʒa] __
	[di] __	or	[ti] __		[ʃi] __	or	[ʒi] __
	[du] __		[tu] __		[ʃu] __		[ʒu] __

	S R		S R		S R		S R
	[sa] __	or	[za] __		[na] __		[jɔ] __
	[si] __		[zi] __		[ni] __		[jɛ] __
	[su] __		[zu] __		[nu] __		[jʌ] __

	S R		S R		S R
	[laʊ] __		[æt̄] __		[æd̄] __
	[laɪ] __		[ɪt̄] __		[ɪd̄] __
	[lɔɪ] __		[ʌt̄] __		[ʌd̄] __

	S R		S R		S R		S R
Can alternate	[da-na] __		[ʃi-li] __		[sæ-næ] __		[bʌ-dʌ] __
	[ʃi-si] __						

Can vary pitch of voice over a range of at least eight semitones when repeating these syllables.

	S R		S R		S R		S R
Step 3.	[ga] __		[ka] __		[tʃa] __		[dʒɑ] __
	[gi] __	or	[ki] __		[tʃi] __	or	[dʒi] __
	[gu] __		[ku] __		[tʃu] __		[dʒu] __

	S R		S R		S R		S R
	[æŋ] __		[ræ] __		[æk̄] __		[æḡ] __
	[ɪŋ] __		[rɪ] __		[ɪk̄] __	or	[ɪḡ] __
	[ʌŋ] __		[rʌ] __		[ʌk̄] __		[ʌḡ] __

	S R		S R		S R		S R
Can alternate	[ri-gi] __		[tʃa-ra] __		[su-gu] __		[ræ-læ] __

Can produce syllables in this step in a loud voice _____ quiet voice_____ whisper_____ .

Can vary pitch of voice over at least eight semitones when repeating these syllables.

Step 4.   Can alternate:

S R	S R	S R	S R
[ba-pa] _ _	[æb-æp] _ _	[fi-vi] _ _	[tʃai-dʒai] _ _
[da-ta] _ _	[æd-æt] _ _	[θi-ði] _ _	
[ga-ka] _ _	[æg-æk] _ _	[ʃi-ʒi] _ _	
		[si-zi] _ _	

S R
[pʌ-tʌ-kʌ]   _ _
[bʌ-dʌ-gʌ]   _ _
[fa-θa-ʃa]   _ _

Can differentially produce aɪs-aɪz _____ kæp-kæb _____ in whisper.

Can vary pitch of voice over eight semitones when repeating these syllables _____ .

WORD-INITIAL BLENDS

Rate each blend according to criteria set for simple consonants.

Step 1.   Two-organ sequential blends.

S R	S R	S R
[sma-smi-smu] _ _	[spa-spi-spu] _ _	[swa-swi-swu] _ _

Can vary intensity __ and pitch __ of voice while repeating any set of these syllables.

Step 2.   Single-organ sequential blends.

S R	S R	S R
[ska-ski-sku] _ _	[sla-sli-slu] _ _	[sna-sni-snu] _ _

S R	S R
[sta-sti-stu] _ _	[θra-θri-θru] _ _

Can vary intensity __ and pitch __ of voice while repeating any set of these syllables.

Step 3.   Two-organ coformulated blends.

S R	S R	S R
[bla-bli-blu] _ _	[bra-bri-bru] _ _	[fla-fli-flu] _ _

	S R		S R		S R
[fra-fri-fru]	_ _	[kwa-kwi-kwu]	_ _	[pla-pli-plu]	_ _
[pra-pri-pru]	_ _	[twa-twi-twu]	_ _		

Can vary intensity __ and pitch __ of voice while repeating any set of these syllables.

Step 4. Single-organ coformulated blends.

	S R		S R		S R
[dra-dri-dru]	_ _	[gla-gli-glu]	_ _	[gra-gri-gru]	_ _
[kra-kri-kru]	_ _	[ʃra-ʃri-ʃru]	_ _	[tra-tri-tru]	_ _

Can vary intensity __ and pitch __ of voice while repeating any set of these syllables.

Step 5. Complex blends.

	S R		S R		S R
[skra-skri-skru]	_ _	[skwa-skwi-skwu]	_ _	[spra-spri-spru]	_ _
[stra-stri-stru]	_ _				

Can vary intensity __ and pitch __ of voice while repeating any set of these syllables.

WORD-FINAL BLENDS

Rate each blend according to criteria set for simple consonants.

Step 1. Continuant-continuant blends.

	S R		S R		S R		S R		S R		S R
[ɪfs]	_ _	[ɪlm]	_ _	[ɪln]	_ _	[ɪlz]	_ _	[ʌmz]	_ _	[ʌns]	_ _
[ɪnz]	_ _	[ʌŋz]	_ _	[ʌsl̩]	_ _	[ɪθs]	_ _	[ɪsn̩]	_ _	[ɪvz]	_ _

Can vary intensity __ and pitch __ of voice while repeating any set of these syllables.

Step 2. Continuant-stop blends.

	S R		S R		S R		S R		S R		S R
[aft]	_ _	[ald]	_ _	[ʌlp]	_ _	[alt]	_ _	[ʌmp]	_ _	[and]	_ _
[ant]	_ _	[ʌŋk]	_ _	[ask]	_ _	[ʌsp]	_ _	[ʌvd]	_ _	[ʌzd]	_ _

Can vary intensity __ and pitch __ of voice while repeating any set of these syllables.

Step 3. Stop-continuant blends.

S R	S R	S R	S R	S R	S R
[ɪbl̩] _ _	[æbz] _ _	[ɪdl̩] _ _	[ɪdz] _ _	[ɪgl̩] _ _	[ɪgz] _ _
[ɪkl̩] _ _	[æks] _ _	[ɪpl̩] _ _	[æps] _ _	[ɪtl̩] _ _	[ɪtn̩] _ _

Can vary intensity ___ and pitch ___ of voice while repeating any set of these syllables.

Step 4. Stop-stop blends.

S R	S R	S R	S R
[ækt] _ _	[æpt] _ _	[ægd] _ _	[æbd] _ _

Can vary intensity ___ and pitch ___ of voice while repeating any set of these syllables.

Step 5. Complex blends.

S R	S R	S R	S R	S R
[ɪfts] _ _	[ækts] _ _	[ɛmbl̩z]	_ _ [æmpl̩] _ _	

S R	S R	S R	S R
[ɑndz] _ _	[ɔɪnts] _ _	[æŋkl̩] _ _	[ʌpl̩z] _ _

S R	S R	S R	S R
[ɑskt] _ _	[ætn̩d] _ _	[ɪspt] _ _	[ɪtn̩z] _ _

Can vary intensity ___ and pitch ___ of voice while repeating any of these syllables.

OBSERVATIONS

Comments on points of general difficulty such as breathy or harsh voice quality, hypernasality, etc., or specific physical problems such as dys-arthria, cleft palate, etc.

_____

_____

_____

_____

IMMEDIATE TEACHING GOALS
(as determined from above)

_____

_____

_____

_____

Evaluation carried out by:

_____

_____

_____

REFERENCES

Baer, D. M., & Sherman, J. A.   Reinforcement control of generalized imitation in young children. *J. Exp. Child Psychol.*, 1, 37–49, 1964.

Bankson, N. W., & Byrne, M. C.   The relationship between missing teeth and selected consonant sounds. *J. Speech Hear. Disord.*, 27, 341–348, 1962.

Barrett, R. G.   A test to assess the intelligibility of speech of the congenitally deaf. *Teach. Deaf*, 45, 151–156, 1947.

Berko, J.   The child's learning of English morphology. *Word*, 14, 150–177, 1958.

Bjuggren, G.   A method to test the intelligibility of the speech of pre-school children with severe hearing impairment. *Acta Oto-Laryngol. Suppl.*, 110, 83–88, 1954.

Carter, E. T., & Buck, M.   Prognostic testing for functional articulation disorders among children in the first grade. *J. Speech Hear. Disord.*, 23, 124–133, 1958.

Clarke School for the Deaf.   *Speech Development: Curriculum Evaluation and Development Program.* Northampton, Mass.: Clarke School for the Deaf, 1971.

DiSimoni, F. G.   Perceptual and perceptual-motor characteristics of phonemic development. *Child Dev.*, 46, 243–246, 1975.

Ewing, A. W. G., & Ewing, E. C.   *Teaching Deaf Children To Talk.* Manchester: Manchester University Press, 1964.

Farman, J. J.   The Farman-Phillips Speech Intelligibility Diagnostic Test. *Volta Rev.*, 56, 168–170, 1954.

Fisher, H. B., & Logemann, J. A.   *The Fisher-Logemann Test of Articulation Competence.* Boston: Houghton Mifflin, 1971.

FitzSimons, R.   Developmental, psychosocial, and educational factors in children with nonorganic articulation problems. *Child Dev.*, 29, 481–489, 1958.

Gallagher, T. M., & Shriner, T. H.   Articulatory inconsistencies in the speech of normal children. *J. Speech Hear. Res.*, 18, 168–175, 1975.

Gerweck, S., & Ysseldyke, J. E.   Limitations of current psychological practices for the intellectual assessment of the hearing impaired: A response to the Levine study. *Volta Rev.*, 77, 243–248, 1975.

Girardeau, F. L., & Spradlin, J. E. (Eds.)   *A Functional Analysis Approach to Speech and Language*. (ASHA Monographs #14) Washington, D.C.: American Speech and Hearing Assoc., 1970.

Glaser, R.   Instructional technology and the measurement of learning outcomes: Some questions. *Am. Psychol.*, 18, 519–521, 1963.

Goldman, R., & Fristoe, M.   *Test of Articulation*. Minnesota: American Guidance Service, 1969.

Goss, R. N.   Language used by mothers of deaf children and mothers of hearing children. *Am. Ann. Deaf*, 115, 93–96, 1970.

Greene, M. C. L.   Speech of children before and after removal of tonsils and adenoids. *J. Speech Hear. Disord.*, 22, 361–370, 1957a.

Greene, M. C. L.   *The Voice and Its Disorders*. London: Pitman, 1957b.

Guilford, J. P.   *Psychometric Methods*. New York: McGraw-Hill, 1954.

Harvold, E. P.   Speech articulation and oral morphology. In *Speech and the Dentofacial Complex: The State of the Art*. (ASHA Reports, #5, 69–75) Washington, D.C.: American Speech and Hearing Assoc., 1970.

Haycock, G. S.   *The Teaching of Speech*. Washington, D.C.: Volta Bureau, 1933.

Horton, C. E., Crawford, H. H., Adamson, J. E., & Ashbell, T. S.   Tongue-tie. *Cleft Palate J.*, 6, 8–23, 1969.

Jakobovits, L. A., & Gordon, B.   *The Context of Foreign Language Teaching*. Rowley, Mass.: Newbury House, 1974.

John, V. P.   The intellectual development of slum children: Some preliminary findings. *Am. J. Orthopsychiatry*, 33, 813–822, 1963.

Johnson, W., Darley, F. L., & Spriestersbach, D. C.   *Diagnostic Methods in Speech Pathology*. New York: Harper and Row, 1963.

Johnston, M., & Harris, F. R.   Observation and recording of verbal behavior in remedial speech work. In H. N. Sloane and B. D. MacAulay (Eds.), *Operant Procedures in Remedial Speech and Language Training*. Boston: Houghton Mifflin, 1968.

Kirshner, A. J.   *Training That Makes Sense*. San Rafael, Calif.: Academic Therapy Publications, 1972.

Kresheck, J. D., & Socolofsky, G.   Imitative and spontaneous articulatory assessment of four-year-old children. *J. Speech Hear. Res.*, 15, 729–733, 1972.

Lahey, B. B. (Ed.)   *The Modification of Language Behavior*. Springfield, Ill.: Thomas, 1973.

Lambert, W. E.   *Language, Psychology and Culture*. Stanford, Calif.: Stanford University Press, 1972.

Larr, A. L., & Stockwell, R. P.   A test of speech intelligibility. *Volta Rev.*, 61, 403–407, passim, 1959.

Lee, L. L.   A screening test for syntax development. *J. Speech Hear. Res.*, 35, 103–112, 1970.

Lee, L. L.   *Developmental Sentence Analysis*. Evanston, Ill.: Northwestern University Press, 1974.

Levine, E. S.   Psychological tests and practices with the deaf: A survey of the state of the art. *Volta Rev.*, 76, 298–319, 1974.

Ling, D.   Amplification for speech. In D. R. Calvert and S. R. Silverman, *Speech and Deafness*. Washington, D.C.: A. G. Bell Assoc. for the Deaf, 1975.

Ling, D., & Ling, A. H.   Communication development in the first three years of life. *J. Speech Hear. Res.*, 17, 146–159, 1974.

Ling, D., & Naish, S. J.   Threshold variations in repeated audiograms. *Volta Rev.*, 77, 97–104, 1975.

MacDonald, J. D., & Blott, J. P.   Environmental language intervention: The rationale for a diagnostic and training strategy through rules, context, and generalization. *J. Speech Hear. Disord.*, 39, 244–256, 1974.

Mager, R. F.   *Preparing Instructional Objectives*. Belmont, Calif.: Fearon Publishers, 1962.

Mase, D. J.   Etiology of articulatory speech defects. (Teachers College Contribution to Education, 921) New York: Columbia University, 1946.

McDonald, E. T.   *Articulation Testing and Treatment: A Sensory-Motor Approach*. Pittsburgh: Stanwix House, 1964.

Mowrer, D. E.   Evaluating speech therapy through precision recording. *J. Speech Hear. Disord.*, 34, 239–244, 1969.

Myklebust, H. R.   *Auditory Disorders in Children*. New York: Grune & Stratton, 1954.

Myklebust, H. R.   *The Psychology of Deafness*. New York: Grune & Stratton, 1960.

Northern, J. L., & Downs, M. P.   *Hearing in Children*. Baltimore, Md.: Williams & Wilkins, 1974.

Oller, D. K., & Kelly, C. A.   Phonological substitution processes of a hard-of-hearing child. *J. Speech Hear. Disord.*, 39, 65–74, 1974.

Owrid, H. L.   Measuring spoken language in young deaf children. *Teach. Deaf*, 58, 24–34, 1960.

Pendergast, K., Dickey, S., Selmar, J., & Soder, A.   *Photo Articulation Test*. Danville, Ill.: Interstate Printers & Publishers, 1969.

Peterson, S. J.   Nasal emission as a component of the misarticulation of sibilants and affricates. *J. Speech Hear. Disord.*, 40, 106–114, 1975.

Prutting, C. A.   *Articulatory behavior and syntactical acquisition in hard of hearing children*. Unpublished Ph.D. diss., University of Illinois at Urbana-Champaign, 1970.

Rockey, D.   *Phonetic Lexicon*. New York: Heyden, 1973.

Schlesinger, H. S., & Meadow, K. P.   *Sound and Sign*. Berkeley, Calif.: University of California Press, 1970.

Shelton, R. L., Arndt, W. B., Kreuger, A. L., & Huffman, E.   Identification of persons with articulation errors from observation of non-speech movements. *Am. J. Phys. Med.*, 45, 143–150, 1966.

Shelton, R. L., Johnson, A., & Arndt, W. B.   Variability in judgments of articulation when observer listens repeatedly to the same phone. *Percept. Mot. Skills*, 39, 327–332, 1974.

Siegel, G. M., Winitz, H., & Conkey, H.   The influence of testing instruments on articulatory responses of children. *J. Speech Hear. Disord.*, 28, 67–76, 1963.

Smith, M. W., & Ainsworth, S.   The effects of three types of stimulation on articulatory responses of speech defective children. *J. Speech Hear. Res.*, 10, 333–338, 1967.

Snow, K., & Milisen, R. L.   The influence of oral versus pictorial presentation upon articulation testing results. *J. Speech Hear. Disord. Monogr. Suppl.*, 4, 29–36, 1954.

Spriestersbach, D. C., & Sherman, D.   *Cleft Palate and Communication.* New York: Academic Press, 1968.

Taylor, H.   The phonograph as an aid in articulation teaching. *Am. Ann. Deaf*, 59, 337–339, 1914.

Telage, K., & Fucci, D.   Vibrotactile stimulation: A future clinical tool for speech pathologists. *J. Speech Hear. Disord.*, 38, 442–447, 1973.

Templin, M. C., & Darley, F. L.   *The Templin-Darley Tests of Articulation.* Iowa: Bureau of Educational Research and Service, University of Iowa, 1969.

Turton, L. J.   Diagnostic implications of articulation testing. In W. D. Wolfe and D. J. Goulding (Eds.), *Articulation and Learning.* Springfield, Ill.: Thomas, 1973, pp. 195–218.

Tyack, D., & Gottsleben, R. *Language Sampling and Analysis.* Palo Alto, Calif.: Consultant Psychologists Press, 1974.

Voelker, C. H.   An experimental study of the comparative rate of utterance of deaf and normal hearing speakers. *Am. Ann. Deaf*, 83, 274–284, 1938.

Vorce, E.   *Teaching Speech to Deaf Children.* Washington, D.C.: A. G. Bell Assoc. for the Deaf, 1974.

Warren, D. W.   Restorative treatment of the dentofacial complex. In *Speech and the Dentofacial Complex: The State of the Art.* (ASHA Reports, #5, 132–145) Washington, D.C.: American Speech and Hearing Assoc., 1970.

Weir, R.   Some questions on the child's learning of phonology. In F. Smith and G. A. Miller (Eds.), *The Genesis of Language.* Cambridge, Mass.: M.I.T. Press, 1966.

West, J. J., & Weber, J. L.   A phonological analysis of the spontaneous language of a four-year-old hard-of-hearing child. *J. Speech Hear. Disord.*, 38, 25–35, 1973.

West, R., Ansberry, M., & Carr, A.   *The Rehabilitation of Speech.* New York: Harper and Row, 1957.

Winitz, H.   *Articulatory Acquisition and Behavior.* New York: Appleton-Century-Crofts, 1969.

Winitz, H., & Bellerose, B.   Self-retrieval and articulatory retention. *J. Speech Hear. Res.*, 18, 466–477, 1975.

Woodward, H. M. E.   Criterion-referenced testing and the measurement of language growth. *Volta Rev.*, 77, 229–240, 1975.

Worster-Drought, C.   Speech disorders in children of school age. *J. R. Inst. Public Health Hyg.*, 17, 190–200, 1954.

Zink, G. D.   Hearing aids children wear: A longitudinal study of performance. *Volta Rev.*, 74, 41–51, 1972.

Zola, I. K.   Culture and symptoms: An analysis of patients' presenting complaints. *Am. Soc. Rev.*, 31, 615–630, 1966.

=======/10/=======

Teaching Order
and Evaluation:
A Synthesis and a Model

A Speech Teaching Model

An effective speech teaching model must represent the serial and parallel orders in which speech patterns are developed as well as economic and precise evaluation procedures which allow us to determine what phonetic and phonologic patterns have been learned. Some bases for such a model have been presented in the preceding chapters. The model we propose, shown as Figure 10.1 (following pages), represents speech teaching as a process which requires the serial development of skills through seven major stages of acquisition. It includes two distinct levels of acquisition at each stage: the phonetic and the phonologic. They are represented as being essentially parallel paths of development. The model is structured on the principle that phonetic level acquisition, fostered if necessary by teaching appropriately ordered target behaviors and subskills, underlies the development of the child's phonology.

The teaching of speech is viewed as an activity mainly, though not exclusively, carried out at a phonetic level. At the phonologic level the main requirements are constant exposure to adequate models of production, insistence on the use of speech skills as they are acquired at the phonetic level, and reinforcement of speech patterns accurately produced. The model accords with the view that teaching at the phonologic level should be concerned not so much with speech production per se as with spoken language development and with the integration of lexical, morphological, and syntactic development into the speech system (see Chapter 7).

Each of the seven stages of speech acquisition specified in our model consists of a number of target behaviors. These behaviors were discussed in Chapter 8. Further, to achieve each of these target behaviors, the child must master a series of specific subskills. Figure 10.2 illus-

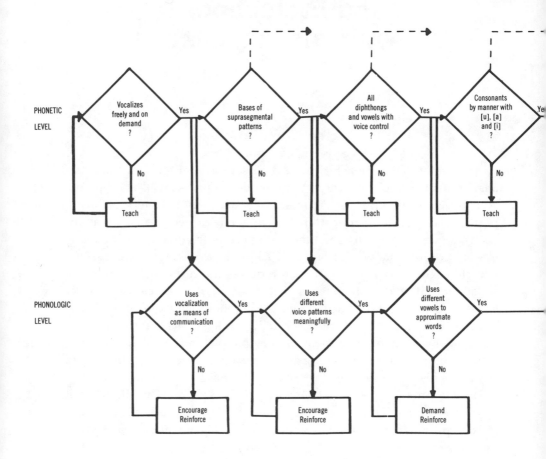

Figure 10.1

A seven-stage model for speech acquisition in hearing-impaired children. Diamonds represent evaluation and oblongs represent intervention procedures. Dotted lines indicate that when 70 % of the work at a particular stage is completed, work at the next stage may be initiated.

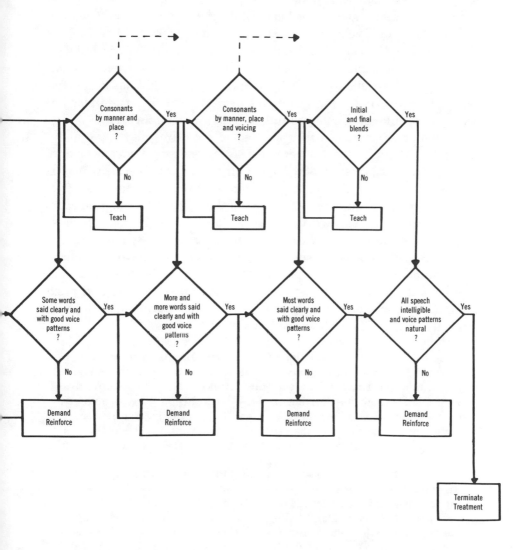

trates how particular target behaviors and the subskills which underlie them relate to our model. In this figure we use Stage 4 as an example. It consists of seven target behaviors: namely, production of the seven front consonants which differ mainly in manner of production and which we recommend should be developed as soon as the essential range of vowels in Stage 3 has been established. In this figure we have indicated that to develop any given target behavior the teacher must select the first of the various subskills involved (the number, n, will vary from one target to another), plan her teaching strategy, carry it through, and then evaluate the result of her work. If the subskill has been mastered, she may proceed to teaching the next; if not, she must re-plan her work, using different strategies and materials, and begin again.

The processes involved in teaching the nasal [m] may serve to indicate the nature of the teacher's task in developing target behaviors through ensuring mastery of the subskills which underlie them. Nasality, as indicated in Chapter 2, is a common problem among hearing-impaired children, as is denasalization of the [m] in phonologic speech. To avoid such problems we need to select and teach subskills with great care to ensure automatically correct target production. By following the proposed model we can be sure that the antecedent behaviors required for adequate production are present. These behaviors are vocalization on demand (Stage 1); control of voice duration, intensity, and pitch (Stage 2); and production of several vowels and diphthongs (Stage 3). Subskills required for [m] acquisition are listed below:

Subskill 1 is the direct production of [m] in isolation. (Isolated production of an [m] is permissible because it can be used syllabically as in "mmm!") In addition to behaviors already acquired, this subskill only requires that we establish nasal emission during voicing. For this purpose, an auditory model should serve all but the totally deaf child since the [m] has stronger low-frequency components than any other consonant. For the totally deaf child a vibratory-tactile cue (finger on bridge of nose) will suffice.

Subskill 2 is the repeated production of [m] in isolation. This requires that the child be able to produce an [m] several times on one breath. The actual number of sounds on a trial and their intensity should be varied. The purpose here is to ensure that the child can initiate voicing for the [m] while maintaining the lips and velum in the appropriate position. The exercise should lead to relaxation of the lips and tongue and to focusing of the child's attention on only the sound being produced.

Subskill 3 is the production of [m] in a final position following the vowels [u], [a], and [i]. It requires the continuation of voicing and the initiation

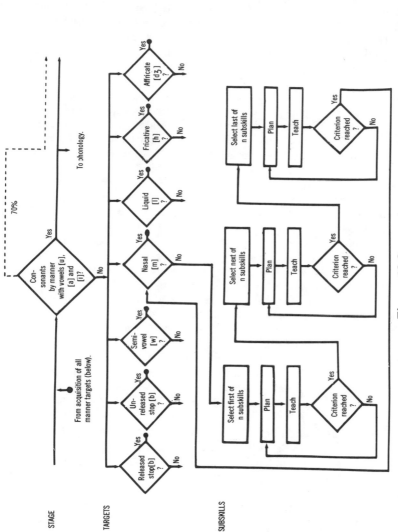

Figure 10.2

Relationship of target behaviors and subskills to the speech acquisition model shown as Figure 10.1. Each of the major stages may similarly be broken down into n targets, and each target into n subskills. Diamonds represent evaluation steps, and oblongs, activities related to teaching. Training on different targets may be provided concurrently, as indicated by positive target evaluation leading to Yes, rather than to another target. The dotted line indicates that work on consonants by manner and place may be begun when evaluation shows that 70% of target behaviors and subskills in this stage have been taught.

of nasal emission following lip closure. This subskill is the first in the series that involves control of velopharyngeal valving. To establish oral-nasal control, it is essential to ensure oral (non-nasal) resonance during vowel production. If there is a problem in this regard, the child should initially be encouraged to feel the oral breath stream, which is more tangible for [u] and [i] than for [a]. If necessary, these vowels may initially be released with [h] to accentuate their tangible oral quality. This subskill cannot, however, be considered as being acquired until the child can produce the syllables [um], [am], and [im] without tactile cues. The purpose of teaching the [m] in the final position prior to teaching it in an initial position is to ensure that its production is free of the lip tension associated with stop targets. Teaching [m] first in an initial position would invite intrusive plosion as in [mba] since more than the required amount of tension is typically present in the acquisition of speech sounds until the child has learned how to produce them correctly with the least effort.

Subskill 4 is the *repeated* production of vowel-initiated syllables ending in [m]. The repeated production of such syllables on one breath and with continuous voicing ensures production of the [m] in a medial (intervocalic) position. It also lays the foundation for acquisition of the sound in an initial position since, in a string of syllables (e.g., [amamam]), the [m] is released into a vowel. The smooth (non-plosive) consonant-to-vowel transition obtained through the acquisition of this subskill provides both the orosensory-motor patterns and the auditory-proprioceptive foundation for later contrast with the bilabial stops. The criterion set for this subskill should be repetition at the rate of at least three syllables per second with a variety of vowels including [u], [a], and [i]. The purpose of combining the sound with at least these three vowels is to ensure that the child does not acquire the notion that the lip posture for [m] is unvaried. Lip closure for [m] in normal speech occurs when the lips are rounded as in [um], spread as in [im], or neutral as in [am].

Subskill 5 is the production of [m] as a releasing consonant in syllables formed with various vowels including [u], [a], and [i]. This production may be developed through reference to the previous subskill. For the child to acquire this subskill, it is usually only necessary to have him terminate the string of syllables with a vowel (e.g., [imimi] instead of [imimim]) and to repeat the final syllable. Great care should be taken to ensure that the vowel is not unduly nasalized.

Subskill 6 is the repeated production of [m] in an initial position in a string of syllables, each containing the same vowel: e.g., [mumumu]. Again, reference to *Subskill 4* usually ensures its speedy acquisition. Repetition at a rate of at least three syllables per second is required to reach criterion for completion of training on this and subsequent subskills.

Subskill 7 is the repeated production of [m] in an initial position in a string of syllables containing different vowels: e.g., [mimuma]. This subskill is required to ensure the flexibility of lip-closing gestures in a variety of vowel contexts and of tongue target positioning for vowels during bilabial closure.

Subskill 8 is the alternation of syllables containing [m] with syllables containing other sounds: e.g., [mabimabi]. This subskill ensures that movements of the tongue, lips, and velum are fluently coordinated. There should be no undue nasalization of the vowels. Should there be a problem in this regard, alternation of [m] with a fricative (e.g., [f]) should resolve it since velopharyngeal closure is required for the adequate production of fricatives.

Subskill 9 involves humming over a range of at least a musical fifth (eight semitones).

Subskill 10, the final subskill essential to the development of the [m] target, is the production of various syllables initiated with [m] at high, mid, and low pitch over a range of at least eight semitones. This subskill assists in the development of normal intonation patterns in phonologic level speech.

Evaluation and Planning Within the Model

The phonetic and phonologic level evaluation procedures described in the previous chapter may be used to determine what target behaviors within each stage have been acquired. These procedures lead to the identification of targets which cannot be produced consistently within the context of the test and hence to the definition of immediate teaching goals. In planning her work, the teacher may allow some overlap between certain adjacent stages (see Chapter 8). This is indicated in Figure 10.1 by the non-terminating broken lines. Thus, one may reasonably plan to work on vowels while continuing to teach the child to control voice pitch, or to introduce the first step of consonant teaching while completing work on vowel production. However, the teacher should not plan to work on targets that are not in adjacent stages.

In our phonetic level evaluation (see Chapter 9) we recorded speech target behaviors as being produced consistently, inconsistently, or not at all. Our goal is consistently accurate production. In other words, our criterion for success on all items is 100% accuracy. For segmental production this criterion applies both when the pattern is repeated in syllables and when the pattern is alternated in syllables at the rate of at least three items per second. It must therefore also apply as a measure of success in teaching each subskill. Even if production is speedy and accurate we cannot be sure that it is automatic—i.e., that it does not require the child's conscious attention.

If a particular pattern is not sufficiently automatic at a phonetic level, then the child's use of this pattern at a phonologic level cannot be expected. In the event that a speech pattern is satisfactorily produced during phonetic level testing but does not quickly become incorporated into the child's phonology, further practice with the pattern in the presence of an attention-distracting task may be planned. For example, the child might be expected to alternate the target sound with another pattern accurately and speedily and, at the same time, to carry out a sorting task such as separating out the four suits from a shuffled deck of playing cards. The technique is also useful as a diagnostic measure. If it can be done successfully, then one can be sure that the reason the child does not use the sound phonologically is either that he is unaware of how the sound should be used or that its use in spoken language has not been sufficiently encouraged and reinforced (see Chapter 7). The delay between the child's achieving consistent use of the pattern at the phonetic level and his phonological use of it should be minimal, as indicated in our model (see Figure 10.1).

In order to teach each subskill effectively the teacher must first plan her work (see Figure 10.2). The first step is to decide what sensory avenue(s) provide(s) the particular child with the most appropriate means of discriminating the target pattern when spoken by others (see Chapters 3 and 4) and by what sensory-motor means the child will best be able to differentiate the target from other patterns when he himself produces it (see Chapters 5 and 6). The decision as to strategy should ultimately depend on the child's sensory-motor capacities and, to some extent, on the subskill to be taught (see subsequent chapters). The next step for the teacher in planning her work is to decide what apparatus and materials (if any) she will require for optimal effectiveness and to determine how they will be used. Preference should be given to things that are attractive to the child, sufficiently varied to maintain his interest, and simple to manipulate—bearing in mind that the work need not necessarily be formal. For example, we were once asked how to teach tongue placement for [u] to a class of 4-year-olds. We advised the teachers to help the children make feathered headdresses and then to teach them to do an Indian war dance while vocalizing and waggling a finger in the mouth between rounded lips. Evaluation following the game showed that all children were then able to produce [u] with satisfactory tongue placement. The game was much more fun than attempting to match a pattern on an oscilloscope—and much more effective. The teacher's final step should be to plan the type and schedule of reinforcement that she will employ if a formal approach is required.

To carry out both evaluation and training, the teacher requires well developed auditory-phonetic skills. She must be able to judge sounds accurately and consistently. A teacher who is unable to hear and produce subtly different speech patterns can no more expect a satisfactory outcome to her work than a tailor who uses an elastic inch tape in measuring his cloth. Consistent and accurate judgments are essential if one is to determine whether the child's performance is adequate and, if not, to specify the nature of his production errors. Ability to imitate the child's production is useful in this regard since, by reference to one's own speech, the type of discrepancy present in others' speech becomes more readily apparent. Therefore, if the teacher is not already adept at mimicry, she should set out to become so.

The Model: A General Case

One purpose of a model such as that proposed above is to provide a framework within which speech acquisition can be systematically and effectively fostered regardless of the child's age, degree of hearing impairment, or current speech status. With the very young child one would not seek to develop subskills in such a formal way as with an older child, but one would nevertheless ensure their acquisition. One would also ensure that the older child could vocalize freely and on demand before attempting to teach control of duration, intensity, and pitch: the target behaviors underlying the production of suprasegmental features.

Whether children are hard-of-hearing or totally deaf, the stages of acquisition specified in Figure 10.1 need to be followed—and in the order depicted. Differences in approach would be related to the strategies one adopts to ensure the development of the subskills underlying desired target behaviors. Similarly, the model is applicable regardless of the status of the child's speech on admission to training. Indeed, it provides the evaluative framework required to determine speech status and to define areas of acquisition that require the teacher's attention.

Working from such a model does not demand adherence to a particular approach: it provides guidelines equally appropriate for those who espouse a natural (i.e., auditory-global) approach and those who prefer to follow a more analytic-synthetic path in their teaching. In our own work, we adopt the principle of least intervention: if the child, through adequate exposure to speech patterns, can within a reasonable time span acquire successive target behaviors without specific teaching of subskills, then intervention at the subskill level is not undertaken. On the other hand, we are ready to intervene by teaching subskills that are not readily acquired through more global exposure to speech. The child's needs as determined through informed observation and specific evaluation within the framework of the model provide the guidelines for treatment, not a curriculum which requires such and such a target to be taught by a particular age or in a particular grade.

As this model indicates, speech acquisition can be considered globally as a series of seven major phonetic and phonologic stages; as a number of more clearly defined target behaviors, some of which may be taught concurrently; and as numerous sets of phonetic subskills, each of which can serve as the basis for criterion-referenced teaching. Full description of the model would require complete definition of all stages, specification of all target behaviors, and identification of all underlying subskills. Such a description cannot be attempted here, since we have yet to explore the target behaviors and subskills required in greater detail. They, together with the strategies which may be used to develop them, will be discussed in the following chapters.

Another purpose of the proposed teaching model is to provide a framework for systematic research. As structured, the model postulates seven major stages of speech acquisition. Although this structure accords with current knowledge, the division into seven stages is somewhat arbitrary. The model also depicts a range of phonetic target behaviors which underlie each stage. Can all target behaviors involved in speech be defined? What of the subskills underlying each target behavior? Can they be specified with accuracy? On what basis should they be ordered? What physiological mechanisms underlie their acquisition? What sensory cues related to each should be made available to children with particular types of hearing deficit? What problems underlie the mastery of certain subskills? Can children be expected to employ sound phonologically when they can produce the pattern phonetically only in isolated syllables? To what extent is practice in repeating and alternating sounds in syllables reflected in phonologic development? To what extent does subskill acquisition for one target behavior affect the development of other target behaviors? How well can training on certain subskills prevent the development of faults typically found in the speech of hearing-impaired children? The model suggests these and many more questions which require research that might lead to improvements in teaching speech—and to the formulation of a superior teaching model. As we examine each aspect more fully in future chapters, these questions should be borne in mind.

Summary

A model for the teaching of speech to hearing-impaired children is introduced and discussed with reference to material presented in earlier chapters. The model depicts seven major stages of phonetic and phonologic level speech acquisition. Each stage is shown to contain a variety of speech target behaviors. Underlying each of these target behaviors is a suggested set of subskills. We discuss how evaluation and planning may be integrated by the teacher to yield effective strategies for teaching these subskills in accordance with each child's demonstrated needs and sensory-motor capacities. We emphasize that the model is applicable regardless of the child's age, hearing level, or speech status.

/11/

Breath and
Voice Control

The breath stream is the primary source of all speech energy. Its passage through the partly open glottis (the space between the vocal cords) results in a whisper. Its pressure upon the vocal cords when they are adducted (brought together) creates the vibration we hear as voice. The skilled speaker does not simply control his breath stream: he coordinates it with the laryngeal and articulatory adjustments which shape the speech signal. In the natural acquisition of speech, the required coordinations are gradually mastered. Voluntary vocalization—the behavior called for in the first stage of our model—requires relatively simple coordinations. At each successive stage of development (see Figure 10.1) increasingly complex coordinations are involved. We cannot, therefore, teach breath and voice control as self-contained skills prior to teaching speech. We can advance their development only through relating speech breathing and voice target behaviors to the progressive acquisition of phonetic and phonologic speech.

Although the breath and voice patterns which underlie speech production are much less salient than segmental sound patterns, we nevertheless attend to them in speech reception. We use the characteristic breath-grouping of words to derive information on the deep structure of an utterance, and we use the speaker's voice patterns to obtain cues not only on the intended message but also on the speaker's emotional state, sex, age, and even physical characteristics. Breath and voice patterns therefore have a pervasive importance in all aspects of speech communication. Accordingly, we shall suggest breath and voice control targets both in this and in subsequent chapters as each stage of the proposed model is considered. In this chapter, the emphasis is given to the mechanisms underlying the use of breath and voice in speech rather

184

than to procedures for teaching subskills relating to breath and voice patterns. Only if these mechanisms are adequately understood can one devise or exploit procedures to prevent the development of habitual errors or prescribe effective remedial techniques to overcome breath and voice problems that have been allowed to occur.

Mechanisms of Breathing

Respiration

In quiet breathing, about half a liter of air is exchanged on the dozen or so breaths that are taken each minute (Comroe, 1965). The two muscles primarily involved in the process of inspiration are the diaphragm, which forms the base of the thorax (chest cavity), and the external intercostals, the muscle tissue which fills the spaces between (and essentially serves to lift) the ribs. The diaphragm is responsible for most air intake. Its action can be seen as an outward movement of the abdominal wall. Although the diaphragm normally functions in tandem with the external intercostals, the two muscles can function independently (Konno and Mead, 1967). In deep breathing (forced inspiration), muscles accessory to the diaphragm and to the external intercostals become active. These accessory muscles are not usually used in speech production. Hence, deep breathing exercises as a preparatory basis for speech are likely to establish unnatural speech breathing patterns.

As the inspiration phase of the breathing cycle nears completion, and as the expiration phase begins, the diaphragm and the external intercostals serve to resist the elastic forces of the thorax and lungs which return them to a resting level. Expiration below the resting level of the thorax-lungs system requires active use of four other muscles: the internal intercostals, the rectus abdominus, the external oblique, and the lattisumus dorsi. Thus, resistive muscle force is required at the beginning of a speech event to restrain expiration, and positive muscle force is required at the end of a speech event to sustain it (Draper, Ladefoged, and Whitteridge, 1959).

Speech Breathing

Although speech can be produced with the same volume of air that is required for quiet breathing, and the same musculature serves both functions, respiratory breathing and speech breathing differ in three important ways. First, in respiratory breathing inspiration is only slightly more rapid than expiration, but in speech breathing—which requires fewer breathing cycles per minute—it is markedly so. (See Lenneberg, 1967, for detailed discussion.) Second, in respiratory breathing air is usually taken in through the nose, but in speech breathing inspiration is normally via the mouth. Third, expiration in respiratory breathing is relatively smooth, whereas in speech breathing it may also be pulsatile. As sound patterns are stressed, exhalation must also be pulsed to supply the necessary subglottal and intraoral pressures. The required pulses appear to be supplied at high- and mid-range lung volumes by controlled relaxation of the external intercostals, and at low lung volumes by activity of the internal intercostals (Hixon, 1973).

Because different muscle systems are involved at different stages of the expiration phase of the breathing cycle, hearing-impaired children should initially be encouraged to produce vocalizations of fairly long duration. This ensures the development of control over the different muscular forces which operate at different lung volumes. If isolated, short-duration vocalizations are accepted and these vocalizations are produced only above the thorax-lung resting level, then control of only the diaphragm and external intercostals and of their restraining function may be established. Vocalization must also employ the muscle complex which serves to sustain expiration below the thorax-lung resting level. Practices such as teaching sounds in isolation, reading words one to a breath, and eliciting single-word naming responses all tend to limit, rather than to enhance, the development of adequate speech breathing control. The development of coordinations for pulsing the breath stream over the normal range of lung volumes is similarly inhibited by such teaching tactics.

Problems commonly related to hearing-impaired children's breath control during speech (Carr, 1964; Numbers, 1967) are clearly unrelated to lung capacity. The normal range of lung volumes used in speech production is quite limited. Only rarely does speech require more than 20-25% of the lungs' vital capacity—the volume of breath which can be expelled following deep inspiration. In quiet speech, inspiration to about 60% and expiration to about 35% of vital capacity is normal. In loud speech, the range from about 80% to 60% of vital capacity is usually employed (Hixon, Goldman, and Mead, 1973).

Speech Breathing Target Behaviors

There is little in the specialist literature on hearing-impaired children relating to the definition of speech breathing target behaviors and few acceptable suggestions on the development of subskills which underlie them. Where reference is made to the topic, recommendations often indicate a generally poor understanding of the mechanisms involved. Kinsey (1883), Henderson (1930), and Haycock (1933, p. 45), for example, all advocated deep-breathing and blowing exercises. Such exercises were condemned by A. M. Bell (1914) as being of no avail except for the treatment of consumption and by Hudgins (1937) as being more appropriate to the gymnasium than to the classroom. In the light of modern knowledge one must agree with Bell and Hudgins. Even among normal speakers, blowing and phonation skills are not significantly related (Ptacek and Sander, 1963). We agree with Hudgins (1946) that the speech breathing problems common to hearing-impaired children are due not to inadequate lung capacity or blowing skill, but to lack of control in the emission of breath over a range of lung volumes. We view such control as a goal involving three target behaviors: (1) the maintenance of a steady breath flow for continuous vocalization; (2) the production of a pulsed breath stream in coordination with laryngeal and articulatory valving for sounds and syllables in running speech; and (3) the organization, through feedforward control, of intake and expenditure of breath in relation to the linguistic structure of the utterance. It is doubtful whether any of these target behaviors can be developed except in the context of speech production involving both whispering and voicing. This view accords with the opinion of Greene (1901), A. M. Bell (1914), and Hudgins (1937, 1946).

Hudgins (1937) provided more detailed suggestions for the development of speech breathing than any other writer in the field. He was not entirely self-consistent in that the program of training he proposed included non-speech exercises. The first exercise specified by Hudgins (1937) was the ability to inflate the chest and to hold this position with the mouth and glottis open for a reasonable period without escape of breath. Once established, this exercise was extended to include panting—the inhalation and expulsion of small puffs of air while the chest remained inflated and the glottis open. The second exercise was the release of a series of puffs of air through the open glottis on one breath. The third was the approximation of the vocal cords during controlled exhalation such that prolonged vowels would result. The fourth was the production of four to six vowels on one breath, with the vocal cords continuously approximated and each vowel being arrested by chest action alone. The fifth exercise was similar to the fourth, except that patterns of loud and quiet syllables were demanded. The sixth required the alternation of whispered and voiced vowels, an exercise to develop the intrinsic laryngeal muscles. The seventh, a further refinement of glottal control, was to alternate the syllables [ha] and [a], thus to develop aspiration. Hudgins' final step combined sequences of nonsense syllables.

Of the eight exercises proposed by Hudgins (1937), the last six—those which include voicing—are incorporated into our model. We require the third subskill at Stage 2, the fourth at Stage 3, and the remainder at later stages when syllables are repeated and alternated. Hudgins' list of subskills is, of course, far from comprehensive. For example, to complete even the third stage of our model satisfactorily one must develop a subskill relating to control of vocal intensity when vocal pitch is varied. This is because subglottal pressure must vary with vocal pitch if vocal intensity is to be maintained. At more advanced stages, subskills which relate to the breath-grouping of linguistic units must be developed. We do not regard the first two of Hudgins' proposed subskills as essential to a developmental program, although they may be useful as remedial procedures when faults have been allowed to become habitual. If they are to be used remedially—and we have doubts as to whether they should be—then two parallel non-speech subskills ought to be added: the restraining of breath intake with glottis open below the lung-thorax resting level, and the pulsation of breath in this lower range of the breathing cycle. The two non-speech exercises Hudgins suggested may lead children wrongly to deduce that speech is carried out only at lung volumes above the lung-thorax resting level. It is doubtful whether such exercises can be generalized to actual speech.

Achievement of the coordinations involved in speech appears to us to require more extensive micro- and macro-organization of breathing skills than can be accomplished through conscious effort toward breath control. At the micro-organization level, intricate compensations for the small variations in pressure and breath flow which result from laryngeal and articulatory valving must be made. These demand the development of reflex mechanisms about which we still know relatively little (Matthews, 1964; Hixon, 1973). At the macro-organization level, utterances must be breath-grouped according to their linguistic structure. Again, we know relatively little about the feedforward processes involved in such organization.

Mechanisms of Voicing

The vibration of the vocal cords, which gives rise to the production of voice, is due to the rapid alternation of forces: the pressure of the breath stream from below the larynx which parts the cords, and the aerodynamic energy (the Bernouilli force) which—together with the elastic properties of the tissues—restores them to a closed position (Lieberman, 1967). The stronger the elastic properties of the vocal tissues, the greater the proportion of time will be that the vocal cords are closed during the vibratory cycle, the richer in harmonic structure the voice will be, and the less breath one will require for phonation (Sonesson, 1960). The intrinsic laryngeal muscles which serve to adduct the vocal cords must therefore be maintained in good tonic condition. This requires their frequent use. Vocal rest results in flaccidity of the vocal tissues and in the production of breathy speech (Zilstorff, 1968). Hearing-impaired children who make infrequent use of voice often lack intrinsic laryngeal muscle tonicity and, as a result, have breathy voices accompanied by random fluctuation in fundamental pitch (F_0). Such fluctuation of voice among hearing-impaired children has been reported by Carlin (1968).

Voice Pitch

The pitch of voice (F_0) is determined by the length, mass, and tension of the vocal cords and by subglottal pressures. Due to greater length and mass of the vocal cords, the voice of an adult male is, in general, lower than that of an adult female, which in turn tends to be lower than that of a child. Studies of vocal pitch among both children and adults have been summarized by McGlone (1966) and by Hoops (1969, p. 58). They show that the mean pitch of children's voices decreases slightly from 7 to 14 years of age within the range of from 300 to 240 Hz. At adolescence, the voice pitch typically drops by about 30 Hz among females and by about 100 Hz among males. The relatively abrupt changes in the male voice at adolescence result from a rapid increase of about one-third in the size of the larynx (Negus, 1929). These changes pose problems for few normally hearing boys (Greene, 1972), but hearing-impaired boys may experience considerable difficulty in relearning controlled voice production at puberty unless specific training is provided to help them establish new and appropriate auditory and kinesthetic targets. Without such training, voice tends to be abnormally high-pitched. Voelker (1935), Green (1956), Hood (1966), and Boone (1966) all have reported voices with higher-than-normal F_0 among hearing-impaired adolescents. This is a matter of some concern, since maintaining voice at an abnormally high pitch induces considerable vocal strain.

Controlled change in the overall pitch of voice is required to produce the intonation patterns that are typically present in speech. These changes are effected in three ways: through modifying the elasticity by adjusting the length and mass of the vocal cords, through modifying subglottal pressure, or through both (Shipp and McGlone, 1971). Specifically, pitch may be raised by shortening the length over which the vocal cords vibrate, by reducing their mass, by increasing their tension, by increasing subglottal pressure, or by any combination of these mechanisms. Pitch may be lowered by the reverse procedures. A given pitch may be maintained either by keeping all mechanisms constant or by simultaneously changing one or more of these mechanisms while compensating for the change with others: for example, by decreasing tension and increasing subglottal pressure.

With such a variety of mechanisms available, the teacher may adopt various methods of inducing pitch change in the child's voice. For example, lowering the head toward the chest will change the position of the larynx so that tension on the vocal cords is reduced and their mass is increased, a procedure suggested by Connery (1919). Other mechanisms remaining constant, this procedure will lower voice pitch. A bass singer attempting to reach an extremely low note in his range often uses such a head-to-chest technique to achieve his target. Raising the head tends to have the opposite effect on voice produced in the chest register. The kinesthetic sensation associated with differing pitches thus produced may then guide the child toward making the desired laryngeal adjustments without head movement.

Intonation Patterns

Inducing the child to produce pitch change is a relatively simple matter. Helping the child to develop feedforward and feedback control of pitch to generate appropriate intonation patterns may be much more difficult unless the child has sufficient low-frequency residual hearing and uses a hearing aid with an adequate low-frequency response to establish voice control through auditory proprioceptive experience (Ling, 1964). Residual hearing capacity need not be extensive for this purpose. The frequency range of 100 to 500 Hz is sufficient to encompass the F_0 range normally met in male and female adults and children (see above).

In generating intonation patterns, we are normally conscious only of the acoustic results, not of the mechanisms by which they are achieved. Indeed, the mechanisms underlying the production of intonation are so complex that they cannot be analyzed through introspection. Hence, it is impossible to achieve more than gross control of the voice through conscious reference to kinesthetic patterns. Fine control depends on the development of reflex mechanisms (Judson and Weaver, 1965, p. 78). Adjustment of the musculature to change voice pitch may also affect vocal intensity. For example, both pitch and intensity are changed if the tension on the vocal cords is modified and all other mechanisms are held constant, and both of these increase in proportion to subglottal pressure. The fine control of intonation, which involves compensatory adjustments for the maintenance of vocal intensity, requires the coordination of from 12 to 24 neck muscles and of an even larger number of thoracic and abdominal muscles (Gray and Wise, 1959, p. 181). It is small wonder that Voelker (1935), Green (1956), and Hood (1966), in studies of the voices of children who made little or no use of residual audition, found their intonation to span less than half the normal range of 8-12 semitones! The child's attention to the intonation patterns he achieves as an outcome of his efforts rather than to the means by which he achieves them should clearly constitute the target behavior we seek to develop. His awareness of the outcome should preferably be through audition. If this is unrealistic for the child, visual representation of intonation such as may be provided by the use of hand cues or a pitch indicator (Anderson, 1960) becomes essential.

Vocal Cord Adjustment

The vocal cords may assume a variety of positions. In the position assumed for deep inspiration, they are fully abducted. For chest register voicing, they are adducted to a midline position in such a manner that their edges are approximated but free to vibrate along their entire length. In whispering they may be partially approximated. To produce a falsetto voice the vocal cords are so firmly adducted that they are free to vibrate over only a small portion of their length. These positions are illustrated in Figure 11.1, in which the vocal cords are represented

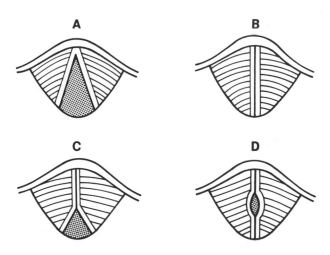

Figure 11.1

Diagrams show positions assumed by the vocal cords for (A) deep inspiration, (B) chest register voicing, (C) forceful whispering, and (D) falsetto voicing. The vocal cords are schematically represented as seen from above.

as one would see them from above by means of a laryngostroboscope.

Abductive-adductive action of the vocal cords is rather slow in relation to the rate at which segments occur in running speech and in relation to the delay in voice onset time (VOT) of 20 msec. or so which differentiates word-initial, voiced, and unvoiced stops (see Chapter 8). It takes about 100 msec. for the vocal cords to move from position (A) (fully abducted) to position (B) (midline approximation) (Soron and Lieberman, 1963). Accordingly, the ability to voice a segment in running speech with the necessary precision requires the development of feedforward processes which schedule the adductive movement to begin while a preceding unvoiced segment is still being produced. The abductive movement required to produce unvoiced sounds following voiced segments similarly requires pre-planned and fluent coarticulation.

Target Behaviors Relating to Voice

The target behaviors relating to voicing are initially simple and become more and more complex at each of the stages of speech acquisition specified in our model (Figure 10.1). At the first stage, there are two target behaviors: abundant, spontaneous vocalization, and vocalization on demand. At the second stage, three voice target behaviors are required: gross control of voice duration, control of vocal intensity, and control of pitch. At the third stage, we seek finer control of all three aspects of voice specified for Stage 2 but, in addition, require this control to be exercised during the production of clearly differentiated diphthongs and vowels. At the fourth and fifth stages, the new target behaviors required are the synchronization of voice onset with the initiation of consonants in syllables, the pulsatile voicing for the alternation and coordination of syllables released with voiced and unvoiced consonants, such as [bʌhʌbʌhʌ], and the synchronization of voice cessation with the arrest of syllables by an unreleased stop, such as [ʌp̄ ʌp̄ ʌp̄]. In Stage 6, the additional voice target behaviors required are control of relative voice onset time (VOT) to ensure the differentiation of homorganic cognate pairs such as [p-b] and [f-v], and control of the relative duration of the vowel (or preceding voiced consonant) to signal the voiced-voiceless contrast of postvocalic consonants—e.g., *rice-rise*. (See Chapter 8.) In the seventh stage of acquisition, there are two new voice target behaviors: reduction of aspiration (VOT) for stops occurring in blends such as [sp], and the control of timing in relation to suprasegmental features.

The voice target behaviors specified above are considered to be in order of increasing difficulty, with development and refinement at each stage of acquisition being dependent upon adequate mastery at the previous stage. As specified, they relate both to phonetic and to phonologic level development.

Summary

In this chapter we describe the mechanisms by which one controls breath and voice. We review the literature on teaching breath and voice control and demonstrate that views previously expressed do not accord with current knowledge. We provide evidence to support our view that such control can be adequately developed only in the context of phonetic and phonologic speech production, and we describe the target behaviors relating to breath and voice control at each successive stage of speech development.

REFERENCES

Anderson, F. An experimental pitch indicator for training deaf scholars. *J. Acoust. Soc. Am.*, 32, 1065–1074, 1960.

Bell, A. M. Vocal physiology, the principles of speech, and dictionary of sounds. *Volta Rev.*, 16, 65–78, 1914.

Boone, D. R. Modification of the voices of deaf children. *Volta Rev.*, 68, 686–692, 1966.

Carlin, T. W. Spectrographic presentation of the vocal quality of partially hearing school children. *Int. Audiol.*, 7, 96–101, 1968.

Carr, J. Early speech development of deaf children. In *Proc. Int. Congr. Educ. Deaf*. Washington, D.C.: U.S. Govt. Printing Office, 1964, pp. 261–267.

Comroe, J. H. Jr. *Physiology of Respiration*. Chicago: Year Book Medical Publishers, 1965.

Connery, J. M. A demonstration in voice training. *Volta Rev.*, 21, 108–109, 1919.

Draper, M. H., Ladefoged, P., & Whitteridge, D. Respiratory muscles in speech. *J. Speech Hear. Res.*, 2, 16–27, 1959.

Gray, G. W., & Wise, C. M. *The Bases of Speech*. (3rd ed.) New York: Harper Bros., 1959.

Green, D. S. *Fundamental frequency characteristics of the speech of profoundly deaf individuals*. Unpublished Ph.D. diss., Purdue University, 1956.

Greene, D. Breath and voice. *Am. Ann. Deaf*, 46, 477–487, 1901.

Greene, M. C. L. *Disorders of Voice*. Indianapolis: Bobbs-Merrill Co., 1972.

Haycock, G. S. *The Teaching of Speech*. Washington, D.C.: Volta Bureau, 1933.

Henderson, J. M. Outline of a speech lesson. *Volta Rev.*, 32, 134–136, 1930.

Hixon, T. J. Respiratory function in speech. In F. D. Minifie, T. J. Hixon, & F. Williams (Eds.), *Normal Aspects of Speech, Hearing and Language*. Englewood Cliffs, N.J.: Prentice-Hall, 1973, pp. 73–125.

Hixon, T. J., Goldman, M. D., & Mead, J. Kinematics of the chest wall during speech production: Volume displacements of the rib cage, abdomen and lung. *J. Speech Hear. Res.*, 16, 78–115, 1973.

Hood, R. B.   *Some physical concomitants of the perception of speech rhythm of the deaf.* Unpublished Ph.D. diss., Stanford University, 1966.

Hoops, R. A.   *Speech Science.* (2nd ed.) Springfield, Ill.: Thomas, 1969.

Hudgins, C. V.   Voice production and breath control in the speech of the deaf. *Am. Ann. Deaf*, 82, 338–363, 1937.

Hudgins, C. V.   Speech breathing and speech intelligibility. *Volta Rev.*, 48, 642–644, 1946.

Judson, L. S. V., & Weaver, A. T.   *Voice Science.* (2nd ed.) New York: Appleton-Century-Crofts, 1965.

Kinsey, A.   *A Full Course of Exercises in Articulation for Deaf Children.* London: W. H. Allen, 1883.

Konno, K., & Mead, J.   Measurement of the separate volume changes of rib cage and abdomen during breathing. *J. Appl. Physiol.*, 22, 407–422, 1967.

Lenneberg, E. H.   *Biological Foundations of Language.* New York: Wiley, 1967.

Lieberman, P.   Intonation and the syntactic processing of speech. In W. Wathen-Dunn (Ed.), *Models for the Perception of Speech and Visual Form.* Cambridge, Mass.: M.I.T. Press, 1967, pp. 314–319.

Ling, D.   Implications of hearing aid amplification below 300 cps. *Volta Rev.*, 66, 723–729, 1964.

McGlone, R. E.   Vocal pitch characteristics of children aged one and two years. *Speech Monogr.*, 33, 178–187, 1966.

Matthews, P. B. C.   Muscle spindles and their motor control. *Physiol. Rev.*, 44, 219–288, 1964.

Negus, V. E.   *The Mechanism of the Larynx.* St. Louis: C. V. Mosby, 1929.

Numbers, M. E.   A plea for better speech. In *Proc. Int. Conf. Oral Educ. Deaf.* Washington, D.C.: A. G. Bell Assoc. for the Deaf, 1967, pp. 543–555.

Ptacek, P. H., & Sander, E. K.   Maximum duration of phonation. *J. Speech Hear. Disord.*, 28, 171–182, 1963.

Shipp, T., & McGlone, R. E.   Laryngeal dynamics associated with voice frequency change. *J. Speech Hear. Res.*, 14, 761–768, 1971.

Sonesson, B.   On the anatomy and vibratory pattern of the human vocal folds. *Acta Oto-Laryngol. Suppl.*, 156, 1960.

Soron, H. I., & Lieberman, P.   Some measurements of the glottal-area waveform. *J. Acoust. Soc. Am.*, 35, 1876–1877, 1963.

Voelker, C. H.   A preliminary strobophotoscopic study of the speech of the deaf. *Am. Ann. Deaf*, 80, 243–259, 1935.

Zilstorff, K.   Vocal disabilities of singers. *Proc. Royal Soc. Med.*, 61, 1147–1150, 1968.

/12/

Vocalization and Voice Patterns: Targets, Subskills and Teaching Strategies

The first two stages of acquisition designated in our model (see Figure 10.1) share common mechanisms of breath and voice production. Both are therefore treated in this chapter. In the first stage of speech acquisition we seek to obtain an abundance of vocalization and to lay the foundations of communication involving voice. In the second stage our objective is to develop control over the duration, intensity, and pitch of voice. While it is convenient for us to treat the two stages as separate steps, it is evident that they are not entirely independent. The abundant vocalization obtained at the first stage will contain variations in duration, intensity, and pitch, but these variations will be largely involuntary. Thus, to specify two stages of acquisition and specific target behaviors relating to voicing is not to imply different mechanisms of production, but to recognize that it is expedient to evaluate progress at certain points along the continuum of development toward voluntary voice control.

The purpose of this chapter is to define the target behaviors called for in the first two stages of speech acquisition, to specify the subskills which underlie them, and to describe various types of teaching strategies that can be used to develop the child's mastery of each. We relate the strategies we suggest to the acoustic sensory correlates of each of the target behaviors and subskills we specify. We do this because the most effective teaching strategies for a given child have to be determined in accordance with the auditory, tactile, and visual cues that can be made available to him. Efficiency demands that the child with useful residual hearing be taught as far as possible through audition and that those who are totally deaf be provided with effective tactile and visual means of receiving the speech patterns we wish them to reproduce. We concentrate on the development of the nonsegmental skills which underlie later segmental and suprasegmental performance. At this point we make but brief mention of the many target behaviors relating to vocalization and voice which have to be developed within the context of the more complex speech patterns the child will produce in later stages of acquisition. We give detailed description of strategies which can be used both to promote production of nonsegmental patterns and to treat faults relating to vocalization and voice which may have been allowed to develop. We consider that the strategies described should serve only as examples and believe that the teacher should be expected to devise many more.

Spontaneous Vocalization and Vocalization on Demand

Target Behaviors: Their Acoustic and Sensory Correlates

Arbitrarily defined, the target behaviors we required at Stage 1 (see Chapter 10) are (1) the spontaneous production of at least 12 voluntary vocalizations in the course of a three-minute observation period when the child is stimulated through active play, (2) the consistent use of voice to attract attention, and (3) vocalization in response to a question or when asked to imitate. For all three targets the quality of the vocalization should be pleasant—not harsh, brief, or shrill. The phonetic quality of the vocalization produced at this stage of training is less important than its abundance. It matters little whether the child vocalizes with back, central, or front vowels providing that he vocalizes frequently. The acoustic properties of the vocalization that concern us here, therefore, are those relating to laryngeal tone.

The child must be made aware of the vocalization he produces if he is to achieve the target behaviors specified for this stage. Although vibration is present in the chest, throat, and head when voice is produced, it may not be adequate for our purposes. If the child's attention is focused on such vibration, he may seek to maximize it by adopting strategies that impede the development of good voice quality—for example, by exercising abnormal pharyngeal tension. Since we do not wish the child to adopt such strategies or to become conscious of the mechanisms underlying vocalization (see Chapter 11), we should seek to direct the child's attention to the audition of his voice or to the reception of cues through a vibratory device. Hearing is the preferred modality. Because the fundamental (F_0) and the first formant of most vowels and diphthongs fall within the frequency range of 200 to 1,000 Hz, all except totally deaf children may be expected to receive adequate cues through residual audition providing appropriate hearing aids have been fitted.

The presence of voicing cannot be directly observed through vision. Although transformation of voice patterns into visual images can be achieved (see Chapters 3 and 4), devices which yield such transformations cannot readily be employed to encourage spontaneous vocalization in children.

Subskills and Teaching Strategies

There is but one speech subskill involved in vocalization: the production of voice which results when breath is released and the vocal cords are adducted. In the normal course of events, every child vocalizes involuntarily: always in laughter; usually when crying, coughing, sneezing, or exercising strenuously; and sometimes in active play. The child must derive pleasure from vocalization if he is to use voice voluntarily and abundantly. The pleasure he derives may be intrinsic to the act—obtained from hearing and feeling his own voice, and/or extrinsic to it—received as reinforcement contingent upon vocalization.

Spontaneous Vocalization: Most hearing-impaired children use voice spontaneously and voluntarily at least to some extent at the beginning of training. A child who has been deaf from birth may, however, enter school effectively mute because he has received too little intrinsic or extrinsic reinforcement. His vocalization will then be limited to involuntary voicing. Similarly, a child who has lost hearing early in life, say as a result of meningitis, will also lose much of the intrinsic pleasure associated with hearing his own voice. Unless he is quickly fitted with a hearing aid to restore intrinsic reinforcement and unless he receives much more extrinsic reinforcement than formerly, he too may become effectively mute. To develop voluntary vocalization in such cases, the teacher must determine the sense modality most appropriate for the child, provoke involuntary vocalization, and then reinforce it.

The child's use of vocalization can usually be developed through the training of his residual hearing. Because audition is the modality of choice, no effort should be spared to ensure that the child hears as much as possible of his own and others' vocalization. The extent to which the child will respond to voice when wearing hearing aids cannot be reliably determined from an audiogram. Pragmatic assessment of auditory response in the course of training the child to vocalize is therefore required. Tactile cues should be employed only if it is evident that the child does not use audition. Even then, attempts to obtain responses through audition should continue since many children who hear nothing without hearing aids need to be trained to respond to sound when aids are first used. If responses through audition are obtained following the provision of tactile cues, the child should then be stimulated and reinforced through audition alone. Continued use of touch could, under these circumstances, detract from attention to hearing.

There are several ways in which a variety of involuntary vocalizations may be provoked. Thus, the teacher must decide which type of involuntary voicing she should select as the most appropriate antecedent behavior, how she will provoke it, and how she will reinforce it. Generally she should select the involuntary vocalization most closely comparable in quality to the voluntary pattern which she seeks to establish. Usually this is found in laughter. Tickling, physical play, and slapstick games are most likely to provoke laughter, just as formal seating, passive participation in dull or sedate activities, and work or play in isolation are most likely to inhibit it. Additional means of provoking voice may be necessary, however, since voice other than in the context of laughter must be produced before the two can be dissociated.

Of the possible alternatives, voice in the context of exertion may be the most practical. Activities involving exertion lead to both intake of breath and approximation of the vocal cords. In strenuous lifting or pushing, one impounds air in the lungs by closing the glottis (the space between the vocal cords) in order to render the chest a sufficiently rigid base for effective leverage (Gray and Wise, 1959, p. 163). Since the vocal cords cannot be approximated for longer than one can hold one's breath, exertion tends to produce the conditions necessary for voicing. Games such as tug-of-war and one-arm table wrestling are fun for the older child and usually provoke vocalization that can be reinforced. If the teacher involves herself in these games, she then has some control over the level and duration of exertion and can thus optimize her chances of eliciting the required behavior. The teacher should use exertion games judiciously; otherwise the child may readily and wrongly associate voicing with overall body tension. Facial distortion during exertion games should be carefully avoided.

Extrinsic reinforcement of vocalization may take many forms (see Chapter 7). From early infancy and throughout childhood, the most appropriate way to encourage voice production is through social conditioning. Rheingold, Gewirtz, and Ross (1959) provided a complex of auditory (echoic), visual (smiling), and tactile (patting, stroking) reinforcement each time young normally hearing babies vocalized. Vocalization increased substantially through this type of adult intervention. Similar procedures were successfully used by Lach, Ling, Ling, and Ship (1970) to maintain and extend the early vocalizations of hearing-impaired children. Schwartz, Rosenberg, and Brackbill (1970) studied the relative effectiveness of the auditory, visual, and tactile components involved in social conditioning of vocalization. They found that all three yielded equally good results. Non-social reinforcement—i.e., sights, sounds, or movement presented by remote control contingent upon the child's vocalization—is also effective (Ramey and Watson, 1972). However, human presence tends to increase its effectiveness (Todd and Palmer, 1968). The most effective reinforcement for vocalization appears to be live voice produced by a person in contact with the child. This is probably because the reinforcing voice may also serve as a model for the desired behavior. Indeed, modification of the child's F_0 in the direction of the F_0 used by the person providing reinforcement has been reported (see Lieberman, 1967, p. 45).

In the development of vocalization, one should reinforce the child with natural language, not simply with the vowel-like utterances one seeks to obtain from the child. If through the teacher's use of natural language the child spontaneously acquires clearly differentiated voice patterns, vowels, and some consonants as he learns to vocalize, all the better. If he does not, then he will acquire them later, if the teacher follows the stages of acquisition described in our model (Figure 10.1). Echoing a simple vocalization to show pleasure and thus provide social reinforcement of desired behavior is quite a natural thing to do; restricting one's own speech to utterances required of the child at a given stage of acquisition is not.

Vocalization on Demand: One cannot demand vocalization until it can be spontaneously produced. Only when the child can vocalize freely should he be expected to use voice to attract attention or to vocalize as a prerequisite to the fulfillment of his needs. As soon as voluntary vocalization is established, however, it is essential that it be used to supplant previously existing nonverbal behaviors such as pulling and pointing. This can be achieved by responding sluggishly or not at all to nonverbal behaviors and reacting quickly, vividly, and pleasantly to any attempt at vocal interaction.

Voice Patterns: The Bases of Suprasegmental Structure

Target Behaviors: Their Acoustic and Sensory Correlates

The three target behaviors required at this, the second, stage of speech acquisition are (1) gross control over duration of voicing, (2) control over voice intensity, and (3) control of voice pitch. The more abundantly the child has vocalized in Stage 1, the more likely it is that voice patterns varying in duration, intensity, and pitch will have emerged. If the child's spontaneous vocalization is reinforced in a variety of situations, it tends to be varied. If it is reinforced only in one type of situation, it tends to become monotonous. Figuratively one speaks of the "still, small voice of calm," "shrieks of pleasure," and "murmurs of delight," and voices are described as raised in anger, loud in protest, droning in monotony, and raucous with mirth. Such expressions give recognition to the fact that voice reflects mood. Because hearing-impaired children in the early stages of speech acquisition lack voice control, the extent to which the duration, intensity, and pitch of vocalization change with mood is often greater than that observed in normally hearing children of comparable age. A rich, emotionally stimulating environment therefore provides the most promising basis for the spontaneous voicing from which our target behaviors may be developed.

To develop the vocal target behaviors specified, the teacher must, at the outset, determine through what sense modality the child will most adequately perceive differences in the duration, intensity and pitch of voice—her own voice as well as his. If residual hearing is present, it should be used as the principal avenue for teaching at this stage since both exteroceptively and proprioceptively it provides the least ambiguous information on nonsegmental voice features. Direct vision provides no information on duration, intensity, or pitch of voice, while touch provides reasonably clear information only on vocal duration (see Chapters 3 and 4). Residual hearing need not extend beyond 500 Hz to encompass the acoustic range of either the teacher's or the child's F_0. Hearing up to 1,000 Hz will encompass not only the F_0, but several harmonics of voice. With appropriate amplification, therefore, it may be expected that most hearing-impaired children will be able to acquire the voice patterns demanded at this stage through residual audition. The advantage in continuing to concentrate attention on the auditory patterns at this stage is that it trains the child to develop habits of listening which will be required and extended in later stages of speech acquisition. For the rare child with total deafness, the visual and/or tactile modalities must be exploited. Chapters 3 through 6 indicate how they may be used most effectively.

Subskills and Teaching Strategies

Subskills Relating to Vocal Duration: A child may be considered as having acquired basic control over duration of voice when he can, on one breath, imitate groups of up to four distinct vocalizations varying in duration. The subskills underlying this target include ability to:

1. sustain a vocalization for at least three seconds;
2. imitate separate vocalizations differing in duration, each on one breath;
3. imitate up to four separate vocalizations differing in duration, all on one breath.

These three subskills are of importance both to the acquisition of other second-stage target behaviors and to the achievement of breath and timing control fundamental to further speech development. Ability to sustain a vocalization for at least three seconds' duration ensures that we have sufficient vocal material for subsequent development of differentiated intensity and pitch patterns. Similarly, the breath-grouping of utterances of various durations is essential to the regulation of breath in the production of a vocal stream which, in later speech, will be modulated by and coordinated with articulatory activity.

Teaching Strategies: Vocal Duration: The phonetic quality of the vocalization produced is unimportant to our immediate goals. Usually, central or mid-front vowels are produced early in speech acquisition because they involve neutral lip and tongue positions. If the child produces different vowels and certain consonants spontaneously during training aimed at control of vocal duration, he should be encouraged to maintain them. As with earlier conditioning, the teacher's echoic response coupled with an expression of pleasure provides strong reinforcement and incentive toward their maintenance and further development.

Subskill 1: The production of vocalizations which are sustained for at least three seconds. Voluntary vocalization developed from involuntary voicing may initially be harsh and brief. It will become less so only with extensive use. This may be encouraged with either social or instrumental conditioning. Games in which sustained vocalizations lead to reinforcing outcomes are particularly effective. For example, as the child vocalizes, the teacher may move a desired toy toward him, pour sand or liquid into a long vessel with the objective of making it overflow if voice is sustained for three seconds, draw a line along the chalkboard toward increasingly distant points, or walk along a line and then measure the distance covered. The imaginative teacher can invent many such duration-related activities. Electrically operated toys may similarly be employed. Thus, a train can be made to run or a windmill to turn for as long as the child produces voice. Such toys may be switched on and off either by a voice-operated relay or by hand. Games involving other children are also possible variants and may contribute to the children's increased use of residual audition. For example, musical chairs can be played by listening to a child's vocalization as well as by listening to music.

Subskill 2: The ability to imitate and to approximate separate syllables differing in duration, each on one breath. Imitation of vocal duration can be developed from imitation of nonverbal behaviors. Imitation is a natural response among children, and its encouragement in one setting will result in its generalization to others (Baer and Sherman, 1964). Imitation in building a structure with blocks, for example, helps to develop imitation of hand movements, which in turn encourages imitation of other body and head movements, facial expressions, and lip gestures. Because imitation is such a pervasive force in development, phonetic variety—which we do not specifically seek to develop at this stage—is nevertheless likely to occur. Reinforcement of responses that approximate the teacher's vocal model usually results in development of this subskill. Strategies similar to those proposed for the previous subskill may also be employed. Tactile rather than visual cues may initially help to convey the notion of relative duration to the child. For example, tracing one's finger down the child's arm while producing a long vocalization and patting his hand when producing a short vocalization readily leads to the association of touch and voicing in most children. When the auditory-tactile model has been provided, the teacher indicates that it is the child who has to voice according to the duration of the given tactile cue. As soon as the notion of relative duration has been conveyed in this (or some similar) way, an auditory rather than an auditory-tactile model should be employed with those children who have adequate residual hearing. Practice in this subskill without either visual or tactile cues is an excellent exercise in training the use of audition.

Subskill 3: The imitation of up to four separate vocalizations differing in duration, produced on one breath. Grouping vocalizations of differing duration on one breath is a simple step providing that the previous two subskills have been mastered. The teacher's first strategy should be to attempt to obtain imitation of the required pattern through audition. If this fails, then strategies involving visual, tactile, or visual-tactile cues in conjunction with audition may be employed. Tracing one's finger down the child's arm from elbow to wrist over a period of three seconds while he vocalizes will provide the child with the time set within which he will be expected to work. Movement of the finger toward the child's elbow will quickly become a signal for him to take in enough breath to sustain voicing of this duration. Stopping the movement (and hence the voicing) for a brief interval part way down the arm and then continuing will usually lead the child to produce two vocalizations on one breath. Since the child has already inhaled sufficient breath to sustain a long-duration vocalization, he will not need to inhale during such a pause. After establishing vocal patterns consisting of two vocalizations of similar duration on one breath over a three-second period, the number and variety of vocalizations required on one breath may be gradually increased. As soon as the child is able to complete the subskill with whatever visual and tactile cues have been used, he should—if he has adequate audition—be trained to carry out the task from an auditory model only. To this end, it may be necessary to fade the non-auditory cues gradually; for example, the teacher may begin by providing an auditory-tactile model instead of an auditory-tactile-visual model.

The development of this subskill should not be hurried, since the production of several short vocalizations on one breath demands the formation of new feedforward patterns which underlie pulsatile breath release, laryngeal valving, or both. Indeed, there is some danger that the performance of this subskill, if hurriedly developed, could result in vocal strain, particularly if the child is tense. Such danger may be avoided by ensuring that the child is not tense and that short syllables in a series are released with aspiration as in [ha] rather than with a hard glottal attack. If aspiration is not readily obtained, then a series of short syllables might be released with [b]. To encourage babbling of syllables initiated with [b] is not to enter Stage 4 prematurely; at that stage we seek not merely the production of a consonant but also its differentiation from other consonants and its alternation with them in various vowel contexts.

Subskills Relating to Vocal Intensity: Basic control of vocal intensity may be considered as being achieved if the child can imitate a series of several vocalizations varying in intensity, from loud speech to a whisper, on one breath. The subskills underlying this target include ability to produce:

1. brief, loud utterances;
2. brief, quiet utterances;
3. a whisper;
4. loud, quiet, or whispered utterances of at least three seconds' duration;
5. a series of several discrete, but breath-grouped, vocalizations varying in intensity.

Two aspects of vocal intensity are important in speech: overall level and relative peak level. Overall level, the mean intensity of speech, should vary according to the demands of the environment. In close, face-to-face conversation under quiet conditions one speaks more quietly than at a distance and in the presence of ambient noise or competing conversation. Relative peak level, the extent to which syllables in a word or words in a sentence are produced more loudly than others, should vary according to the stress patterns determined by the basic linguistic and semantic structure of an utterance. While the overall intensity is not—within the limits of audition—important to intelligibility, relative peak levels are. Stress on the wrong syllable of a word or on the wrong word in a sentence can adversely affect intelligibility, render an utterance ambiguous, or substantially change its meaning. Vocal intensity is not, of course, the only component of linguistic stress. Variations in duration and pitch also contribute to the relative salience of speech components (Fry, 1958).

The reasons for teaching the child to regulate voice intensity at this—the second—stage of speech acquisition are various. First, because the mechanisms underlying voice intensity and vocal pitch are closely associated (see Chapter 11), it is important that the child be able to produce various intensity levels and to differentiate them from each other before we attempt to develop pitch control. In this way, confusion between the two aspects—intensity and pitch—may be avoided. Second, teaching the child to whisper helps to focus his attention on audition unless he is totally deaf. Whispered and voiced sounds are homophenous. If the child with useful residual hearing focuses to an undue extent on speechreading, he will not be able to differentiate between whispered and voiced speech patterns. Further, as we shall see when discussing voice pitch, the whisper may be used to prevent the development of habitual falsetto voice. Third, the breath-grouping of up to four syllables differing in vocal intensity helps to foster the development of feedforward processes relating to intake and expenditure of breath such as are required in running speech. Additionally, work on vocal intensity as described above ensures the tonic condition of the intrinsic laryngeal musculature essential to the regulation of vocal pitch.

Teaching Strategies: Vocal Intensity: Differentiation of voice levels may have developed, at least in part, in the course of previous training during which vocalization and control over its duration have been established. If so, then the task at this level may only involve reinforcement of the desired behaviors. If not, then strategies such as those outlined below may be employed.

Subskill 1: Production of brief, loud utterances. Brief, loud utterances can be encouraged through such games as "waking up the teacher." In this game the teacher pretends to sleep and will open her eyes only when the child produces a sufficiently loud voice. The notion of what is required can be developed through imitation. Similarly, voice-operated or hand-switched toys can be employed so that they function only when the child's voice reaches the required level. The child may be trained at this stage to raise his voice as the distance between himself and the listener is increased.

Subskill 2: Production of brief, quiet utterances. It is assumed that the child will have learned to produce normally quiet voice during previous training. The advance to be made with this subskill is to produce quiet voice in contrast to loud voice. Strategies such as those described for the previous subskill may be employed. Thus, the teacher may "stay asleep" while the child vocalizes or babbles with a quiet voice and "wake up" only to loud utterances. The notion that the child can exercise some control over people in his life through vocalization is an important aspect of such play.

Subskill 3: Production of whispered speech. Even children whose hearing does not extend beyond 1,000 Hz can hear a forced whisper if their hearing aids have sufficient gain and if the microphone is close to the speaker's mouth. A whisper at three inches from the microphone is as intense as a shout from a few yards. This is because intensity is reduced by about six decibels with every doubling of distance between the microphone and the speaker. The simplest strategy for developing whispered speech is imitation through the use of residual hearing. Children who have insufficient residual hearing to learn through imitation involving audition may be taught to whisper through the use of touch. Blowing out a flame or producing a breath stream that can be felt by the hand in the absence of vibration will readily yield an adequate whisper.

Subskill 4: Production of loud, quiet, or whispered utterances of at least three seconds' duration. This subskill requires the integration of two sets of previously developed behaviors, one relating to voice level and the other to vocal duration. The strategies employed in teaching these sets of behaviors separately can be modified to encourage the child to maintain a given voice level for the required duration. For example, the child can "make the teacher walk" a given distance only if the voice level (loud, quiet, or whisper) is maintained, or a hand-switched toy can be made to operate only so long as a particular level of voice is produced.

Subskill 5: Production on one breath of a series of vocalizations varying in intensity. The purpose in developing this subskill is to coordinate vocal cord abduction-adduction with the release of breath. More breath is required for whispering than for voicing. Hence, this subskill also calls for differential regulation of transglottal flow. This subskill may be considered as being acquired when both whispered and voiced sounds can be produced on one breath. A strategy which rapidly leads to production of sounds at different levels on one breath involves the teacher's placing a candy under one of three cups, rotating the cups while the child is watching, and then pointing to each cup in turn, asking the child to indicate—by using different levels of voice—which cup hides the candy. For the empty cups the child would whisper, for example, [bʌbʌbʌbʌ], and for the cup which hides the candy, he would voice this pattern (or vice versa). If all syllables are not produced on one breath, the strategy is begun again. If the child is correct, he wins the candy. Alternatively, the child can play at being a tiger stalking his prey (another child). While stalking, he whispers and when pouncing, he shouts. Only if he touches his prey while voicing does he get to "keep" his prey. Other "tag" games can also be adapted.

Subskills Relating to Vocal Pitch: The target behavior required for satisfactory completion of Stage 2 is the production of three vocalizations on one breath, each at a discrete pitch in a range of at least eight semitones. The subskills underlying this target behavior include the production of:

1. discrete vocalizations on separate breaths, approximating the highest and lowest points in the desired vocal range;
2. vocalizations continuously varying in pitch between these two points (low-high, high-low);
3. discrete vocalizations, on separate breaths, approximating the high, low, and mid points in this range;
4. vocalizations continuously varying between the high, mid, and low points in the child's pitch range (high-mid, mid-high, low-mid, mid-low);
5. discrete vocalizations on one breath, approximating each of the three established points (high-mid-low, low-mid-high, mid-low-high, and mid-high-low), independently varying in vocal intensity.

Concurrently with training in later stages, the child should be taught to make increasingly finer pitch adjustments so that at least simple tunes can be sung. Moreover, the subskills taught in Stage 2 should be integrated with all further aspects of training. Thus, each vowel and syllable should be produced over the established range of vocal pitch in order to ensure independent laryngeal and articulatory control and a requisite level of automaticity. If the child's attention to pitch adversely affects his sustained production of a vowel, his repeated production of a vowel, or his repeated production of a syllable, then sufficient automatic control of target production has not been established and further training at the phonetic level is indicated. Once control of voice pitch has been acquired at the phonetic level, the child should be encouraged to use pitch variation in his phonologic speech so that his utterances accord with the intonation contours typical of the spoken language of his community.

Teaching Strategies: Vocal Pitch: Control of vocal pitch is most readily acquired by the child if residual hearing is used to the fullest possible extent. Many children with adequate residual hearing for the acquisition of pitch control fail to acquire pitch because their hearing aids do not provide adequate gain below 300 Hz. As already noted in our discussion of mechanisms underlying voice control, pitch change requires that compensatory adjustments are made to hold vocal intensity constant. Both pitch and loudness can be simultaneously processed through hearing, whereas through touch their interaction is confusing (see Chapters 3 and 4). Voice pitch has no direct visual correlate except perhaps movement of the larynx in speakers who have a prominent thyroid cartilage (Adam's apple). Visual aids may be used to indicate F_0 (Anderson, 1960; Holbrook and Crawford, 1970; Pickett, 1971), but all except the most complex of such instruments register voice pitch without reference to vocal intensity. Thus, tactile or visual training relating to pitch may encourage pitch change only in the context of proportional changes in vocal intensity. Too easily, then, the child who makes no use of his own or the teacher's auditory system may acquire the notion that "high" equals "loud" and "low" equals "quiet." Therefore, if tactile or visual aids are used to monitor voice pitch, they should be regarded only as a supplement to the ear, which is a far better analyzer than most current alternatives.

All subskills relating to vocal pitch require that the child control the tension of the vocal cords while they are adducted. Haycock (1918) suggested that most hearing-impaired children vary the tension on the vocal cords and hence modify voice pitch spontaneously in relation to their emotional state at the time of speaking. He further suggested that such variability could be used as a basis for the development of voluntary pitch control. We concur. Thus, an active, exciting environment will encourage the child to produce sounds varying in pitch. If patterns produced are differentially reinforced ("That's a high voice. Good! Do it again." etc.), production of varied pitch can be brought under voluntary control.

Habitual use of monotonous voice usually indicates that the environment has not been sufficiently stimulating, that the child is not using residual hearing to the full, that he has not been provided with sufficient speech models which vary in pitch, that he has not been adequately encouraged to vocalize freely, or that he has not been systematically reinforced for producing varied voice patterns. An informal, active approach which features all the conditions mentioned above is essential to the natural development of voice pitch control. More formal methods such as those described below should, except for the totally deaf child, be considered only as supplementary teaching strategies.

Subskill 1: Production of discrete vocalizations on separate breaths, approximating the highest and lowest points in the desired vocal range. Since hearing is the best method of monitoring pitch change, the child should first be asked to identify high-pitched and low-pitched voice produced by the teacher. The reference points selected should differ by at least eight semitones. A high-pitched voice may be associated with a hand stretched high above the head, and a low-pitched voice with a hand lowered well below waist level. When the child can identify the pitch of the teacher's voice correctly with visual cues, he should then be trained to identify pitch through residual hearing alone. Children with a considerable amount of residual hearing may be expected to master the task quite rapidly and to imitate the teacher if successful auditory identification of "high" and "low" voice is systematically reinforced. Very few children are too deaf to acquire pitch control through audition if hearing aids with extended low-frequency response are used. Some may, however, imitate pitch patterns only if they are first taught to change the tension on the vocal cords and to modify subglottal pressure. There are several strategies through which children with little or no hearing can be taught these adjustments.

One of the strategies which may be used to decrease pitch is to lower the chin toward the chest and relax the arms and shoulders. The procedure reduces tension on the vocal cords and increases their mass. If the child's attention is focused on the acoustic quality of the vocalization produced during this activity, the body and head movements can be reduced while the required voice pitch is maintained. Once the child can produce a low-pitched voice with ease, he can be asked to alternate vocalizations having "low" and "medium" pitch. The laryngeal sensations arising from such alternation will usually provide the child with enough information to deduce how to go further and to make the necessary laryngeal adjustments which result in higher-than-normal pitch. Usually, the higher-than-normal pitch will initially be accompanied by head-raising and neck-stretching, extraneous behaviors which—once pitch change has been produced—should not be allowed to persist.

A decrease in the pitch of voice can also be produced by a more direct strategy: namely, by placing pressure on the thyroid cartilage. The action again decreases tension on the vocal cords and increases their mass. The procedure need not be objectionable and can be carried out by the child himself. Oscillating the pitch of voice by alternating pressure on the thyroid cartilage makes a normal voice resemble the quavering production typical of an older person. Children, including hearing-impaired children, often enjoy impersonation and find voice oscillation fun. The procedure may also help to obtain variable pitch control from children who habitually use the chest register but produce only monotonous voice.

The disadvantage of this strategy is that it imposes voice pitch change on the child. Even when the child himself presses on his throat there is a passive adjustment of the larynx. Hence, there is less intrinsic sensation from which the child may learn to make the necessary adjustments in the absence of external pressure. The only way that a child can learn to modi-

fy voice pitch satisfactorily is by making the necessary adjustments in vocal cord tension and subglottal pressure through proprioceptive sensation
arising in the larynx itself. For this reason, the strategy described below
may be more effective than that in the preceding paragraph.

If the child has no useful residual hearing, or if he cannot initially modify voice pitch without tactile cues, he may be asked to feel the upward
and downward motion of the teacher's larynx as she alternately produces
a high and a low voice; then, through feeling his own larynx, he can
attempt to match the laryngeal movement. Success in this will certainly
produce pitch change in the desired direction and will also yield the proprioceptive sensation required for controlled pitch variation even in the
absence of residual audition.

Once the child has been taught to vary pitch of voice through the sense
of touch, then every effort should be made to have him monitor pitch
change through hearing. Many children who cannot initially imitate the
teacher's pitch of voice through hearing prior to tactile intervention can
do so following such training. Whether the child can hear pitch change or
not, extensive practice is required to ensure that the orosensory-motor
patterns which underlie controlled pitch production become firmly established. Visual pitch indicators are useful only when the child can change
the pitch of his voice. In other words, they may help a child to monitor
pitch changes when they are produced, but they cannot teach him how to
effect such changes in the first place. Visual pitch indicators that simply
show whether or not the child has produced the intended target on a giv-
en trial are advantageous once some ability to modify pitch has been acquired. Visual displays that provide moment-by-moment information are
not recommended, since irrelevant changes in such displays tend to distract the child's attention, or provide reinforcement for random vocal behavior. They do little to foster the feedforward control of pitch that we
seek to develop.

*Subskill 2: Production of vocalizations continuously varying in pitch between the
lowest and highest points in the child's vocal range.* This subskill can be developed satisfactorily only when high and low points in the vocal range have
been established. A smooth, continuous excursion from low to high or
high to low is difficult to perceive through touching the larynx, though it
may be heard by most children and visually indicated in a variety of
ways. For example, the teacher may indicate the rate and smoothness of
the desired pitch excursion by representing it graphically or by raising or
lowering her hand. If the child does not succeed in effecting a smooth
transition from one pitch to another, this too can be indicated by some
type of visual feedback.

Voice breaks occasionally occur when this subskill is first attempted.
Such breaks tend to take place if the low point in the child's vocal range
has been established in the chest register and the high point is a falsetto.
Even if this is not the case, they may occur as pitch is raised, as it is lowered, or both. When breaks occur in only one direction, the teacher

should initially work at establishing control in the other. When control has been established in one direction, pitch breaks in the other are less likely to occur. It may be assumed that the child has adequate control when he is able to vary the pitch of voice smoothly from the highest to the lowest point in the vocal range, both rapidly (in one second) and slowly (over three seconds). If pitch breaks persist, then reference points lower in pitch should be established.

Subskill 3: Production of discrete vocalizations on separate breaths, approximating the high, low, and mid points in the child's vocal range. The most appropriate strategies for teaching this subskill are similar to those described for teaching Subskill 1. If possible, the child should first be trained to discriminate auditorily between three vocalizations varying in pitch (high, mid, low) and then to identify the order in which the teacher produces any set of the three vocalizations (high-low-mid, mid-low-high, etc.). The three vocalizations may be represented visually: for example, by three wood-block towers of differing height to which the child may point and thereby identify the stimulus pattern presented. When the child can respond reliably, he should be asked to imitate the model provided by the teacher. Since the child should come to the task with normally pitched vocalization (established at the previous stage) as well as high-pitched and low-pitched voice (established as Subskill 1), he should have no problem in learning this subskill. Children who require tactile cues may be taught this subskill by means of strategies similar to those described for Subskill 1.

Subskill 4: Production of vocalizations continuously varying between the high, mid, and low points in the child's pitch range. This subskill may be developed through reference to previously learned subskills. If tactile or visual cues are necessary, they may be provided, for example, by establishing the child's hand as a referent for low pitch, his elbow for mid pitch, and his shoulder for high pitch. The teacher may touch each in turn to obtain discrete pitch production in the previous subskill, and then—by moving the finger up and down between shoulder, elbow, and hand—she can indicate the direction, rate, and continuity of the pitch change desired. Undesired discontinuity (voice breaks) may be signaled by breaking contact between the teacher's finger and the child's arm. The advantage of using this strategy is that, in the auditory discrimination phase of training, the child can trace the pattern representing what he hears on the teacher's arm while keeping his eyes shut to exclude extraneous visual cues.

Subskill 5: Production of discrete vocalizations on one breath, approximating each of the three established points, independently varying in vocal intensity. The strategy here is first to obtain quiet and loud vocalizations separately at each level of pitch. As soon as distinctly different vocal intensities can be produced at each pitch, various combinations of pitch and intensity (such as quiet + low; loud + high; quiet + high; loud + mid) may be demanded. This subskill requires independent control of laryngeal tension and subglottal pressure of the type required for producing suprasegmental structure in phonologic speech. One may teach the necessary differentiations through the games and subskills already described. For example, in "wake the teacher," the teacher might respond only if the child's voice is loud and low or high and quiet. This subskill usually presents little difficulty because the concepts of loud, quiet, high, and low have already been acquired whether the child has verbal labels for them or not. Of course, complete control of voice pitch will not have been mastered by the child when this subskill has been learned. Further refinement in pitch control will be demanded in later stages.

Remedial Treatment of Deviant Patterns

Deviant patterns in the speech of hearing-impaired children are most likely to occur when too great and too early an emphasis is placed on the development of articulation skills, and when too little attention is paid to obtaining well controlled breath and voice production. If problems affecting resonance and articulation are present, then the first step in remediation is to determine the extent to which they are due to inadequate respiration and phonation. Certain typical errors of production such as intrusive voicing, weak second formant structure in vowels, implosion of stops, prevoicing of stops, failure to make voiced-voiceless distinctions, and insufficient turbulence in the production of fricatives may be due to inadequate control of source energy—breath flow and voice—rather than to articulation errors per se. Thus, a variety of articulatory faults may be treated indirectly through the development of the various subskills already specified in this chapter. Indeed, for the most part, remedial treatment should follow the developmental stages described in this text. Deviant patterns occur mainly because the prerequisite behaviors for development of new skills have not been adequately established or because new skills have not been systematically incorporated into a wide range of phonetic and phonologic contexts.

Breathy Voice

Breathy voice quality, a common characteristic of speech of hearing-impaired children, occurs when there is relatively little tension on the vocal cords, which therefore open and close mainly in response to aerodynamic flow (the Bernouilli force). In this condition, the glottal pulses which resonate the supraglottal cavities have a weak, triangular waveform, and the resulting voice spectrum is weak in upper partials. When more muscle tension is exerted, the vocal cords are less readily parted by subglottal pressure and more readily close in synchrony with the Bernouilli force. The glottis in this latter condition opens for less than half of the vibratory cycle (how much less depends on the degree of muscle force), and the resulting glottal pulses—having a sharper onset-offset time—result in a voice with strong high-frequency components. Whereas the spectrum of breathy voice may have a slope of −16dB/8ve, the spectrum of a stronger voice may have a slope of −10dB/8ve or less. In the latter condition, the upper formants of the vowels will be considerably more audible than when voice is breathy (see Chapter 11).

Breathiness is usually due to failure to approximate the vocal cords firmly, as shown in Figure 11.1, position B. This may be corrected through exercises involving exertion (see above) or games in which the child is led to hold his breath in anticipation of voicing. For example, he may be asked to signal the beginning of a race between two other children through voicing. He holds his breath, with his mouth open ready for voicing, and vocalizes when the teacher signals readiness. The vocal cords, adducted in preparation, will be sufficiently tense for a strong voice to result. Repetition of this and other games requiring such anticipatory adjustments will improve the tonicity of the laryngeal muscles and establish adequate voicing habits. This type of game, which also helps to eradicate habitual release of breath prior to adduction of the vocal cords, should supplement a program in which frequent use of voice is demanded. Most voice problems in hearing-impaired children stem from restricted use of vocalization, and their remediation cannot be effected by exercises alone.

Pharyngeal Tension

Tension of the pharyngeal walls accounts for a considerable proportion of the vocal resonance problems met among hearing-impaired children. Pharyngeal tension tends to inhibit modification of vocal pitch because tension in the pharyngeal structures usually extends to the larynx. It also modifies the shape of the cavity behind the tongue and hence changes the intensity and frequency of the vowel formants. Such tension may be induced through speech exercises involving exertion or may occur in the course of learning to modify vocal pitch through feeling the larynx. Much as the child learning to write may unnecessarily tense groups of muscles in the upper arm, a child learning to control the voice through touch and kinesthesis may unnecessarily involve the pharyngeal structures in his early efforts to vocalize. If the teacher provides adequate opportunity for the child to produce voice freely in play and in the absence of tension the problem will usually take care of itself. If, on the other hand, specific articulation skills are imposed on a child in whom pharyngeal tension is evident, it may become habitual. Because monotonous pitch and pharyngeal tension tend to occur together, work toward establishing an adequate and easily produced range of voice pitch usually results in reduction of the problem.

Vocal Abuse

Vocal abuse occurs when the strain imposed during the act of voicing leads to inflammation and/or structural changes in the larynx. The most common cause of strain in speech is undue laryngeal tension. It may arise through habitually hard glottal attack, through continuation of exercises involving exertion beyond the point where they have served their purpose (see above), through generalized body tension, or through the habitual use of inappropriate voice pitch. Remedial treatment involves establishing new habits of voicing, the most important of which is vocalizing while keeping all but the essential muscle groups relaxed. The teaching of speech should never be undertaken in such a way that the strategy used leads to the child's becoming tense through apprehension. Fun and laughter, during which overall tension is minimal, lead to much more natural voice than fear of failure.

Habitual use of too high a voice pitch induces considerable vocal strain and may cause nodules to form on the vocal cords. Both prevention and treatment call for the child's use of a more appropriate range of voice pitch. Zaliouk (1960) proposed that optimal chest register pitch should be established by having the child produce vibration over the whole facial mask during the production of [m]. Rozanska (1966) counseled that the child should feel the voice in the chest rather than in the head or face. Providing that the vibration during [m] is tangible in the bones of both the nose and the chin, we find, as Zaliouk suggested, that voice F_0 falls in about the center of the pitch range appropriate for the speaker. Adjusting the voice so that it may be continually felt in the chest may produce too low a pitch and hence an alternative source of strain.

Feeling vibration of the voice in the chest may serve as reinforcement for correct production of a low-pitched sound, but only rarely does it succeed in eliciting the desired voice pitch in the first place. The strategy is usually effective only when the child can, but does not, use a range of pitch patterns. Absence of vibration in the chest merely indicates to the child who can only produce falsetto voice, for example, that his production is not what is required. Like holding a cold mirror under the nose to indicate—through its steaming up—that unwanted nasal emis-

sion is present, the procedure clearly demonstrates the child's in-
adequacy but does nothing to indicate what steps the child should take
to remedy the defect.

Falsetto Voice

Falsetto voice (Figure 11.1, position D) is commonly acquired and habitually used by children who have no residual hearing or make no use
of what hearing they have. Falsetto defects are quite easily prevented
by making full use of low-frequency audition. If no useful residual hearing is present, acquisition of the fault may be avoided by developing
skill in the rapid alternation of voiced and unvoiced sounds at a phonetic level and by the use of phonologic level speech at approximately normal rates. To produce falsetto voice, one must first approximate the vocal cords (Figure 11.1, position B) and then tense them to a much greater
extent than is required for chest register vocalization. These adjustments take considerable time—time that is simply not available to the
child who has been encouraged to use both voiced and unvoiced
sounds in speech habitually produced at a normal or near-normal rate.

For the remediation of falsetto voice, we recommend measures similar to those suggested for its prevention: the rapid alternation of voiced
and unvoiced sounds and the establishment of a normal rate of speech
production. In essence, the problem underlying falsetto production is
one of unnecessary laryngeal tension during voicing. The child whose
use of falsetto voice is habitual may be resistant to learning speech without laryngeal tension. As an intermediate step, we may therefore introduce a type of speech which involves a different kind of laryngeal
tension: the forced whisper.

In forced whispering the vocal cords are adjusted as shown in Figure
11.1, position C. Whispering of this type involves as much tension as
the falsetto voice; but before any other position of the vocal cords can be
adopted following a forced whisper, they must be relaxed. Once the
child has achieved mastery of the forced whisper and can maintain it for
several utterances, he can be expected to produce a string of syllables of
which, say, four out of five are forcefully whispered and only one—the
second, third, or fourth syllable on the string—is voiced. If the whispered syllables are produced with sufficient force and at a rate of four to
five syllables per second, a natural chest register will be achieved on the
one voiced syllable. The number of voiced syllables may be gradually
increased only when a relaxed chest register voice has been consistently
achieved and reinforced. It is important that the child's acquisition of
the new pitch target is, as far as possible, error-free. This permits the

sensory-motor components of relaxed voicing to become thoroughly familiar to the child. Only when these components are familiar can relaxed voicing in a less restricted context be expected.

Another method of inhibiting falsetto voice and initiating chest register production is to raise the head so that the neck is stretched backwards. Although this procedure tends to raise the voice during chest register production, it renders falsetto almost impossible. Since the tension on the vocal cords during falsetto is at maximum in a face-forward position, the same degree of tension cannot be maintained while raising the head. Accordingly, a greater degree of laryngeal muscle relaxation is forced upon the child. However, there is an advantage in deriving a natural, chest register voice from the forced whisper rather than from change in head position: no physical manipulation is imposed on the child. Although the desired sensory-motor control can be developed through manipulative procedures, it is more likely to result through the use of techniques which require the child's active participation in the realization of the target behavior (see Chapter 3).

Voice Patterns in Phonologic Speech

The production of speech patterns in relation to time largely determines their intelligibility and governs their natural quality. This is as true at the sentence level as at the phoneme level. English is commonly regarded as a stress-timed language. Thus, in the sentence, "The boy went down the road to the park," the words *boy*, *road*, and *park* receive stress and the intervals between these words tend to be of similar duration. This timing pattern, discussed by Pike (1945) and by Abercrombie (1967), among many others, requires that unstressed words, syllables, and phonemes lying between stress points be changed in duration to fit the overall pattern. In the above sentence, for example, three syllables occur between *boy* and *road* as compared with two between *road* and *park*; accordingly, more time is available for the phonemes present in the second group of unstressed words than for those in the first.

This type of timing is not found in all languages. French is syllable-timed rather than stress-timed and hence has a quite different rhythm. Martin (1972) suggests that the rhythmic structure of English speech, which is created by giving salience to the most important words in a sentence, provides an essential link between production and perception of a message. Thus, the speaker, in providing rhythmic stress, allows the listener to predict the locus of the next highly informative unit of an utterance. The adjustments in duration required to achieve rhythmic stress are principally achieved through modifying the degree to which adjacent sounds are coarticulated (Lindblom, 1965).

Stress-timing alone does not determine the relative length of a speech sound in an utterance. The number of syllables in a phrase and the position of the sound in relation to a linguistic boundary also influence the duration of sounds in normal speech. Thus, the duration of a vowel in a word of two syllables is normally about 70% of the duration it would assume in a monosyllable. In words of more than two syllables, the duration of the vowel might be as little as 50% of its normal monosyllabic duration (Barnwell, 1971). The duration of a consonant such as [s] can similarly be affected by the number of syllables in an utterance (Klatt, 1974). Further, sounds in words immediately preceding a pause all tend to expand in duration (Lehiste, 1972). Although stress-timing influences are present in the speech of very young normally hearing children, the effects of utterance length on phoneme duration appear only gradually in their speech from about 6 years of age (DiSimoni, 1974).

Duration in relation to pause and disjuncture is also important in speech. Fine differences in the spacing of words and syllables serve as a cue to the grammatical construction of an utterance to much the same extent as do contrastive stress and intonation contour (Bolinger and Gerstman, 1957). Disjunctures at the sentence level are relatively gross, and one should attempt to develop them as soon as two or more words are combined. Quite subtle disjunctures occur at word and syllable levels and their accurate incorporation into the child's speech cannot be expected to occur before the final stage of acquisition has been almost completely mastered.

Bolinger (1964) did not regard intonation as being crucial to communication; he pointed out that if it were, we should not be able to understand anyone who speaks in a monotone. This is like saying that voicing is not crucial to communication because we can understand whispered speech. Much as vocal cord vibration and its absence are normally used to contrast such words as *pat* and *bat*, so too is intonation usually used to contrast questions and statements and to clarify or emphasize meaning at the phrase and sentence levels. To the extent that intonation carries information provided in parallel by the segmental stream, it is redundant; but this is not the case when intonation may be used to modify the meaning of an utterance.

The role of intonation in the acquisition of language has received relatively little attention. Voice patterns that vary in pitch are normally used well before words are learned (Bever, Fodor, and Weksel, 1965; Kaplan, 1969), and they appear to facilitate acquisition of both speech reception and speech production skills (Smith and Goodenough, 1971).

Intonation patterns apparently provide a framework within which the segmental components can be better remembered (Blasdell and Jensen, 1970), aid in the segmentation of an utterance, and indicate underlying grammatical construction and semantic content (Lieberman, 1967). Voice produced at an optimum pitch for the speaker and with intonation is far more pleasant to listen to than speech which is poorly pitched and monotonous, probably because it carries more information on the personal qualities of the speaker (Greene, 1972). Most hearing-impaired children can be trained to modulate the pitch of voice, and many can learn to sing in tune (Presto, 1943; Rooney, 1944).

Summary

This chapter defines target behaviors involved in vocalization and in the production of nonsegmental voice patterns as depicted in the first two stages of our model of speech acquisition. Subskills which underlie these target behaviors are specified, and examples of strategies that might be used to teach them are provided.

We show that the acoustic properties of vocalization and of nonsegmental voice patterns are such that they should be audible to all except totally deaf children if appropriate hearing aids are worn. The teaching strategies suggested therefore emphasize the use of residual hearing supplemented, if necessary, by tactile and visual cues. The need to develop vocalization informally and through play rather than through formal teaching strategies is stressed, and it is suggested that, at best, formal work can only augment component skills acquired within the framework of an informal approach. Finally, we suggest a range of strategies that might be used in the remedial treatment of deviant voice patterns commonly present in the speech of hearing-impaired children.

REFERENCES

Abercrombie, D. *Elements of General Phonetics*. Chicago: Aldine Publishing Co., 1967.

Anderson, F. An experimental pitch indicator for training deaf scholars. *J. Acoust. Soc. Am.*, 32, 1065–1074, 1960.

Baer, D. M., & Sherman, J. A. Reinforcement control of generalized imitation in young children. *J. Exp. Child. Psychol.*, 1, 37–49, 1964.

Barnwell, T. P. *An algorithm for segment durations in reading machine context*. Research Laboratory of Electronics, M.I.T., No. 479, Cambridge, Mass., 1971.

Bever, T. G., Fodor, J. A., & Weksel, W. Theoretical notes on the acquisition of syntax: A critique of 'contextual generalization'. *Psychol. Rev.*, 72, 467–482, 1965.

Blasdell, R., & Jensen, P.   Stress and word position as determinants of imitation in first-language learners. *J. Speech Hear. Res.*, 13, 193–202, 1970.

Bolinger, D. L.   Around the edge of language: Intonation. *Harvard Educ. Rev.*, 34, 282–296, 1964.

Bolinger, D. L., & Gerstman, L. J.   Disjuncture as a cue to constructs. *Word*, 13, 246–255, 1957.

DiSimoni, F. G.   Influence of utterance length upon bilabial closure duration for /p/ in three-, six- and nine-year-old children. *J. Acoust. Soc. Am.*, 55, 1353–1354, 1974.

Fry, D. B.   Experiments in the perception of stress. *Lang. Speech*, 1, 126–152, 1958.

Gray, G. W., & Wise, C. M.   *The Bases of Speech*. New York: Harper, 1959.

Greene, M. C. L.   *Disorders of Voice*. Indianapolis: Bobbs-Merrill Co., 1972.

Haycock, G. S.   The development of pitch in the voice of congenitally deaf children. *Volta Rev.*, 20, 258–261, 1918.

Holbrook, A., & Crawford, G. H.   Modification of vocal frequency and intensity in the speech of the deaf. *Volta Rev.*, 72, 492–497, 1970.

Kaplan, E. L.   *The role of intonation in the acquisition of language.* Unpublished Ph.D. diss., Cornell University, 1969.

Klatt, D.   The duration of [s] in English words. *J. Speech Hear. Res.*, 17, 51–63, 1974.

Lach, R., Ling, D., Ling, A. H., & Ship, N.   Early speech development in deaf infants. *Am. Ann. Deaf*, 115, 522–526, 1970.

Lehiste, I.   The timing of utterances and linguistic boundaries. *J. Acoust. Soc. Am.*, 51, 2018–2024, 1972.

Lieberman, P.   *Intonation, Perception and Language*. Cambridge, Mass.: M.I.T. Press, 1967.

Lindblom, B. E. F.   Dynamic aspects of vowel articulation. *In Proc. 5th Int. Congr. Phonetic Sciences, Muenster, 1964*. New York: Karger, 1965, pp. 387–388.

Martin, J. G.   Rhythmic (hierarchical) versus serial structure in speech and other behavior. *Psychol. Rev.*, 79, 487–509, 1972.

Pickett, J. M.   Speech science research and speech communication for the deaf. In L. E. Connor (Ed.), *Speech for the Deaf Child: Knowledge and Use*. Washington, D.C.: A. G. Bell Assoc. for the Deaf, 1971.

Pike, K. L.   *The Intonation of American English*. Ann Arbor, Michigan: University of Michigan Press, 1945.

Presto, M.   An experiment in voice control. *Volta Rev.*, 45, 490–493, 1943.

Ramey, C. T., & Watson, J. S.   Nonsocial reinforcement of infants' vocalizations. *Dev. Psychol.*, 6, 538, 1972.

Rheingold, H. L., Gewirtz, J. L., & Ross, H. W.   Social conditioning of vocalizations in the infant. *J. Comp. Physiol. Psychol.*, 52, 68–73, 1959.

Rooney, A. G.   Voice work for the young deaf child. *Volta Rev.*, 46, 558–560, passim, 1944.

Rozanska, E. v. D.   An approach to teaching speech to the deaf. *Volta Rev.*, 68, 758–761, 1966.

Schwartz, A., Rosenberg, D., & Brackbill, Y.   Analysis of the components of social reinforcement of infant vocalization. *Psychonomic Sci.*, 20, 323–325, 1970.

Smith, F., & Goodenough, C.   Effects of context, intonation and voice on the reaction time to sentences. *Lang. Speech*, 14, 241–250, 1971.

Todd, G. A., & Palmer, B.   Social reinforcement of infant babbling. *Child Dev.*, 39, 591–596, 1968.

Zaliouk, A.   Falsetto voice in deaf children. *Curr. Probl. Phoniatr. Logop.*, 1, 217–226, 1960.

/13/

Vowels
and
Diphthongs

Vowels are formed when sound produced at the glottal source—voice, whisper, or breathy voice—is selectively filtered and resonated in the vocal tract. The spectrograms shown as Figure 13.1 illustrate the characteristics of the vowel [ɛ] when it is produced with each of these three types of glottal energy. When the vowel is voiced, the periodic opening and closing of the glottis gives rise to a series of harmonics which appear on the left spectrogram as horizontal bars. Those harmonics enhanced by resonance in the vocal tract (the darker lines) show the formant frequency values. In this case the frequency of F_1 falls at about 850 Hz, that of F_2 at about 2,000 Hz, and that of F_3 at about 2,700 Hz. When the vowel is whispered, the glottis, instead of vibrating, causes the transglottal air flow to become turbulent. The sound associated with such turbulence is aperiodic, a random mixture of many frequencies. Those sounds resonated by the vocal tract are enhanced, and they also appear as formants on the center spectrogram. Because the vocal tract configurations for the voiced and whispered [ɛ] are similar, the formants are also similar. When breathy voice is used, there is both a periodic and a turbulent source of energy, and a vowel sharing the properties of both the voiced and the whispered [ɛ] occurs. As shown in the spectrogram at the right, it has features in common with both its voiced and whispered counterparts because the source energy has been filtered or resonated by a similarly shaped vocal tract.

The shape of the vocal tract is affected by all speech organs—the larynx, pharynx, velum, palate, cheeks, jaw, tongue, and lips—but those that are principally responsible for creating the cavities and apertures that govern vowel formant structure are the tongue and the lips. They

220

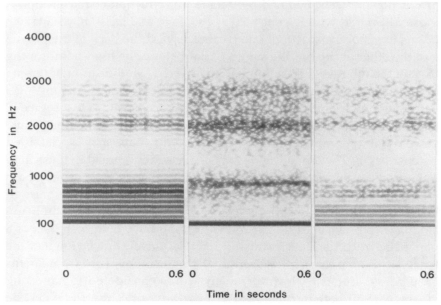

Figure 13.1

Spectrograms of the vowel [ɛ] spoken by the writer showing: left, the voiced vowel which has strong harmonic structure; center, the whispered vowel which has no harmonic structure; and, right, a breathy-voiced vowel which has both periodic and aperiodic characteristics.

are the most mobile of the several structures involved, the more so because they can also be moved passively by raising or lowering the jaw. In the production of the 15 vowels and four diphthongs which are most commonly encountered in English and with which we shall deal in this text, movements of the tongue and lips are correlated. As the constriction produced by the tongue increases and moves toward the front of the mouth for the vowels [æ], [ɛ], [e], [ɪ], and [i], so are the lips slightly spread. As the tongue is elevated toward the back of the mouth for the vowels [a], [ɔ], [o], [ʊ], and [u], so are the lips increasingly rounded.

The most crucial variable in vowel production is the point at which the tongue creates the greatest degree of constriction in the vocal tract. For most vowels this is the highest point in the tongue's profile during steady-state production. The exceptions are the back vowels such as [o] and [ɔ] where the constriction may be greater in the pharynx than between the tongue's highest point and the palate. However, if vowels are taught with the tip of the tongue resting on or near the lower front teeth, raising the appropriate part of the tongue to the required height with the adequate muscular tension will usually result in their correct production. Vowels modified by tongue tip retraction or retroflexion—those associated with [r], such as [ɝ], [ɚ], [ar], and [ɔr]—may have two points of major constriction: one created toward the back of the tongue and the other at the tip. We suggest establishing the high point for the back of the tongue with the tongue tip lowered. Modification of tongue tip position may be introduced following production of [r] later on.

Certain vowels may also be differentiated according to the degree of tension intrinsic to the tongue and jaw during their production. Thus, vowels that have similar tongue height and lip shape may be classified as tense or lax. The tongue tends to be more widely spread in tense than in lax vowels, and in phonologic speech tense vowels are usually both louder and longer than their lax counterparts. The tense-lax pairs in English are [i] - [ɪ], [e] - [ɛ], [u] - [ʊ], [ʌ] - [ə], and [ɝ] - [ɚ]. In many languages the tense-lax dimension is unimportant, both members of a pair being regarded as variants of a single vowel; but in English the tense-lax dimension is often used to distinguish one word from another: e.g., *beet* from *bit*. However, many words considered to have long vowels contain both members of the tense-lax pair. Thus, *spoon* may be pronounced as /spun/ or /spʊun/ and *key* may acceptably be said as /ki/ or /kɪi/ (Raphael and Bell-Berti, 1975).

The formant frequencies of a vowel will vary according to the size of the vocal tract, particularly its length; but the relative shape of the vocal tract, and hence the overall form of the acoustic pattern, will be similar for all speakers. Thus, whether the speaker is a man, a woman, or a child, the highest point reached by the tongue will be high in the back of the mouth for [u] and high in the front of the mouth for [i]. Accordingly, the first two formants of [u] will both be in the low-frequency range while those of [i] will be widely spaced, F_1 low and F_2 high. Ladefoged and Broadbent (1957) considered that a listener establishes formant values for a given vowel by a normalization process involving reference to a speaker's pronunciation of other vowels in the first few syllables of an utterance. To use a visual analogy, the average person would deduce that the symbol "*1*" is a numeral in the series *123* and a letter in the word *1ove* simply by reference to the other symbols in the set. Once the nature of the symbol has been deduced, it matters little whether the written form is small or large, thin or fat, upright or sloping. Similarly, once a normal listener has established reference points for a speaker's formant structure, vowels may be pronounced quietly, loudly, or in a whisper, at close range or at a distance, without much risk of identification error. Lieberman (1973) suggests that the listener uses the vowels [i], [a], and [u] and the semivowels [j] and [w] as a means of "calibrating" the size of the speaker's vocal tract, but Studdert-Kennedy (1975) suggests that normalization may call for such vowels in a consonant environment. The normalization process in vowel recognition as it relates either to a hearing-impaired person's auditory recognition of others' speech or to a normally hearing person's discrimination of speech produced by hearing-impaired subjects has not been directly studied.

Vocal tract configuration is rarely static in everyday speech, and a speaker may not make identical articulatory adjustments for a particular vowel even in saying the same word twice. Indeed, if the same word is said in two different contexts, two distinctly different pronunciations are apt to result. Nevertheless, each skilled speaker is likely to have developed an articulatory target—an ideal—for each vowel whether that target is reached on a given occasion or not. The extent to which "ideal" vowel targets are approached in the context of consonants depends on the consonants employed (Lindblom and Studdert-Kennedy, 1967) and on the extent to which the vowel receives stress (Mermelstein, 1973). There is relatively little variability or overlap in formant structure when vowels are sustained (Peterson, 1952). The sustaining of vowels, therefore, provides optimum opportunity for the hearing-impaired child to establish auditory awareness of them and to acquire the orosensory-motor patterns that underlie their adequate production.

Unless "ideal" vowel targets are established through sustained production, severely hearing-impaired children can have no concept of a reference point toward which the tongue and other articulators should be moved or of the position at which they should be maintained if steady-state production is called for in a particular speech context. Without such a concept, hearing-impaired children tend to neutralize all vowels (Angelocci, Kopp, and Holbrook, 1964). Those which tend to be neutralized most are the front vowels (Mangan, 1961). In these, the tongue plays a more crucial role than the lips. Of course, a tendency toward neutralization exists in normal speech, and the schwa [ə] may legitimately be substituted for most vowels in certain unstressed syllables. The tendency reaches the point of abnormality if the schwa is the principal vowel used: for example, if /ə/ rather than /ɪ/ is employed as a substitute for /i/, and if every vowel is begun or terminated with the tongue in a neutral position so that all vowels become diphthongized.

Diphthongs

A diphthong results when two vowels are produced as a glide. In slow speech the two vowels may be produced as steady-state portions of the diphthong, but at normal speaking rates neither vowel is distinctly produced since the tongue and lips move continuously through-out the diphthong. It is merely a convenient fiction to label a diphthong in terms of its two component vowels. For example, both the [a] and the [ɪ] may be identified when [aɪ] occurs in slow speech, but in fast speech the tongue may not start from an [a] position and may frequently under-shoot the [ɪ] target. This is irrelevant to the listener, who knows from the audible glide that it is a diphthong and can identify which diph-thong was intended from the direction and rate of formant frequency change (Gay, 1968, 1970). In producing a diphthong in a stressed posi-tion the tongue may overshoot its target. For instance, instead of [aɪ], the speaker may actually say [ai]; and instead of [aʊ], he may say [au]. In short, when diphthongs occupy stressed positions, a tense rather than a lax component vowel may be produced.

The difference between one dialect and another is due mainly to dif-ferences in the way vowels and diphthongs are used. For example, most American speakers pronounce the word *basin* as /beɪsn̩/ or /besn̩/, whereas most Australians pronounce it as /baɪsn̩/; and while speakers in the northern U.S. employ a single vowel in most short words such as *can*, speakers born in the southern states more frequently employ a diphthong. Most of the basic vowels and diphthongs discussed in this chapter occur in all dialects of English. Variations according with local usage should be encouraged so that the child's pronunciation conforms to that of his community.

Articulatory Targets and Formant Values

The approximate positions assumed by the principal speech organs during the production of each vowel are summarized in Table 13.A. This table indicates the position of the tongue when it is arched to its highest point in the mouth, the disposition of the lips, the extent to which the jaw is raised or lowered, and the relative tension intrinsic to the musculature. Additionally, Table 13.A shows the typical center fre-quency of the first two formants of each vowel as produced by a child. (The frequency values shown are estimates derived mainly from data reported by Peterson and Barney, 1952.)

No table or figure can adequately indicate the three-dimensional shaping of the vocal tract or convey the dynamic nature of vowel pro-duction. For this reason we avoid showing diagrams that, without ex-tensive explanation, may mislead the reader. We consider the data pre-sented in Table 13.A to be an adequate guide to the teacher in devel-oping vowels, providing that:

1. she ensures that the child's tongue tip rests on or near the lower

TABLE 13.A

Approximate speech organ adjustments and children's formant frequency values for vowel target behaviors.*
Targets arranged in accordance with teaching steps recommended in Chapters 8 and 9.

Step 1 Vowels	[a]	[i]	[u]
Tongue arching	low-central	high-front	high-back
Lips	neutral	neutrally spread	rounded
Jaw	open	close	close
Musculature	lax	tense	tense
Formants (Hz)	$F_1 = 1{,}020$, $F_2 = 1{,}750$	$F_1 = 370$, $F_2 = 3{,}200$	$F_1 = 430$, $F_2 = 1{,}170$

Step 2 Vowels	[ɔ]	[ɛ]	[ʊ]	[I]
Tongue arching	mid-back	mid-front	high-back	high-front
Lips	slightly rounded	neutral	rounded	neutrally spread
Jaw	open	mid-close	close	close
Musculature	tense	lax	lax	lax
Formants (Hz)	$F_1 = 840$, $F_2 = 1{,}060$	$F_1 = 690$, $F_2 = 2{,}610$	$F_1 = 540$, $F_2 = 1{,}410$	$F_1 = 530$, $F_2 = 2{,}730$

Step 3 Vowels	[æ]	[ʌ]	[ɑ]	[o]	[e]
Tongue arching	low-front	low-central	low-back	mid-back	mid-front
Lips	neutral	neutral	neutral	rounded	neutral
Jaw	open	mid-close	open	mid-close	mid-close
Musculature	lax	tense	lax	tense	tense
Formants (Hz)	$F_1 = 1{,}010$, $F_2 = 2{,}320$	$F_1 = 850$, $F_2 = 1{,}590$	$F_1 = 1{,}030$, $F_2 = 1{,}370$	$F_1 = 760$, $F_2 = 1{,}250$	$F_1 = 610$, $F_2 = 2{,}680$

Step 4 Vowels	[ɜ]	[a]	[ɚ]	[ɝ]
Tongue arching	mid-central	low-central	mid-central	mid-central
Lips	neutral	neutral	neutral	neutral
Jaw	mid-close	mid-close	mid-close	mid-close
Musculature	tense	lax	lax	tense
Formants	$F_1 = 560$, $F_2 = 1{,}820$	$F_1 = 600$, $F_2 = 1{,}680$	$F_1 = 580$, $F_2 = 1{,}740$	

*Diphthong targets may be specified relative to their component vowels.

225

front teeth for all vowels except those associated with [r] and that the velum is raised during the production of all vowels;

2. by feeling the movements and position assumed by her own tongue in vowel production, she becomes thoroughly familiar with how it is arched for each vowel so that, through mimicry of the child's speech, she is able to identify how the child is forming the vowel he produces;

3. she develops the various subskills underlying each vowel as described later in this chapter;

4. she discourages exaggeration (The teeth should not be more than a centimeter apart when the jaw is "open").

However, the teacher who finds visual representation of vowel positions helpful is advised to supplement the data provided here by consulting other texts—e.g., Carrell and Tiffany (1960), Singh and Singh (1976).

Acoustic Properties of Vowels and Their Sensory Correlates

The data on formant frequencies presented in Table 13.A relate to vowels produced by children. The formant frequencies of vowels produced by female adults who have somewhat longer and larger vocal tracts tend to be about 20% lower, and those of vowels produced by adult males may be as much as 40% lower. Values for children's formants are the most important in the present context, for in teaching speech we need to know what components of the vowels the child might hear when he himself produces them. We may be sure that if the formant of a particular vowel produced by the child is within his range of hearing, it will also be audible to him when produced as a model by his teacher. In this regard, it is important to note that the child's range of hearing as determined by pure-tone audiometry is not a precise guide to his hearing for vowel formants (see Chapter 3). On one hand, the conventional audiogram provides no direct information about the audibility of sound at frequencies other than those tested; on the other, the values shown in Figure 13.1 represent the center frequencies of formants that may have bandwidths of over 150 Hz (Stevens and House, 1961). Partly because each formant extends over a substantial range of frequencies, vowels are more audible to most hearing-impaired children than their audiograms may suggest.

Most vowels spoken in isolation can be identified by normal listeners if both the first and second formants are audible, although identification of the high-front vowels may be improved if F_3 can also be heard (Delattre, Liberman, Cooper, and Gerstman, 1952). Table 13.A shows that audibility of the first two formants of all vowels calls for hearing up to 3,000 Hz. It also shows that F_2 frequency values increase systematically as the tongue moves forward in the mouth. F_2 is therefore lower for the back than for the front vowels. The order in which the vowels may be arranged according to F_2 frequency (low to high) is reflected in the sentence, "Who would know more of art must learn and then take his ease." It is because hearing impairment is usually greater for high than for low frequencies that errors made by hearing-impaired listeners in speech identification tasks are more frequently associated with front than with back vowels (Rosen, 1962; Schultz, 1964).

Several of the front and back vowels have F_1 values that are quite similar. This is shown in Figure 13.2, in which broad-band spectrograms of the vowel pairs [i] and [u], and [ɛ] and [ɔ] are used to illustrate the commonality of F_1 energy in each pair. The hearing-impaired listener to whom only sounds under 1,000 Hz are audible will be able to hear these vowels but will be likely to confuse them through hearing alone if they are presented out of context. With training in the context of syllables, the individual will be less likely to make such confusions since consonant-to-vowel formant transitions may also be audible. This can be demonstrated with normally hearing subjects by using an electronic filter to suppress all frequencies above 1,000 Hz. Under such filter condi-

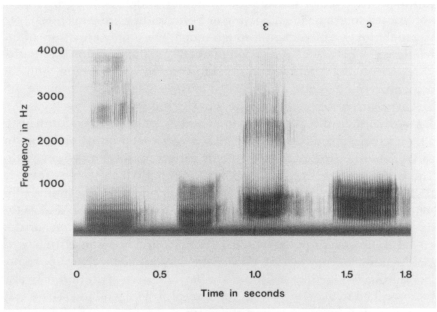

Figure 13.2
Spectrograms of vowels with similar F_1 frequencies.

tions, [u] and [i] are almost indistinguishable, yet [bu] and [bi] can be differentiated with ease. It is because consonant-to-vowel transitions aid auditory differentiation that we recommend releasing sustained vowels with a consonant. Of course, children who can hear only F_1 information must use other sense modalities as a supplement to residual audition if they are to acquire adequate vowel reception and vowel production skills.

Vision is a particularly useful supplement to residual hearing for vowels because tongue and lip placement are directly related. The child with residual hearing extending up to 1,000 Hz can be expected to hear F_1 of all vowels. However, in order to discriminate between those back and front vowels which have similar F_1 values (see Figure 13.2), the child must supplement F_1 information with cues provided by lip shape. The rules by which such a child could learn to differentiate vowels on an auditory-visual basis might be expressed as follows: low F_1 + lips rounded = [u]; low F_1 + lips spread = [i]; high F_1 + lips neutral = [a], and so on. Indeed, we have found that children with very limited hearing who have learned to monitor voice pitch (see Chapter 12) can usually utilize vision together with hearing for F_1 information in this way. Their previous training in the identification and modification of F_0 permits them to identify and to modify the pitch of the first formant. Children who cannot utilize F_1 information, either because they have not learned to use residual hearing or because they are totally deaf, can be taught tongue placement through touch. Once they are aware of the relationship between lip and tongue configuration, vision alone provides adequate *exteroceptive* information for vowel reception, and the orosensory-motor patterns associated with tongue and lips provide sufficient *proprioceptive* information for vowel production.

Whether the child can hear both F_1 and F_2, only F_1, or no formants at all, he will need considerable experience in vowel production before he can differentiate the orosensory-motor patterns associated with vowels. These patterns are much more motor-kinesthetic than tactile. Thus, in [i] there is a strong motor-kinesthetic component as the front of the tongue is raised toward the hard palate, as the jaw is lifted, and as the lips are spread to a neutral position. The orotactile sensation for this vowel is, however, quite restricted. The jaw and lips offer virtually no tactile cues. One may feel the sides of the tongue touching the upper molars during production of [i], but similar orotactile sensation may also be associated with other vowels, for example [ɪ], [ɛ], and [æ]. There may be a diminution of pressure of the sides of the tongue on the teeth as lower lax vowels are produced, but the effect is small. If tongue placement is exaggerated so that the tongue assumes a very close position, that assumed for [j], some vibratory sensation may be available. Such a teaching strategy may be used to approximate [i]; but since the vibratory sensation does not occur in normal production, it cannot be used to maintain the [i] in speech. In short, the only orosensory-motor cues that appear to be fully effective for [i] are those associated with motor-kinesthetic patterns, and it appears to be on the basis of these patterns that one establishes feedforward control and feedback of performance in the absence of hearing.

The strength of motor-kinesthetic patterns as compared with the weakness of tactile correlates characterizes the pattern of sensation for all vowels. The jaw and the tongue are increasingly more relaxed for [ɪ], [e], [ɛ], and [æ] than for [i], and there is a kinesthetic sensation indicating the front-raising of a less widely spread tongue; but there are no marked tactile cues. The lower sides of the tongue may touch the bottom molars in the production of central vowels, and differentiation between front and central vowels can therefore be made on the basis of this sensation; but tactile cues do not permit discrimination of one central vowel from another. Considerably fewer tactile cues are available for back vowels as compared with central and front vowels. The sensation leading to correct tongue placement for these vowels must therefore be almost entirely motor-kinesthetic. The motor-kinesthetic patterns associated with lip movement strengthen as the lips are rounded and protruded for back vowel production.

Oral sensation associated with articulators other than the tongue and lips should not be ignored in vowel production. Appropriate laryngeal and pharyngeal adjustments can only result if the child is encouraged to experiment with speech production in such a way that he experiences the wide range of motor-kinesthetic patterns associated with different degrees of laryngeal and pharyngeal tension. Only through proprioception can he learn that the tension on the larynx required to maintain a particular voice pitch, and the degree of lateral pharyngeal wall movement, are greater for low than for high vowels (see Minifie, Hixon, Kelsey, and Woodhouse, 1970). The child must also learn through the experience of producing oral vowels that velopharyngeal closure is an essential target in their production in English. Resonance is markedly changed if nasal escape occurs during vowel production: vocal tract damping is increased with the result that formant peaks become flattened, areas of zero energy appear between formants, and high frequency harmonics are weakened. Thus, although some nasalization of vowels may be expected when they are coarticulated with adjacent nasal consonants, the target for the velum during vowel production should be a highly elevated if not closed position. Since the tactile, kinesthetic, and motor patterns associated with velar movement are all relatively weak, extensive experience of correct vowel production is required before velopharyngeal closure can be effected automatically. Finally, because adjustments required of the tongue and lips are relative to jaw position, exaggerated jaw movements that result in inappropriate motor-kinesthetic patterns must never be encouraged.

Subskills and Teaching Strategies

Subskills Related to Vowel Production

All vowels require the use of the subskills developed at previous stages: vocalization and whisper to produce the source energy; and elementary control over the duration, intensity, and pitch of voice. The additional subskills called for in the production of each vowel are:

1. differential shaping of the vocal tract to produce the required formant structures;

2. the ability to maintain each target vocal tract configuration for at least three seconds;

3. rapid repetition of each vowel target;

4. rapid alternation of the articulators so that they can assume their target positions for each vowel easily from whatever position they previously occupied; and

5. independent control of the larynx (source) and the articulators (filter).

The child who has come to this stage (Stage 3 of our model) with extensive experience in vocalizing and producing varied voice patterns is also likely to have acquired some distinctly differing vowels, though mastery of all five subskills specified above cannot be expected without specific training. The extent to which vowel differentiation occurs spontaneously usually depends on the amount of residual hearing that is present and the extent to which it has been used. The wider the frequency range of the child's hearing, the greater the variety of vowels he will be likely to produce if appropriate hearing aids and extensive exposure to speech have been provided. The child's orosensory-motor differentiation of spontaneously produced vowel patterns will also depend on the effectiveness of the reinforcement that has been supplied.

Teaching Strategies Related to Vowel Production

The strategies one should adopt in developing the subskills which underlie vowel production must be determined for each child according to the extent of his residual hearing and his ability to use it. All other variables such as age and previous experience are of secondary importance. All five subskills relating to vowel production can be developed through the use of residual audition and the provision of adequate reinforcement if the child's hearing extends over the frequency range of the vowel formants specified in Figure 13.1. Thus, children with hearing up to 3,000 Hz may be expected to imitate and identify all vowels through the use of audition. Through hearing they may also learn to sustain and repeat each vowel target, to alternate one vowel with another, and to produce each of the vowels while varying the duration, intensity, and pitch of voice. Only when attempts to teach the five vowel subskills through audition have failed should one employ either touch or vision to develop them.

One should not rush into teaching any of the five subskills underlying vowel production by either tactile or visual means. Before strategies primarily involving touch and vision are adopted, the child must first have abundant spontaneous vocalization and elementary control of voice patterns; it must also be evident that he cannot develop the range of vowels and diphthongs specified for the first teaching step through interactive play involving auditory imitation. Too frequently we have seen teachers approach this and other aspects of speech teaching without having made exhaustive efforts to exploit residual hearing, without having provided regular and plentiful auditory models of the desired behavior, and without having given appropriate reinforcement for vocalizations varying in phonetic quality. Such failure on the part of the teacher (and the parents) to optimize conditions for natural speech development may critically and permanently impair the child's attitude toward speech communication.

Subskill 1: Differential Shaping of the Vocal Tract

Auditory Strategies: Appropriate shaping of the vocal tract for each vowel calls for orosensory-motor differentiation of each target behavior. By far the simplest and most effective strategy is to teach whatever vowels one is able to teach through auditory imitation so that auditory and orosensory-motor differentiation are simultaneously fostered. Not all children, of course, have sufficient hearing to acquire all vowels through audition, but such acquisition is not an all-or-none affair. For example, the back vowels—in which both formants are relatively low-pitched—may be audible and discriminable to a child when the front vowels are not, and the first formants may fall within a child's range of hearing even if the second formants cannot be heard.

When incomplete or no vowel formant structure is available to the child through audition, one must adopt teaching strategies involving touch, tactile aids, vision, or visual aids to promote development of the required subskills. It is important to note that when auditory strategies can be used they are equally effective whether one seeks to develop or to maintain vowel differentiation, whereas non-auditory strategies are not. For example, touch is much more effective than vision in teaching the totally deaf child to produce most vowels, but vision becomes the more effective modality for vowel reception once target behaviors have been acquired.

Auditory strategies must be based on the full use of residual hearing. This implies the need to teach the child to discriminate between vowels so far as possible without the use of touch and vision. The first step is to provide the child with an abundance of auditory models in the course of interactive communication. This requires techniques very similar to those specified for the development of abundant vocalization (see Chapter 12). With the very young infant, different toys can be associated with different vowels: a train with the sound made by its whistle, [u-u]; a jet airplane with its whine, [i-i]; and so on. Farm animals can be similarly associated with the noises they make: a cow with [mu], a lamb with [ba], or a duck with [kwæ]. Identification of the toy from the sound associated with it and imitation of the sound by the child should be reinforced. A variety of hand-switched toys can also be used so that, for example, on imitation of [a] a doll blinks its eyes, on imitation of [i] a kaleidoscope turns, on production of [u] a train moves forward, and so on. In addition to such training the child must be encouraged to produce the different vowels developed during play.

Auditory training of the type described above should be partly diagnostic. One should set out not only to teach the child to listen and respond to different vowels but also to determine which vowels the child can hear, at what distance particular vowels are audible, and which vowels are discriminable. For example, having the child build a tower by adding a block each time he hears the teacher produce a particular vowel will allow the teacher to determine how close she must be to the child to obtain a response and, hence, how near she must stay to the child if she hopes to have him learn from and imitate auditory models (see Leckie and Ling, 1968). Imitation may be fostered by reversing the role of teacher and child. If the child confuses [u] and [i] consistently in listening during such an activity, one may conclude that F_2 of the vowel [i] is inaudible. If [ɛ] and [ɔ] are also confused, then F_2 of the vowel [ɛ] probably lies outside the child's frequency range. The need to systematize auditory training through reference to the formant structure of the vowels has been recognized by many workers including Wedenberg (1951) and Jeffers (1966).

Auditory strategies similar to those described above should also be used with older children although the materials employed should be congruent with the children's maturity and interests. Programmed instruction may also be employed (see Doehring and Ling, 1971). One should not seek to develop auditory discrimination by itself, however. The evidence to date suggests that the result is most advantageous if auditory and orosensory-motor differentiation of speech are developed synchronously. Since a whisper at a few inches from the microphone of the child's hearing aid is as loud as a shout from a distance of a few yards, whispering should be one of the auditory strategies used to develop vowel and diphthong production. As shown in Figure 13.1, the formant structure is acoustically clear when vowels are whispered. Because there is no harmonic structure to whispered vowels, F_2 is remarkably more salient in whispered than in voiced speech sounds. Thus, attention can readily be focused on F_2 components if they lie within the frequency range audible to the child. The formant glides associated with whispered diphthongs are, if anything, even more salient than those of whispered vowels and, accordingly, offer excellent models with which to guide the child toward appropriate shaping of the vocal tract. The voicing of target behaviors shaped by means of whispering should, of course, be immediately encouraged and reinforced.

Auditory-visual strategies (listen + look) should be adopted only if confusion between vowels having similar F_1 frequencies persists. In such cases, awareness of F_1 and of the relationship between tongue position and lip configuration (see above) may emerge without tactile intervention. If it does not, then auditory-visual strategies should be resumed once tactile strategies have been used to demonstrate the relationship which exists between tongue and lips.

Tactile Strategies: Tongue height and tongue configuration for most vowels can be felt by the child if he places a finger on the teacher's tongue as she speaks. The child may be expected to imitate the tongue height and tongue position assumed by placing a finger of his other hand into his own mouth. This strategy has been discussed in Chapters 3 and 8 and its efficacy confirmed through experimental study (Ling and Bennett, 1974–75). Tongue target configuration taught by this strategy involves four steps for the child: first, feeling with a finger the movement toward, and the steady-state position of, the teacher's tongue; second, imitating tongue configuration by using another finger to feel tongue position in his own mouth; third, maintaining the tongue position after the finger is withdrawn; and fourth, assuming the desired tongue position without using the fingers as a guide. The last two steps call for visual reference to lip position and motor-kinesthetic memory.

The strategy described above is particularly effective as a means of focusing the child's attention on the motor-kinesthetic patterns that underlie the production of both vowels and diphthongs. The correct tongue placement for [i], for example, can be rapidly achieved if it is developed through using the diphthong [ai] (a variant of the English [aɪ]) simply because the motor-kinesthetic sensation is particularly strong. The movement felt by the finger in this case is forceful, and it unambiguously defines the target track for the diphthong and the target position for each component vowel. The strategy is most appropriate for teaching tongue targets for the front vowels to children whose residual hearing is very limited. To most children it is much less objectionable than manipulation and also more effective because the finger provides the feedback that is not available from spatulas or from similar instruments such as those described by Borden and Novikoff (1974).

Direct tactile experience obtained by feeling the tongue with a finger can also provide information on tongue width and tongue tension. As mentioned earlier, these variables serve to differentiate certain vowels that have similar tongue height and lip shape: the tense and lax vowels [i] and [ɪ], [e] and [ɛ], [u] and [ʊ], [ʌ] and [ə], [ɝ] and [ɚ] . The tongue is tangibly more widely spread and feels much harder in tense vowels than in their lax counterparts.

The intrinsic firmness of the tongue required for tense vowels may be indicated to the child by less direct tactile means through exerting pressure with the fingertips on the child's chin. Once an approximate tongue configuration has been achieved by the child the teacher may, for example, press his fingers down firmly on her chin for [i] and lightly for [ɪ]. In this way the child simultaneously feels that her jaw also assumes a slightly more open position for the lax member of the vowel pair. The strategy usually results in effective imitation because there is a tendency to oppose a force with an equal and opposite force. In much the same way the requisite tension in the vowel may be obtained if the teacher requires the child to say the tense member of a pair as she pushes her hand firmly against his to obtain a strong resistance or gently against his to demonstrate relatively less tension.

In the initial stages of vocal tract shaping, the child's attention may be drawn to the relatively few orotactile cues that are available in vowel production. These include feeling the tongue tip resting on the lower front teeth in all vowels and feeling the sides of the tongue against the upper molars in front vowels and against the lower molars in central vowels. Placing the fingertips near the mouth and feeling the oral breath stream that results with correct production of high-back and high-front vowels helps to avoid nasality. Since the breath stream is stronger when vowels are whispered than when they are voiced, the strategy is most effective in whispered speech.

Tactile aids which provide formant frequency information as part of a cutaneous display (Kirman, 1974) might be used to teach all five vowel subskills, but such aids are not yet generally available. Simple vibrators are of no help in this regard since the skin is relatively insensitive to differences in frequency.

Once tongue position for a given vowel has been established through touch, tactile strategies should be discarded and others substituted. The child should be reinforced so that he learns to maintain vowel production through the normal proprioceptive mechanisms—the orosensory-motor patterns associated with tongue placement and whatever residual hearing is present. Hearing even for the first formant alone is of enormous value, not only in the maintenance of the target behaviors learned, but also in the development of skills to be acquired at subsequent stages.

Visual Strategies: Tongue positions for vowels cannot be adequately visualized unless an exaggerated model is provided. We hesitate to use visual exaggeration as a strategy since tongue postures other than those taught through an exaggerated visual pattern must be learned if the child is later required to produce the sound with normal jaw adjustment. An exaggeration can yield but an imprecise notion of the target behavior required. True, a gross approximation of tongue position is better than no approximation at all, but more direct strategies involving touch and kinesthesis are available. The tactile strategies described above do not call for initial exaggeration. We personally find the mirror to be neither necessary nor useful in vowel development, although it may be helpful in the remediation of long-standing faults that involve habitual exaggeration. Such remediation is discussed later on.

Vocal tract shaping may be taught through the use of rather complex visual teaching aids that present either a formant display (Pickett and Constam, 1968) or pictures of the vocal tract such as may be derived from X-rays or from real-time computer analysis of the sounds produced (Wakita, 1973). Less direct, but much simpler, alternatives to such devices include a three-dimensional model which allows the teacher to manipulate an artificial tongue within a visible mouth cavity (Bonet, 1620); analogies in which the position assumed by one hand relative to the other indicates tongue placement in relation to the palate (Ewing and Ewing, 1964); and, of course, line drawings. Visual cues to the oral nature of the high-front and high-back vowels may be provided by showing the child how a lightweight object (a feather, a scrap of paper, or a Ping-Pong ball) can be moved by the breath stream. However, the most effective use of vision in teaching this and other subskills relating to vowel production probably remains that of providing visual reinforcement for successive approximations to target behaviors.

Subskill 2: Maintenance of Target Vocal Tract Configuration

Sustaining each vowel for several seconds serves three purposes: it establishes an "ideal" target position for the speech organs involved; it lays the foundation for tongue position to be maintained during the first stage of consonant teaching; and it provides articulatory control of sufficient duration to allow the development of independent laryngeal and articulatory adjustments.

If auditory strategies have been successfully used to develop differential shaping of the vocal tract, then they may also be used to promote maintenance of the target vowel. The child should initially be reinforced for each successful attempt. Strategies similar to those used to promote control of vocal duration may be employed (see Chapter 12). If tactile strategies have been used to develop a target vowel they may also be required to foster control over the duration of its production. Most children should be able to produce vowels previously taught by touch simply through reference to auditory (F_1) and visual cues. Should this not be the case, one should, first, have the child feel the tongue as it assumes its target configuration (as in initial teaching of the sound); second, have him feel the tongue as it is maintained in its target position; and, third, require him to maintain the target position without tactile cues.

Of the utmost importance is that the child should learn to perform this subskill in such a way that source energy is produced only while the target vocal tract configuration is maintained. The onset of voice (or whisper) should be timed to coincide with the achievement of target configuration, and its offset should occur prior to release of tongue target posture. If a pure vowel is the target, then no diphthongization should be allowed to occur. If successive approximation is allowed to occur so that the target vowel is achieved or terminated with other vowels, the effect is comparable to that produced by the beginning violinist who slides his finger up or down the string before reaching the desired note. Much as a melody rendered by such a violinist is unpleasant for the lis-tener to hear and difficult to identify, so is the speech of a child allowed to diphthongize vowels displeasing to the ear and difficult to under-stand. Faults arising from inappropriate diphthongization in the speech of hearing-impaired children have been frequently noted (see Chapter 2). In the study reported by Markides (1970), 56% of the vowels produced by his 58 deaf subjects were regarded as errors, and most of these errors were due to diphthongization. The causes and treatment of habitual diphthongization will be discussed later in this chapter.

One can sustain vowels to the limit of one's breath supply, but one cannot sustain diphthongs. This subskill is not, therefore, applicable to the development of diphthongs.

Subskill 3: Rapid Repetition of the Vowel Targets

Once the first few vowel targets (those in Steps 1 and 2) have been achieved and each can be sustained in isolation for about three seconds without diphthongization, they should be initiated with a labial con-sonant, preferably [b]. Most children, however severe their hearing im-pairment, will imitate [b] or other labial consonants during the earliest stages of speech acquisition. The [m] should not be used until there is no risk of introducing habitual nasality through assimilation. When the child can produce sustained syllables such as [ba], [bu], and [bi], he should be taught to produce a string of such syllables on one breath. This task requires the maintenance of the tongue in the appropriate po-sition for the vowel while the lips are moved independently. If carried out without diphthongization, the procedure develops the basic motor-kinesthetic patterns required for correct syllabification and at the same time provides additional acoustic cues which may aid in the auditory discrimination of the syllables. Many faults in the speech of hearing-impaired children are due to the production of syllables without due regard for the tongue and jaw positions assumed for the vowels. Stew-art (1969) labels such positions "articulatory settings." Faulty articula-tory settings yield both motor-kinesthetic and acoustic patterns that are inappropriate. The strategy of using correctly produced vowels as the articulatory settings for labial consonants serves to avoid such problems. Further, it lays the foundation for producing lingual sounds while the tongue's extrinsic musculature is maintaining an appropriate position for the vowel and the tongue's intrinsic musculature is moving that portion of the tongue required to form the consonant (see Perkell, 1969).

Subskill 4: Rapid Alternation of Vowel Target Positions

This subskill serves first to augment the motor-kinesthetic patterns associated with each vowel; second, to ensure that the speech organs are trained to assume their target positions whatever their previous position; and, third, to ensure that movements associated with vowel formation can be made at rates equivalent to those commonly observed in running speech (i.e., three syllables per second).

The motor-kinesthetic patterns we seek to develop are central to the control of vowels in speech whether we use audition or not. The more movement there is associated with adjustment of vocal tract configuration, the more vivid and hence more perceptible these patterns will be. Alternation of non-adjacent vowels (vowels not occurring next to each other in the sentence, "Who would know more of art must learn and then take his ease.") is therefore recommended. Vocal tract configuration for the various vowels and ability to sustain it have been developed as prior subskills. To teach the child to alternate one established vowel target with another, the teacher may associate a particular vowel with the child's left hand and another with his right; if the teacher lifts the child's left hand while saying [i] and then his right hand while saying [u], the child is provided with the appropriate model to imitate. The two vowels may be alternated initially on separate breaths; next, quite slowly on the same breath; and, finally, at the rate of at least two vowels per second on one breath. At an even more advanced level, strings of several vowels should be alternated. For this more advanced work, colored blocks may be substituted for the hands, or small candies may be associated with each vowel. The child may receive some or all of the blocks or candy when the task has been successfully completed.

If vowels are taught only in isolation or randomly in the context of consonants, the child will not be likely to derive strong motor-kinesthetic patterns from his speech experience; nor will he be called upon to adjust the vocal tract to a given configuration from the variety of positions met in everyday speech. In isolated vowel production, for example, the likelihood is that the tongue's excursion to every target position will be from a central schwa-like posture. Such is not the case in running speech where, in sentences such as "Give me one too, please," the tongue does not approximate the schwa posture at any point.

Subskill 5: Independent Control of the Larynx and the Articulators

Our objective is not simply to develop a normal vowel system, but to enable the child to speak within the framework provided by supraseg-mental structure. He must therefore be trained to produce all vowels with various patterns of duration, intensity, and pitch. This subskill may be developed through strategies similar to those described in the previous chapter. The advance to be made at this stage involves maintaining and alternating differentiated vowels (as compared with un-differentiated vocalization) while varying voice patterns.

Order and Evaluation of Target and Subskill Development

Phonetic Level: The order in which we propose that vowels and diph-thongs should be taught was specified in Chapter 8. We suggested that their development be fostered in four distinct teaching steps. In Step 1 we recommended teaching [a], [i], [u], [aʊ], and [aɪ]. All five sub-skills underlying the three vowels should be taught before progressing to Step 2. In short, the vocal tract configuration for each vowel should be developed, each target should be sustained for about three seconds, the three vowels should be alternated, and each should be produced with variations of duration, intensity, and voice pitch. Concurrently, the two diphthongs should be taught, alternated, and finally produced slowly and quickly, in a whisper and with quiet and loud voice, and with discretely and continuously varied voice pitch ranging from low to high. When evaluation (see Chapter 9) shows that these targets and sub-skills have been achieved, concern should shift to the targets called for in Step 2—namely, [ɔ], [ɔɪ], [ɛ], [ʊ], and [ɪ]. When, following a similar approach to that outlined above, these new targets and subskills have been achieved, the first step in consonant teaching and the third step in vowel development (the [æ], [ʌ], [a], [o], and [e] targets) should be tackled concurrently. The fourth step in vowel development involving [ɝ] and [ɚ] may be left until consonantal [r] production has been established.

Phonologic Level: As soon as the first two or three phonetic level subskills underlying a particular vowel or diphthong have been mastered, the child should be encouraged to use the target in phonologic speech. There are many ways in which various vowels can be used and their imitation encouraged in everyday situations. For example, [au] can be used when a child is hurt or pretending to be hurt, [u] if he is surprised or expressing pleasure. These should be used frequently and with appropriate intonation. At a slightly later stage, the young child may be expected to say [au] for *cow* as readily as he attempts to imitate [u] for *moo*, but this should not be taught until the vowel target can be produced without difficulty. Phonetic level rehearsal of the remaining subskills and phonologic use of the sound should, in short, proceed concurrently until production is automatic. The problem of putting a vowel or diphthong into a meaningful framework after it has been taught phonetically is minimal. It simply involves providing the child with adequate models and reinforcing production in meaningful situations sufficiently often to permit the child to make the required associations. It matters little at this stage that in the child's first meaningful associations words may lack consonants, providing that the correct phonologic model is constantly presented and that similar transfer to a phonologic level is encouraged once the missing consonants have been developed phonetically. Thus, the child may initially use /bʌ/ for *bucket, bus,* and *been* but, by a process of incremental learning, progressively differentiate them. The process can be observed in normally hearing children.

We stress that the child's awareness of the correspondence between phonetic and phonologic use of a sound cannot occur without adequate exteroceptive experience. It is therefore essential that the child be exposed to abundant spoken language patterns which relate to his immediate interests and activities. These patterns must be presented in such a way that they can be optimally perceived by the child: within his range of hearing if he possesses any residual audition; within his auditory and visual field if he has to supplement audition with vision; and within his visual field while he is looking if he has to rely on vision alone. The fact that one may have to use touch to teach vocal tract configuration for each vowel does not mean that one should speak to the child in isolated vowels. Phonologic evaluation of the child's speech should be used to indicate which vowels and diphthongs are present in his attempts to communicate and which require more specific phonetic level teaching. It must be remembered that a natural language approach at the phonologic level is not precluded even if one has to adopt a vigorous, structured approach in order to develop phonetic level skills. Since consonants can not be adequately taught until a variety of vowels has been developed, early emphasis must be given to vowel acquisition.

Remedial Treatment of Deviant Patterns

Among the deviant patterns typically affecting vowel production in the phonologic speech of hearing-impaired children are substitution, neutralization, prolongation, diphthongization, exaggeration, nasalization, and interdependent rather than independent laryngeal and articulatory control—the latter being most strongly characterized by context-dependent pitch. In this section we shall discuss each of these sources of error, mention of which is made in Chapter 2. We shall examine the possible causes underlying specific faults and suggest ways in which they may be prevented or remedied. By and large, the most appropriate remedial treatment for any fault in vowel or diphthong production appears to be the redevelopment of the sound along the lines suggested earlier in this chapter. It is rarely possible to find shortcuts in the remediation of faults that have become habitual, for errors occur mainly through lack of requisite subskills that demand orderly acquisition.

Substitution

Vowel substitution may occur because the child does not have the correct vowel in his phonetic repertoire, because the subskills underlying the particular target have not been acquired or practiced to a sufficient level of automaticity, or because the child does not know how to pronounce the words in which the fault occurs. The problem calls for evaluation as described in Chapter 9 and remediation based on the outcome of such evaluation.

If the fault is at the phonetic level, then mastery of each of the five subskills specified above must be developed. To this end, the strategies already described for initial teaching should be applied. Following mastery at the phonetic level, the child should be taught everyday words, phrases, and sentences which include the vowel or diphthong in question. In short, phonetic-to-phonologic transfer should be demanded as soon as the requisite subskills have been acquired at a phonetic level. The written form should be avoided at this stage in view of the notorious lack of correspondence between the spoken and orthographic forms of vowels in English. Habitual use of the vowel in a number of everyday words will provide a key vocabulary to which the teacher may refer the child when introducing new words. If the error occurs only at a phonologic level, which is generally not the case, then the building of a key vocabulary and work on pronunciation are usually sufficient for remediation. In phonologic development, phrases and sentences as well as words should be emphasized to provide the suprasegmental framework within which vowels can be varied in duration, intensity, and pitch.

Neutralization

Neutralization may be defined as the extensive use of vowels approximating the neutral schwa [ə] in place of those which require a more specific vocal tract configuration. It is, therefore, strongly akin to the problem of substitution. Indeed, at the phonetic level neutralization may be regarded as being equivalent to substitution, for at this level it occurs only if the child has not acquired the full range of specific target vowels and the subskills that underlie them. The evaluation procedures described in Chapter 9 are required to determine whether the problem lies at this or at a phonologic level.

Neutralization may occur at the phonetic level as a result of speaking with a falsetto voice. When F_0 is higher than the normal F_1 frequency, the vocal tract—even if correctly shaped—cannot resonate at the normal F_1 frequency simply because none of the harmonics generated by the falsetto voice is present in that frequency range. This is why female singers cannot produce normal vowels over the upper portion of their pitch range. The [u] and [i] vowels are the most likely to suffer since they have the lowest F_1 frequencies, and they are heard as a neutral vowel. Thus, voice in the normal frequency range must be established before vowels can be developed. Additionally, of course, the abnormal tension present in all muscles during production of a falsetto voice tends to displace the speech organs and to create a distorted vocal tract as well as inappropriate motor-kinesthetic patterns, both of which have to be avoided if vowels are to be produced accurately.

Neutralization which occurs only at a phonologic level may stem from articulatory carelessness, insufficient automaticity in the production of the vowel, unfamiliarity with the usual form of pronunciation of the word, or misapplication of the rules governing neutralization of vowels in running speech. Carelessness in speech is much less common than other causes. The child who speaks usually wishes to be understood. Thus, carelessness tends to occur only if those with whom the child communicates habitually adjust their standards to accommodate to faulty speech rather than demand that the child use the more appropriate patterns that lie within his phonetic repertoire. Insufficient automaticity may be due to too little practice at a phonetic level, to restricted opportunity to use acquired patterns phonologically, to too little demand to do so, or to all three. It may be remedied by ensuring that the situation in all respects is reversed. Unfamiliarity with the usual form of pronunciation is a problem that may be dealt with by the strategies suggested for remediation of substitution.

Neutralization of certain unstressed vowels is a normal process in

English. Thus, the sentence, "This problem is of some concern," may legitimately be rendered as:

/ðɪs prɑbləm əz əv səm kənsɜ n/ or /ðɪs prɑblɪm ɪz ɑv sʌm kɑnsɜ˞n/.

In the first case, the schwa /ə/ has been substituted for other vowels on no less than five occasions. Such substitution is acceptable, but only in rapid, rhythmic speech and in contexts which cannot be rendered ambiguous in meaning through its use. When speech is slow, use of the schwa is largely avoided. Indeed, it is difficult for the normal speaker to employ the schwa in slow speech. At normal (neither fast nor slow) speaking rates the schwa serves to differentiate between emphatic and unemphatic material, between the key words in a sentence—those that are given salience—and others that carry less meaning.

Neutralization becomes a major problem when the hearing-impaired child's speech contains no differentiating stress patterns and when his speech is abnormally slow. The solution is therefore twofold: first, the child should be trained to employ suprasegmental structure and to use specific vowels accurately in words receiving stress; second, he should be trained to use speech that approximates a normal rate. Training in the subskills according to the strategies described in Chapters 12 through 15 is required in both regards. One must work toward automaticity at both the phonetic and the phonologic levels of production.

Prolongation

Prolongation is a fault that may be allowed to pervade all aspects of speech, consonants as well as vowels. That it is widely prevalent among hearing-impaired children is an indictment of current teaching procedures. Hearing impairment is essentially a sensory problem, and in but a small proportion of cases is it associated with organic deficits of motor function. Most hearing-impaired children can be as effective as their hearing peers in acquiring motor behaviors which demand rapid rates of performance if they are required to do so. Since speech production (articulation) is largely a motor task, there is no inherent cause for the duration of sounds to be affected by hearing impairment. If the child can be taught to speak at all, he can be taught to do so at normal rates. Prolongation is, in the main, due to inadequate speech teaching.

There are many ways in which speech teaching may be inadequate and may therefore cause prolongation. The most common causes are that:

1. attention has been focused on segmental elements to the detriment of suprasegmental structure;

2. the essential target behaviors have not been clearly specified or systematically developed by the teacher;
3. articulation rather than coarticulation has been fostered;
4. the child's phonetic repertoire is inadequate to meet his phonologic needs;
5. subskills demanding rapid repetition and alternation have not been practiced to a sufficient level of automaticity; hence the child's attention is on *how* he says things rather than *what* it is he wishes to express;
6. speech sound production has been associated with orthographic or other symbol systems which serve to interfere with the feedforward planning of motor speech sequences;
7. attention has been focused on feedback rather than feedforward processes;
8. sufficient models of speech at a normal rate have not been provided;
9. speech at a normal rate has not been expected as a standard;
10. residual hearing, which provides abundant cues on rhythm and rate, has not been exploited;
11. the child's language has not been sufficiently developed to permit him to structure a series of ideas in acceptable linguistic form as he expresses them sequentially in speech.

In view of the diversity of possible causes of prolongation, no single strategy can be expected to be effective either in its prevention or remediation. This is why attempts to ameliorate timing problems in the speech of hearing-impaired children by treating prolongation as an isolated phenomenon can but result in failure. In the light of this analysis, many of the attempts that have been made (see Chapter 2) can be seen as experimentally naive and pedagogically unsound. To counteract any tendency toward prolongation of sounds, phonologic speech at the normal rate must be consistently provided as a model and expected of the child as soon as his nonsegmental and segmental phonetic level skills are sufficiently developed. Attention in teaching should be directed toward the development of automaticity and feedforward processes which encompass both speech and language. The association of speech with a largely irrelevant and confusing symbol system should be avoided. Finally, whatever existing audition should be used to the utmost.

Diphthongization

Diphthongization of certain vowels may legitimately occur in English. Thus, as previously mentioned, the word *too* may be acceptably rendered /tʊu/ and the word *bee* pronounced /bɪi/. Speech production is faulty when vowel targets other than /i/ and /u/ are diphthongized unless the diphthongs systematically conform to the speaker's regional dialect.

Faults of diphthongization most commonly found in the speech of hearing-impaired children involve the neutral vowel. They arise when the child glides to his vowel target from a vocal tract configuration approximating that for the schwa [ə] and terminates his vowel with a similar glide to a neutral position. The fault differs from that of neutralization, where the correct target is never reached; for in diphthongization the target vowel is reached, but by way of other vowels.

Diphthongization involving glides to or from the neutral vowel is time-consuming. It may therefore be associated with prolongation. Diphthongization is inelegant and inefficient in that the tongue has to travel much further than necessary to complete its task. Imagine, for example, a salesman who lives in Chicago (a neutral position) and who travels back to that city after every assignment instead of covering all calls on a round trip. Picture his mileage (and his bank balance) if he were to follow an itinerary such as: Chicago, Vancouver, Chicago, Seattle, Chicago, San Francisco, Chicago, Phoenix, Chicago, instead of simply returning to his home base only once after having visited each of the other cities in turn. That hearing-impaired children tend to return the tongue to its neutral base position after each attempt to reach a target vowel may be attributed, like prolongation, to inadequate teaching. The vocal tract configurations for each vowel have been taught in isolated or single syllables (one assumes), but they have not been alternated with one another to ensure that the tongue and lips can reach their target positions rapidly and by the shortest route.

Diphthongization may be difficult to ameliorate. If the child has been allowed to acquire the fault, then all vowels should be redeveloped through the procedures described earlier in this chapter. In other words, the child should recapitulate the learning process as if he had only undifferentiated vocalization to start with; he should thus master all five subskills associated with each vowel at a phonetic level. Once vowel targets have been redeveloped at this level, they should be used phonologically at normal speaking rates in words and phrases commonly used by the child. One must ensure that unwanted diphthongs become habitually replaced with vowels. This latter step is usually the most difficult one, since the child who has been allowed to diphthongize vowels over an extended period will have established strong associations between particular auditory-motor-kinesthetic and linguistic patterns. Such associations account for its being easier to teach the correct speech pattern in new words than to correct a speech pattern in previously malarticulated words (see Chapter 7).

Exaggeration

Exaggerated movements of the jaw which lead to abnormal tongue and lip target behaviors occur with considerable frequency among hearing-impaired children. The problem is exacerbated by prolongation, which allows time for the articulators to assume extreme positions. It contributes to diphthongization because changes in vocal tract configuration during extensive excursions of the jaw give rise to audible formant glides. As with many other speech faults, there is no inherent connection between exaggeration and hearing impairment. The problem arises mainly because inappropriate teaching strategies have been used and because the faults have been reinforced through neglect.

Among the strategies that lead to exaggeration are the initial teaching and subsequent rehearsal of speech target behaviors principally or exclusively through reference to vision. Most speech sounds cannot be visualized unless exaggeration is employed. Thus, such visual strategies provide the very models that, when imitated by the child, are recognized as faulty. If exaggerated visual models have been provided for imitation, they should be faded in all subsequent work. In other words, training in specific subskills should deliberately feature reduction of the initially exaggerated form.

Two further common faults in vowel production may be fostered by teaching visually through exaggerated patterns: namely, tongue retraction and pharyngeal tension. To produce a front vowel such as [i] with exaggerated jaw-opening demands that the tongue's mass be brought much further forward and that a different (more central) portion of the tongue be elevated than in normal speech. The tongue has to be retracted from this position to allow the jaw to close, and pharyngeal tension is introduced when the child attempts to raise the wrong portion of his tongue to produce an [i] constriction too near the center of the palate. If these faults occur, one must resort to the tactile strategies described above to obtain correct tongue placement. To reduce pharyngeal tension, one must provide extensive practice in the production of sounds while ensuring that the child's body is relaxed (this does not mean slumping in a chair) so that extraneous tension is avoided.

Exaggeration, if habitual, indicates that the child has been reinforced for producing inappropriate patterns. This may be a matter of neglect; the teacher and parents may give encouragement for speech but be unaware of the abnormality or exaggeration which they may even unconsciously come to share with the child. On the other hand, exaggeration may be deliberately fostered on the assumption that it facilitates visual communication through speechreading. It is doubtful whether this assumption can be justified. Although more of the segmental elements can be seen in exaggerated speech, they will be seen in a distorted form; and the rhythmic structure—which contributes greatly to the understanding of speechread material—is less well conveyed, if not destroyed. Moreover, the child who speaks and speechreads only an exaggerated form is placed at a severe disadvantage when faced with the task of communicating with people outside his school and home.

The remediation of habitual exaggeration requires the concurrent use of two strategies: the child must be taught to use less exaggerated patterns, and he must be consistently provided with normal speech models with which his own speech must be expected to conform. In other words, work at both the phonetic and phonologic levels is required. Some texts suggest that exaggeration can be remedied by placing the hand under the child's chin to provide consciousness of the limit to which jaw excursion is permitted. It has even been suggested that the teacher should hold one hand under the child's chin and the other on top of the child's head, thus restricting jaw movement by a "vise-like" grip (Bishop and Johnson, 1967). Such strategies are not recommended. First, they involve laying hands on the child; second, they may engender even more exaggeration because of the child's tendency to oppose an externally applied force with an equal and opposite force. Vowels taught through visual exaggeration should be corrected by reference to the visual patterns of normal speech, and all five vowel subskills should be rehearsed without exaggeration. Attention during this process should be gradually shifted from the visual to the auditory and motor-kinesthetic patterns associated with each target until production becomes automatic. If normal patterns cannot be obtained except through tactile means, then the subskills specified earlier in this chapter should be rehearsed while the child holds a pencil or similar object between his teeth, rather as a smoker holds his pipe. This ensures that the muscles responsible for producing the excursion of the jaw are relaxed during speech and that the motor-kinesthetic patterns associated with tongue position and movement become the child's predominant guide to vowel production.

As work at the phonetic level proceeds, the teacher, parents, and others in everyday contact with the child should ensure that their speech is not exaggerated and that the child's phonologic speech incorporates the more normal patterns taught at a phonetic level. Emphasis should be given to the production of speech at a normal rate. As with the correction of prolongation, the correction of exaggeration in familiar words and phrases poses the greatest difficulty because previously faulty articulatory patterns will have become strongly associated with the word's meaning and—if sounds have been represented by orthographic symbols—also with the written form. Strategies such as rehearsing phonologic speech sequences (words, phrases, and sentences) while an object is held between the teeth may be required in order to break down such associations and to establish more appropriate speech behaviors. They should, however, be introduced only when exaggeration has been eliminated at a phonetic level and should be used only briefly in specific training sessions. Corrections of an habitual fault should not be attempted when the child is in the process of communicating by speech since it could readily discourage the child from making further attempts. Responses to communicative speech should always be such that they provide the child with greater motivation (see Chapter 7).

Nasalization

Nasalization of vowels occurs when the velopharyngeal port is sufficiently open to route a substantial proportion of the breath stream through the nasal cavities. Providing that the velum is not lowered to such a degree that there is as much or more restriction within the oral cavities as in the nasopharynx, significant nasalization does not occur. In other words, complete velopharyngeal closure—though perhaps a desirable target—is not essential to the production of oral vowels (Coleman, 1963). The relationship between the degree of velopharyngeal closure and perceived nasality is by no means simple. For example, in vowels where there is considerable constriction, such as [i], a greater degree of velopharyngeal closure is called for than in those involving less constriction of the oral vocal tract (Moll, 1962; Matsuya, Miyazaki, and Yamaoka, 1974). Furthermore, perceived nasality depends to some extent on the context of speech. Thus, Colton and Cooker (1968) found that when normally hearing persons spoke slowly, their speech was perceived as more nasal than when they spoke at the usual rate. They suggested that increasing the speaking tempo of hearing-impaired subjects might produce a concomitant reduction in perceived nasality.

The reason why hearing-impaired children tend to produce nasal vowels unless particular care is taken to prevent the fault is not clear. It is possible that nasality provides stronger orosensory patterns than orality and hence more intrinsic feedback in the absence of audition, but there has been no work to substantiate this theory. Certainly, the use of available residual hearing will effectively counteract the development of nasalization, providing that there are no organic defects such as cleft palate and difficulty in closing the velopharyngeal port as a result of adenoidectomy (see Gelder, 1974). The speech of children taught in accordance with the model proposed in this text does not tend to be nasalized. This is because the use of audition is emphasized, because velar target position for all vowels is raised, because vowels that have a tangible breath stream—[i] and [u]—are among the first to be developed, and because consonants differing in manner of production are contrasted early in the speech teaching process. We disagree with the opinion of Moll and Daniloff (1971) that velar targets are "closed" for non-nasal consonants, "open" for nasal consonants, and "unspecified" for vowels; we suggest that the literature indicates that a closed velum is a basic target behavior in vowel production—although target position may not be reached due to assimilation and coarticulation (see Kent, Carney, and Severeid, 1974). Although velar closure can usually be observed in normal speakers (McClean, 1973), it may be rare among hearing-impaired subjects whose speech is habitually nasalized. Thus, McClumpha (1966) in a cinefluorographic study found not only that velar closure was rarely achieved by his deaf subjects but also that the velum in the deaf speakers was much smaller than in normal speakers. This finding suggests that nasality is a fault that feeds upon itself: that failure to use the velar musculature leads to an asthenic—if not atrophied—organ and hence to less likelihood of its being used effectively.

The remedial treatment of nasalization in speech calls for a simultaneous attack on the problem at both the phonetic and the phonologic levels. At the phonetic level the most effective procedure is to ensure the presence of the high-front [i] and high-back [u] so that tangible breath stream can be used to foster orality. These vowels should be sustained and alternated while the breath stream is used to provide sensation on the fingertip, to move lightweight objects (feather, paper), or to disturb a flame. This is far more effective than pinching the child's nostrils or having the child feel vibration on his nose, strategies that tend to focus attention on nasal emission (from which he is probably seeking feedback anyhow). One should emphasize not what the child is doing wrong but rather what he can do to get things right.

As soon as the child can produce the basic vowels at an automatic level without tactile feedback, the first few consonants should be introduced (see Chapter 14). Emphasis should primarily be given to syllables released with fricatives, semivowels, and plosives to maintain the tangibility of the oral breath stream. The [m] may then be introduced, but syllables ending in [m] should be released with an audible fricative to ensure velopharyngeal closure prior to vowel production: e.g., [fam], [fim], [θʌm]. Similarly, syllables beginning with [m] should be arrested with a fricative: e.g., [mʌf]. Great care should be taken to repeat such syllables at normal rates and to alternate syllables containing [m] with syllables containing fricatives: e.g., [fa-ma], [θi-mi]. Similar rehearsal with other vowels and fricatives is essential when teaching nasal sounds at other stages of consonant development: e.g., [sa-na], [θa-na].

Two facts relating to nasality should be borne in mind. First, the range of sounds available in the earliest stages of our proposed model is adequate for teaching the four basic velar targets and movements unambiguously. These targets are as follows:

1. *Velum raised*—all vowels, all consonants except nasals.
2. *Velum lowered*—the three nasal consonants, [m], [n], and [ŋ].
3. *Velum initially raised, finally lowered*—syllables such as [fʌm], [sim], [ʃan], [bæn], [paŋ], and [tɪn].
4. *Velum initially lowered, finally raised*—syllables such as [mʌʃ], [nɪʃ], [maθ], and [naɪs].

Second, prevention of hypernasality is better than cure. We stress the importance of babbling non-nasal syllables (vowels released with plosives and unvoiced fricatives) as early as possible in training. We do not encourage babbling of syllables such as [mʌmʌmʌ] until the child has established orality rather than nasality as a norm. Over 90% of the sounds produced in normal speech are non-nasal. Hence, orality is the rule and nasality the exception. Of course, if [məməmə] is the first series of sounds produced by the young hearing-impaired child, one must initially reinforce it; but the sooner [bʌbʌbʌ] and other syllables can be substituted, the better, for then we may cease to reinforce what may otherwise prove to be the foundation for nasalization in later speech.

Treatment for excessive nasalization (hypernasality) is generally more effective if one uses speech as a medium than if one attempts to establish velar control in a non-speech context. Indeed, if the oral-peripheral examination (see Chapter 9) has shown that velopharyngeal closure can be effected, then the strategies described above are sufficient to establish the four velar targets at the phonetic level. Work by Shelton, Knox, Elbert, and Johnson (1970) has shown that there is little carry-over into speech from velar exercises undertaken in a non-speech context (see Chapter 6). This may, in part, be due to the fact that the velum alone is not the only organ involved in velopharyngeal closure. The lateral pharyngeal walls also move medially and assist in closure during speech (Zwitman, Sonderman, and Ward, 1974). Similar findings have been reported by Moller, Path, Werth, and Christiansen (1973).

However, when velopharyngeal closure cannot be effected in a speech context but can be obtained in non-speech contexts, one has no alternative but to initiate treatment with non-speech exercises. They may strengthen an asthenic velum much as isometric exercises involving the biceps can strengthen the arm. If the exercises are part of a carefully planned program, the results may—through a process of behavior shaping—be transferred to speech. Thus, Massengill and Quinn (1974) treated velopharyngeal incompetence through sucking exercises. Over a six-month period of training, an 18-year-old patient learned to effect velopharyngeal closure by holding a piece of paper at the end of a drinking straw. The procedure restored the musculature of the velum sufficiently to permit the patient to make stop consonants and thence to begin speech-context training.

Transfer of velar target behaviors from non-speech contexts to speech is notoriously difficult. The velum must be lowered when breathing in or out through the nose, but gravity assists in this. To involve the velar musculature sufficiently for strengthening the downward movement, vigorous sniffing or blowing out through the nose rather than quiet intake of breath is essential. Yawning, sucking, blowing, and whistling all require a raised velum. Alternating sniffing with yawning, sucking, blowing, or whistling may therefore help to strengthen velar action. As speech requires outward rather than inward transglottal air flow, blowing and whistling most closely approximate the requirements for speech. Most children, including those who are hearing-impaired, love to whistle and should be taught to do so because this skill usually involves more pharyngeal action to aid in closure than does blowing.

Transfer to speech may be sought by coupling phonation with either skill—blowing or whistling. The technique has been advocated by Shprintzen, McCall, and Skolnick (1975). We have also found whispering to be an effective bridge between blowing exercises and speech as well as an effective antidote to nasalization of vowels. The formants of whispered vowels become much less audible if damped by nasalization; hence, those children with useful residual hearing can usually discriminate between nasal and non-nasal sounds in whispered speech. Those who have no useful residual hearing are better able to feel the breath stream in whispered than in voiced vowels; hence, their oral nature can be more readily demonstrated.

Nasalization cannot be corrected in phonologic speech unless the vowels can be produced without nasality at a phonetic level. Once oral vowels have been established through phonetic level exercises, familiar words and phrases which contain no nasal consonants may be practiced while the child feels the oral breath stream with a wet finger. Considerable effort may be required before oral vowels are automatically produced in phonologic speech if nasalization has become habitual.

Context-Dependent Pitch

In normal speakers, there is a tendency for F_0 to vary slightly in relation to the vowel used (Lehiste and Peterson, 1961). Among hearing-impaired children, particularly those to whom vowels have been taught before control of voice pitch has been established, F_0 may be substantially influenced by the tongue and jaw positions adopted in vowel production. Among such children a markedly higher pitch tends to be associated with the raised, fronted tongue posture for [i] than with the dropped jaw and retracted tongue posture for [ɑ]. When such is the case, the development of independent laryngeal and articulatory control calls for the gradual shifting from one vowel to another as pitch is maintained at the desired level.

To develop a high pitch on all front vowels, one first obtains production of the high-pitched [i]. Then, [i] is alternated with [eɪ]. When pitch can be held stable using these two vowels, a third, more central vowel [ɛ] is introduced and alternated with [i] and [eɪ]. The procedure is repeated with adjacent vowels until the central vowel [a] can be alternated with [i] and with intermediate vowels, pitch being held constant.

To obtain low pitch on all front vowels the strategy is reversed. Beginning with the low-pitched vowel [a], the child alternates it in turn with [æ], [ɛ], [eɪ], and [i], the teacher ensuring that voice pitch is maintained. The strategy may be extended to include all vowels.

By following the procedures described above, one may establish a voice pitch contrast from which the child can develop the first of the subskills required for pitch control. As soon as the child can produce several vowels at each of two discrete pitch levels, he should be trained to control pitch on all vowels in accordance with the schedule of subskills described in the previous chapter.

Multiple Faults

Any two or more of the faults described above may occur together and, unfortunately, frequently do. The spectrogram shown in Figure 13.3(a) shows a normal pronunciation of the word *baby* as spoken by an adult male. Figure 13.3(b) illustrates the effect when it is said with the

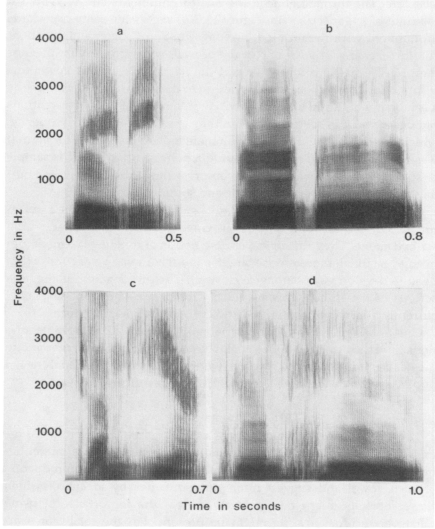

Figure 13.3

Broad-band spectrograms showing: (above), the word "baby" (a) as spoken normally, and (b) with prolongation and neutralization; and (below), the phrase "Come here" (c) as spoken normally, and (d) with nasalization and prolongation.

prolongation and neutral vowel substitution typical of a poorly taught hearing-impaired speaker. Dealing with either problem alone would not yield intelligible speech. Indeed, increasing the rate of this particular sample of speech by means of a tape recorder with time compression capability simply made the word shorter, not clearer.

Figure 13.3(c) shows a normal (adult male) production of the words *come here.* The formant glide of the final diphthong is clearly visible at the right of the spectrogram. Figure 13.3(d) shows the same two words pronounced with nasalization, prolongation, and some neutralization. All three characteristics of "deaf speech" were present in the one sample. The nasalization weakened the /k/ in *come* and all vowel formants, particularly those toward the end of the word *here* where even the weak orality of the /h/ was lost due to prolongation. Formant transitions can be seen in this spectrogram, but they tend to be lower in frequency, which indicates that while this adult male moved his tongue forward, it was not moved sufficiently far to produce the required /ɪ/. This sample of speech was improved by time compression; it did not become normal, but the words were intelligible and sounded less nasal.

Children who exhibit multiple faults such as those illustrated in Figure 13.3(d) can respond quickly to remedial teaching of the type described above. They already have some notion of tongue placement (but need to establish more precise targets) and have some velar control (but need to develop velopharyngeal closure). The prolongation is the least serious of the three problems, all of which must be dealt with concurrently, first at a phonetic level and then in phonologic speech.

One final word: the spectrograms shown above are simply illustrations on which to hang discussion. They are useful to the writer and to the reader but not to the teacher, who should be able to analyze her pupils' speech by means of a much superior instrument: her ear.

Summary

The mechanisms by which vowels and diphthongs are produced are explained and the sensory and acoustic properties of vowel target behaviors examined. We specify five subskills underlying the production of each vowel and suggest numerous strategies by means of which these subskills might be taught. We stress the importance of using whatever residual hearing might be present. For the totally or near-totally deaf child, we suggest that tactile rather than visual strategies would be more appropriate to teach the vowels, although vision might be more important than touch to maintain them. Finally, we discuss the prevention and remedial treatment of various types of deviant vowel production typically found in the speech of hearing-impaired children. We insist that there are few shortcuts in this remedial treatment of faults. Our view is that if vowels are faulty, they must be redeveloped through much the same strategies as we have proposed for initially teaching them. The remedial strategies suggested largely conform with this view.

REFERENCES

Angelocci, A. A., Kopp, G. A., & Holbrook, A. The vowel formants of deaf and normal-hearing eleven- to fourteen-year-old boys. *J. Speech Hear. Disord.*, 29, 156–170, 1964.

Bishop, M. E., & Johnson, S. *Factors Influencing and Techniques for Achieving Intelligible Speech in Deaf Children*. Utah State School for the Deaf, 1967.

Bonet, J. P. *Reduccion de las letras y arte para ensenar a hablar los mudos*. Madrid: Francisco Abarca de Anguls, 1620.

Borden, G. J., & Novikoff, D. P. What is an orthophoniste? *Asha*, 16, 203–206, 1974.

Carrell, J., & Tiffany, W. R. *Phonetics: Theory and Application to Speech Improvement*. New York: McGraw-Hill, 1960.

Coleman, R. O. *The effect of changes in width of velopharyngeal aperture on acoustic and perceptual properties of nasalized vowels*. Unpublished Ph.D. diss., Northwestern University, 1963.

Colton, R. H., & Cooker, H. S. Perceived nasality in the speech of the deaf. *J. Speech Hear. Res.*, 11, 553–559, 1968.

Delattre, P., Liberman, A. M., Cooper, F. S., & Gerstman, L. J. An experimental study of the acoustic determinants of vowel color; observations on one- and two-formant vowels synthesized from spectrographic patterns. *Word*, 8, 195–210, 1952.

Doehring, D. G., & Ling, D. Programmed instruction of hearing-impaired children in the auditory discrimination of vowels. *J. Speech Hear. Res.*, 14, 746–753, 1971.

Ewing, A. W. G., & Ewing, E. C. *Teaching Deaf Children To Talk*. Manchester: Manchester University Press, 1964.

Gay, T. Effect of speaking rate on diphthong formant movements. *J. Acoust. Soc. Am.*, 44, 1570–1573, 1968.

Gay, T. A perceptual study of American English diphthongs. *Lang. Speech*, 13, 65–88, 1970.

Gelder, L. van Open nasal speech following adenoidectomy and tonsillectomy. *J. Commun. Disord.*, 7, 263–267, 1974.

Jeffers, J. Formants and the auditory training of deaf children. *Volta Rev.*, 68, 418–423, passim, 1966.

Kent, R. D., Carney, P. J., & Severeid, L. R. Velar movement and timing: Evaluation of a model for binary control. *J. Speech Hear. Res.*, 17, 470–488, 1974.

Kirman, J. H. Tactile perception of computer-derived formant patterns from voiced speech. *J. Acoust. Soc. Am.*, 55, 163–169, 1974.

Ladefoged, P., & Broadbent, D. E. Information conveyed by vowels. *J. Acoust. Soc. Am.*, 29, 98–104, 1957.

Leckie, D., & Ling, D. Audibility with hearing aids having low-frequency characteristics. *Volta Rev.*, 70, 83–86, 1968.

Lehiste, I., & Peterson, G. E. Some basic considerations in the analysis of intonation. *J. Acoust. Soc. Am.*, 33, 419–425, 1961.

Lieberman, P. On the evolution of language: A unified view. *Cognition*, 2, 59–94, 1973.

Lindblom, B. E. F., & Studdert-Kennedy, M. On the role of formant transitions in vowel recognition. *J. Acoust. Soc. Am.*, 42, 830–843, 1967.

Ling, D., & Bennett, C. W.   Training severely hearing-impaired children in vowel imitation. *Hum. Commun.*, 3, 5–18, 1974–75.

Mangan, K. R.   Speech improvement through articulation testing. *Am. Ann. Deaf*, 106, 391–396, 1961.

Markides, A.   The speech of deaf and partially-hearing children with special reference to factors affecting intelligibility. *Br. J. Disord. Commun.*, 5, 126–140, 1970.

Massengill, R., & Quinn, G.   Adenoidal atrophy, velopharyngeal incompetence and sucking exercises: A two year follow-up case report. *Cleft Palate J.*, 11, 196–199, 1974.

Matsuya, T., Miyazaki, T., & Yamaoka, M.   Fiberscopic examination of velopharyngeal closure in normal individuals. *Cleft Palate J.*, 11, 286–291, 1974.

McClean, M.   Forward coarticulation of velar movement at marked junctural boundaries. *J. Speech Hear. Res.*, 16, 286–296, 1973.

McClumpha, S.   *Cinefluorographic investigation of velopharyngeal function in selected deaf speakers*. M.A. thesis, University of Florida, 1966.

Mermelstein, P.   Some articulatory manifestations of vowel stress. *J. Acoust. Soc. Am.*, 54, 538–540, 1973.

Minifie, F. D., Hixon, T. J., Kelsey, C. A., & Woodhouse, R. J.   Lateral pharyngeal wall movement during speech production. *J. Speech Hear. Res.*, 13, 584–595, 1970.

Moll, K. L.   Velopharyngeal closure on vowels. *J. Speech Hear. Res.*, 5, 30–37, 1962.

Moll, K. L., & Daniloff, R. G.   Investigation of the timing of velar movements during speech. *J. Acoust. Soc. Am.*, 50, 678–684, 1971.

Moller, K. T., Path, M., Werth, L. J., & Christiansen, R. L.   The modification of velar movement. *J. Speech Hear. Disord.*, 38, 323–334, 1973.

Perkell, J. S.   *Physiology of Speech Production: Results and Implications of a Quantitative Cineradiographic Study*. Cambridge, Mass.: M.I.T. Press, 1969.

Peterson, G. E.   The information-bearing elements of speech. *J. Acoust. Soc. Am.*, 24, 629–637, 1952.

Peterson, G. E., & Barney, H. L.   Control methods used in a study of the vowels. *J. Acoust. Soc. Am.*, 24, 175–184, 1952.

Pickett, J. M., & Constam, A.   A visual speech trainer with simplified indication of vowel spectrum. *Am. Ann. Deaf*, 113, 253–258, 1968.

Raphael, L. J., & Bell-Berti, F.   Tongue musculature and the feature of tension in English vowels. *Phonetica*, 32, 61–73, 1975.

Rosen, J.   *Phoneme identification in sensorineural deafness*. Unpublished Ph.D. diss., Stanford University, 1962.

Schultz, M. C.   Suggested improvements in speech discrimination testing. *J. Aud. Res.*, 4, 1–14, 1964.

Shelton, R. L., Knox, A. W., Elbert, M., & Johnson, T. S.   Palate awareness and nonspeech voluntary palate movement. In J. F. Bosma (Ed.), *Second Symposium on Oral Sensation and Perception*. Springfield, Ill.: Thomas, 1970.

Shprintzen, R. J., McCall, G. N., & Skolnick, M. L.   A new therapeutic technique for the treatment of velopharyngeal incompetence. *J. Speech Hear. Disord.*, 40, 69–83, 1975.

Singh, S., & Singh, K. S.   *Phonetics: Principies and Practices*. Baltimore: University Park Press, 1976.

Stevens, K. N., & House, A. S.   An acoustical theory of vowel production and some of its implications. *J. Speech Hear. Res.*, 4, 303–320, 1961.

Stewart, R. B.   The speech of children with high frequency losses of hearing—a small phonetic study. *Sound*, 3, 40–43, 1969.

Studdert-Kennedy, M.   Speech perception. In N. J. Lass (Ed.), *Contemporary Issues in Experimental Phonetics*. Springfield, Ill.: Thomas, 1975.

Wakita, H.   Direct estimation of the vocal tract shape by inverse filtering of acoustic speech wave forms. *I.E.E.E. Trans. Audio Electroacoust.*, AU-21, 417–427, 1973.

Wedenberg, E.   Auditory training of deaf and hard of hearing children. *Acta Oto-Laryngol. Suppl.* 94, 1951.

Zwitman, D. H., Sonderman, J. C., & Ward, P. H.   Variations in velopharyngeal closure assessed by endoscopy. *J. Speech Hear. Disord.*, 39, 366–372, 1974.

/14/

Consonants:
Their Acoustic Properties
and Sensory Correlates

Consonants differ from vowels in several important ways. They are produced with greater restriction of the vocal tract and call for more varied and, in many cases, faster and more precise adjustments of the articulators. While all vowels can be produced in isolation, many consonants cannot. Acoustically there are also marked differences. There is a greater intensity range between the loudest and quietest consonants than between the loudest and quietest vowels. Consonants similarly vary to a greater extent than do vowels in respect to their durational and frequency characteristics. Certain consonants may therefore be harder to produce than vowels, and some will be much less audible to the child with limited hearing. However, the orosensory-motor patterns associated with most consonants are relatively stronger than those intrinsic to vowel production since additional tactile components are generated by the contact of one speech organ with another.

Consonants may be classified according to three articulatory dimensions: manner, place, and voicing. *Manner* distinctions refer to whether consonants are plosives, stops, nasals, semivowels, liquids, fricatives, or affricates. *Place* distinctions specify the point of greatest constriction in the vocal tract during articulation. Thus, sounds may be described as bilabial, labiodental, linguadental, alveolar, palatal, velar, or glottal. *Voicing* is a binary dimension. If the vocal cords vibrate as the sound is produced it is regarded as voiced, and if they do not, as unvoiced. The consonants with which we are concerned in this text, as classified according to these three dimensions, are shown in Table 14.A.

The classification of consonants as shown in Table 14.A tempts one to make a somewhat simplistic interpretation of the speech teaching task. As sounds are articulated, the data in the table are adequate; as sounds

TABLE 14.A

Consonants classified according to manner of production, place of production, and voicing.

		Bilabial	Labiodental	Linguadental	Alveolar	Palatal	Velar	Glottal
Plosives/Stops	Unvoiced	p			t		k	
	Voiced	b			d		g	
Fricatives	Unvoiced	ʍ	f	θ	s	ʃ		h
	Voiced		v	ð	z	ʒ		
Nasals	Voiced	m			n		ŋ	
Semivowels	Voiced	w				j		
Liquids	Voiced				l, r			
Affricates	Unvoiced					tʃ		
	Voiced					dʒ		

are coarticulated, they are not. Consider the following examples. Aspiration can be heard (and felt) following the release of /p/ in the word *pan*, but it does not occur following /p/ in the word *span*. The [f] and [v] are classified as fricative, but they are not inevitably characterized by turbulence. In running speech /v/ as in the word *very* may have no fricative turbulence and /f/ as in the word *fat*, very little (Reddy, 1967). They may, indeed, be pronounced as if they were labiodental stops. Further, not all nasals are voiced. Following /s/ as in the word *small* the /m/ may be partly or wholly unvoiced. The /n/ may similarly become unvoiced in a word like *snow*. The semivowels and liquids are modified in much the same way through assimilation. Thus, the /j/ glide in the word *human* and the /r/ in the word *trap* are rarely, if ever, produced with the vocal cords vibrating.

These and other variations in the production of consonants are extremely common. The allophonic variants we have discussed above could be represented in Table 14.A by IPA symbols. However, as allophonic variations due to assimilation and coarticulation are discussed in the text, it is sufficient here simply to mention the dangers of using a broad phonetic transcription and to repeat our warning against associating orthographic or other symbols with speech sounds (see Chapter 4). It is because allophonic variations are characteristically present in consonant production that fluent, intelligible speech cannot be developed through reference to the written form.

Acoustic analysis of consonants in the context of both synthetic and natural speech shows that they consist of both variant and invariant types of energy. The variant energy is derived from formant transitions which occur as a result of coarticulation with adjacent vowels (see Liberman, 1957; Liberman, Cooper, Shankweiler, and Studdert-Kennedy, 1967). The invariant energy is derived from the way in which the vocal tract is constricted as the consonant itself is articulated (Jassem, 1965; Fant, 1967, 1968; Cole and Scott, 1974a, b). Thus, there are two major sources of acoustic energy by means of which most consonants can be identified. Both provide multiple cues. For example, cues on manner may be present in the F_1 and F_2 (and in some cases F_3) transitions, and more than one part of the spectrum of a given consonant may provide information on its identity. In short, the speech signal is characterized by many types of redundancy (Studdert-Kennedy, 1975).

Systematic teaching of speech to hearing-impaired children through the maximum use of residual hearing demands that the data presented in this chapter are known. Although nothing new on the acoustic and sensory correlates of speech is presented, the information accumulated has not previously been summarized in this manner for the teacher. It should therefore serve as a useful reference source and as a foundation to which new material can be added as more work is published. Most readers will find that the information in this chapter is too complex to digest on first reading. As we deal with the teaching of consonants in later chapters we shall, therefore, continue to refer to this material. The reader should then find that the general principles which underlie the acoustic and sensory correlates of speech will emerge from what may initially appear to be an overabundance of detail.

Manner, Place, and Voicing

Manner Distinctions

Manner cues are more important than either place or voicing cues in the differentiation of words in English (Denes, 1963). Furthermore, many of these cues occur in the lower end of the speech frequency range and hence are likely to be audible to most hearing-impaired listeners. The identification of a consonant as having a particular manner of production is of major importance in speech perception since the more certain one is about the identity of a class, the less likely one is to make errors within that class (Wang and Fillmore, 1961). The importance of providing auditory information on manner to the hearing-impaired person was stressed by Walden (1971, p. 122), who pointed out that whereas information on place could be fairly readily perceived through speechreading, information on manner and voicing could not. Electromyographic studies confirm that manner cues are difficult, if not impossible, to speechread. For example, Harris, Lysaught, and Schvey (1965) found no significant differences in muscle potential during the formation of [p], [b], and [m]. Although Sussman, MacNeilage, and Hanson (1973) found certain differences, they were not of the type that could be perceived visually.

Acoustic Cues Relating to Manner of Production: Plosives are produced by completely closing some portion of the vocal tract and then releasing the pressure built up in the process as a sharp burst. The invariant acoustic cues associated with plosives are, not surprisingly, a short period of silence (about 30 msec.) and a subsequent burst (Halle, Hughes, and Radley, 1957). In word-initial plosives, the frequency of the burst varies according to both the place of production of the plosive and the vowel which follows it. The vowel has the greater influence on the burst characteristics. In medial positions the burst frequency may

also be somewhat modified by the vowel preceding the plosive. As Delattre (1958) points out, such findings show that the smallest invariant
acoustic unit in speech is the syllable.

Several variant cues distinguish plosives from other classes of consonants. The F_1 consonant-to-vowel transition begins at a lower frequency than the transition associated with other manners of production. This property is due to the complete closure of the vocal tract in
the formation of plosives (Stevens and House, 1956). The duration of all
formant transitions is also shorter in plosives than in consonants having another manner of production, and the speed of plosive formant
transitions is therefore greater (Delattre, Liberman, and Cooper, 1955;
Liberman, Delattre, Gerstman, and Cooper, 1956). Of particular importance here is that plosive characteristics can be recognized very clearly
as such from F_1 transitions alone (Smith, 1974). Thus, they should be
audible to children who have only low-frequency residual hearing. Plosives can certainly be discriminated from other consonants in low-pass
filtered speech when sounds above 500 Hz are excluded (Gay, 1970).

Stops are produced much like plosives except that they are unreleased
and therefore have no burst characteristics. Stops may be recognized by
the rapid formant transitions leading to an abrupt termination of the
preceding vowel. Work by Sharf and Beiter (1974) indicates that formant transition cues are much more important to the identification of
stops than to the identification of plosives. Because total closure of the
vocal tract is involved in the production of stops, the F_1 transition is,
like that of plosives, lower than for other classes of consonants.

Nasal consonants are produced by stopping the oral tract with either
the tongue or the lips and lowering the velum, thus coupling the oral
and nasal cavities. The invariant cues associated with nasal consonants
are a low-frequency murmur—a steady-state formant which usually
falls between 200 and 300 Hz (Delattre, 1958; Nakata, 1959); upper formants that are relatively weaker than those in vowels; and the presence of
antiformants—bands of zero energy in the spectrum (Fant, 1960). The
very low formant is due to the large capacity and small aperture of the
resonating system. The relative weakness of nasal formants is probably
due to increase in the surface area of soft tissue with nasals and the resulting absorption of energy. The antiformants are due to the closed-off
space in the blocked oral tract which serves as an extremely effective
acoustic filter. Since there is no build-up of intraoral pressure in nasals,
acoustic bursts are not produced (Fujimura, 1961).

The variant cues associated with nasal consonants are discontinuity
of F_1 and damping (reduction in peak intensity) of the formants of adja-

cent vowels (Delattre, 1954). The discontinuity of F_1 shows on spectrograms as a sudden shift between the low nasal murmur and the F_1 of the vowel. It is caused by the rerouting of the breath stream and the resulting change in resonance as the velum is lowered or raised. Damping of the formant structure of the vowel occurs when the velopharyngeal port is not adequately closed, and in normal speech this is commonly associated with the coarticulation of nasal consonants and vowels. The action of the velum is, in any case, sluggish (Bjork, 1961), and in hearing-impaired speakers it may be particularly so (see the section on nasalization in Chapter 13).

Because both invariant and variant cues associated with nasal consonants are present in the low-frequency range, they are audible to most children with residual audition if appropriate hearing aids are worn. Studies by Miller and Nicely (1955) and by Gay (1970) show that the nasal consonant feature is the most resistant to low-pass filtering and that the presence of sound below 450 Hz is sufficient to permit the recognition of consonants as nasal even in the presence of noise. Predictably, the acquisition of nasal consonants and the reduction of nasalization in other speech sounds is superior when one uses hearing aids having extended low-frequency response rather than aids which amplify sound only above 300 Hz (Ling, 1964). On the basis of low-frequency cues alone, one may discriminate between nasal and stop/plosive consonants; this may be done more readily if the sounds are contrasted in syllables so that the variant information provided by coarticulation is also available.

The *semivowels* [w] and [j] are formed in the same way as the vowels [u] and [i], but with greater vocal tract constriction. They do not occur in word-final positions. Since the frequency of F_1 is directly related to the degree of vocal tract constriction, F_1 for both semivowels is lower than for either vowel. The duration and speed of formant transitions (about 75 msec.) differentiate among diphthongs, semivowels, and plosive consonants. When the transition is long and slow (over 100 msec.), diphthongs are heard. When transitions are brief and fast (less than 50 msec.), the plosive [b] or [g] may be heard (Liberman *et al.*, 1956). Thus the identity of the semivowels is at best obscured in speech characterized by prolongation (see Chapter 13). Additionally, the constriction of the vocal tract may lead to a slightly turbulent breath stream which results in a low-frequency fricative noise for [w] and a high-frequency fricative noise for [j]. Such noise is not always present; hence the major acoustic cues are variant and arise through the coarticulation of the semivowel with adjacent vowels.

The low-frequency energy of the semivowels renders them audible and discriminable from plosives and nasals when sounds above 500 Hz are filtered out. Even in noise, the low-frequency onset characteristics of the plosives and semivowels are highly contrastive, as is the continuity/discontinuity dimension separating semivowels from nasal consonants. Most children with low-frequency residual hearing can therefore be expected to discriminate among these manners of production if fitted with hearing aids having some low-frequency gain.

The *liquids* [l] and [r] are produced with a relatively open vocal tract, the tongue creating a partial occlusion and a diversion of the breath stream within the oral cavity. Since the degree of vocal tract opening determines F_1 values, the F_1 formants of the liquids are higher than those of the other classes of consonants described above; they typically fall at or above 400 Hz unless palatalized (Fant, 1960, p. 163). The acoustic cues which characterize the liquids are the relatively high F_1 frequency; the short (30–50 msec.) steady-state energy preceding the relatively long glide to the vowel (50–75 msec. for [l] and even longer for [r]); and steady-state formants above F_1 which are weaker than those of vowels, yet stronger than those of nasals (Cooper, Delattre, Liberman, Borst, and Gerstman, 1952; O'Connor, Gerstman, Liberman, Delattre, and Cooper, 1957). Due to their higher F_1 frequency values, the liquids are less likely to be audible to children with only low-frequency residual hearing. If they are audible, however, they are usually quite discriminable from consonants having other manners of production (Owens and Schubert, 1968).

The *fricatives* are produced by creating such a small aperture in the vocal tract that the breath stream becomes turbulent and thus causes noise at the point of constriction. The frequency of the noise depends on the size of the cavity and the aperture anterior to the constriction. Other things being equal, the nearer the front of the mouth the constriction is, the smaller the cavity and the higher the frequency of the fricative will be (Hughes and Halle, 1956; Fant, 1960; Hixon, Minifie, and Tait, 1967; Stevens, 1971). Accordingly, [h] in any vowel environment tends to have some low-frequency energy, and the [s] is considerably higher than the [ʃ]. The [s] is practically destroyed if frequencies above 3,500 Hz are eliminated (Fletcher, 1929, p. 331).

Turbulent noise is the one invariant cue to fricative production. The duration of this noise is typically long (100 msec. or more), although its duration varies considerably according to whether the fricative is voiced or unvoiced (Gerstman, 1957). The duration and intensity of noise in fricatives are usually greater than those in plosive bursts. The intensity of the noise also varies according to the duration, stress, and position of the fricative in the syllable, word, or sentence (Umeda, Monsen, and Molter, 1973). The rate at which the intensity of the noise increases in initial fricatives is much slower than in initial affricates (see below).

Variant cues are important to the identification of fricatives. Vowels preceding fricatives tend to be longer in duration, greater in power, and lower in fundamental frequency than vowels preceding stops (House and Fairbanks, 1953; Lintz and Sherman, 1961). Many severely hearing-impaired children find all fricative noise inaudible. Even so, the variant cues provided in syllables and in running speech may be adequate for such a child to identify a consonant as fricative by a process of elimination if cues to other manners of production are audible. No other class of consonant has such long duration coupled with lack of distinctive low-frequency energy.

The *affricates* [tʃ] and [dʒ] are formed by releasing a stop with a fricative. The invariant cues to affricates are the brief duration of silence (about 50 msec.) preceding an almost equally brief noise burst which, on account of the preceding stop, has sudden onset (Gerstman, 1957). These cues are sufficient to differentiate them from plosives, which share the pre-burst silent interval but have shorter bursts (less than 30 msec.), and from fricatives, which have no pre-burst silent interval and much longer noise characteristics with less sudden onset. The variant cues associated with affricates are similar to those associated with stops: namely, rapid vowel-to-consonant formant transitions. These consonants have no other known low-frequency energy which distinguishes their manner of production.

Sensory Correlates of Manner Distinctions: A variety of sensory cues may be derived from speech. Such cues have been discussed in some detail in Chapters 3, 4, and 6 and have been mentioned elsewhere throughout this text. The purpose here is to focus attention on those that relate specifically to manner distinctions in consonant production so that appropriate guidelines may be provided for selecting strategies to teach the subskills underlying the targets specified in Step 1 (see Chapter 15). The strategies adopted for a particular child must be selected according to his sensory capabilities, particularly the extent of his residual hearing.

Auditory cues on manner of production may be derived from almost every component part of the acoustic spectrum (see above). Audition is therefore the modality of choice in teaching manner distinctions. The child with hearing up to 4,000 Hz may be expected to make use of the multiplicity of cues present: those that are both invariant and variant. He may, in short, be expected to hear and to discriminate between plosives, stops, nasals, semivowels, liquids, fricatives, and affricates. Such a child may usually be taught exclusively through audition.

In contrast to the child with an extensive range of hearing, the child with hearing below about 1,000 Hz will receive fewer multiple cues on manner. Not only will much of the invariant energy be inaudible—particularly that associated with fricatives, affricates, and plosive bursts—but the variant cues associated with the F_2 transitions of at least the front vowels will be lost. Nevertheless, he may derive sufficient auditory cues for discrimination among the plosive, stop, nasal, semivowel, and liquid manners of production from the variant and invariant energy present below 1,000 Hz and even below 500 Hz. In our discussion of the acoustic cues on manner (above) we made several passing references to the use of residual hearing and pointed out the specific cues that could be identified from low-frequency energy. It is important to note that such energy is strongest for the front consonants—those that are bilabial, labiodental, and linguadental in origin. It is partly for this reason that we selected these sounds as the first consonants to be taught.

Because the auditory modality provides both proprioceptive and exteroceptive cues, it is inherently superior to either touch or vision as a means of learning speech. Most visual correlates of manner are difficult—if not impossible—to speechread, and tactile correlates of manner are relatively imprecise.

Direct visual cues on manner of production are present only for the labiodental fricatives [f] and [v] and for the linguadental fricatives [θ] and [ð]. Otherwise, sounds of different manner are homophenous: for example, the nasal [m] is visually similar to the bilabial plosives and stops; and the semivowel [w] may be readily confused with [r] if the latter is produced with any degree of lip-rounding. If the child cannot learn to distinguish the manner characteristics of homophenous sounds through hearing, or if sounds of a certain manner (e.g., fricatives) are inaudible, he must be provided with supplementary cues that allow him to differentiate them. Visual cue systems and visual aids that may be utilized to this end have been discussed in Chapters 3, 4, and 6.

Tactile cues on manner of production may be employed to differentiate between homophenous pairs if the child cannot distinguish manner cues through hearing. Plosives may be indicated through feeling the burst energy on the fingertips. (Unvoiced plosives provide the strongest burst energy since the breath stream is not impeded by laryngeal valving in voiceless sounds.) Stops may be indicated by sharp cessation of tangible breath stream; nasals, by the presence of vibration in the bony structures of the nose; and semivowels, fricatives, and affricates, by their particular breath stream characteristics. Tactile aids may also be used to provide vibratory cues as to manner of production. The use of touch has been discussed in Chapters 3 and 4.

Place Distinctions

Place of production is our principal concern in teaching the target behaviors specified in Steps 2 and 3 (see Chapter 16). It is in these steps that we seek to generalize from the front (mainly labial) consonants of different manner to the alveolar, palatal, and velar consonants of similar manner—those produced with the tongue. As with manner cues, the acoustic energy signifying place distinctions may be either variant (associated with consonant-to-vowel or vowel-to-consonant transitions) or invariant (intrinsic to the articulation of the consonant itself). Most of the acoustic energy providing information on place of production lies in the mid-frequency and high-frequency range. Difficulty in the auditory discrimination of place increases dramatically as frequencies below about 2,000 Hz are eliminated by filtering (Gay, 1970) and as the signal-to-noise ratio decreases below 6 dB (Miller and Nicely, 1955). Optimum acoustic conditions must therefore be maintained for developing auditory discrimination of place distinctions. These call for speaking close to the microphone of the child's aid in a quiet voice or in a whisper.

Acoustic Cues Relating to Place of Production: *Plosives* have been more extensively studied than other types of consonants. Cues on their place of production are provided by variant energy, i.e., formant frequency change, and by invariant energy, i.e., the frequency of the plosive burst (Delattre, 1958).

Formant frequency changes, principally F_2 transitions, can provide sufficient cues for auditory discrimination of place in most vowel contexts (Delattre *et al.*, 1955), although F_3 transitions may also contribute cues, especially for plosives releasing front vowels (Harris, Hoffman, Liberman, Delattre, and Cooper, 1958). Place of production can be recognized from transitions of F_2 because they vary systematically according to the point at which the vocal tract is occluded. Thus, transitions point toward (but do not begin at) a frequency locus at about 700 Hz for labials, 1,800 Hz for alveolars, and 3,000 Hz for velar sounds with all but the back vowels (Liberman, Delattre, Cooper, and Gerstman, 1954). The reason that velar plosives with back vowels differ from those with front vowels is that the lip-rounding associated with back vowels lowers all formants and formant transitions. Loci for back vowels are found below 1,000 Hz. The velar plosives [k] and [g] may therefore be taught more easily through audition to the child with a limited auditory range if they are combined with back vowels.

The frequency of the plosive burst also varies systematically according to place of production. Thus, bursts above 3,200 Hz are associated with [t] and [d]; those with energy below 400 Hz, with [p] and [b]; and those in the intermediate range of 800 to 3,000 Hz, usually with [k] and [g], but sometimes with [p] and [b] if releasing front vowels (Liberman, Delattre, and Cooper, 1952; Stevens and House, 1956; Hoffman, 1958). For normally hearing listeners and with natural rather than synthetic speech, the plosive burst may often provide stronger cues as to place than formant transitions (Fisher-Jorgensen, 1954; Malécot, 1968; Ainsworth, 1968). The evidence available indicates that, as a rule, both types of acoustic cues are utilized, although bursts for labial and alveolar plosives are more important as cues than are bursts for velars (Winitz, Scheib, and Reeds, 1972).

The discrimination of plosive and other place distinctions by hearing-impaired listeners is, predictably, poorer as frequency range becomes more restricted and as high-tone hearing loss increases. Subjects with sloping audiograms showing high-frequency hearing loss therefore discriminate place cues less well than manner or voicing cues, whereas those with flat audiograms may discriminate all three types of cues equally well (Siegenthaler, 1949). There is, however, an interaction between place discrimination and vowel environment. In the context of vowels with low-frequency F_2 values such as [u], hearing-impaired listeners may hear place cues that are unavailable when F_2 values of the adjacent vowel are high as in [i] (Cox, 1969). Work by Rhodes (1966), Rhodes and Corbett (1970), and Rosen (1962) also indicates that when many of the high-frequency place cues cannot be heard by hearing-impaired listeners, parallel cues in lower frequencies may be used to discriminate place of production.

Stops provide fewer place cues than plosives simply because they are produced without burst. The auditory identification of unreleased stops therefore depends entirely on the variant energy contained in the F_2 and F_3 vowel-to-consonant transitions which occur as a result of forward coarticulation (LaRiviere, Winitz, and Herriman, 1975). They are essentially, but not exactly, mirror images of the transitions associated with plosives (Halle *et al.*, 1957; Andrésen, 1960; Wang and Fillmore, 1961; Broad and Fertig, 1970; Fisher-Jorgensen, 1972). Not surprisingly, the absence of burst energy leads to the association of more place errors with stops than with plosives in most studies of speech discrimination, even those carried out with hearing-impaired listeners (Pickett, Martin, Johnson, Smith, Daniel, Willis, and Otis, 1972).

Nasal consonants may be identified as bilabial [m], alveolar [n], or velar [ŋ], either through the variant F_2 and F_3 transitions to and from the adjacent vowel or through their invariant formant structure. Normal listeners apparently use both types of cues rather than one or the other. This was demonstrated by Malécot (1956), who interchanged the three consonants in various syllables by means of tape splicing. When either the transitions or invariant structure cues associated with [m] were presented, [m] was heard. With [n] the results were similar. However, both transitions and invariant cues were required before [ŋ] could be positively identified. The differences found may be due to the fact that the oral cavity's filter effect is not so great when the constriction is velar.

Comparison of perceived distinctions between stops and nasals indicates that although formant transitions associated with the two classes of consonants are similar, those associated with nasals are less effective than those associated with stops (Cooper *et al.*, 1952). This may in part be due to the weakening of the F_2 and F_3 transitions which occurs when vowels are somewhat nasalized through coarticulation. It may also be due to the listener's seeking to identify place of production from the invariant acoustic energy of the nasals. The variant energy associated with F_2 transitions lies mainly between 800 and 1,300 Hz for [m], 1,500 and 2,000 Hz for [n], and 2,000 and 2,500 Hz for [ŋ] (Hecker, 1962). The invariant F_2 energy appears to be centered at about 1,100 Hz for [m], 1,700 Hz for [n], and 2,300 Hz for [ŋ] (House, 1957; Nakata, 1959). Since the formant bandwidths of nasal sounds are relatively broad, the child with hearing up to 1,000 Hz might be expected to hear something of the F_2 energy of [m] and hence to discriminate between [m] and the other two nasal consonants. Hearing up to 2,000 Hz would, however, be required to identify [n] and (by a process of elimination) to discriminate nasal place distinctions.

The semivowels both have relatively strong F_1 and F_2 transitions by means of which they may be identified. The [w] is both bilabial and velar since the lips are rounded and the tongue dorsum is raised toward the velum during the initial phase of its production. This vocal tract configuration yields two low formants: F_1 originating from about 300 Hz, and F_2 from about 750 Hz. Both formants glide almost continuously toward those associated with the vocal tract configuration of the following vowel. If [w] is followed by [u], both formants rise as lip-rounding decreases and fall again as the lips are again rounded for [u]. The [j], which is a palatal consonant with no lip-rounding, initially has a low F_1 (about 300 Hz) and a high F_2 (over 2,500 Hz) which, like those of the [w], glide continuously toward those of the following vowel. The acoustic properties of semivowels have been studied in word-initial positions by O'Connor *et al.* (1957) and by Ainsworth (1968), and in intervocalic positions by Lisker (1957a, b).

The [w] and [j] have similar F_1 characteristics and may therefore be confused if hearing impairment precludes audition of F_2 energy. The two sounds are usually discriminable if hearing up to 1,000 Hz is present since at least part of the F_2 glide of [w] toward the central and front vowels will then be audible, and part of the F_2 glide of [j] toward central and back vowels will be equally so.

The liquids [l] and [r] are both classed as alveolar sounds. To the extent that they are alveolar, their discrimination cannot be regarded as being based on place cues. However, [l] is usually produced with some palatalization (elevation of the tongue toward the palate), particularly in the context of back vowels; and the initial [r], often retroflexed, involves some degree of velarization and lip-rounding. Acoustically, the two consonants have first and second formants that originate at about similar frequencies: F_1 at or above 350 Hz, and F_2 at or above 950 Hz. However, their second formants change at different rates: following brief (about 50 msec.) steady-state energy at the original frequency, the F_2 of [l] glides to the F_2 of the following vowel in about 40 msec., while the F_2 of [r] has an initial steady-state component of about 35 msec. and a glide duration of about 50 msec. (Dalston, 1975). The principal difference between [l] and [r] is, however, in the frequency of F_3 (O'Connor *et al.*, 1957). While the F_3 of [l] remains relatively stable at about 3,000 Hz, the F_3 of [r] glides from its point of origin at around 1,500 Hz to the F_3 of the adjacent vowel. This mid-frequency F_3 glide, due to tongue retroflexion and/or lip-rounding in [r], is rendered more audible if it is enhanced through whispering. If, for example, whispered [lae] and [rae] are compared, the absence versus the presence of an F_3 glide can be clearly distinguished. The [r] and the [l] in intervocalic position yield F_3 transitional cues similar to those produced when these liquids occur in an initial position (Lisker, 1957b).

The child with hearing that extends up to about 1,000 Hz can, then, only make auditory discriminations between [l] and [r] on the basis of durational differences. These are of a very fine order, and they are more difficult for children than for adults (Koenigsknecht, 1968). Furthermore, durational differences may be masked by variations in speed of production. Thus, a rapidly produced [ra] can actually yield shorter transitions than a more slowly produced [la]. If possible, therefore, frequency of F_3 transitions should be used as the basis for contrasting liquids in teaching. This contrast is available to the child with hearing up to about 1,500 Hz if [l] and [r] are produced in the context of central or back vowels since these have the lowest F_3 values. It is quite simple to demonstrate with such children that the [l] and [r] discrimination becomes easier and easier to make as the adjacent vowel shifts from [i] to [ɛ] to [æ] and then to [ɔ].

The *fricatives* provide strong place cues through the frequency characteristics of both their variant and their invariant energy. Place cues are not, however, the only means by which one identifies fricatives. Both intensity and durational characteristics also contribute to their recognition. The strongest cues, however, are those derived from the variant, transitional energy (Sharf, 1968).

The [ʍ] has low-frequency energy due to lip-rounding, and its fricative quality—if any—is limited to the first few milliseconds of its production. Its transitions are similar to those of its voiced counterpart, the semivowel [w].

The [h] is caused by turbulence at the glottis; hence the whole vocal tract is free to resonate according to the configuration assumed for the following vowel. Since the back and central vowels have the lowest F_2 energy, the [h] is best taught in conjunction with these vowels. In any case, it should be audible to the child with residual hearing which extends up to about 1,000 Hz because it also has relatively strong F_1 energy. The child previously taught to whisper vowels should have no trouble in producing a satisfactory [h] and, if hearing up to 1,000 Hz is present, in discriminating [h] from [ʍ]. In the former, the frequency transitions parallel those of the following vowel, whereas in the latter, the formant transitions rise as the lips are unrounded to release the vowel. Because the degree to which the vocal tract is open largely determines F_1 frequency, the [h] produced in the context of vowels with exaggerated jaw-opening will tend to be higher in frequency than those produced in a more normal context. The reader may verify this simply by whispering [h] with various degrees of jaw-opening. Thus, the unexaggerated [h] will be more audible than the exaggerated [h] to children whose hearing is restricted to the low frequencies.

The [θ] and [ð] fricatives are readily confused with [f] and [v] when the transitions are removed (Harris, 1958; Cole and Scott, 1974b). This may be because both pairs have a similar concentration of energy in their second formants which lie close to 1,500 Hz (Heinz and Stevens,

1961; Jassem, 1965). The [θ] is usually somewhat weaker than the [f] (Strevens, 1960); but in the production of isolated syllables, such a difference tends not to be made. There is a substantial amount of energy in both pairs of sounds between 7,000 and 8,000 Hz. The main basis for discrimination between the two pairs of sounds is, therefore, the variant transitional energy. Some fricative energy may be present in the transitions below 1,000 Hz as the formants move down toward a back vowel. Above 1,000 Hz, the spectra of voiced and voiceless fricatives are similar (Hughes and Halle, 1956).

The [ʃ] and [ʒ] sounds are characterized by a wide band of fricative energy which, in steady state, extends from about 1,500 Hz to over 7,000 Hz. The energy in these sounds usually peaks at about 2,600 Hz. Thus, their invariant frequency characteristics are quite unlike those of the other fricatives discussed above and those associated with [s] and [z], discussed below (Harris, 1958). These fricatives, [ʃ] and [ʒ], have greater acoustic power than other fricatives (Strevens, 1960); accordingly, the energy present in the frequency transitions renders them among the most audible. In repeated syllables such as [ʃu], when a considerable degree of lip-rounding is maintained, the characteristic frequency of the fricative energy is lowered, thus bringing the sound within the range audible to children with hearing up to 1,000 Hz. While the [ʃ] can be found initially, medially, and finally in English words, the [ʒ] occurs only in a medial position. The position of the preceding as well as the following vowel influences the formant frequency of both sounds when they are situated intervocalically. Thus, the [ʃ] can be heard to glide downward in pitch as in [iʃu] and upward in pitch as in [uʃi]. This coarticulation effect is again quite readily perceived if the two examples are whispered.

The [s] and the [z] have most fricative energy at between 3,600 and 7,000 Hz and, due to antiresonances, relatively little immediately below the major peak, which is usually located at the lower end of this range. The frequency of the peak energy is lowered by lip-rounding in the context of [u] and raised by lip-spreading in the context of [i]. The fricative components for [s] and [z] are somewhat stronger than those for [θ] , [ð], [f], and [v] because the orifice created by the tongue is more nearly round and hence creates turbulence more efficiently (Fant, 1960). These fricatives, like [ʃ] and [ʒ], are clearly identifiable when removed from vowel transition context (Harris, 1958), although vowel transitions normally aid in their identification. Because their energy is concentrated relatively high in the speech frequency range, [s] and [z] are audible only if hearing extends upward well beyond 3,000 Hz. The transitional energy may help the listener to identify the presence of these sounds if hearing up to about 2,500 Hz is present.

Many individual hearing aids provide no significant gain over 3,200 Hz. Children who have adequate hearing for [s] and [z] may therefore find the sounds inaudible on this account. Since it is much simpler to teach these fricatives through hearing than through other sense modalities, the solution is to change the individual aid or, if none can be found that provides sufficient gain, to use a speech training aid with headphones that have a sufficiently wide frequency response. TDH-39 earphones, for example, afford high gain to at least 7,000 Hz. A normal [s] produced by the writer has a peak intensity of just over 30 dB re. audiometric zero (ANSI, 1964) when spoken at a distance of two yards. If the child has a 90 dB hearing loss at 4,000 Hz, he would therefore require a hearing aid with at least 60 dB gain before the sound could reach his threshold of audibility. Speaking closer to the microphone of the hearing aid would, of course, allow one to reach such a threshold with less gain (see Ling, 1975, for further discussion of such problems).

The affricates [tʃ] and [dʒ] are both palatal and are differentiated from each other by voicing, a dimension which will be discussed below.

Sensory Correlates of Place Distinctions: The purpose of this section is to summarize the variety of sensory cues that can be used to facilitate the child's acquisition of place distinctions. These have been reviewed in detail in Chapters 3, 4, and 6 and mentioned in various parts of the text including this chapter. These distinctions are principally called for in the production of targets in the second and third steps of consonant development specified in the next chapter.

Auditory cues on place of production are carried principally, though not entirely, by the variant acoustic energy contained in F_2 and F_3 transitions. This is true for all consonants regardless of manner of production and explains our emphasis on the teaching of consonants in the context of units of at least syllabic length. Such cues are not made available to the child if consonants that can be produced out of vowel contexts are taught only in isolation.

Sound has three dimensions: frequency, intensity, and duration. The analysis of acoustic properties of consonants, presented in the preceding section of this chapter, indicates that, of the three dimensions, frequency carries the most important information on place of production. For relatively complete information on place of consonant production, one requires hearing up to at least 4,000 Hz. However, many variant and invariant cues are present at lower frequencies, and these are summarized in Table 14.B. This table presents data that demonstrate the enormously important influence of vowel environment. Many cues on place that are unavailable in the context of front vowels if hearing extends to only 2,000 Hz are audible in the context of back and central vowels. Similarly, many more cues on place of production are available below 1,000 Hz in the context of back vowels than in the context of either central or front vowels. Only one unambiguous place cue is available under 500 Hz; namely, the burst associated with the bilabial plosives in a back vowel context.

Table 14.B presents data relating to the frequency of the acoustic cues on place but not to their relative intensity. Although the semivowels and liquids can have much the same intensity as the vowels, the invariant acoustic energy in most consonants is much weaker. This is particularly true of the high-frequency energy which carries information on place of production. It is the principal reason why place cues are so readily masked by noise. Since hearing impairment tends to increase with frequency, the problem is more acute for those with hearing impairment than for the normal listener. One can compensate to some extent by using hearing aids that provide most amplification in the high-frequency range, but the child's ability to tolerate high levels of sound and to discriminate speech at high levels of intensity imposes limits in this regard. Whether one speaks loudly or quietly, the mid- and high-frequency place cues are produced at much the same intensity. It is mainly the low-frequency energy that varies according to speaking level. The reader may verify this by listening to the level of the vowels versus the fricative and the plosive bursts in a sentence such as, "What's the matter then?" when it is shouted and spoken quietly. The dynamic range from the loudest to the quietest sound is increased in shouting because there is an increase in vowel and voice intensity but not an overall increase in all speech components. To emphasize place cues one should therefore talk quietly and close to the microphone of the aid.

Up to this point we have emphasized how important it is for a child to have hearing aids with sufficient low-frequency response to permit him to hear the acoustic cues on vocal duration, vocal intensity, vocal pitch, the F_1 of all vowels, and consonant manner distinctions. Our concern has been to stress that those children with very little audition above 500 Hz can, in fact, receive many such cues if hearing aids with extended low-frequency response are provided. Of course, parallel information on voice patterns and manner of production is provided by acoustic energy in the higher frequencies—which also carry information on place of production. If the low frequencies alone are amplified,

TABLE 14.B

Place of production. Summary of the variant cues (those associated with F_2 and F_3 transitions, designated T_2, T_3, respectively) and the invariant cues (those intrinsic to the consonant) that are normally available below 1,000 Hz, 2,000 Hz, and 3,000 Hz. Consonants classified as "front" include the bilabials, labiodentals, and linguadentals; as "mid," the alveolars and palatals; and as "back," the velars and glottals. [1]

Manner	Variant Place Cues			Invariant Place Cues		
	Front	Mid	Back	Front	Mid	Back
3,000 Hz						
Plosives	$T_2 + T_3$	$T_2 + T_3$	$T_2 + T_3$	bursts	bursts*	bursts
Stops	$T_2 + T_3$	$T_2 + T_3$	$T_2 + T_3$			F_2
Nasals	$T_2 + T_3$	$T_2 + T_3$	T_2	$F_2 + F_3$	$F_2 + F_3$ F_2 [j]	
Semivowels		F_2 [j]				
Liquids		T_3 [l] + [r]			F_3[l] + [r] [s]*	
Fricatives	T_2 [θ] + [f]**	[s]*	[h]			
2,000 Hz						
Plosives	T_2	T_2**	T_2*	bursts		bursts**
Stops	T_2	T_2**	T_2*		F_2	
Nasals	T_2**	T_2**	T_2**	F_2*		
Semivowels	T_2 [w]	T_2 [j]**				
Liquids		T_3 [r]**			F_3 [r]	
Fricatives	T_2 [θ] + [f]*	[ʃ]	[h]**			F_1 [h]**
1,000 Hz						
Plosives	T_2**	T_2*	T_2*	bursts		bursts*
Stops	T_2**	T_2*	T_2*			
Nasals	T_2*	T_2*	T_2*	F_2		
Semivowels	T_2 [w]*					
Liquids		T_2 [l] + [r]*			F_2 [l] + [r]	
Fricatives			[h]*			

*Only with back vowels.
**Not with front vowels.
[1]Most consonants have acoustic energy below the frequencies shown, which may serve to distinguish between one manner of production and another, and which provides cues on voicing.

or are amplified to too great an extent relative to the high frequencies, place information either will not be transmitted or, through upward spread of masking, will be rendered inaudible to those who could otherwise hear it (see Ling, 1963; Martin and Pickett, 1970). There is a problem in this regard if one selects aids that emphasize the low frequencies on the false assumption that if some low-frequency gain is good, more must be better. There is usually no problem in using aids which have a response from 100 Hz or so providing that the gain of the hearing aid increases substantially with frequency. Aids of this type were described by Ling (1964). If they cannot be used to advantage in teaching place distinctions, vision or touch should be used.

Visual cues on place of consonant production are the least ambiguous of those cues that are available through speechreading (see Chapter 3). Accordingly, there has been no call for technical aids to indicate place of production. However, it is important to stress that the exact place and extent of constriction for alveolar, palatal, and velar sounds cannot be visualized. Once the child can produce these sounds and has learned to coarticulate them with others, then he may infer their production from speechreading; but vision alone cannot provide sufficient cues for their acquisition. Much as an [m] and a [b] look alike on the lips, so are the tongue gestures for [t], [d], [n], [s], [z], [l], and [r] visually similar.

If manner distinctions can be taught through residual hearing, then vision in combination with audition can supply enough information to differentiate sounds that share place of production. If they cannot, it may be possible to use vision and orosensory-motor patterns together to foster generalization from previously acquired front consonants. For example, given that [m] has been acquired, [n] may be taught by first having the child maintain the tongue tip on the alveolar ridge through visual imitation; next, having him close the lips to produce [m]; and finally, having him part the lips while maintaining the nasal manner of production. Analogously, [d] may be developed by providing visual cues on place and reference to the orosensory-motor patterns associated with bilabial plosion for [b]; and [s] may be similarly developed from [θ]. Although the child cannot see that a narrow gap between the tongue and the alveolar ridge is required for [s], he may infer this; his previous experience with [f] and [θ] in contrast with [t] has established that fricatives call for constriction at the appropriate place of production rather than for occlusion—an orosensory-motor pattern associated with plosives and stops. If place distinctions cannot be acquired through hearing alone, through hearing and vision, or through vision plus orosensory-motor experience, then tactile strategies must be employed.

Tactile cues on place of production have to be more specific than those required to demonstrate manner differences. Whereas manner distinctions can be felt from the breath stream or from vibration on the face, tactile differentiation of place involves putting a finger directly into the mouth. By this means both manner and place can be felt simultaneously. Tactile strategies are rarely required to teach place of consonant production if the speech sounds have been developed in an orderly fashion and if hearing and vision have been properly employed. However, there are many children who have unnecessary and persistent problems with the production of a [k], for example, because direct tactile cues were not provided. The tongue's contact with and pressure upon the velum, and the characteristics of plosive release in a syllable such as [ka], can be unambiguously conveyed by having the child place a finger into the teacher's mouth and feel where and how she produces the sound. Less direct tactile strategies, such as pressing one's finger under the child's chin and then taking the finger sharply away to indicate plosive release, can lead the child to have permanent misconceptions about velar targets. No technological aids that assist in the tactile discrimination of place features have so far been developed.

Voicing Distinctions

The voiced-voiceless distinction in consonant production is our principal concern in teaching the target behaviors specified in Step 4 (see Chapter 17). As with cues on manner of production, cues on voicing are carried largely by low-frequency acoustic energy; hence they are available to children with minimal residual hearing. Much of the information on voicing is carried in a parallel fashion by changes in the intensity, frequency, and duration of the speech signal. Durational cues tend to be the most salient. Some of these have been discussed in earlier chapters.

Acoustic Cues Relating to Voicing: In *initial plosives* the voiced-voiceless distinction is mainly cued by voice onset time (VOT). This is the time that elapses between the release of the constriction in the vocal tract (i.e., the onset of plosive burst) and the onset of vocal cord vibration. In English, [b] has a VOT of about 0 msec. This means that voicing and plosive burst coincide, or approximately so. The unvoiced cognate [p] does not begin until the voiceless burst is complete and the articulators have moved well toward their positions for the following vowel. For English [d-t] and [g-k] distinctions there are similar differences in VOT. Although vocal cord vibration tends to lag slightly behind plosive release in [d] and [g], the VOT associated with their voiced cognates is almost always some 20 to 40 msec. longer (Lisker and Abramson, 1964, 1967).

Plosive energy also contains other voiced-voiceless cues. These include differences in burst energy (Halle *et al.*, 1957) and differences in fundamental pitch (Haggard, Ambler, and Callow, 1970). Plosives that are voiced tend to have weaker bursts than those that are unvoiced because transglottal airflow is impeded during phonation. For much the same reason, voice pitch at onset of voicing tends to be lower in the voiced than in the unvoiced plosives.

In *stops* the duration of the preceding vowel appears to be the most important cue. Listeners perceive word-final stops as voiceless when they are preceded by vowels of short duration and as voiced when they are preceded by vowels of long duration (Raphael, 1972). Differences in vowel duration preceding voiced and voiceless stops result in differences in the rate of formant transitions, which tend to be much faster for voiceless consonants (Slis, 1970).

In medial position the duration of the preceding vowel provides cues of the same type as those reported for word-final stops above. Additionally, the closure duration for the unvoiced stop in a medial position is greater than that for the voiced stop. For example, Lisker (1957b) compared the closure interval in word pairs such as *rabbit-rapid* and *ruby-rupee* and found that closure duration averaged 75 msec. (range 65–90 msec.) for [b] and 120 msec. (range 90–140 msec.) for [p]. Closure durations are even more markedly different when stops are used to arrest one word and plosives to release the next, as in *robe bag* and *hip pocket*. Lisker also noted that voice intensity at the onset of phonation was greater following unvoiced than voiced stops and that aspiration (turbulent noise) often followed an unvoiced stop/plosive but was never present following its voiced counterpart.

Even though voicing may continue throughout the short closure interval associated with voiced stops (as in *ruby* or *robe bag*), the low-frequency formants of the surrounding vowels are completely suppressed during stop closure. Listeners use the duration of such vowel suppression as a cue to the voiced-voiceless distinction (Pickett, 1968). The extent to which voicing can continue during stop closure depends on the place of stop production. It can continue longer with [b] than with [d] and longer with [d] than with [g]. This is because transglottal airflow is impeded less by the build-up of intraoral pressure as the cavities in the vocal tract become larger.

In *fricatives* voicing and turbulence occur almost simultaneously if the sound is voiced and with a VOT lag of about 75 to 100 msec. if the sound is unvoiced. In voiced fricatives at least one formant is present at or below 700 Hz, and the lower harmonics generated by the larynx are audible (Delattre, 1958). The intensity of the turbulence is stronger in unvoiced fricatives than in their voiced counterparts because the breath stream is impeded by the larynx when the sound is voiced.

Intervocalic and word-final fricatives share many of the voicing cues mentioned for stops. Intervocalically, the vowel formants are suppressed for the duration of the constriction. This tends to be somewhat longer for fricatives than for stops. In unvoiced fricatives virtually no energy is present under 1,000 Hz whereas in voiced fricatives the F_0 and low-frequency harmonics are present, as is a formant at or below 700 Hz. The low-frequency components of voiced fricatives have considerable strength since the transglottal flow is not greatly impeded in their production. The relative duration of the preceding vowel and the duration of the fricatives themselves both serve as a cue to voicing when the fricatives occupy an intervocalic or final position. As with stops, an unvoiced fricative is cued by a short preceding vowel, and voiced fricatives tend to be shorter than their unvoiced cognates (Denes, 1955; Raphael, 1972).

Affricates are signaled as being voiced or voiceless by much the same types of cues as are the stops and fricatives, whose properties they share. In initial position, the major cue is voice onset time. In medial position, duration of the preceding vowel and duration of the silent interval preceding burst both contribute to the voiced-voiceless distinction, as does suppression of the formants of surrounding vowels during the closure and burst interval. As with plosives, the burst energy associated with unvoiced [tʃ] is greater than that of the voiced [dʒ].

Sensory Correlates of Voicing Distinctions: *The auditory cues* which may be derived from the variant and invariant energy of consonants are plentiful. As shown by the above review of the acoustic properties pertaining to voiced and unvoiced consonants, many of these cues are durational and fall within the low-frequency range. Many of these that are associated with frequency are also to be found below 500 Hz. Intensity cues, though perhaps of less importance than others, may nevertheless contribute to voiced-voiceless distinctions. Because several parallel cues on voicing are usually available in the low-frequency range, it is not surprising that voicing distinctions are well preserved in noise and under conditions of low-pass filtering (Singh, 1971; Smith, 1974; Rosenthal, Lang, and Levitt, 1975).

Auditory discrimination of the voiced-voiceless distinction by hearing-impaired listeners tends to be relatively good (Siegenthaler, 1949; Rosen, 1962; Rhodes, 1966; Cox, 1969). Indeed, when speech below 500 Hz is presented to normally hearing and to hearing-impaired listeners, both groups may discriminate voicing equally well (LaBenz, 1956; Pickett *et al.*, 1972). These findings suggest that even children with minimal low-frequency audition can learn to hear and to produce the voiced-voiceless distinction in speech if provided with appropriate hearing aids and training. This view is supported in studies reported by Aston (1972) and by Bennett and Ling (1973). Children with similar hearing levels who have been provided with intensive visual training usually produce speech that contains a high proportion of voicing errors (Morley, 1949; Stark, 1972; Irvin and Wilson, 1973).

Visual cues on voicing as received by speechreading are particularly weak. There are no visual correlates of the frequency and intensity cues which signal the voiced-voiceless distinction. Durational cues are therefore the only possible source of visual information on voicing. There have been no studies to determine how well such durational cues may be processed through speechreading. Visual aids should be of some help in distinguishing between voiced and voiceless consonants, and several such aids are available (see Chapter 6).

Tactile cues on voicing may be derived through feeling the presence or absence of vocal cord vibration on the larynx, chest, or face of the speaker. This tactile correlate of voicing has been traditionally employed in teaching speech to hearing-impaired children. However, as indicated above in the discussion of acoustic cues on voicing, the presence or absence of vocal cord vibration during the production of consonants is only one of the many cues on voicing. Thus, if the teacher provides only skeletal vibration cues during the production of voiced and unvoiced consonants, the child can develop but a primitive notion of the voiced-voiceless distinction. The frequency cues on voicing present in the acoustic signal cannot be conveyed to the skin except by a complex coding process (see Chapter 3). However, a vibratory transform of the acoustic signal can carry cues on duration and intensity. If the child's audition is too limited for him to acquire voicing distinctions through hearing, then a device designed to present duration and intensity cues to the skin should be used. It should be remembered that at least as many cues on voicing are carried by the variant energy associated with consonants as by the invariant energy intrinsic to them. In order to exploit such cues, consonants must be presented in the context of units of at least syllabic size.

Summary

In this chapter we describe the acoustic properties and sensory correlates of consonant production in relation to manner, place, and voicing distinctions. We point out which cues might be received by hearing-impaired children through the use of residual audition depending on the frequency range available to them. We stress that there are multiple acoustic cues to the identity of consonants and that many cues on manner of production and voicing are available below 1,000 Hz.

REFERENCES

Ainsworth, W. A.   First formant transitions and the perception of synthetic semivowels. *J. Acoust. Soc. Am.*, 44, 689–694, 1968.

Andrésen, B. S.   On the perception of unreleased voiceless plosives in English. *Lang. Speech*, 3, 109–119, 1960.

Aston, C. H.   Hearing-impaired children's discrimination of filtered speech. *J. Aud. Res.*, 12, 162–167, 1972.

Bennett, C. W., & Ling, D.   Discrimination of the voiced-voiceless distinction by severely hearing-impaired children. *J. Aud. Res.*, 13, 271–279, 1973.

Bjork, L.   Velopharyngeal function in connected speech. *Acta Radiol. Suppl.*, 202, 1961.

Broad, D. J., & Fertig, R. H.   Formant-frequency trajectories in selected CVC-syllable nuclei. *J. Acoust. Soc. Am.*, 47, 1572–1582, 1970.

Cole, R. A., & Scott, B.   Toward a theory of speech perception. *Psychol. Rev.*, 81, 348–374, 1974a.

Cole, R. A., & Scott, B.   The phantom in the phoneme: Invariant cues for stop consonants. *Percept. Psychophys.*, 15, 101–107, 1974b.

Cooper, F. S., Delattre, P. C., Liberman, A. M., Borst, J. M., & Gerstman, L. J.   Some experiments on the perception of synthetic speech sounds. *J. Acoust. Soc. Am.*, 24, 597–606, 1952.

Cox, B. P.   *The identification of unfiltered and filtered consonant-vowel-consonant stimuli by sensori-neural hearing-impaired persons*. Unpublished Ph.D. diss., University of Pittsburgh, 1969.

Dalston, R. M.   Acoustic characteristics of English /w, r, l/ spoken correctly by young children and adults. *J. Acoust. Soc. Am.*, 57, 462–469, 1975.

Delattre, P.   Les attributs acoustiques de la nasalité vocalique et consonantique. *Studia Linguistica*, 8, 103–109, 1954.

Delattre, P.   Les indices acoustiques de la parole: Premier rapport. *Phonetica*, 2, 108–118, passim, 1958.

Delattre, P., Liberman, A. M., & Cooper, F. S.   Acoustic loci and transitional cues for consonants. *J. Acoust. Soc. Am.*, 27, 769–773, 1955.

Denes, P. B.   Effect of duration on the perception of voicing. *J. Acoust. Soc. Am.*, 27, 761–764, 1955.

Denes, P. B.   On the statistics of spoken English. *J. Acoust. Soc. Am.*, 35, 892–904, 1963.

Fant, G.　Acoustic Theory of Speech Production. The Hague: Mouton, 1960.

Fant, G.　Auditory patterns of speech. In W. Wathen-Dunn (Ed.), Models for the Perception of Speech and Visual Form: Proceedings of a Symposium. Cambridge, Mass.: M.I.T. Press, 1967, pp. 111–125.

Fant, G.　Analysis and synthesis of speech processes. In B. Malmberg (Ed.), Manual of Phonetics. Amsterdam: North Holland Publ. Co., 1968, pp. 173–277.

Fisher-Jorgensen, E.　Acoustic analysis of stop consonants. Miscellanea Phonetica, 2, 42–59, 1954.

Fisher-Jorgensen, E.　Identification of unreleased Danish stop consonants. In Annual Report #6, Perceptual Studies of Danish Stop Consonants. Copenhagen: Institute of Phonetics, University of Copenhagen, 1972, pp. 89–103.

Fletcher, H.　Speech and Hearing. New York: van Nostrand, 1929.

Fujimura, O.　Bilabial stop and nasal consonants: A motion picture study and its acoustical implications. J. Speech Hear. Res., 4, 233–247, 1961.

Gay, T.　Effects of filtering and vowel environment on consonant perception. J. Acoust. Soc. Am., 48, 993–998, 1970.

Gerstman, L. J. Perceptual dimensions for the friction portions of certain speech sounds. Unpublished Ph.D. diss., New York University, 1957.

Haggard, M. P., Ambler, S., & Callow, M.　Pitch as a voicing cue. J. Acoust. Soc. Am., 47, 613–617, 1970.

Halle, M., Hughes, G. W., & Radley, J-P. A.　Acoustic properties of stop consonants. J. Acoust. Soc. Am., 29, 107–116, 1957.

Harris, K. S.　Cues for the discrimination of American English fricatives in spoken syllables. Lang. Speech, 1, 1–7, 1958.

Harris, K. S., Hoffman, H. S., Liberman, A. M., Delattre, P., & Cooper, F. S.　Effect of third-formant transitions on the perception of the voiced stop consonants. J. Acoust. Soc. Am., 30, 122–126, 1958.

Harris, K. S., Lysaught, G. F., & Schvey, M. M.　Some aspects of the production of oral and nasal labial stops. Lang. Speech, 8, 135–147, 1965.

Hecker, M. H.　Studies of nasal consonants with an articulatory speech synthesizer. J. Acoust. Soc. Am., 34, 179–188, 1962.

Heinz, J. M., & Stevens, K. N.　On the properties of voiceless fricative consonants. J. Acoust. Soc. Am., 33, 589–596, 1961.

Hixon, T. J., Minifie, F. D., & Tait, C. A.　Correlates of turbulent noise production for speech. J. Speech Hear. Res., 10, 133–140, 1967.

Hoffman, H.　Study of some cues in the perception of the voiced stop consonants. J. Acoust. Soc. Am., 30, 1035–1041, 1958.

House, A. S.　Analog studies of nasal consonants. J. Speech Hear. Disord., 22, 190–204, 1957.

House, A. S., & Fairbanks, G.　The influence of consonant environment upon the secondary acoustical characteristics of vowels. J. Acoust. Soc. Am., 25, 105–113, 1953.

Hughes, G. W., & Halle, M.　Spectral properties of fricative consonants. J. Acoust. Soc. Am., 28, 303–310, 1956.

Irvin, B. E., & Wilson, L. S.　The voiced-unvoiced distinction in deaf speech. Am. Ann. Deaf, 118, 43–45, 1973.

Jassem, W.　The formants of fricative consonants. Lang. Speech, 8, 1–16, 1965.

Koenigsknecht, R. A. *An investigation of the discrimination of certain spectral and temporal acoustic cues for speech sounds in three-year-old children, six-year-old children and adults.* Unpublished Ph.D. diss., Northwestern University, 1968.

LaBenz, P. J. Potentialities of auditory perception for various levels of hearing loss. *Volta Rev.*, 58, 397–402, 1956.

LaRiviere, C., Winitz, H., & Herriman, E. Vocalic transitions in the perception of voiceless initial stops. *J. Acoust. Soc. Am.*, 57, 470–475, 1975.

Liberman, A. M. Some results of research on speech perception. *J. Acoust. Soc. Am.*, 29, 117–123, 1957.

Liberman, A. M., Cooper, F. S., Shankweiler, D. P., & Studdert-Kennedy, M. Perception of the speech code. *Psychol. Rev.*, 74, 431–461, 1967.

Liberman, A. M., Delattre, P., & Cooper, F. S. The role of selected stimulus-variables in the perception of the unvoiced stop consonants. *Am. J. Psychol.*, 65, 497–516, 1952.

Liberman, A. M., Delattre, P. C., Cooper, F. S., & Gerstman, L. J. The role of consonant-vowel transitions in the perception of the stop and nasal consonants. *Psychol. Monogr.*, 68, 1–13, (Whole No. 379), 1954.

Liberman, A. M., Delattre, P. C., Gerstman, L. J., & Cooper, F. S. Tempo of frequency change as a cue for distinguishing classes of speech sounds. *J. Exp. Psychol.*, 52, 127–137, 1956.

Ling, D. The use of hearing and the teaching of speech. *Teach. Deaf*, 61, 59–68, 1963.

Ling, D. Implications of hearing aid amplification below 300 cps. *Volta Rev.*, 66, 723–729, 1964.

Ling, D. Amplification for speech. In D. R. Calvert and S. R. Silverman, *Speech and Deafness.* Washington, D.C.: A. G. Bell Assoc. for the Deaf, 1975.

Lintz, L. B., & Sherman, D. Phonetic elements and perception of nasality. *J. Speech Hear. Res.*, 4, 381–396, 1961.

Lisker, L. Minimal cues for separating /w, j, r, l/ in intervocalic position. *Word*, 13, 256–267, 1957a.

Lisker, L. Closure duration and the intervocalic voiced-voiceless distinction in English. *Language*, 33, 42–49, 1957b.

Lisker, L., & Abramson, A. S. A cross-language study of voicing in initial stops: Acoustical measurements. *Word*, 20, 384–422, 1964.

Lisker, L., & Abramson, A. S. Some effects of context on voice onset time in English stops. *Lang. Speech*, 10, 1–28, 1967.

Malécot, A. Acoustic cues for nasal consonants. *Language*, 32, 274–284, 1956.

Malécot, A. The force of articulation of American stops and fricatives as a function of position. *Phonetica*, 18, 95–102, 1968.

Martin, E. S., & Pickett, J. M. Sensorineural hearing loss and upward spread of masking. *J. Speech Hear. Res.*, 13, 426–437, 1970.

Miller, G. A., & Nicely, P. E. An analysis of perceptual confusions among some English consonants. *J. Acoust. Soc. Am.*, 27, 338–352, 1955.

Morley, D. E. *An analysis by means of sound spectrograph of intelligibility variations of consonant sounds spoken by deaf persons.* Unpublished Ph.D. diss., University of Michigan, 1949.

Nakata, K. Synthesis and perception of nasal consonants. *J. Acoust. Soc. Am.*, 31, 661–666, 1959.

O'Connor, J. D., Gerstman, L. J., Liberman, A. M., Delattre, P. C., & Cooper, F. S.   Acoustic cues for the perception of initial /w, j, r, l/ in English. *Word*, 13, 24–43, 1957.

Owens, E., & Schubert, E. D.   The development of constant items for speech discrimination testing. *J. Speech Hear. Res.*, 11, 656–667, 1968.

Pickett, J. M.   Sound patterns of speech: An introductory sketch. *Am. Ann. Deaf*, 113, 120–133, 1968.

Pickett, J. M., Martin, E. S., Johnson, D., Smith, S. B., Daniel, Z., Willis, D., & Otis, W.   On patterns of speech feature reception by deaf listeners. In G. Fant (Ed.), *International Symposium on Speech Communication Ability and Profound Deafness*. Washington, D.C.: A. G. Bell Assoc. for the Deaf, 1972.

Raphael, L. J.   Preceding vowel duration as a cue to the perception of the voicing characteristics of word-final consonants in American English. *J. Acoust. Soc. Am.*, 51, 1296–1303, 1972.

Reddy, D. R.   Phoneme grouping for speech recognition. *J. Acoust. Soc. Am.*, 41, 1295–1300, 1967.

Rhodes, R. C.   Discrimination of filtered CNC lists by normals and hypacusics. *J. Aud. Res.*, 6, 129–133, 1966.

Rhodes, R. C., & Corbett, L. S.   Learning of speech discrimination skills by young hypacusics. *J. Aud. Res.*, 10, 124–126, 1970.

Rosen, J.   *Phoneme identification in sensorineural deafness*. Unpublished Ph.D. diss., Stanford University, 1962.

Rosenthal, R. D., Lang, J. K., & Levitt, H.   Speech reception with low-frequency speech energy. *J. Acoust. Soc. Am.*, 57, 949–955, 1975.

Sharf, D. J.   Distinctiveness of 'defective' fricative sounds. *Lang. Speech*, 11, 38–45, 1968.

Sharf, D. J., & Beiter, R. C.   Identification of consonants from formant transitions presented forward and backward. *Lang. Speech*, 17, 110–118, 1974.

Siegenthaler, B. M.   A study of the relationship between measured hearing loss and intelligibility of selected words. *J. Speech Hear. Disord.*, 14, 111–118, 1949.

Singh, S.   Perceptual similarities and minimal phonemic differences. *J. Speech Hear. Res.*, 14, 113–124, 1971.

Slis, I. H.   Articulatory measurements on voiced, voiceless and nasal consonants: A test of a model. *Phonetica*, 24, 193–210, 1970.

Smith, A. D.   *The importance of the first two formants in the perception of consonants*. Unpublished Ph.D. diss., McGill University, 1974.

Stark, R. E.   Teaching /ba/ and /pa/ to deaf children using real-time spectral displays. *Lang. Speech*, 15, 14–29, 1972.

Stevens, K. N.   Airflow and turbulence noise for fricative and stop consonants: Static considerations. *J. Acoust. Soc. Am.*, 50, 1180–1192, 1971.

Stevens, K. N., & House, A. S.   Studies of formant transitions using vocal tract analog. *J. Acoust. Soc. Am.*, 28, 578–585, 1956.

Strevens, P.   Spectra of fricative noise in human speech. *Lang. Speech*, 3, 32–49, 1960.

Studdert-Kennedy, M.   Speech perception. In N. J. Lass (Ed.), *Contemporary Issues in Experimental Phonetics*. Springfield, Ill.: Thomas, 1975.

Sussman, H. M., MacNeilage, P. F., & Hanson, R. J.   Labial and mandibular dynamics during production of bilabial consonants: Preliminary observations. *J. Speech Hear. Res.*, 16, 397–420, 1973.

Umeda, N., Monsen, R. B., & Molter, M.   Fricatives: Their physical properties and allophones. *J. Acoust. Soc. Am.*, 53, 378, 1973 (A).

Walden, B. E.   *Dimensions of consonant perception in normal and hearing-impaired listeners.* Unpublished Ph.D. diss., Purdue University, 1971.

Wang, W. S-Y. & Fillmore, C. J.   Intrinsic cues and consonant perception. *J. Speech Hear. Res.*, 4, 130–136, 1961.

Winitz, H., Scheib, M. E., & Reeds, J. A.   Identification of stops and vowels for the burst portion of /p, t, k/ isolated from conversational speech. *J. Acoust. Soc. Am.*, 51, 1309–1317, 1972.

/15/

Manner Distinctions
in Consonant Production

The target behaviors with which we shall deal in this chapter are those involving manner distinctions between front consonants. The subskills we shall propose may be viewed as items in a program designed to help the child generalize the use of each consonant from one phonetic context to another. If the child can produce a given consonant in one context but not in others, such a generalization program is called for (see McDonald, 1968; Gerber, 1973). If the child cannot produce the consonant in any context, then the teacher must find some means first to evoke the sound and second to elicit it reliably. In this chapter we shall discuss the many strategies by means of which the teacher can:

1. evoke the desired consonant;
2. elicit the sound reliably in at least one phonetic context once it has been evoked, and
3. generalize production of the consonant to all other contexts so that the various allophones of the sound can be used correctly and without conscious effort in communicative speech.

In order to evoke a sound, one must first ensure that the child has developed all the prerequisite behaviors for its production and, next, select and employ a strategy that will help the child to coordinate these behaviors. To elicit the sound reliably in at least one phonetic context, the teacher must present the child with a model to imitate and, if necessary, may supplement her model by prompting the child with whatever cues unambiguously specify the critical articulatory dimensions of the sound. For the child to generalize production of the sound, he must be taught to produce and rehearse it in a series of different contexts, each of which demands behaviors that are similar but not identical to those that have already been acquired.

Teaching Techniques

If a consonant cannot be evoked through direct imitation, one's first step should be to determine whether the child clearly understands, and is prepared to try to do, what is expected of him. If neither of these is in doubt, the second step is to ascertain whether he can perceive the model sufficiently well; i.e., whether he fails to imitate because he is not receiving enough unambiguous sensory cues. If the teacher is satisfied on these accounts, she may conclude that the child either lacks certain of the prerequisite target behaviors for the production of the sound or does not have the ability to coordinate such behaviors. She must then determine the exact source of the problem through analysis of the child's current speech status (see Chapter 9). If the program suggested in this text has been followed and if vocal play has been sufficiently encouraged, the only necessary procedure in teaching manner distinctions between front consonants should be coordinating new and previously acquired behaviors. The strategies which may be adopted to evoke new target behaviors, to coordinate them with previously acquired skills, and thus to promote the imitation of consonants include vocal play, explanation of component skills, verbal instructions, demonstration, analogy, and manipulation.

Vocal play has been recommended in previous chapters. It must be consistently encouraged both at home and at school. A wide range of sounds including different voice patterns, various vowels, and many of the consonants discussed in this chapter will be evoked and differentiated if the child is encouraged to vocalize abundantly and is appropriately reinforced. Encouraging the child to generate sounds spontaneously in the course of vocal play (and through his attempts at communication) establishes the use and control of the speech organs. Even though it may not by itself be sufficient, it is an essential component strategy for all hearing-impaired children, and it may be the only feasible strategy for the very young child.

Explanation of component skills is usually ineffective in the early stages of speech acquisition. There are two reasons for this: first, most young hearing-impaired children have too little language to understand the type of detailed explanation called for; second, even if they could understand, few could apply the knowledge gained through explanation. For example, it is rare to find even normally hearing English-speaking children and adults who are able to produce the French vowels [y] or [ø] simply from verbal instructions. Moreover, few normal speakers can, without intensive training, specify the tongue position required to produce sounds if the tongue cannot be visualized (Daniloff, Montgomery, Percifield, and Hampton, 1975; Daniloff and Adams, 1975).

Verbal instructions are to be recommended providing that they are relatively simple. The child should certainly be expected to respond correctly to requests and commands such as, "Show me your teeth, please," "Don't round your lips so much," or "Press a bit harder." However well they may be understood, such instructions are—for reasons given above—unlikely to lead to correct placements or movements of the tongue.

Demonstration of the type that involves providing a model of the desired behavior can be effective only insofar as it can be accurately heard, seen, or felt by the child. Since there is usually a way to render components of sounds either visible or tangible if they cannot be heard, demonstration is the most commonly used and successful of all strategies. Other than manipulation, it is also the most direct and, of course, is an essential ingredient for imitation. Demonstration involves the danger of simultaneously providing both appropriate and irrelevant cues. Thus, the teacher who is not on her guard may unconsciously flinch as the child touches her nose, grimace as the child feels her tongue, or simply purse her lips more for a plosive than for a stop. She should be aware that the child may associate such behaviors with those that she actually wants him to learn.

Analogy is an extremely important tool. Analogies can be auditory, visual, or tactile depending on the child's sensory capacities and on the nature of the behavior to be taught. For example, an auditory analogy might be used to show the commonality of nasality in sounds such as [m] and [n], or [b] and [d]; a visual analogy, using one hand to represent the palate and the other the tongue, might be used to demonstrate relative points of occlusion for [t] and [k]; or a tactile analogy, using the fingers on the chin to feel vibration, might be used to indicate that both [v] and [z] are voiced. The most effective use of analogy is to show that a sound or behavior that is known shares a particular characteristic with the sound or behavior that is being learned.

Manipulation may be defined as the shaping of a speech behavior through force imposed on one or more of the speech organs. There are three types of manipulation: that in which instruments (tongue depressors and the like) are used; that involving the teacher's "laying on of hands"; and that in which the child himself uses an instrument or his finger to adjust the tongue, lips, or jaw. Of the three types, the last is to be preferred since experience which is actively obtained is superior to that which is imposed and, as a rule, is much less objectionable to the child. Manipulation is usually unnecessary. It has no place in the teaching of front consonants; but, if sparingly used, it can be effective in evoking consonants such as [r] where the positioning of the tongue is obscured. For example, working from the tongue's position for [l], the tip may be pushed back until retroflexed. This is usually difficult to achieve if the teacher tries to position the child's tongue with an instrument or her finger; but if she lets the child push the tip of her tongue back with his finger and then invites him to push his own tongue back in the same way, the sound can usually be evoked with ease.

One should not evoke consonants in isolation if they can be elicited in a vowel context. Further, one should not persist in using strategies such as those described immediately above once the sound has been evoked. They should be unnecessary if the child has imitated and repeated the sound (or syllable) and received reinforcement. If the sound cannot be elicited through imitation once it has been evoked, some form of visual or tactile prompting may be used.

Prompting

Prompting activities involve the association of a particular manner of production with specific objects or actions. In touching her nose to denote nasality or in patting the child's left hand to specify a plosive and stroking his right hand to indicate a fricative, the teacher is using prompting activities. All cue systems are essentially prompting activities. They should be used only when the child cannot discriminate between sounds without such help and are of value only when sounds can be reliably evoked. Prompts should be discarded as soon as possible during subskill acquisition since their continued use may impede the development of coarticulation skills. Only in this chapter shall we provide specific descriptions of prompting activities. Those we suggest can best be used in teaching speech to young school-age children; but they are also intended to serve as examples which the imaginative teacher can adapt and extend to her work with children at any stage of speech acquisition and in any age group, whether she uses auditory, visual, or tactile strategies or some combination of these modalities.

Auditory Strategies

In the previous chapter it was shown that the differentiation of consonants according to manner of production can be successfully accomplished through audition if hearing up to 1,000 Hz is available. Indeed, we indicated that certain manner distinctions can be made on the basis of acoustic cues that occur below 500 Hz. Thus, the auditory discrimination of most manner distinctions is a realistic goal for the majority of hearing-impaired children, even for many whose hearing is limited to the low-frequency range. As pointed out in Chapter 3, some children who respond only to low-frequency sounds may do so because they *feel* rather than *hear* sound (see also Risberg, Algefors, and Boberg, 1975). Further, some children may actually hear rather than feel sound, but nevertheless may be unable to differentiate sounds auditorily. Such children cannot be identified on the basis of an audiogram, even assuming that a reliable audiogram can be obtained. We therefore reiterate that the speech teaching process should be considered as diagnostic therapy—an activity in which the child's hearing capacity is evaluated, in the course of training, on the basis of his ability to differentiate speech stimuli through audition.

Before attempting to teach any consonant through audition, one should first check to ensure its audibility. With continuant sounds such as nasals and fricatives, this can be done by asking the child to clap his hands or put one block on top of another when he hears the sound, as in play audiometry. With other types of sounds one may verify audibility by asking the child to differentiate between a vowel produced in isolation and the same vowel released or arrested with the consonant; e.g., [a] versus [ba], [wa], or [ap̄]. One should, by this means, determine the distance over which the sound is audible to him and then teach within this distance. One must initially assume that if a sound is audible to the child, it will also be discriminable from other consonants differing in manner of production or will become so with training. The subskills, as arranged, provide a hierarchical structure for training in both the auditory discrimination and the production of each consonant.

If the child has a limited range of hearing and has been fitted with a hearing aid that does not provide some gain for the frequencies below 300 Hz, then some vowels such as [u] and [i] will not be adequately amplified since their first formants will be partially filtered out by the hearing aid. This means that some vowels will be heard by the child, if at all, as being much quieter than others. In such a case, unnecessary difficulty will be experienced in teaching certain consonants with certain vowels and in developing the stress contrasts called for in some subskills. The relative audibility of vowels may be checked by measuring the distance over which the child can hear the vowels [u], [a], and [i]. If there are marked differences in the distance over which these sounds are audible when spoken by the teacher in a conversational-level voice, then the hearing aid should be adjusted or a more appropriate one provided. Sufficient low-frequency gain is also essential for teaching subskills involving modulation of vocal pitch through audition because, if a vowel is inaudible, then pitch changes associated with that vowel will also be inaudible. Indeed, sufficient (not overmuch) gain below 300 Hz is required if most children with very limited hearing are to learn most of the subskills specified in this entire teaching step through the use of audition.

If a certain sound can be heard by the child only over a very limited distance, one may ensure that he both hears and focuses his attention on the auditory cues required for all subskills by taking his body-worn hearing aid in the hand and speaking quietly, close to the microphone. The teacher may then hold the microphone close to the child's mouth so that he may hear his imitation of the model. Care should be taken to ensure that the breath stream in the plosive burst is not directed into the microphone. This would cause distortion which could mask the normal frequency characteristics of the burst and obscure the consonant-to-vowel transitions. There should be no need to use such a strategy to focus attention on audition if the child is appropriately fitted with a head-level hearing aid.

If an auditory-vocal imitation of the teacher's model is within the child's potential, it is probably most readily achieved by the suppression of visual cues during at least part of the teaching session. The teacher may block visual cues during speech training by obscuring her mouth with the child's hearing aid (if using the strategy described above), by masking her face with a piece of card, by sitting beside rather than in front of the child, by having him close his eyes, or by having him avert his head. The purpose is to focus his attention on auditory cues rather than on their visual correlates. Of course, there is no point in suppressing speechreading cues if they do not contribute to the differentiation of the patterns being taught. This would be the case if one were contrasting syllables such as [ba] and [ma] or contrasting voiced and whispered stimuli. However, in contrasting stimuli such as [a] and [pa], [ʌ] and [ʌp̄], or [æ æ æ] versus [æt̄ æt̄ æt̄] when the objective is to determine whether the child can perceive the influence of the consonant on the vowel, vision would have to be suppressed since differentiating features could be seen. The teacher should be sure that the child fully understands the nature of the task before she asks him to perform it without the benefit of vision. Children who have not learned to use hearing as an orienting sense are reluctant to work without visual input and are particularly reluctant to work with their eyes closed since, when they cannot see, they have much less contact with their environment. For this reason a child is usually much less reluctant to close his eyes for a listening task if the teacher holds his hand or otherwise "keeps in touch."

Choice of Strategy

Auditory strategies are, of course, the preferred strategies. Only if auditory strategies fail to yield results after fair trial should one consider alternatives. Even then, discriminations learned visually or through touch should continually be attempted by the child through audition alone. There is, for example, no justification for teaching plosives through vision or touch if the child can learn to discriminate the difference between [a] and [ba] auditorily. There is similarly no merit in continuing to work through vision or touch if, once a subskill has been introduced by alternative strategies, the child can then make the required discriminations through audition. The influence of motor speech on perception is such that children may often come to discriminate differences auditorily after they have learned to produce such differences in their speech.

Consideration of the nature of the visual cues required to discriminate and to make the consonant manner distinctions suggests that little or no help can be provided by using a mirror. The child can usually imitate the visible speech organ gestures involved without seeing himself do so. Further, the gestures that are visible do little to indicate what specific characteristics differentiate between manners of production.

In teaching speech our principal goal is to establish accurate orosensory-motor patterns by means of which the child may differentiate one sound or syllable from another. Whether the child has useful residual hearing or not, such patterns are of primary importance in providing feedback and in establishing feedforward control of production. Consonants must therefore be developed with the utmost precision and consistency so that the orosensory-motor patterns associated with them do not vary, except systematically in respect to context and vocal effort. Not all teaching strategies are equally effective in leading to such precision.

When auditory strategies cannot be used, a visual or tactile alternative should not be selected haphazardly. One strategy may lead very much more quickly than another to an habitually correct articulation of a particular sound. For example, fricatives such as [f] and [θ] are made by forcing the breath stream through a narrow aperture, thus creating turbulence. It is obvious that one would use visual strategies to teach their place and degree of constriction to a totally deaf child since these characteristics can be easily seen. However, the airflow required to produce turbulence cannot be seen in speechreading. It may be indicated visually by showing that a lightweight object such as a small piece of paper can be made to move in the breath stream, or tactually by having the child feel the breath flow with a wet finger. If the child produces too little breath stream to generate turbulence, should one use a visual or a tactile strategy to teach the sound? We would use the tactile strategy since it does not call for exaggerated airflow. Much more force than is normally used in speech is required to move a small piece of paper. The reader may verify this by saying [fʌfʌfʌ] in a normal manner while employing each strategy. The tactile strategy, since it does not call for exaggeration, provides the more fitting orosensory-motor patterns, which include the sensation generated by the appropriate degree of intraoral breath pressure that should accompany all constrictive consonants.

Strategies such as those described above should seldom be needed in teaching consonants to hearing-impaired children, although their frequent use is rarely questioned. The child's use of a substantial breath stream and good voice patterns should be established before consonants are taught as such. When consonants are taught, they should be initially learned not as particular sounds but as different ways to modulate the stream of breath and voice. Sufficient attention to breath flow and adequate rehearsal of subskills that call for plenty of breath to support the prolonged—but rapid—repetition and alternation of syllables will do much to avoid the abnormal dynamics of breathing commonly found in the speech of hearing-impaired persons (see Hutchinson and Smith, 1976). We describe strategies to indicate breath stream in our discussion of various consonants in the following pages; but we suggest that if they have to be used frequently, attention should be refocused for at least part of each speech teaching period on the targets treated in earlier chapters. This is not to say that long-duration teaching sessions are recommended. Indeed, they are to be avoided; for what we seek are numerous, relatively small increments of learning of the type that can best be fostered by working systematically for two or three minutes several times each day.

Coarticulation

We emphasize the development of coarticulation skills for two reasons. First, the vowel environment in which the consonant is produced may yield important acoustic cues to assist the child in its production. Second, even if the child is too deaf to benefit from such cues, his speech must contain these cues if it is to be intelligible. This is why we recommend systematic work to develop consonants in syllables at the phonetic level. It has been shown that children are better able to learn to hear consonant sounds when these sounds are presented in nonsense syllables than when they are presented in words (McNeil and Stone, 1965); that there are systematic consonant-vowel interactions in speech production (House and Fairbanks, 1953); and that such interactions lead to the syllable's being perceptually processed by normally hearing listeners as a single unit (Wood and Day, 1975).

Goals and Criteria

The consonants to be developed within each teaching step should be taught concurrently so that effective use may be made of manner contrasts. In other words, the teacher should select and rehearse subskills for two or three different consonants from the same teaching step in each two- or three-minute training session. Subskills for [b], [m], and [θ], for example, might be rehearsed in one session and subskills for [m], [w], and [h] in another. Orderly description in this text demands that we treat consonants one by one within each teaching step. The opposite is demanded of the teacher (see Chapter 8).

No consonant can be considered as being acquired until each of the subskills underlying the target behavior has been mastered with 100% accuracy. This level of accuracy should be established over at least 10 trials during teaching sessions and again in the course of periodic evaluation (see Chapter 9). Only when the child is able to perform each subskill without error can one expect the subskill to become automatized, and only when a high level of automaticity has been developed can one expect generalization of subskills (a) to other consonants of similar manner but different place, and (b) from the phonetic level to phonologic speech. Automaticity calls for rehearsal beyond the demands of accuracy (see Chapter 7). It is evidenced by ability to perform a task without conscious attention and at reasonable speed. Production of the consonant with minimal effort and repetition and alternation at rates approximating those in normal speech (at least three syllables per second) are therefore to be achieved.

TEACHING STEP 1:
Target Behaviors, Subskills, and Teaching Strategies
Relating to Front Consonants
[b, p], [p̄, b̄], [m], [w, ʍ], [h, f, v, θ, ð]

The Plosives [b] and [p]

Targets and Subskills

Both [b] and [p] are bilabial consonants, the first voiced and the other unvoiced. The target behaviors required are among the simplest in consonant production: arrest of the breath stream through bilabial closure of sufficient duration (30-50 msec.) to build up intraoral pressure, and its sudden release which results in a burst of energy. The following subskills are required for adequate production of [b] and [p]:

Subskill 1: Production of [b] or [p] in single syllables releasing various vowels including [i], [a], and [u].

Subskill 2: Production of [b] and [p] in a series of repeated syllables formed with one vowel or another (e.g., [bubububu], [bibibibi], etc.).

Subskill 3: Production of [b] or [p] in a series of repeated syllables formed with various vowels (e.g., [bibabu], [bʌbɪbæ], etc.).

Subskill 4: Alternation of syllables released with [b] or [p] and syllables released with other consonants in Step 1 (e.g., [bamabama], [bifibifi], etc.).

Subskill 5: Production of [b] or [p] in syllables varying in intensity.

Subskill 6: Production of [b] or [p] repeated in intervocalic position with either the first or second vowel stressed.

Subskill 7: Production of [b] or [p] in repeated or alternated syllables varying over at least eight semitones in pitch.

Subskill 1 ensures that the child effects bilabial closure regardless of whether the lips are neutrally spread as in [i] or rounded as in [u]. If the child is taught [b] or [p] with only the central vowels, he may acquire the notion that these sounds must be initiated with the lips in an unspread and unrounded posture. If this notion is acquired, then diphthongization of the following vowel inevitably occurs.

Subskill 2 ensures that tongue position is maintained during repeated bilabial closure. All vowels in the child's repertoire should be used in the development of this subskill, and no neutralization of the vowel should be allowed to occur (see Chapter 13).

Subskill 3 ensures that the tongue assumes its target position for the following vowel during the closure phase of the consonant: in other words, that the sounds in the syllable string are coarticulated.

Subskill 4 calls for the rapid and accurate achievement of the target regardless of the intervening articulatory gestures.

Subskill 5 involves the incorporation of previously learned subskills relating to vocal intensity, to the end that the child can use these consonants in a whisper, in a quiet voice, and in a loud voice. It lays the foundation for the voiced-voiceless contrast and also for Subskill 6.

Subskill 6 involves shaping the speed, force, and duration of bilabial closure according to the demands of the context. In the sequence [ǽbi, ǽbi], for example, stress on the first syllable calls for slower, weaker, and longer-duration closure than does [æbí, æbí]. The difference is important phonologically. Thus, the above example would lead to the appropriate differentiation of *Abbey* and *a bee* in phonologic speech. Various vowel combinations should be used to perfect this subskill.

Mastery of Subskill 7 ensures that the sound can be produced easily in the context of any intonation pattern. It also serves to focus the child's attention on some other aspect of speech production as he produces the target sound. This subskill ensures the high level of automaticity required for generalization of plosive patterns to other consonants of similar manner and to their use in phonologic speech.

Teaching Strategies

The subskills listed above are all concerned with plosives in initial and medial positions. We do not advocate teaching plosives in a final position because the procedure almost inevitably leads to intrusive voicing. Words ending in /b/ or /p/ are legitimately pronounced with the final sound unreleased; hence we recommend teaching postvocalic stops rather than postvocalic plosives. An alternative approach to the problem of intrusive voicing was proposed by Scott (1900), who substituted the plosive [p] for [b] in word-final position. This is, however, no solution because habitual postvocalic plosion can destroy the natural rhythm of speech. The procedure we recommend is not new. It has been employed by Roe (1915); Christmas (1926); and Rawlings (1935, 1936).

Auditory strategies are the most appropriate for teaching [b] and [p], even to those children who have minimal residual hearing. There are sufficient acoustic cues under 500 Hz to allow auditory discrimination between these plosives and to permit auditory differentiation among plosives and other consonants. If auditory rather than visual strategies are used, visually similar sounds like [b] and [m] will not be confused.

Audition is especially useful in teaching Subskill 2 since F_1 of [u] and

F_1 of [i] both fall below 500 Hz. If the tongue shifts during repeated production, the F_1 glide should be audible. The same is true if any diphthongization of vowels occurs in Subskill 3. In Subskill 4 the acoustic cues differentiating [b] or [p] and [m] are particularly salient since parallel changes in frequency, intensity, and duration under 500 Hz occur as these sounds are alternated. Subskill 5 cannot be learned visually, and children who have been trained to look rather than to listen cannot tell whether these sounds are voiced or whispered. It is particularly important that Subskill 5 should be taught through audition if possible since its mastery provides the foundation for discrimination of the voiced-voiceless feature. In Subskill 6, intensity and durational changes in low-frequency energy are usually audible to all children except those who are totally deaf. Subskill 7 can usually be taught through audition to all but totally deaf children since pitch cues are available under 500 Hz.

Visual strategies for teaching [b] and [p] include the provision of cues for speechreading and the use of visual aids to demonstrate manner of production. Although speechreading gives unambiguous cues for bilabial closure, it provides no direct cues on the presence of plosive burst. To demonstrate plosive burst one may use objects that can be seen to move as a result of the burst (e.g., paper, feather, flame). Alternatively, the burst pattern can be displayed on an oscilloscope. Even simpler is the use of combined visual and tactile cues, allowing the child to see the bilabial closure and to feel the burst energy directly on his fingertips. Such strategies are adequate for the first four of the subskills specified, but not for the remainder. Subskills 5, 6, and 7 can be accomplished by the child who has no residual hearing only if prompts on voice are also presented (see Chapter 12).

Visual prompts may be useful for teaching several of the subskills listed above. For example, in Subskill 4 one may associate the plosive selected with a blue cup and the nasal [m] (or other sound chosen for alternation) with a red cup. The cups may then be tapped in turn at the rate the sounds are initially to be alternated. A candy hidden under the cup may be used for reinforcement on completion of a successful rehearsal of the subskill. Similarly, different-sized or different-colored cups, cards, or other objects can be associated with a whisper, a quiet voice, and a loud voice in Subskills 5 and 6. In Subskill 7, high pitch may be represented by a tall glass and lower pitches by successively smaller glasses which hold (or, inverted, cover) a candy. Diagrams may also be used. A mirror is not required to foster imitation of a visual model.

Tactile strategies include those that allow the child to feel both bilabial closure and plosive burst directly with a fingertip and to sense the voice pattern changes that are intrinsic to Subskills 5, 6, and 7. Cues associated with changes in duration and intensity may also be presented through a vibrotactile aid. Prompting activities involving touch include associating particular parts of the child's body with different sounds. For example, in teaching Subskill 4, the nasal [m] may be associated with touching one knee and the [b] or [p] with touching the other. The teacher may then demonstrate through touch the sound required and the rate of alternation initially expected. The force of a sound can also be demonstrated by pressing hard on one knee to indicate a stressed vowel and pressing gently on the other to contrast it with an unstressed vowel. Thus, Subskills 5 and 6 may easily be developed through the provision of a tactile analogy. Force of closure—whether it is effected by lips or by tongue—is related to overall vocal effort. Thus, weak articulations may be strengthened by working not just on the sound but on the whole syllable.

The Stops [p̄] and [b̄]

Targets and Subskills

Both [b̄] and [p̄] are unreleased bilabial stops, the first voiced and the other unvoiced. The one target behavior required is simple bilabial closure to arrest the preceding vowel. The two sounds are differentiated not so much by the presence or absence of vocal cord vibration during closure as by the relative speed of closure and by the duration of the previous vowel. In general, the duration of vowels preceding [p̄] is shorter than the duration of those preceding [b̄]. We suggest that one should first teach [p̄] in the context of short vowels both to avoid risk of intrusive voicing and to foster rapid speaking rate. The following subskills underlie the production of both bilabial stops:

Subskill 1: Arresting of various vowels including [ɪ], [ʌ], and [ʊ] through bilabial stop closure in single syllables.

Subskill 2: Arresting of a series of syllables formed with one vowel or another through bilabial stop closure (e.g., [ʌp̄ʌp̄ʌp̄], [ɪp̄ɪp̄ɪp̄], etc.).

Subskill 3: Alternation of syllables arrested with [p̄] or [b̄] and released with a fricative (e.g., [ʌp̄θʌ], [ɪp̄fə], etc.).

Subskill 4: Alternation of syllables arrested with [p̄] and released with a fricative, one stressed, the other not.

Subskill 5: Alternation of syllables as in the previous two subskills with production of each syllable at a different pitch over a range of at least eight semitones.

As with the corresponding plosives, it is essential for the child to learn that closure is to be effected regardless of the lip-rounding or lip-spreading associated with the previous vowel. Care should be taken to teach this and to avoid burst release in developing Subskill 1.

The performance of Subskill 2 calls for the integration of several pre-viously acquired behaviors: first, the maintenance of tongue posture during bilabial closure; second, the avoidance of plosive burst release prior to the onset of subsequent vowels; and third, control of the breath stream so that the series of syllables can be released on the same breath.

Subskill 3 requires that the first syllable be arrested and the second initiated without burst or intervening aspiration. It demands feed-forward control and coordination of breath release with articulation, and it should be rehearsed with whispered and voiced vowels.

The purpose in teaching Subskill 4 is to develop speed, force, and breath control in relation to closure. As the first syllable is stressed—for example, in [ʌ́pðu]—the voice will normally be raised in pitch (due to the increased subglottal pressure required to make the vowel louder than normal) and the stop closure will be more vigorous than in [ʌp̄θú].

The development of Subskill 5 ensures two things: first, that the child will be able to employ the bilabial stop within the context of any in-tonation pattern; and second, that sufficient automaticity has been ac-quired to permit his attention to be focused on pitch without detriment to the correct use of the bilabial stop, i.e., without aspiration between the first and second syllables.

Teaching Strategies

In carrying out trials of the approach recommended in this text, some teachers have questioned whether the stops should be taught con-currently with the plosives. Their objection to concurrent teaching is that children tend to confuse the two aspects of production. If this is the case, we consider that sufficiently unambiguous perceptual training will quickly result in their sorting out one from the other. Further, we suggest that such confusion, usually met in children who are highly vis-ual and who have been taught through use of the written form, would probably become more difficult rather than simpler to sort out if com-parison of the two were postponed. Further, if the plosive form is well established before the stop form is taught, the former will tend to re-place the latter in phonologic speech with the result that intrusive bursts will impair rhythmic quality. The question remains open.

Auditory strategies for teaching the stop subskills have much in com-mon with those for teaching the plosive subskills. With the stops there are fewer acoustic cues, but of those that are available most are within the low-frequency range. Some F_2 and all F_1 transitions fall under 1,000 Hz, and there is a sharp cessation of the lower harmonics associated with voicing, particularly in syllables ending with [p̄]. These cues are usually sufficient for the identification of the sound as a stop, even by children with minimal residual hearing, if sufficient auditory training and experience are provided. Since bilabial closure is an entirely visible speech gesture, it is only through the suppression of vision that one can be sure whether the child can hear the difference between [ʌp̄] and [ʌ], i.e., whether strategies involving other sense modalities are necessary.

Visual strategies can be devised to help the child develop all five subskills. The first subskill—arresting of various single vowels through bilabial stop closure—may be achieved simply through speechreading providing that the stop is not confused with the nasal [m]. If it is, and if the confusion cannot be overcome through the use of audition, the simplest means to ensure its correct use is to produce [b] or [p] in an intervocalic position, e.g., [ʌpʌ]. This accomplished, one should associate the first syllable with raising the finger and the second syllable—initiated by the plosive—with lowering it. Then, by stopping the finger in a raised position and allowing the child to release the second syllable only when the finger is dropped, one divides the intervocalic consonant into two separate phases: the one arrested by the stop and the other released with a plosive—i.e., [ʌp̄, pʌ]. Because the child will recognize that the breath must be restrained at the end of the stop phase (to produce the expected plosive), nasal escape will not normally occur. After the child has achieved the stop, reinforcement and generalization training will assure the production of Subskills 1 and 2.

Pointing out to the child that he is making a nasal instead of a stop is reasonable. Telling the child to produce something other than a nasal without telling him how to go about it is to invite frustration and rebellion. Once the stop-versus-nasal distinction has been made, the stop can be associated with placing a finger on the lips and the nasal with placing a finger on the nose. With the help of such visual prompts, the child may be expected to alternate the two and thus to acquire clearly differentiated orosensory-motor patterns for the two types of sounds. Once the stop is produced satisfactorily, it is helpful to have the child use it phonologically. There should be no difficulty in helping the child to clothe his production of [ʌp̄] with meaning. The word *up* is one of the first expressions to be acquired and used dynamically by normally hearing infants.

Subskill 3 may be taught by a strategy similar to that proposed for

Subskills 1 and 2. In this case, holding the finger in a raised position is equated with resisting plosion, and lowering it is associated with the release of the fricative. Likewise, in Subskill 4 the rate and extent of hand movement can be used to indicate the speed and vigor with which the stop should be made and the intensity of production required for each syllable. Subskill 5 calls for strategies similar to those suggested for pitch control in combination with those suggested above. A technical device which provides a visual display could be selected or devised as an aid to teaching almost any subskill, not simply those described above. Few would be any more effective than the teacher's use of hand cues, toys, colored cups, blocks, paper hats, tokens, balls, cards, or buttons that may be employed as prompts for a particular manner or place of production or for voicing. Simple associative strategies work, and the range of such strategies or of the visual cues that can be used is limited only by the bounds of the teacher's imagination, creativity, and enthusiasm. It is because one can use such a variety of objects attractive to children that vision is an excellent means of providing reinforcement.

Tactile strategies for teaching stops include that of enabling the child to feel sharp bilabial closure and the concurrent cessation of voice through placement of the fingers on the face as in the Tadoma method (see Chapter 3). Such a strategy is effective for teaching Subskills 1, 2, and 3. Because the intensity of the vibration felt depends on the vowel used, one would need to use the same vowel in both the initial and final syllables if such a tactile strategy is to be effective for Subskill 4. Since change in pitch of voice can be felt as change of location of vibration in the facial structure, Subskill 5 may also be taught through the Tadoma technique. Simple vibratory aids could also be used to teach Subskills 1 through 4, but a complex vibratory device—one driven by energy derived from the speaker's voice pitch—would be required to teach Subskill 5.

The Nasal [m]

Targets and Subskills

The [m] is a bilabial nasal consonant, usually voiced. There are two target behaviors involved in its production: bilabial closure and opening of the velopharyngeal port. Although the lateral pharyngeal walls usually assist in velopharyngeal closure and must therefore be relaxed in the production of nasal sounds, we propose to treat the velopharyngeal target simply as one involving the velum. Because we are concerned with coarticulation, we cannot consider only the lowering of the velum for the nasal consonant (a movement which is usually initiated during the preceding vowel); we must also be concerned with the raising of the velum to effect closure for production of the vowel. The coloring of the adjacent vowels by nasal consonants, due to sluggish velopharyngeal action, provides acoustic cues to their manner of production (see above). Training in the various subskills relating to [m] must therefore be structured to develop appropriate velar action before, during, and following the production of the consonant.

The subskills proposed for [m] have been presented and discussed by way of detailed example in Chapter 10. They are summarized below:

Subskill 1: Production of a single [m] in isolation.

Subskill 2: Repetition of several [m] sounds in isolation.

Subskill 3: Production of [m] in final position following the vowels [i], [u], and [a].

Subskill 4: Repetition of [m] in postvocalic position following either [i], [a], or [u], the repetitions to be effected on one breath.

Subskill 5: Production of [m] in initial position preceding the vowels [i], [u], and [a].

Subskill 6: Repetition of syllables initiated with [m].

Subskill 7: Repeated production of [m] in initial position in a series of syllables containing different vowels (e.g., [mimamu]).

Subskill 8: Alternation of syllables containing [m] with syllables containing other consonants (e.g., [mabamaba], [fimifimi], etc.).

Subskill 9: Humming over a range of at least eight semitones.

Subskill 10: Production of syllables containing [m] varying in pitch over a range of at least eight semitones.

Teaching Strategies

Auditory strategies for teaching the subskills which underlie production of [m] should be successful for all but totally deaf children. This is because the murmur associated with [m] and other nasals falls at or below 300 Hz and is sharply discontinuous with F_1 of the preceding or following vowel. It should, then, be taken as axiomatic that if a child has measurable hearing, an [m] will be audible if an appropriate hearing aid is worn. If the child's hearing aid does not provide some gain below 300 Hz and if the patterns of resonance and antiresonance which occur at higher frequencies are also inaudible, one cannot, of course, expect identification of nasals or discrimination between them and consonants having a different manner of production.

If the [m] is audible there should be no difficulty in teaching Subskills 1 through 4 by imitation since the child will already have learned the prerequisite skills of vocalization on demand and of production of the vowels involved. In Subskills 5 and 6 there is a danger that the child will produce [b] or [mb] instead of [m] if training in the first four subskills has been too hurried or if attention has not been sufficiently focused on hearing the [m]. If this fault does occur, the teacher should backtrack and establish the previous subskills more strongly. In Subskills 6 and 7 auditory attention should be focused not only on the [m], but also on the quality of the vowel to ensure that neither undue diphthongization nor nasalization occurs. In Subskill 8 alternation of [ba] and [ma] should be undertaken with particular care so that their differentiation becomes ingrained. The teacher should be sure to present the [b] first on some occasions and the [m] first on others so that the child has to listen carefully to the model provided. Subskill 9 should be very well established before Subskill 10 is attempted since if the latter is attempted too quickly, the increased laryngeal tension associated with high pitch may generalize to the lips with the result that [b] or [mb] rather than [m] will be produced. Because of this risk it is better to practice Subskill 10 first with [m] following various vowels, next with [m] in an intervocalic position, and last with [m] releasing various vowels.

Visual strategies are less effective with [m] than are either auditory or tactile strategies because nasality cannot be visualized through speechreading. The bilabial target can be seen, but the velar target cannot. Velar movement can be observed if one looks in the mouth. However, the amount by which the velum should be lowered to produce nasality or the extent to which it should be raised to produce orality in consonants cannot be judged with the mouth open. Furthermore, the production of a nasal consonant is not in itself a difficulty. The problem is the differentiation of nasality and orality and, more specifically, the timing of the velar excursion for appropriate velopharyngeal valving.

Nasality can be demonstrated by means of a visual display driven from an accelerometer coupled to the bridge of the nose. However, nasal vibration during the production of [m] may as readily be felt directly with the finger. The most appropriate use of vision in teaching the 10 subskills specified is, therefore, in prompting production of [m] with a visual cue (such as touching the nose) and in providing reinforcement.

Tactile strategies are certainly the most effective means of teaching [m] to the totally deaf child since production of [m] results in (a) vibration which is of maximal intensity at the bridge of the nose, and (b) emission of breath through the nostrils. It is the only sound that can be evoked with these tangible characteristics when the lips are closed. Its production should be established in Subskills 1 and 2 in conjunction with a visual cue so that the prompt alone will later suffice to elicit the sound. In other words, touch should be discarded as soon as the child is aware of the orosensory-motor patterns associated with the sound.

Subskill 3 should not be introduced to the child until he is sufficiently familiar with the orosensory-motor patterns associated with [m] to be able to produce the sound when prompted visually to do so. That is to say, Subskill 3 should not be introduced until he can produce [m] without having to feel his nose in order to determine whether vibration and nasal breath stream are present. At this point, he should be able to terminate various vowels with [m]; and, if the vowels have been adequately developed, he should have no difficulty in keeping them oral. If there is such difficulty, the vowel should be initiated with [h] or another fricative. The two sounds—the vowel and the [m]—may be produced first on a different breath, next on the same breath with a brief pause between them, and finally as a single syllable. The rate of production may be increased as training proceeds if the child is provided with a tactile or visual prompt. For example, the teacher can associate lifting the child's left hand with the vowel and lifting his right hand with the [m]. The shorter the delay between her raising the child's left and right hands, the faster and closer together the two sounds should be produced. Subskill 3 cannot be considered as being mastered until the two sounds are blended normally without undue tension. Subskills 4 and 5 can be taught by means of similar strategies.

In Subskill 5 the [m] is introduced in an initial position. If the child has had adequate previous training with [m] and is sufficiently familiar with its postvocalic production, he will not tend to confuse [m] with [b] or to introduce an intrusive [b]. Should he do so, further training in previous subskills must be provided. It may also be helpful to practice earlier subskills immediately before attempting initial [m] production in order to provide a behavioral set. It is particularly important to practice Subskill 5 with high-back [u] and high-front [i] vowels since they require more definite velopharyngeal closure than does [a]. Practice with these vowels yields the strongest orosensory-motor patterns associated with velar action, provides essential exercise for strengthening the velar musculature, and develops the basic coordination required for effective velopharyngeal valving in coarticulated speech. If the vowels following [m] do become nasalized, they should be terminated with a fricative. If, in spite of reference to previous subskill training, the child produces [mb] rather than the desired [m], he may be taught to produce the [m] smoothly by tactile analogy—stroking the hand or knee as the [m] releases the vowel, as compared with patting the hand or knee when the [mb] is substituted. This strategy is preferable to introducing an [h] between the [m] and the vowel for three reasons: (a) it is still possible for the child to say [mbha]; (b) the practice tends to encourage prolongation; and (c) [mha] is in itself unacceptable and may become established as a fault.

Only when Subskill 5 has become automatized to the extent that [m] can be produced with all vowels in long and short syllables and without undue tension should one introduce Subskill 6, which calls for repetition of syllables initiated with [m]. To prevent intrusive plosion one should have the child begin by repeating only three or four syllables to a breath at the rate of about one per second. The rate should be increased gradually so that error-free performance is maintained. This subskill should eventually be performed at a rate of about three syllables per second for up to five seconds with all vowels. If the vowel is unduly nasalized, a fricative may be used to terminate each syllable until correct velopharyngeal valving has been established. The fricative should be dropped as soon as possible. For reasons given above, it is particularly important to practice [mimimi] and [mumumu]. Visual-tactile cues can initially be used to convey the notion of smooth release of the vowel, but at faster rates such props should be discarded. Once the child can initiate vowels with [m] at slow rates, he should be expected to develop speed and feedforward control of his articulators and to rely solely upon the orosensory-motor patterns generated to provide feedback.

In Subskill 6 the tongue should be maintained in its target position during bilabial closure. If it is not, then neutralization tends to occur. This may be corrected by feeling the tongue position with a finger as in the original teaching of a vowel. Thus, the high-front arching of the tongue can be felt equally as well in [mimimi] as in [i]. In Subskill 7 the tongue should move to assume its position for the following vowel during bilabial closure. A similar subskill is required in plosive production. If the tongue has not reached its target position before release of the nasal [m], then diphthongization tends to occur. Again, this type of problem can be dealt with by having the child feel tongue movement while the lips are approximated.

Subskill 8 is of critical importance in establishing the rapid and well coordinated velar function that is called for in coarticulated speech. Tactile cues should not be necessary if previous subskills have been mastered, and their continued use is likely to be disadvantageous simply because the child cannot cue as fast as one requires him to carry out the speech task. That cueing beyond the initial stages induces slow rates of production and prolongation is easy to demonstrate. Let the reader try to point the finger alternately to nose and lips while repeating [ba-ma], doing both as rapidly as possible. It will be clear that (a) alternations of [ba-ma] will be much faster, and (b) coordination of finger with mouth at even moderate rates is difficult. In short, to continue to provide any other than auditory prompts beyond the introductory stage of teaching will burden the child unnecessarily and may prevent him from achieving this or any other subskill.

Subskills 9 and 10 require production of [m] over a range of at least eight semitones. Both call for new types of coordination between the laryngeal and articulatory musculature. Tactile strategies for obtaining pitch change as discussed in Chapter 12 and tactile strategies for [m] production as discussed above may be jointly employed to teach the required behaviors.

The Semivowels [w] and [ʍ]

Targets and Subskills

The [w] is a bilabial oral consonant which also requires tongue arching toward the velum. There are, therefore, two target behaviors involved. The bilabial target is initial lip-rounding followed by rapid neutralization of lip position and final assumption of the lip target associated with the following vowel. The tongue target is initial approximation of the tongue dorsum to the velum, much as in the vowel [u], and a relatively smooth glide to the target position required for the following vowel. This consonant can only be produced in a syllable: more specifically, when followed by a vowel. It can therefore occur only initially, medially, and in blends. The sound is represented in traditional orthography by the letter "w"; but when this letter occurs at the end of a word as in *now*, it does not signal the phonetic [w] but instead signals a diphthong—in the given example, the diphthong [aʊ]. If [w] is taught in association with orthography, intrusive voicing toward the neutral vowel is encouraged in word-final position.

The [w] is most simply considered as an extremely tense form of the vowel [u]. It is best developed through reference to this vowel regardless of whether auditory, visual, or tactile strategies are required to teach it. The [ʍ] may, for all practical purposes, be considered as a glide equivalent to the unvoiced [w], but with a greater fricative component. In blends initiated with unvoiced consonants (e.g., [tw], [kw], and [sw]) the sound is usually unvoiced. The following subskills may be specified:

Subskill 1: Production of [w] in single syllables releasing central and front vowels.

Subskill 2: Repetition of syllables initiated with [w] releasing central and front vowels.

Subskill 3: Production of [w] in single and repeated syllables releasing back vowels.

Subskill 4: Production of [w] in intervocalic position in varied vowel contexts (e.g., [uwa], [əwe], etc.).

Subskill 5: Alternation of syllables initiated with [w] and syllables initiated with other consonants.

Subskill 6: Production of a series of syllables released with [w] which vary in pitch over a range of at least eight semitones.

The purpose of teaching [w] first with central and front vowels (Subskills 1 and 2) is to provide the child with the strongest possible orosensory-motor patterns. These arise from the rapid and definite unrounding of the lips and the extensive excursion of the tongue which are characteristic of [w] in such vowel contexts. Different orosensory-motor patterns result from rehearsal of Subskill 3, which demands brief unrounding of the lips and their rapid rerounding for following vowels such as [o] and [u]. This subskill calls for a relatively small amount of tongue movement. Subskill 4 is an extension of Subskills 2 and 3 since the [w] becomes medial in a series of syllables such as [wɛwɛwɛ]. The purpose of the subskill is to ensure that the [w] can be initiated with one vowel and terminated with another.

The purpose of Subskill 5 is to emphasize the nature of the orosensory-motor patterns associated with [w] through direct contrast with syllables released by consonants having other manners of production. A further purpose of Subskill 5 is to develop feedforward control and coordination of the articulators in the speedy production of [w] by simulating the contexts within which the sound has to be produced in running speech.

The purpose of Subskill 6 is to ensure that the [w] can be used flexibly within any intonation pattern. It is particularly useful as an exercise to establish independent control of laryngeal and articulatory function since the tongue and lips are highly mobile throughout the production of a series of syllables such as [wewewe].

Teaching Strategies

Auditory strategies are usually effective except for the totally deaf child since the [w] is initiated well below 500 Hz and the F_1 and F_2 glides to the adjacent vowel are salient acoustic features. Auditory detection of the glides can usually be taught through comparison of a vowel in isolation and the same vowel initiated with [w]—e.g., [a] and [wa]. Particularly strong transitions are yielded when [w] releases central vowels, as in Subskills 1 and 2. Thus, the child with very limited residual hearing may find F_1 of the [w] glide to central vowels among the most audible of all consonant cues. The child who has hearing up to 2,000 Hz should have no trouble with any of these subskills since the F_2 glide to both central and front vowels is also an acoustically prominent feature. The most difficult of the subskills to learn through audition is the third, since the formant glides of [w] associated with back vowels are the least salient. However, since the least salient cues are exclusively in the low-frequency range, they should be audible to all but totally deaf children. In teaching Subskills 5 and 6 it is helpful to focus the child's attention on the acoustic properties of the syllables selected for development. Thus, if [ba-wa] is to be alternated, the child may initially be asked to listen to and thus identify the order in which the syllables are spoken by the teacher. Similarly, the pitch of the items in the model provided for Subskill 6 (high-mid-low, low-high-mid, etc.) should be heard out by the child and described by him before he attempts to imitate.

The child with very limited hearing and little background in using hearing aids might be helped in the first stage of acquisition if the [w] is introduced as a brief [u], a vowel with which he should already be familiar. Thus, [wa] could be evoked through the following three steps: [u + a], [ua], [wa]. Only in rare cases should this progression be necessary, for the [w] has a duration of about 75 to 80 msec. in normal speech. This is about four times as long as the difference in VOT between voiced and unvoiced members of a cognate pair such as [b] and [p]. The sound [w] is, therefore, already among the lowest, longest, and strongest of the consonants and hence among the easiest to hear. Only if the child is totally or near-totally deaf should it be necessary to use visual or tactile strategies to evoke this sound.

Visual strategies are adequate for teaching the lip targets associated with [w], but the tongue target cannot be seen in speechreading. If the child has already learned to associate lip-rounding with arching the tongue toward the velum as in [u], however, the bilabial cue should be sufficient to allow him to imitate and thus sequentially achieve production of the first five subskills. Since there are no direct and unambiguous visual cues to the vocal pitch of the speaker, imitation of pitch—called for in Subskill 6—requires cues other than those provided through speechreading. These may be hand signals associated with level of pitch, electronic devices that serve as pitch indicators, or some equivalent.

Tactile strategies are unnecessary for the labial targets since they are visible, and such strategies should not be needed for the tongue targets if [u] has been adequately taught. They may, however, be required to encourage adequate production of an oral breath stream and sufficient strength of voice. Once the orosensory-motor patterns yielded through rehearsal of Subskills 1 and 2 have become familiar to the child, strategies involving touch should be discarded in favor of those using vision.

The Fricative [h]

Targets and Subskills

The [h] is the most nondescript phoneme in English because it essentially assumes the unvoiced form of the vowel which follows it. The vocal tract targets for [h] are therefore variable. There is a glottal target: namely, sufficient closure to produce turbulence (aspiration). Adequate breath stream to yield the required turbulence is usually provided by a chest pulse. The prerequisite behaviors for the [h] are ability to whisper (see Chapter 12) and ability to produce voiced and whispered vowels (see Chapter 13). Consonantal [h] is constrained in time, having prevocalic and intervocalic durations of about 100 msec. In developing the subskills which underlie production of [h], we are essentially concerned with teaching coordinations of breath and voice onset. The following subskills may be delineated:

> *Subskill 1:* Production of [h] in initial positions releasing back, central, and front vowels in single syllables (e.g., [hu], [ha], or [hi]).
>
> *Subskill 2:* Repetition of syllables initiated with [h] (e.g., [hihihi], [hahaha], etc.).
>
> *Subskill 3:* Repetition of syllables with [h] in intervocalic position (e.g., [uhu], [ahi], etc.).
>
> *Subskill 4:* Alternation of syllables initiated with [h] and syllables initiated with or without other consonants (e.g., [hi-du], [hi-a], etc.).
>
> *Subskill 5:* Production of syllables initiated with [h] and varying in pitch over a range of at least eight semitones.

It is in Subskill 1 that pulsatile breath release for the [h] must be established and coordinated with aspiration (turbulence created at the glottis and in the vocal tract) preceding voice onset time by about 100 msec. Subskill 2 involves the production of a chain of breath pulses during the exhalation phase of the breathing cycle. The pulsatile breath release required for [h] is quite different from the breath release required for repetition of other consonant-vowel syllables. The pulses must be terminated with voicing; hence, this subskill calls for delicate timing in the coordination of the chest and laryngeal musculature.

Subskill 3 requires the child to terminate voicing of the vowel preceding the [h] and to initiate aspiration for the consonant and then voicing for the following vowel, as in [aha]. It demands coordinations involving breath, laryngeal, and articulatory control that are more precise than those required in previous subskills.

Alternation of syllables beginning with [h] and syllables initiated with another consonant (Subskill 4) serves two purposes: it provides the child with optimum opportunity to contrast the orosensory-motor patterns associated with [h] versus those associated with other consonants; and it encourages the initiation of syllables with relatively forceful breath stream. This subskill therefore provides the foundations for breath release in the production of any stressed syllable.

Subskill 5 calls for the child to produce aspiration for [h] with the larynx differentially adjusted according to the pitch of the following vowel. This is essential to the production of [h] in the context of an intonation pattern and is helpful in the prevention of a falsetto voice (see Chapter 12).

Teaching Strategies

Auditory strategies can be successful even with children whose hearing extends to no more than 1,000 Hz since the frequencies at which the [h] aspiration resonates are determined by the vocal tract configuration assumed for the following vowel. Thus, strong formants well below 1,000 Hz can be created by [h] when preceding the back vowels. Auditory vocal imitation should therefore be attempted first with back vowels and the child trained to discriminate between pairs of sounds such as [hu-u] and [ho-o]. After the orosensory-motor patterns associated with [h] have been developed by such means, production can be generalized to [h] preceding other vowels. The strategy of first using back vowels would, of course, be especially necessary for those children with hearing only below 1,000 Hz. It might also be helpful to those with more residual hearing. It could be applied in the teaching of all five subskills.

Audibility of the [h] may be tested by having the child respond to the sound as in free-field play audiometry when it is produced by the teacher in the context of a whispered vowel. The distance over which it can be heard will vary considerably according to the frequency range of the child's hearing and the vowel used. Thus, a whispered [hu] might be audible to a child with hearing up to 2,000 Hz over a distance of about three feet, whereas the whispered [hi] might be audible to the same child only if produced within a few inches of his hearing aid. The distance at which the teacher can work through audition is, of course, not greater than the distance from the microphone at which she can obtain responses.

Visual strategies for teaching [h] are limited to those which demonstrate that objects move in the breath stream when the sound is produced. The sound cannot be seen in speechreading.

Tactile strategies are particularly appropriate in evoking [h] since the breath flow required for this sound is greater than for any other sound and hence is quite tangible with all vowels. Once the first three subskills have been mastered, the child should be expected to learn the remaining subskills without continuous reference to tactile cues since relatively strong orosensory-motor patterns are associated with production of [h]. These and the feedforward mechanisms developed through previous training should permit the mastery of Subskills 4 and 5.

The Fricatives [f, v] and [θ, ð]

Targets and Subskills

These fricatives—which occur in initial, medial, and final position—are among the simplest to produce since they do not call for extremely fine adjustments of the articulators. The [f] and [v] can be made with the upper teeth in contact with almost any part of the lower lip. The most forward point of contact is usually made following a vowel. Following a bilabial, as in the words *up for*, the teeth may actually be behind the lower lip during production. The [θ] and [ð] can be produced with the tongue either in an interdental position or with the tongue tip resting slightly behind the upper incisors. The latter position is most common in running speech.

The [f] and [θ] are unvoiced and the [v] and [ð] are voiced. In everyday speech the unvoiced sounds are frequently substituted for their voiced cognates. Thus, both the [v] and the [ð] before an unvoiced sound are almost always unvoiced. The tendency may be illustrated by comparing the /v/ in *of men* and *of course* and the /ð/ in *with Bill* and *with Henry*. The reverse is often true for [f] and [θ] before voiced sounds. The orthography associated with these sounds is among the most confusing in English spelling. Voicing is not the only feature to change drastically with context. The fricative component may also be omitted when either voiced sound initiates an unstressed syllable. Accordingly, the characteristics of production may vary widely and yet be regarded as within normal limits. This poses problems for the teacher only if she expects the child to conform closely to some "ideal" target when, in fact, no such rigor is demanded in everyday speech. Providing that the child makes a fair approximation to the models she provides in the several contexts called for in the following subskills, both pairs of sounds should be acquired in all their variety.

The main difference between the two pairs of fricatives relates to their coarticulation with adjacent vowels. The tongue is not involved in the production of [f] and [v]. It is therefore free to assume the position required for the following vowel during fricative production, whereas in [θ] and [ð] only the tongue body can move in preparation for the vowel. It is because the tongue can move freely during [f] and [v], but not during [θ] and [ð], that transitions associated with the two pairs of sounds are so different. Even so, their production—apart from articulatory configuration—calls for similar subskills. These are specified below.

In view of the instability of the voicing feature, we suggest teaching the unvoiced rather than the voiced cognates first. Since the unvoiced fricatives have greater turbulent strength than their voiced cognates, the fricative nature of these sounds can be better demonstrated with [f] and [θ] than with [v] and [ð]. Further, the unvoiced sounds contrast more vividly with other sounds in this step than do their voiced counterparts. Because the tongue is not hampered in [f] as it is in [θ], we recommend teaching all subskills for [f] before those for [θ] so that the fricative nature of these consonants can be demonstrated in the simplest way.

Subskill 1: Production of [f], [θ] in isolation.
Subskill 2: Production of single syllables ending in [f], [θ].
Subskill 3: Repetition of several syllables ending in [f], [θ] on one breath.
Subskill 4: Production of several syllables beginning with [f], [θ] on one breath.
Subskill 5: Alternation of syllables beginning with [f], [θ] and syllables beginning with other consonants.
Subskill 6: Production of syllables containing [f], [θ] varying in pitch over a range of at least eight semitones.

In Subskill 1 the child should learn that the required turbulence is produced by gently approximating the articulators and impeding, but not arresting, the breath flow. One's aim should be to have the child experience an abundance of orosensory-motor patterns characterized by relaxed articulatory adjustment. The intraoral pressure required for these sounds calls for minimal effort. Nevertheless, such pressure is sufficient to be sensed by the pressure receptors within the vocal tract. Such patterns characterize the adequate production of all the fricatives. They therefore provide the basis for development of the fricatives to be taught in later steps.

In the first three subskills these fricatives are taught in final position. They arrest various vowels—including [u], [a], and [i]—so that labiodental and linguadental approximations are taught in the context of lip-rounding (for back vowels), neutral lip configuration (for central vowels), or lip-spreading (for front vowels). Except in blends, all fricatives are terminated by relaxation of the articulatory constriction. When these fricatives are taught first in final position, such relaxation becomes habitually associated with their production.

The development of Subskill 3 results in the child's acquiring sufficient coordination of breath, voice, and articulators to produce the sounds in both final and intervocalic positions. In sequences such as [afafaf], for example, the [f] occurs both medially and finally. Moreover, the fricative is released into a vowel in such a series, thus providing the orosensory-motor pattern required for word-initial production.

Rehearsal of Subskill 4 in the context of several vowels ensures that the continuant quality of the [f] or [θ] is preserved in word-initial position and that the degree of lip-rounding or lip-spreading associated with the vowel is reflected during the production of the fricative.

Subskill 5 is particularly important to the development of velar control when the fricative-initiated syllables are alternated with syllables beginning with [m]. Rehearsal of this subskill also develops the more complex feedforward capability that the child will need in phonologic speech.

Subskill 6 demands initiation of voicing at a high, mid, or low pitch as the fricative is terminated. The laryngeal mechanism by which this is accomplished differs somewhat from that called for in other consonant-vowel (CV) combinations since the vocal cords are widely abducted most of the time during production of these fricatives. For all other consonants in this stage the vocal cords are fully or partially adducted during the consonant phase of the CV syllable.

Teaching Strategies

Auditory strategies may be feasible if the child's hearing extends to 1,000 Hz since some fricative energy for both [f] and [θ] is available below this frequency. This energy is stronger if the sounds are produced in the context of back vowels. Audibility of the sounds can be tested by asking the child to respond when he hears the teacher produce the sound as in free-field play audiometry. The distance over which the sound is audible is likely to be restricted to a few inches from the microphone of the child's hearing aid unless substantial hearing is present over 1,000 Hz. Audibility may also be determined by asking the child to discriminate between [fu] and [u], [θa] and [a], etc. If the sounds are audible, then all subskills can be taught through auditory or auditory-visual imitation. Visual cues may be necessary to supplement audition since the two sounds cannot be reliably differentiated even by normally hearing listeners when [f, θ] are produced in isolation.

Visual strategies are appropriate for teaching place of production for [f, v] and [θ, ð] in demonstrating that the upper teeth actually touch the lower lip for [f, v] and that the tongue touches the teeth in [θ, ð]. However, the requisite breath flow to produce turbulence cannot be visualized in speechreading. If the child fails to produce the sounds on this account, and if he is unable to hear any of the fricative components, breath flow may be demonstrated visually in Subskill 1 by showing the child that light objects can be moved or blown from the hand if held close to the mouth. As mentioned earlier, however, a longer and stronger breath flow than is actually needed for these sounds is required to move even light objects if the constrictions required for [f, v] or [θ, ð] are maintained. Thus, the strategy tends to foster prolongation and inappropriate orosensory-motor patterns.

Tactile strategies are unnecessary for teaching place or degree of constriction for [f, v] and [θ, ð] since these characteristics can be so readily visualized. However, feeling the breath stream required to create the desired turbulence is more expedient than the visual strategy described above. No exaggeration of force or duration is required to render the breath stream tangible during the correct production of these fricatives. Hence, the appropriate orosensory-motor patterns associated with these sounds can be fostered most efficiently if vision is used to indicate place and degree of constriction, and touch is used to demonstrate breath flow requirements. The advantage of using touch to demonstrate breath flow requirements is that the extent of turbulence and the duration of the fricative element will vary rather subtly from one subskill to the next. Such variation cannot be demonstrated by visual strategies.

Summary
In this chapter, we describe the target behaviors associated with the front consonants in Teaching Step 1: namely, [b, p], [p̄, b̄], [m], [w, ʍ], [h, f, v, θ, ð]. We specify the subskills underlying these consonants and discuss the nature of teaching strategies that could be used in their development. We suggest that if speech patterns in previous stages of acquisition have been adequately developed, these sounds should be relatively easy to evoke. More attention is therefore given to their rehearsal, repetition, and alternation in vowel contexts than to their evocation.

Because many acoustic cues on manner of production are present below 1,000 Hz, we emphasize the use of residual audition in teaching the child to differentiate these sounds. We provide several examples of visual and tactile prompting activities and stress that even if prompts are initially necessary, their continued use can inhibit the development of automaticity and appropriate orosensory-motor patterns.

REFERENCES
Christmas, J. J. P, T, K as breath stops. *Volta Rev.*, 28, 195–197, 1926.

Daniloff, R. G., & Adams, M. Verbalizable knowledge of certain speech articulations. *J. Commun. Disord.*, 8, 343–347, 1975.

Daniloff, R. G., Montgomery, A. A., Percifield, P., & Hampton, J. Children's articulatory and auditory awareness of differences between vowel sounds. *J. Commun. Disord.*, 8, 335–341, 1975.

Gerber, A. *Goal: Carryover*. Philadelphia: Temple University Press, 1973.

House, A. S., & Fairbanks, G. The influence of consonant environment upon the secondary acoustic characteristics of vowels. *J. Acoust. Soc. Am.*, 25, 128–136, 1953.

Hutchinson, J. M., & Smith, L. L. Aerodynamic functioning in consonant production by hearing-impaired adults. *Audiol. Hear. Educ.*, 2, 16–25, passim, 1976.

McDonald, E. T. *A Screening Deep Test of Articulation*. Pittsburgh: Stanwix House, 1968.

McNeil, J. D., & Stone, J. Note on teaching children to hear separate sounds in spoken words. *J. Educ. Psychol.*, 56, 13–15, 1965.

Rawlings, C. G. A comparative study of the movements of breathing muscles in speech and quiet breathing of deaf and normal subjects. *Am. Ann. Deaf*, 80, 147–156, 1935, *and* 81, 136–150, 1936.

Risberg, A., Algefors, E., & Boberg, G. *Measurement of frequency-discrimination ability of severely and profoundly hearing-impaired children*. STL-QPSR 2-3/1975. Stockholm: Royal Inst. Technol., 1975, pp. 40–48.

Roe, W. C. The "explosive" sounds. *Volta Rev.*, 17, 457–459, 1915.

Scott, E. How to correct defective articulation. *Assoc. Rev.*, 2, 457–462, 1900.

Wood, C. C., & Day, R. S. Failure of selective attention to phonetic segments in consonant-vowel syllables. *Percept. Psychophys.*, 17, 346–350, 1975.

/16/

Place Distinctions
in Consonant Production

M ost of the consonants discussed in this chapter are produced in the same manner as those treated previously but differ from them in place of production. Those included in Teaching Step 2 are lingua-alveolar or linguapalatal sounds, and those described in Teaching Step 3 are lingua-palatal or linguavelar sounds. Because many share manner of production with sounds already taught, one begins these steps with some important prerequisite behaviors already established. As with consonants in Teaching Step 1, sounds within each of the teaching steps specified in this chapter should be developed in parallel so that manner contrasts are maximized. That we treat [d] before [l] or [n] in this text does not imply that this order should be followed in teaching.

The hearing-impaired child's acquisition of a consonant is a process of incremental growth which begins with the acquisition of behaviors requisite to the sound's production and ends when the child is able to use all allophones of the sound correctly and automatically in communicative speech. It is helpful to summarize the steps in the process as they were described in Chapter 15.

1. Development of prerequisite behaviors.
2. Evocation of the sound.
3. Generalization of the sound to different vowel contexts.
4. Use of the sound in simple phonologic contexts.
5. Generalization of the sound to complex phonetic contexts (see subskills).
6. Appropriate use of the sound in fluent communicative speech.

The sounds to be discussed in this chapter all have specific tongue targets. On this account they may be more difficult to evoke than the sounds treated in the previous chapter. Once the sounds have been evoked, the child may find it more difficult to generalize their produc-

316

tion from one vowel context to another. As soon as the child can produce the sounds in different vowel contexts, however, there is no reason why further development (as specified in 4, 5, and 6 above) should not proceed as easily as with front consonants differing in manner of production.

There are several reasons why sounds involving tongue targets (place and trajectory) may be difficult to evoke. First, the variant and invariant acoustic energy associated with these sounds tends to be higher in frequency and hence less audible to children with limited residual hearing. Second, tongue targets are less easy—or impossible—to see. Third, there is less orotactile sensation associated with sounds made toward the back of the mouth. However, there are factors which ameliorate the difficulty of evoking these sounds if speech has been systematically developed up to this point: basic breath and voice control have been established; a range of vowels can be generated, and hence certain tongue targets which facilitate the production of these sounds can be called for; and the child has acquired certain front consonants having analogous manner characteristics, which makes it relatively easy to foster generalization of manner to new sounds.

All consonants vary according to vowel context. Accordingly, ability to coarticulate a consonant with one vowel does not imply ability to coarticulate it with any other. The severely hearing-impaired child may need to be taught each consonant in the context of each vowel. This is not such an arduous task as it might be because most children can readily generalize from their past experience and the effective teacher can help them to do so. Let us assume that the child can coarticulate [k] with the central vowels but cannot say [ki] or [ku]. Since the point of tongue-palate contact for [k] may differ by as much as 8 mm. in different vowel contexts (Houde, 1967), the difficulty is a common one. Providing that the child has first learned to produce a range of vowels as advocated in this text, one can help him to generalize by having him first produce [ka], then [kæ], [kɛ], [ke], [kɪ], and [ki]. Following coarticulation with the front vowels, one may then teach the child to generalize from [ka] to [kɑ], [kɔ], [ko], [kʊ], and finally to [ku]. In short, by establishing coarticulation of the sound with adjacent vowels, one can reach the extreme targets in several simple steps involving tongue contact shift of less than 1 mm. The strategy is more effective than attempting to establish [ki] and [ku] directly. If the procedure is carried out with care over several brief periods of training each day, the child can achieve the targets without error. There is no need to explain to the child that the point of tongue contact shifts with each vowel. As the child repeats the syllable the tongue target for the vowel and the economy of movement demanded by speedy repetition automatically lead to the correct place of articulation for the consonant. The strategy is illustrated in Figure 16.1.

The strategy illustrated in Figure 16.1 is applicable to the teaching of most consonants. It is helpful but not essential for targets in Teaching Step 1. It is often indispensable in Teaching Steps 2 and 3 in which place distinctions are developed. This is because many consonants in these steps are audible to children with a limited range of residual hearing only in the context of back or central vowels since their variant energy, associated with formant transitions, falls in the low-frequency range. Once such consonants can be initiated with certain vowels through audition, the strategy provides the means whereby production

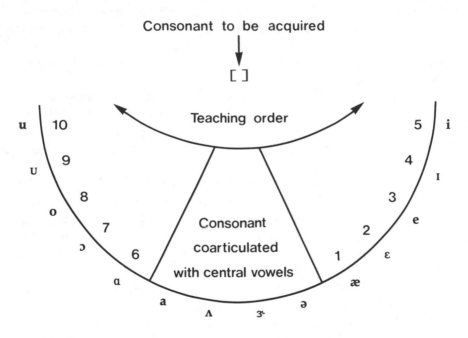

Figure 16.1

A strategy for the progressive generalization of consonants to all vowel contexts. If a consonant has been acquired only in central vowel contexts, its articulation can be generalized to any other context by progressively encouraging its production with adjacent vowels as indicated by the numbers in the diagram. Working toward front vowels first, helps to avoid habitual tongue retraction. The vowels are arranged from left to right in approximate order of ascending F_2 frequency value and position of maximal tongue arching in the mouth.

may be generalized to vowel contexts in which the variant energy may be inaudible.

The strategy described above can only be effective if the consonant is produced in a series of syllables repeated at a rate of at least three per second. Such repetition is required to ensure both that the consonant is correctly coarticulated with the vowel and that the variety of orosensory-motor patterns associated with the sound becomes sufficiently familiar to the child. Only if such patterns are completely familiar to a child can he be expected to coarticulate the sound correctly as he speaks, even in the absence of hearing.

We do not provide specific step-by-step suggestions for incorporating newly learned consonants into phonologic speech. However, it should be clear that the process should initially be as gradual and as systematic as the development of consonants at the phonetic level. English is largely a monosyllabic language. As soon as the child can produce the sound in the context of various vowels, one should then have no problem in helping him to see direct correspondence between the sounds in his phonetic repertoire and those in the phonology of the community (see Chapter 7). For example, [ti], [to], [tu], [æī], [æd], and [no], to use but a few of the first syllables taught early in this step, are words commonly met in everyday speech. One should not wait until all subskills have been developed before encouraging phonetic-to-phonologic level transfer. When all subskills have been developed, the child should not only be using the sound phonologically but should be doing so with accuracy and fluency in communicative speech.

TEACHING STEP 2:
Target Behaviors, Subskills, and Teaching Strategies
Relating to Alveolar and Palatal Sounds
[d, t], [t̄, d̄], [n], [j], [l], [ʃ, ʒ, s, z]

The Plosives [d] and [t]

Targets and Subskills

The plosives [d] and [t] are classified as lingua-alveolar sounds, the [d] generally voiced and the [t] generally unvoiced. As a rule, the tongue target is placement of the tip on the alveolar ridge behind the upper front teeth with the lateral margins in contact with the upper gums and molars. In this position the tongue provides a complete seal which allows the necessary buildup of intraoral pressure for the production of plosive energy burst. The lip and jaw targets are neutral and generally reflect the posture associated with the immediate vowel environment. The velum is raised.

These sounds are not always produced as alveolar consonants. They may be linguadental (made with the tongue between the teeth) if adjacent to the /θ/ or /ð/ as in the word *width*, gingival (made with the tongue touching the edge of the gums) when produced with a front vowel, and even palatal when produced with a back vowel. The /t/ is often heard as voiced in a medial position in words like *little* and *water* as pronounced by many American English speakers, but the /d/ is rarely unvoiced except in substandard speech. As with the [b] and [p], we shall treat production of [d] and [t] as initial and medial plosives. In word-final position, stops rather than plosives will be established. The subskills required for the adequate production of [d] and [t] are as follows:

Subskill 1: Production of [d] or [t] releasing various vowels including [a], [u], and [i] (e.g., [da], [du]).
Subskill 2: Production of [d] or [t] in a series of repeated syllables, formed with one vowel or another (e.g., [dadada], [dididi]).
Subskill 3: Production of [d] or [t] in a series of repeated syllables, with various vowels (e.g., [dadidu], [dodida]).
Subskill 4: Alternation of syllables released with [d] or [t] and syllables released with other consonants taught in Steps 1 and 2 (e.g., [dono], [widi]).
Subskill 5: Production of [d] or [t] in syllables varying in intensity.
Subskill 6: Production of [d] or [t] repeated in intervocalic position with either the first or second vowel stressed.
Subskill 7: Production of [d] or [t] in repeated or alternated syllables varying in pitch over a range of at least eight semitones.

Subskill 1 provides the child with the essential patterns associated with arresting and releasing the breath stream with the tongue at the alveolar ridge. In normal speech the jaw is not used to assist in closure, and care should be taken that the consonant is formed exclusively with the tongue. Rehearsal with all vowels establishes that there are no specific lip or jaw targets and that the tongue targets vary somewhat with the vowel.

In Subskill 2 more precise tongue targets are established since it is only through increasingly rapid repetition within the context of each vowel that the child learns the economy of movement required for fluent coarticulation. Since the tongue tip is wider in [i] than in any other vowel, initial practice in this vowel context may facilitate the acquisition of this subskill. If this is the case, generalization to other contexts should be encouraged through rehearsal with adjacent vowels in the order [ɪ], [e], [ɛ] . . . [u].

Subskill 3 establishes that tongue and lip movements toward the position required for the following vowel are begun during the closure phase of the consonant. Rehearsal of the subskill provides the child with the opportunity to compare and contrast the different orosensory-motor patterns associated with the adjacent syllables.

Subskill 4 extends such comparison to include contrast of the [d, t] with other consonants having the same and different manners and places of production. The orosensory-motor patterns of both the [d] and the other consonant used are emphasized in their alternation in series of syllables such as [da-ba], [do-no], [ti-ʃi], and so on. The [d-n] and the [d-l] contrasts are of particular importance, for unless these pairs are clearly differentiated confusion between [d, n, l] is likely to persist and to carry over into phonologic speech.

Subskill 5 calls for the production of loud, quiet, and whispered syllables initiated with [d, t]. It hence provides the orosensory-motor patterns that enable the child to find the level of lingual pressure required to produce these plosives, whatever the vocal effort associated with the vowel. When syllables containing [d, t] are spoken loudly, the lingual pressure exerted is greater than in the production of quieter syllables (Leeper and Noll, 1972; Brown, McGlone, and Proffit, 1973). This subskill is therefore particularly important for those children with little or no residual hearing, who tend to make good alveolar plosives in association with loud vowels but use inadequate or inappropriate lingual pressure to effect closure in quiet speech. If the child has not mastered this subskill, there is also a tendency for nasal escape to occur during quiet speech because less vigorous production is often associated with failure to raise the velum. If lingual contact is too light in quiet speech, the burst quality is weakened because the breath stream has not been adequately arrested during the closure phase. If lingual pressure is habitually too great, then prolongation of the closure phase tends to occur and movement of the tongue to the adjacent vowel is impeded. Coarticulation is thus adversely affected unless Subskill 5 has provided the child with appropriate orosensory-motor patterns and resulting control of tongue tension, without which Subskills 6 and 7 cannot be effectively developed.

Teaching Strategies

The most effective strategy for evoking [d] and [t] is to provide the child with the appropriate set by demonstrating that these sounds are analogous to the [b] and [p]. If the [b, p] subskills have been developed adequately, then the child will have a clear concept of the articulatory characteristics of plosives: namely, brief vocal tract closure (30 to 50 msec.) to allow a buildup of intraoral pressure, and sharp release of breath as burst energy. The articulatory difference between the [b, p] and the [d, t]—that the lips effect closure for [b, p] while the tongue tip does so for [d, t]—can usually be quickly established if the similarities are first made evident. Auditory, visual, and tactile strategies that may be employed to this end are described below.

Auditory strategies alone can be successful in evoking [d, t] through imitation if the child can hear any two of their three identifying characteristics. These are the durational feature (sudden onset), the burst energy (mostly above 3,000 Hz), and the F_2 transitional energy (some below 1,500 Hz with central vowels and some below 1,000 Hz with back vowels). Thus, the sudden onset of [d] and the transitional energy associated with the back vowels render syllables such as [du], [do], and [dɔ] the most audible to children with a limited range of hearing. The distance over which the child can discriminate syllable pairs such as [u-du], [o-do], and [bɔ-dɔ] should be determined using strategies already described, and auditory imitation should be expected only within that distance. If the child has a sufficiently wide range of hearing (up to 3,500 Hz) he may be expected to discriminate between and to imitate all such syllable pairs regardless of vowel context.

Children with a limited range of hearing should be able to generalize [d, t] production from back or central vowel contexts in which the sounds are audible to front vowel contexts in which they cannot be heard. The strategy by which such generalization may be fostered is, first, to teach the sounds by auditory imitation in the context of vowels which render them audible and, then, to encourage imitation in syllables constructed with vowels that are adjacent to those in which the sound can be produced, as illustrated in Figure 16.1.

Visual strategies for teaching [d, t] are closely akin to those for teaching [b, p], although lingual contact is more difficult to demonstrate than bilabial contact because the tongue is partially masked by the upper teeth. The tongue's position is most readily viewed if the jaw is lowered; hence, the sound is best evoked in the context of [a] or [ʌ]. Even in such a context, the complete occlusion required for the stop phase cannot be visualized; hence, visual imitation is most likely to be successful if the child is asked to produce a series of bilabial plosives immediately before attempting the alveolar sound—e.g., [bʌbʌbʌ, dʌ]. In such a series, the orosensory-motor patterns associated with [b] serve to indicate that analogous closure and plosive burst are required for [d]. As with [b], a visual cue to the burst phase may be provided by showing that an object can be moved by the plosion of [d]. If the child can be taught to produce the [da] or [dʌ] through visual imitation, then he should be able to generalize production of the sound first to syllables formed with adjacent vowels and then to syllables formed with [i] and [u], as illustrated in Figure 16.1. Since the tongue's position becomes increasingly masked by the teeth as the jaw is raised for successive front vowels and by the lips as they are rounded for back vowels, the child's orosensory-motor patterns provide stronger cues than visualization of the teacher's model in such contexts. Once the orosensory-motor patterns associated with [d, t] become familiar to the child through rehearsal of Subskill 1, the remaining subskills can be taught according to the sequence shown.

Tactile strategies are best regarded as a supplement, rather than as an alternative, to visual strategies in teaching [d, t]. The finger can be used to feel the pressure with which the tongue effects closure at the alveolar ridge and to sense the burst energy as the plosive is released. Once this strategy has been used to evoke the sounds, the visual cues provided by the speechread pattern and the orosensory-motor patterns associated with articulation are generally sufficient to sustain production. Persistent use of tactile strategies beyond Subskills 1 and 2 will impair the child's acquisition of the sound in all subskills. One advantage of using the finger to feel tongue pressure and placement in Subskill 2 is that parallel information is transmitted on the immobility of the jaw during repetition of the sounds in a given vowel context.

The Stops [t̄] and [d̄]

Targets and Subskills

For reasons previously explained, we shall treat these sounds as being distinct from their plosive counterparts. We suggest first teaching the [t̄] rather than the [d̄] so that problems relating to voicing are not introduced. This procedure has the additional merit of encouraging rapid rates of closure since the transitions to the [t̄] are generally faster than those to the [d̄]. The sound calls for two main target behaviors: namely, a raised velum and correct tongue placement. Jaw and lip targets are those associated with the preceding vowel. The jaw should not assist in closure. The sounds are best developed through reference to the bilabial sounds [p̄] and [b̄] which share the same manner of production. Thus, the stop characteristics of the consonants can be demonstrated in such series as [ɪp̄ɪp̄ɪp̄, ɪt̄], or [ap̄ap̄ap̄, at̄].

Since the alveolar stops call for a widely spread tongue to effect closure, they are most successfully taught first in the context of central and front vowels in which the tongue is already spread rather than in the context of back vowels for which the tongue is somewhat narrowed. Closure is also facilitated in such a context because the stops tend to be made more with the blade than with the tip of the tongue (i.e., they are gingival rather than alveolar) when coarticulated with front vowels.

Subskill 1: Arresting of various vowels including [ɪ], [ʌ], and [ʊ] with [t̄, d̄] in single syllables.

Subskill 2: Arresting of a series of syllables formed with one vowel or another with [t, d] (e.g., [ɪtɪtɪt̄], [ʌd̄ʌd̄ʌd̄]).

Subskill 3: Alternation of syllables arrested with [t̄, d̄] and syllables released with consonants of different manner and/or place, one stressed, the other not (e.g., [ʌt̄maʌt̄ma], [ɪt̄búɪt̄bú]).

Subskill 4: Alternation of syllables arrested with [t̄, d̄] and syllables released with consonants of different manner, the two syllables varying in pitch over a range of at least eight semitones.

The purpose of Subskill 1 is to establish production of the alveolar stops in various vowel contexts and, through its rehearsal, to familiarize the child with the range of orosensory-motor patterns associated with their production in different vowel contexts. It is during acquisition of the first subskill that the child should learn that no specific jaw and lip targets are associated with the alveolar stops and that the jaw should not be used to assist in closure.

In Subskill 2 the child should, through practice, learn to make the vowel-to-consonant transition with the required economy of effort so that the syllables can be repeated at a rate of at least three per second. A slight pause should be introduced between syllables so that plosive burst is avoided and the following vowel can be produced with sharp glottal release.

The alternation of syllables arrested with [t̄, d̄] and syllables containing sounds of different manner and/or place of production serves to contrast the features that differentiate these sounds from others at both the articulatory and acoustic levels. Such differentiation is accentuated if one syllable is stressed and the other not. As with the alveolar plosives, the degree of lingual pressure used in making these stops tends to vary with the vocal effort expended in making the whole syllable. A weak stop can therefore be strengthened by differentially stressing the two syllables. Both Subskills 3 and 4 call for the development of speech patterns of the type that one should be able to produce in everyday conversation.

Teaching Strategies

Auditory strategies include teaching imitation with or without supplementary visual cues. Since the acoustic energy identifying the [t̄, d̄] is carried by second and third formant transitions (T_2 and T_3), auditory identification of these sounds calls for hearing up to at least 1,500 Hz in back vowel contexts and beyond 2,000 Hz in front vowel contexts. However, in auditory/visual identification such a wide range of hearing is not essential. Many children with hearing up to 1,000 Hz can be trained to recognize the sound as a stop (on the basis of T_1 energy) and can discriminate between [p̄, b̄] and [t̄, d̄] by a process of elimination which may be expressed as "stop + audible T_2 = [p̄]; stop but not [p̄] = [t̄]." The differentiation of [t̄] and [k̄] can be made on the basis of cues provided by speechreading.

One should not work on teaching [t̄, d̄] through audition alone unless the child can use the T_1 energy to identify the sounds as stops, i.e., to specify their manner of production. The child's ability in this should have been determined in the teaching of [p̄, b̄] but may be verified by testing, training, and retesting his auditory discrimination of simple vowels and of vowels terminated with alveolar stops, e.g., [o] versus [ōt] or [a] versus [ad̄].

Visual strategies for teaching the alveolar stops—if restricted to speechreading—are not effective since the [t̄] and [d̄] are visually similar to [s], [z], [l], and [n]. The sounds are best developed visually by having the child produce alveolar plosives in a medial position (e.g., [ada] as in Subskill 6 for [d, t]) and signaling for him to separate the stop and plosive phases of the medial consonant by raising the finger during the first syllable, lowering the finger during the second, and introducing a variable duration pause between the two movements. This procedure has already been described as a strategy for developing bilabial stops. Repeating the procedure first with the bilabial stops and then with alveolar stops usually leads to the rapid acquisition of [t̄, d̄].

Tactile strategies other than feeling the position and force of tongue closure with the fingertip are clumsy compared to the visual strategy described above because they involve placing the fingers in front of the lips and under the nostrils so that the child can feel the sudden cessation of breath flow. Such strategies can help to differentiate [t̄, d̄] from other sounds that are visually similar but should be employed in the context of [i] or [u] since only these vowels provide a sufficiently tangible breath stream. The fingers should not be placed on the nose as a means of differentiating [d̄] and [n] since this tends to encourage rather than discourage the production of the nasal [n].

If a nasal sound is habitually produced instead of a stop, the fault indicates that the child either has an inadequate notion of manner distinction or has problems in velopharyngeal closure. If the former, one should return to rehearsal of the stop-nasal distinction of consonants in Step 1. If the latter, one should alternate syllables containing nasals and fricatives: e.g., [mʌfmʌfʌ], [naʃanaʃa], etc. (See Chapter 13.) Pinching the nose to prevent nasal escape during the articulation of a stop or holding a mirror under the nostrils to indicate nasal escape are strategies to be avoided. They only demonstrate to the child that he is wrong and do nothing to overcome the problems that cause the fault. The only satisfactory solution to such problems is to ensure that the child learns clearly to differentiate between the orosensory-motor patterns associated with nasality and orality. The careful teaching of [m] and [n] and their alternation with consonants having other manners of production are essential in this regard.

The Nasal [n]

Targets and Subskills
   The [n] is a voiced, lingua-alveolar nasal consonant. The tongue target positions for [n] are essentially the same as for the alveolar plosives and stops but are reached less rapidly and with less force. The velopharyngeal port is open, the lips are parted, and the jaw is lowered; but otherwise the lip and jaw targets are neutral and, like those for other alveolar sounds, reflect the demands of the adjacent vowel. There is much the same variation in tongue targets for [n] as in those for [d, t]. With the front vowels tongue contact may be gingival rather than alveolar, and when pronounced in the context of [θ, ð] the sound may be produced interdentally as in the phrase *on the path*. The sound may be used syllabically as in the word /bʌtn̩/. The subskills which underlie adequate production of [n] are similar to those specified for [m].
   The [n] can legitimately be produced in isolation since it is a continuant and can be used syllabically. As with the [m], it is best developed first in a final position so that the child has opportunity to experience the orosensory-motor patterns associated with its nasality and to make the sound without undue tension before using it to release vowels.
   The repetition and alternation of the sound as specified in Subskills 4 to 7 ensure that appropriate motor target behaviors are established. The vowels must not be unduly nasalized in any subskill. If there is a weakness in this regard, fricatives should be used to release or arrest the vowel until appropriate velopharyngeal valving has been established.

Subskill 1: Production of a single [n] in isolation.

Subskill 2: Repetition of several [n] sounds in isolation.

Subskill 3: Production of [n] in final position following a variety of vowels.

Subskill 4: Repetition of [n] in a postvocalic position in syllables repeated on one breath.

Subskill 5: Production of [n] in initial position, preceding various vowels including /u/, /a/, and /i/.

Subskill 6: Repetition of syllables initiated with [n].

Subskill 7: Alternation of syllables initiated with [n] and syllables initiated with other consonants.

Subskill 8: Production of the [n] in syllables varying in pitch over a range of at least eight semitones.

The pitch variation called for in Subskill 8 may be developed from humming as in the previous step, but using [mn-n] rather than [m].

Teaching Strategies

Nasality, as a manner of production differentiated from all other manners of production, has been established in Teaching Step 1 with the nasal [m]. The child should therefore be introduced to [n] through reference to [m].

Auditory strategies are usually effective, though auditory/visual strategies may be required to introduce the sound. The nasal murmur which falls below 300 Hz should be audible to all but totally or near-totally deaf children. Thus, for most children, this auditory cue together with speechreading should specify the [n] unambiguously.

Identification of the [n] through audition alone requires hearing for F_2 and T_2 energy between 1,500 and 2,000 Hz. However, discrimination between [m] and [n] can be expected if the child has hearing only up to 1,000 Hz since the presence of F_2 and T_2 energy associated with [m] at about this frequency renders it distinct from [n]. Once the sound has been taught in Subskill 1 by auditory or auditory/visual means, all remaining subskills can be developed through audition.

Visual strategies for teaching the [n] are limited to demonstrating place of production through speechreading and indicating the presence of nasality through reference to a visual aid designed to display nasal energy. The [n] can nevertheless be easily demonstrated through vision by showing the child the tongue target and having him place his tongue correctly on the alveolar ridge; then, while keeping it in that position, he should alternately close and open the lips. Since [m] has already been acquired, this strategy inevitably results in [mnmnmn]. Prolongation of the final [n] in such a sequence provides the child with a clear concept of the [n] target so that he will have no difficulty in producing the sequence [mnmn, n]. Generalization of the sound to other contexts is fostered through the systematic development of the above subskills.

Tactile strategies are not usually necessary for the [n], but if they are used they should supplement the speechread form. Tongue pressure and placement can be felt with the fingertip, and nasality can be felt through placing a finger on the nose to feel the vibrations. The comments made on the shortcomings of teaching [m] through vibration or visual displays apply equally to [n]. One cannot be concerned merely with the production of nasality; attention must also be given to velar function before, during, and after the production of the nasal consonant in order to ensure adequate coarticulation.

The Semivowel [j]

Targets and Subskills

The semivowel [j] is normally classified as a voiced linguapalatal glide. One should aim to achieve complete velopharyngeal closure during its production. It may be considered as an extremely tense form of [i] and is usually characterized by a short initial fricative element which is distinctly present as it releases the /i/ vowel in a word such as *yeast*. It is frequently unvoiced following /h/ as in the words *hue* and *human*. It is often introduced in speech to avoid a hiatus between two adjacent vowels, as in *the other* and *he ate*. Subskills underlying adequate production are as follows:

Subskill 1: Production of [j] in single syllables constructed with the vowels [u], [a], and [i].
Subskill 2: Repetition of a series of syllables initiated with [j] (e.g., [jajaja], [jujuju]).
Subskill 3: Repetition of [j] in a series of syllables produced in a whisper, with a quiet voice, and with a loud voice.
Subskill 4: Production of [j] in an intervocalic position, one vowel stressed, the other not.
Subskill 5: Production of [j] in syllables varying in pitch over a range of at least eight semitones.

The strongest orosensory-motor patterns associated with [j] derive from the initially tense posture of the tongue and from the glide to the adjacent vowel. The greatest tension is in front vowel contexts, and the strongest glides are associated with contexts of mid- and back-vowels.

Teaching Strategies

Auditory strategies for teaching [j] are successful if the child's hearing extends up to 1,000 Hz since the part of the F_2 energy of [j] in the context of back vowels can be heard below this frequency. Identification of [j] in front vowel contexts requires hearing up to 2,000 Hz; but the transition of the first formant (T_1) is quite audible below 1,000 Hz, and the sound can therefore be quite readily taught by auditory/visual strategies to all but totally or near-totally deaf children.

Visual strategies have the disadvantage that the tongue targets are not visible. However, if the vowel [i] has been well established so that the child has learned that slightly spread lips are associated with the high arching of the tongue toward the front of the mouth, the [j] can usually be taught by visual reference to [i].

Tactile strategies may be required to identify the tongue placement for the initial position of the [j] and to indicate the fricative quality of that portion when the [j] is used in the context of front vowels. They may also be used to indicate, through pressure on the child's hand or knee, the degree of stress called for in Subskill 4.

The Liquid [l]

Targets and Subskills

There are two types of [l] common to English. Both are classified as voiced lingua-alveolar sounds, but one, the initial [l], is termed "light" and the other, the syllabic [l̩], "dark." The difference is that the latter is slightly velarized. That is to say, in the final or syllabic [l̩] the back of the tongue is raised toward the velum to a greater extent than in the initial [l]. This does not affect the type of lingua-alveolar contact made, for in both sounds the tip of the tongue touches the alveolar ridge in such a way that the breath stream is diverted laterally and flows on either side of the point of contact around the lateral margins of the tongue. When [l] occurs in initial and medial positions, tongue contact is maintained for about 30 to 50 msec., and the remainder of the consonant is a glide having qualities very similar to those of a semivowel except that the glide is brief—also 30 to 50 msec.

Unless the velum is raised during production of [l], the sound becomes nasalized. The lips are parted and the jaw is lowered for [l], but they are otherwise not involved in its production. They normally assume the position required by the vowel environment in which the sound is produced.

Vowel environment affects tongue tip placement as in other lingua-alveolar consonants, and the range of contact varies from gingival with front vowels to almost palatal with back vowels. Consonants adjacent to the [l] also exert considerable assimilative influence over its voicing. Thus, following unvoiced consonants the sound tends to become unvoiced. The following subskills may be specified:

Subskill 1: Repetition of [l] in final position in a series of syllables constructed with various vowels (e.g., [alalal], [ululul], [ililil]).

Subskill 2: Production of [l] in an intervocalic position (e.g., [ala], [ulu], [ali]).

Subskill 3: Production of [l] in an initial position in separate syllables (e.g., [la], [lu], [lʊ]).

Subskill 4: Production of [l] in a final position in separate syllables (e.g., [al], [ul], [il]).

Subskill 5: Alternation of two series of syllables, one containing [l] in final position, the other containing [n] in final position (e.g., [ʌlʌlʌlʌl, ʌnʌnʌn], [ɪlɪlɪl, ɪnɪnɪn]).

Subskill 6: Alternation of two series of syllables, one initiated with [l], the other with any other consonant; some series whispered, others produced with loud or quiet voice (e.g., [lɔɪlɔɪlɔɪ, dɔɪdɔɪdɔɪ], [lɛlɛlɛ, ðɛðɛðɛ]).

Subskill 7: Alternation of syllables initiated with [l] and syllables initiated with any other consonant (e.g., [folofolo], [lenelene]).

Subskill 8: Production of syllables initiated with [l] varying in pitch over a range of at least eight semitones.

Although the [l] can be produced in isolation, it occurs in this form only in final blends (see Chapter 18). It is best taught as a mechanism for repeatedly interrupting a prolonged vowel sound rather than as a way to release a vowel. This avoids confusion with any other manner of production, prevents undue tongue tension, and discourages synchronous tongue-jaw movement. The tongue movement required for [l] is relatively simple in that it is ballistic and rather slow. It does not demand the precision of tongue placement required for [s], for example; and although duration of tongue contact is usually about 30 to 50 msec., somewhat longer durations do not affect the quality of the sound in initial or medial positions provided that the glide part of the consonant remains brief.

The high-back and high-front vowels do not provide suitable contexts for evoking the [l] because the teeth or the lips mask the tongue's movement in [i] and [u], respectively. These vowels are also less conducive to initial acquisition on other accounts. In the context of [u] the back of the tongue, being raised for the vowel, tends to "darken" the [l]. In the context of [i] the tongue, being wide at the tip, tends to inhibit lateral airflow. For this reason, one should make sure that the sound is well established in the context of central vowels and work very gradually toward other vowel contexts to ensure error-free learning. The narrowing of the tongue in the context of front vowels is a target unique to the production of the [l] and, since it has not been demanded in earlier stages of speech acquisition, may prove to be difficult for the child to master.

Teaching Strategies

Auditory strategies are effective in developing most subskills if hearing up to 1,000 Hz is present since the F_1 glide, which originates at about 400 Hz, will be audible. Subskills 1 and 2 provide the child with relatively strong orosensory-motor patterns which, in parallel with the acoustic patterns, differentiate [l] from all other consonants and provide a foundation for the development of all subskills. Since T_2 originates at about 1,000 Hz, hearing up to about 2,000 Hz is required to identify [l] with front vowels and to discriminate [l] from [r], which is distinguished by an initially lower [1,500 Hz] third formant.

Visual strategies are particularly useful since, in the context of [a], the narrowness of the teacher's tongue tip as it rests on the alveolar ridge can be seen if she raises her head slightly. So can the movement of the tongue as the sound is produced in a series of syllables such as [alalal]. Once the sound has been obtained in the context of an [a], it must be generalized to other vowel contexts as illustrated in Figure 16.1.

We do not advise the use of visual techniques that in any way exaggerate the consonant. The tongue protrusion and the synchronous jaw and tongue movement that it encourages prevent the child from generating appropriate orosensory-motor patterns relating both to the primary placement of the tongue and to the secondary glide of the tongue to the vowel target.

Tactile strategies are of virtually no avail in teaching [l]. The only ones involving touch that have proved useful to the writer are placing a dab of chocolate syrup on the alveolar ridge to indicate the desired point of contact, having a child hold a Lifesaver or other small candy against the alveolar ridge for the same reason, and encouraging the child to feel the tongue move up and down with a fingertip.

The Fricatives [ʃ, ʒ]

Targets and Subskills

The [ʃ] and [ʒ] are linguapalatal fricatives, the one unvoiced and the other voiced. There are no specific lip targets. Although lip-rounding is often associated with these sounds in British English, it is rarely so in American English. In either case, the lip posture is influenced by vowel context. The jaw is almost closed so that there is but a small space between the teeth. If these sounds are evoked first in the context of central vowels, the child may wrongly conclude that jaw movement is required since the jaw must be lowered when the fricative sound is coarticulated with the vowels. If the child lowers the jaw when these sounds are produced in other contexts, diphthongization will result.

The tongue is raised toward the palate with the lateral margins touching the upper premolars and gums and with the tip and blade lowered in such a way that the breath stream can be directed through a relatively broad aperture on to the alveolar ridge and the teeth. The lower front teeth are important in the production of these sounds since they help to create the turbulence that gives these sounds their sibilant quality. When the lower teeth are missing, the child may be unable to approximate [ʃ] and [ʒ]. The velum is, of course, raised during production.

The [ʃ] occurs in all positions in English words: initial, medial, and final. It also occurs in blends. The [ʒ], however, occurs only in medial position in English words although such words as *garage* or *camouflage* may be pronounced with a word-final [ʒ]. Of the two sounds, the [ʃ] is the more frequently used and has the greater breath stream. We suggest teaching it before [ʒ]. Subskills for [ʃ, ʒ] are as follows:

Subskill 1: Production of [ʃ, ʒ] in isolation.
Subskill 2: Production of [ʃ, ʒ] in final position in single syllables following various vowels (e.g., [ʌʃ], [æʃ], [ɛʒ]).
Subskill 3: Repetition of [ʃ, ʒ] in postvocalic position in a series of syllables constructed with various vowels (e.g., [ʌʃʌʃʌʃ], [ɪʃɪʃɪʃ], [æʒæʒæʒ]).
Subskill 4: Production of [ʃ, ʒ] in intervocalic position in a varied vowel context (e.g., [æʃə] , [ɪʃʊ], [ɛʒə]).
Subskill 5: Same procedure for Subskill 4, except with one vowel stressed, the other not.
Subskill 6: Production of [ʃ, ʒ] in initial position in single and repeated syllables with various vowels.
Subskill 7: Alternation of syllables arrested with [ʃ, ʒ] and syllables arrested with other consonants (e.g., [ʌp̄ʌʃʌp̄ʌʃ], [ɪnɪʃɪnɪʃ]).
Subskill 8: Alternation of syllables released with [ʃ, ʒ] and syllables released with other consonants (e.g., [ʃubaɪʃubaɪ], [ʒideʒide]).
Subskill 9: Production of syllables containing [ʃ, ʒ] varying in voice pitch over a range of at least eight semitones.

Although [ʒ] does not occur initially in English, mastery of the sound

demands that it be produced in that position. We therefore treat generalization training for the two sounds identically. Subskill 1 calls for the
[ʃ] in isolation as it is used in requesting quieting (Shhhh!). Subskills 2
and 3 are concerned with the sound in postvocalic position. Mastery of
these subskills ensures that the child learns to assume the [ʃ, ʒ] tongue
target position accurately and rapidly in any vowel context and to relax
the tongue following production of these fricatives. These subskills are
not easy because the lateral margins of the tongue have to be placed accurately against the upper premolars and gums regardless of whether
the tongue is already spread and close to target position as in [ɛ] or narrowed and far from target position as in [u]. Use in the contexts of mid-
front and low-front vowels is likely to facilitate production of these
sounds. Subskills 4 and 5 develop the child's ability to modify the
tongue's position during the production of [ʃ, ʒ] toward that required
for the following vowel. In such a sequence as [æʃu], for example, the
back of the tongue must begin to rise toward the velum during [ʃ] if the
sounds are to be adequately coarticulated.

The sounds are introduced in initial position in Subskill 6. If production in initial position is required before the sounds are established in
medial and final position, a plosive or an affricate is often substituted.
The delay in introducing the sounds in initial position serves to ensure
that the orosensory-motor patterns the child comes to associate with the
sounds are those of a continuant. Alternation of the sounds with others,
as specified in Subskills 7 and 8, augments the child's experience of
these sounds as continuants and, through contrast, strengthens his
identification of the orosensory-motor patterns by means of which he
differentiates these consonants from others. Rehearsal of Subskill 9
serves to focus the child's attention on voice pitch rather than on production of [ʃ, ʒ] and thus fosters automaticity. It also develops his ability to use intonation in speech.

Teaching Strategies

The [ʃ] and [ʒ] are best evoked through reference to the [θ] and [ð],
which were taught in the previous stage. If the [θ] is produced and the
tongue is sharply retracted as the breath stream is maintained, a [ʃ] usually results because the tongue blade is relatively flat and widely spread
for both sounds and because the [θ] and [ʃ] share an analogous manner
of production. If the tongue is not withdrawn sharply, a [s] may be produced before the [ʃ]. The sound is most readily facilitated in the context
of the vowel [ɛ]. Indeed, if the tongue posture for [ɛ] is maintained and
the jaw is raised until the teeth are closely approximated, a suitable

tongue target for [ʃ] is achieved. If the sound is to be evoked through reference to [ɛ], then one should have the child, first, whisper this vowel in isolation; second, whisper the vowel initiated with a forceful [h]; and finally, during the course of the prolonged whispered [hɛ], raise the jaw until the sound [ʃ] results.

Auditory strategies may be successfully used if hearing extends up to and beyond 1,000 Hz since there is some invariant energy in the [ʃ] just below this frequency. This low-frequency energy is stronger when the sound is produced in the context of back and central vowels and when the lips are slightly protruded than when it is produced in the context of front vowels.

Visual strategies are of limited use in teaching tongue positioning since the necessary gap between the tongue tip and the alveolar ridge can be seen only if the teeth are less closely approximated than they should be in producing [ʃ, ʒ]. The child can, however, see the movements involved if the sound is evoked in reference to either [θ] or [ɛ].

Tactile strategies provide both a direct and an efficient means of evoking [ʃ, ʒ] since the child can readily feel the tongue position with the tip of his finger. If necessary, he may push his tongue up and back from the [θ] position and then, when the teacher tells him that the required placement has been made, withdraw the finger while maintaining the tongue target. The tactile sensation produced by contact of the lateral margins of the tongue should help the child keep the tongue in the required position. The [ʃ] may also be evoked by having the child place a finger under his tongue so that the tip is lifted toward the alveolar ridge. This strategy results in the elevation rather than lowering of the tongue tip and in production of the constriction more with the tip than with the blade of the tongue. However, appropriate tongue tip placement can be obtained if the [ʃ] is evoked in this manner by eliciting the sound thus produced, first with back vowels and then with vowels that call for tongue placement increasingly further forward in the mouth. Such variation in the position of the tongue tip occurs in relation to the vowels when the sound is produced in normal speech.

The Fricatives [s] and [z]

Targets and Subskills

The [s] and [z] are lingua-alveolar fricatives, the [s] unvoiced and the [z] voiced. Like the [ʃ] and [ʒ], these sounds are sibilants because turbulence is partly caused by directing the breath stream on to the teeth. There are no specific lip targets for these sounds. In order to bring the teeth sufficiently close together to produce sibilance, the jaw is raised to a greater extent than in most vowels. There is therefore usually some degree of jaw movement as the sounds release or arrest a vowel, and the extent of this movement tends to be greater with central than with other vowels. If these sounds are rehearsed primarily in the context of central vowels, the child may wrongly associate the sounds' production with greater jaw movement than is actually required.

The tongue target is more complex than that associated with any other sound. The lateral margins of the tongue are placed against the upper gums and premolars to make a seal that prevents lateral emission. At the same time, a groove is formed along the medial line of the tongue so that when the blade of the tongue is placed near the alveolar ridge, the breath stream can exit only by the small aperture thus created. The formation of the groove is of critical importance—not the location of the tongue tip, which can be lowered to touch the bottom front teeth, raised to a point behind the alveolar ridge, or placed in some intermediate position. The groove is more easily formed if the tongue tip is lowered; hence the sounds are usually less difficult to evoke with the tip placed behind the front teeth. If the tongue is protruded during production of [s, z], a lisp results. If it is retracted, then the sounds are lateralized, as in [ḷ, l]. If the groove is not sufficiently narrow, the sounds become diffuse, as in [ʃ, ʒ]. If the groove is too narrow, a whistle may be produced. Such a whistle is often produced by those who wear dentures because lack of tactile feedback normally provided by the upper gums is denied them and they have less control over the tongue target for the sound. Additionally, the hardness and shape of the dental plate contribute to high-frequency resonance. Since the aperture formed between the tongue and the alveolar ridge is small, the [s, z] cannot be produced if there is a significant degree of nasal escape. The velum should therefore be raised and the velopharyngeal port completely closed.

Both the [s] and [z] occur in initial, medial, and final positions. The [s] is common in word-initial blends, and both are common in word-final blends in which they frequently serve as morphemes. As with other fricatives, we suggest teaching the unvoiced sound first. It has greater breath flow than [z] due to the absence of laryngeal valving. Subskills suggested to ensure generalization of the sound to all phonetic contexts are as follows:

Subskill 1: Production of [s, z] in isolation.
Subskill 2: Production of [s, z] in single syllables following various vowels including [u], [a], and [i] (e.g., [us], [æz], [ʌs], [ɪz]).
Subskill 3: Repetition of [s, z] in a series of syllables following various

vowels (e.g., [ʌsʌsʌs], [iziziz], [uzuzuz]).

Subskill 4: Production of [s, z] for a duration of at least three seconds following various vowels (e.g., [ʌsss], [ɑzzz], [isss]).

Subskill 5: Production of [s, z] in intervocalic position in various vowel
contexts (e.g., [æsi], [izi], [uzi]).

Subskill 5: Production of [s, z] in intervocalic position in various vowel contexts (e.g.,[æsi], [izi], [uzi]).

Subskill 6: Same procedure as for Subskill 5, but with one vowel stressed,
the other not.

Subskill 7: Production of [s, z] in initial position in single syllables constructed with various vowels (e.g., [so], [se], [si], [zu]).

Subskill 8: Alternation of syllables ending in [s, z] and syllables released
with other consonants (e.g., [pasapasa], [wiziwizi], [zudu-
zudu]).

Subskill 9: Production of [s, z] in final, medial, or initial position of syllables varying in pitch over a range of at least eight semitones.

The greatest problem with [s, z] is usually one of intrusion or substitution of the [t, d]. Adequate training in the first six subskills does
much to avoid such error by establishing the [s, z] as fricatives and continuants that are terminated by relaxing the tongue. If [s] and [z] are
introduced in an initial position before the child is familiar with the orosensory-motor patterns associated with relaxed production of the
sounds as fricatives and continuants in the final position, [t] or [st] will
be produced rather than [s], and [d] or [zd] will result instead of [z].

There is relatively little tactile-kinesthetic feedback associated with
the [s, z], and it is one of the first sounds to become distorted or omitted
when feedback is reduced by masking or anesthesia. It is also one of the
last sounds to be produced correctly in all contexts by normally hearing
children, even though it may be used in final position quite early by
these same children as a morphological marker. Subskills 8 to 10 should
therefore be thoroughly rehearsed and high levels of automaticity in [s,
z] production achieved before the child is required to produce the
sounds phonologically. Only when there is no difficulty in phonologic
production should the sounds be associated with the written form; otherwise the difficulty rather than the sound will become associated with
the symbol, and the acquisition of the correct sound will be retarded.

Teaching Strategies

Like [ʃ] and [ʒ], the [s] and [z] are best developed through reference
to [θ]. If [θ] is produced and the tongue is drawn back and up very
slowly as the breath stream is maintained, an [s] will be evoked on most
trials as soon as the blade of the tongue approximates the alveolar ridge.

If the sound cannot be evoked by this strategy, it is because of one, or a combination, of the following conditions: sufficient oral breath stream has not been maintained; the lateral margins of the tongue have not been kept in contact with the upper teeth and gums; or the blade has been drawn back but not up. The teacher can diagnose the problem by listening. If sufficient oral breath stream is not maintained, there will be an audible break in turbulence. If there is lateral escape, the result will be a sound like [ɭ]. If the blade of the tongue has not been sufficiently elevated, then a sound more like [h] will occur.

The strategy described above leads to the production of [s] in which the tongue tip is slightly elevated, a position often assumed when [s] is repeated in the context of back vowels by normal speakers. To bring the tongue tip forward, the [s] evoked with tongue tip elevated should be repeated first following back vowels, next following central vowels, and last following front vowels. In this way, the demands of coarticulation will lead to the association of the blade rather than the tip of the tongue with [s] production in the context of front vowels. If the [s] evoked with elevated tongue tip is first repeated in the context of front vowels, an [s] with a lowered tongue tip will be hard to elicit. This might be satisfactory since many normal speakers use such an [s], but the likelihood is that difficulty in producing the [s] will occur in some contexts because it is more difficult to create the midline groove in the tip than in the blade of the tongue.

An alternative strategy for evoking the [s] from the [θ] may be used to teach production of the sound with a lowered tongue tip. In this strategy, the [θ] is produced and the tongue tip is withdrawn slowly over (and in constant contact with) the lower front teeth as the jaw is simultaneously raised to bring the teeth into close approximation. If the sound is evoked in this way, it should be repeated first in the context of front vowels and then generalized through adjacent vowels to [u] (see Figure 16.1). If the [s] evoked by this alternative strategy is rehearsed first with back or central vowels, there is a tendency when it is later attempted with front vowels for the tongue to become bunched behind the teeth so that the groove cannot be made and a stop results.

The [s, z] can also be produced through reference to facilitating vowels. If the vowel [i] is whispered and the tongue position is maintained as the jaw is gently raised to bring the teeth into close approximation, an [s, z] with low-position tongue tip will usually be evoked. If the breath flow is inadequate for production of the fricative, it may be increased by releasing the vowel with [h]. A veritable [hɪss] is, of course, the target behavior. The [s] evoked by this strategy should also be repeated first following front vowels and then generalized by way of adjacent vowels to the [o], [ʊ] and [u].

All fricatives, including [s, z], result from turbulence. This is produced when a sufficiently strong breath stream is forced through a small aperture. If the breath stream is adequate but the aperture is too large, there will be no turbulence. Similarly, if the aperture created by the tongue's constriction of the vocal tract is the correct size but the breath stream is too weak, turbulent flow will not be produced. Armed with this knowledge the teacher can diagnose the reason for a child's failure to produce a fricative target.

Auditory strategies, unless frequency transposing hearing aids are used, are likely to be successful only if hearing extends up to and beyond 3,000 Hz. Below this frequency the sound has relatively little, if any, invariant acoustic energy. If the child has hearing up to 3,000 Hz, it may be possible to evoke the sound in the context of a back or central vowel since some variant acoustic energy just below this frequency would specify the presence, if not the nature, of the fricative. Since many children have hearing that extends beyond 3,500 Hz but have individual hearing aids that do not provide significant amplification beyond 3,000 Hz, the [s, z] may often be obtained through auditory strategies only if speech training aids that have adequate high-frequency response are employed.

Visual strategies could be used to demonstrate how the tongue tip moves from a [θ] toward a [s] position, but only with exaggerated jaw-opening to demonstrate direct placement of the tongue. The position and grooving of the tongue could, of course, be indicated visually by use of a hand analogy, by means of a model, or through line drawings. The grooving of the tongue and hence the sound may be elicited by asking the child to blow through a drinking straw at a Ping-Pong ball or some similar object. The strategy can, somewhat surprisingly, help a child to direct his breath stream between his center teeth and can thus lead to production of [s].

Tactile strategies involving direct touch, other than those required to feel the concentrated breath stream at the center of the mouth, require exaggerated jaw-opening. A finger cannot pass through the space between the teeth during normal [s, z] production. The child may pass his finger slowly down the center of the tongue and, as he withdraws it, close the teeth. The strategy, like blowing through a drinking straw, helps to focus attention on the need for the breath stream—tangible on a wet finger—to be emitted only from the center of the mouth. The use of a tactile aid which presents a frequency-transposed, vibratory analogue of the acoustic energy above 3,500 Hz is useful in teaching these sounds to the totally deaf child.

TEACHING STEP 3:
Target Behaviors, Subskills, and Teaching Strategies
Relating to Palatal and Velar Sounds
[g, k], [k̄, ḡ], [ŋ], [r], [tʃ, dʒ]

The Plosives [g, k]

Targets and Subskills

The [g] and [k] are linguavelar plosives, the former voiced and the latter unvoiced. There are no specific lip or jaw targets for the [g, k]. The tongue targets, as mentioned previously, vary considerably according to vowel context. The velum is raised. Closure of about 50 msec. is required to produce sufficient intraoral pressure for burst to occur as tongue contact with the velum is released.

These sounds are frequently considered to be difficult for hearing-impaired children. In fact, they are not difficult, providing they are evoked through reference to previously acquired plosives, elicited with the aid of unambiguous prompts, and generalized from one context to another systematically by the process illustrated in Figure 16.1. The subskills underlying adequate production of the allophones of [g, k] are as follows:

Subskill 1: Production of [g, k] in single syllables releasing back and central vowels (e.g., [ga], [kʌ])

Subskill 2: Production of [g, k] in single syllables releasing various vowels including [u], [a], and [i].

Subskill 3: Repetition of a series of syllables in which [g, k] releases more than one vowel (e.g., [kikuka], [gɪgægɔ], [gegugɪ].

Subskill 4: Production of [g, k] in medial position (e.g., [aga], [iki], [oke]).

Subskill 5: Same procedure as for Subskill 4, except that certain syllables in each series are stressed.

Subskill 6: Alternation of a series of syllables released with [g, k] and syllables released with other consonants (e.g., [gamagama], [kitikiti], [gubugubu]).

Subskill 7: Production of syllables released with [g, k] which vary in loudness (whisper, quiet voice, and loud voice) and in pitch over a range of at least eight semitones.

The [g, k] is best evoked first with back and central vowels (Subskill 1) because tongue movement to and from the point of linguavelar contact in the context of these sounds produces (a) the strongest orosen-sory-motor patterns and (b) formant transitions that may be heard by children with residual hearing extending only to about 1,000 Hz. How-ever, once evoked and reliably elicited in such contexts, the sound should be quickly generalized to use with front vowels (Subskill 2); oth-erwise the child may habitually produce the sounds too far back in the mouth. If such a tendency exists, it is usually overcome by rehearsal of Subskills 3 and 4 at sufficiently rapid rates (at least three syllables per second). The speedy repetition demands the economy of tongue move-ment that should, with practice of this subskill, ensure correct place-ment and coarticulation.

Subskill 5 calls for the modification of the force of tongue contact. All things being equal, the contact pressure for [g] will be less than that for [k]. This is because the [g] is voiced, and the tongue's task in restrain-ing the breath stream is lightened when the larynx also impedes air-flow. Contact pressure for both sounds, however, increases with the vo-cal effort expended in producing the syllable. A more forceful contact must therefore be developed to produce a loud [go] than a quiet [ko].

The alternation of syllables released with [g, k] and syllables released with other consonants (Subskill 6) is designed to enhance the orosen-sory-motor differentiation of these sounds from others through a pro-cess of contrast. The production of syllables released with [g, k] which vary in pitch fosters automaticity by focusing the child's attention on pitch rather than on [g, k] production and leads to the use of the sound within the intonation patterns of communicative speech.

Teaching Strategies

The principal features differentiating articulation of [d, t] and [g, k] are the point of vocal tract occlusion and the part of the tongue used to produce the occlusion. If the [b, p] and [d, t] plosives have been ade-quately rehearsed, then the child will have developed sufficient famil-iarity with plosive manner to know what type of sound is required. If the sound cannot be evoked through auditory imitation, the place of plosive occlusion and the tongue posture required to teach it must be demonstrated tactually or visually. The sound may then be evoked through analogy with [b, p] or [d, t] in such series of syllables as [ba-baba-ga], [dʌdʌdʌ-gʌ]. Production of the [g, k] is facilitated in the con-text of central vowels because the tongue is neither narrowed as in [u] nor spread as in [i], and the movement of the tongue to and from the velum in the context of central vowels produces the strongest motor-kinesthetic patterns.

The [g, k] is produced with linguavelar contact analogous to that required for the [ŋ]. The [g, k] can, therefore, also be evoked by first teaching the point of linguavelar contact through development of [ŋ]. Once the [ŋ] can be repeated in a series of syllables such as [æŋæŋæŋ] or [ʌŋʌŋʌŋ], familiarity with the motor-kinesthetic patterns associated with the tongue movement together with provision of a plosive set should be sufficient to evoke the [g, k] in a context such as [bʌbʌbʌdʌdʌdʌ-gʌ].

Auditory strategies for teaching [g, k] should focus on the imitation of syllables constructed with back vowels such as [gu], [gɔ], [go] if the child has hearing that does not extend beyond 1,000 Hz. This is because the loci of T_2 in the context of these vowels fall below this frequency, whereas in central and front vowels the T_2 loci are in the region of 3,000 Hz. Further, the plosive bursts associated with [g, k] are lower in frequency in the context of back and central vowels than in the context of front vowels (see Chapter 14).

Visual strategies for evoking [g, k] include demonstration of production through speechreading and, if necessary, the use of visual prompts such as hand analogies, models, or diagrams. A limited amount of information on the tongue target is available through speechreading in the context of central vowels. In other contexts the tongue is masked by the lips, the teeth, or both. The point of velar contact cannot be visualized, but the part of the tongue used to make contact with the velum can be inferred from the portion of the tongue body that is visible. If a plosive set has been clearly established through immediately prior reference to [b, p] and [d, t], the sound can often be evoked by visual imitation. Thus the sequence most likely to evoke the sound would be [bʌbʌbʌ,dʌdʌdʌ,gʌgʌgʌ].

If visual prompting is necessary to elicit the sound in the context in which it was originally evoked, the visual cue supplied should accord with the articulatory characteristics of the sound: i.e., tongue contact with the velum and plosion. Prompts which suggest that the sound is made in the throat (fingers under the chin) should be avoided since they suggest (and frequently lead to) the production of a glottal rather than a velar plosive.

Tactile strategies are usually more effective than visual strategies because the exact point of contact and tongue body shape can be felt quite readily with the finger. The simplest tactile strategy is not to feel the point of tongue contact, however, but to rehearse a series of syllables such as [dʌdʌdʌ] and then ask the child to repeat the same series of syllables with his finger inserted in his mouth just far enough to prevent the blade of the tongue from making contact with the alveolar ridge. Under these conditions, if plosive set has been adequately rehearsed and if the [d] and [t] have been sufficiently established, the dorsum of the tongue will rise to contact the anterior portion of the velum. Once the [g, k] has been evoked in this way, it should be immediately repeated in central vowel context and, when it can be elicited reliably in this context, used with other vowels. If this strategy fails, the child should feel the point and force of closure as the teacher makes the sound by placing his finger in her mouth. By placing another finger in his own mouth, he may then imitate the movement precisely.

Linguavelar contact may be imposed by having the child force the tongue root upward by exerting pressure on either side of the trachea and releasing the pressure sharply as soon as contact is made. The strategy is unpleasant and is recommended as a last resort. We have never had occasion to use it.

The Stops [k̄] and [ḡ]

Targets and Subskills

The targets for [k̄] and [ḡ] are the same as those for [g, k] except that these stops have no burst phase. Closure rates are normally faster for the [k̄] than for the [ḡ]. We suggest teaching the [k̄] before the [ḡ] in order to foster rapid rates of closure.

Subskill 1: The use of [k̄, ḡ] to arrest syllables constructed with the short vowels [ɪ], [ʌ], and [ɛ].

Subskill 2: Production of various series of syllables in which [k̄] and [ḡ] are used to arrest one vowel or another (e.g., [ɪk̄ɪk̄ɪk̄], [æḡæḡæḡ]).

Subskill 3: Alternation of syllables arrested with [k̄, ḡ] and syllables released with other consonants (e.g., [ʌgmaʌgma], [ɪk̄tu,ɪk̄tu], [ɛḡfɔɛḡfɔ]).

Subskill 4: Production of syllables arrested with [k̄, ḡ] which vary in pitch over a range of at least eight semitones.

The purpose in first teaching the sound in the context of short vowels (Subskill 1) is to induce rapid rates of closure. A hiatus (pause) should be introduced between the [k̄, ḡ] and the following vowel when the sounds are repeated in a series of syllables (Subskill 2); otherwise plosive burst will result. Such burst must be avoided between the stop and the following consonant in Subskill 3. Alternation of the stop with either [m] or [n] in this subskill is particularly recommended because it helps to develop the rapid lowering and forceful raising of the velum and hence to strengthen velopharyngeal closure. Subskill 4 is an excellent exercise for developing independent control of the larynx and tongue. If independent control of the tongue and larynx is not developed, raising the tongue as in [k̄, ḡ] will cause a rise in vocal pitch. Maintenance of a steady pitch (high, mid, or low) during the preceding vowel should therefore be encouraged.

Teaching Strategies

These sounds have articulatory features in common with the plosives [g, k], the nasal [ŋ], and the stops [t̄, d̄]. They may therefore be evoked through reference to any or all of these sounds. The same strategies for teaching tongue placement for [g, k] or [ŋ] may be employed for [k̄, ḡ].

Auditory strategies may be used successfully if hearing extends up to or beyond 1,000 Hz since the transitions associated with the back vowels are audible in this frequency range. Audibility of the stop characteristic may be verified by asking the child to discriminate between such syllables as [u] and [uḡ], or [o] and [ok̄]. If the stop can be evoked through auditory imitation with the back vowels only, its production may be generalized to other vowel contexts in which it is inaudible by the process illustrated in Figure 16.1.

Visual strategies that are applicable do not include speechreading. The most effective use of vision in teaching [k̄, ḡ] is to have the child produce the plosive counterpart in intervocalic position as in [aga], raising the finger in synchrony with production of the initial vowel and lowering the finger as the second vowel is released. When the association of finger movement with vowel production has been made, the speed at which the child should produce the syllables can be prompted by the teacher. If she then stops the finger unexpectedly before the second vowel is released, she will obtain [aḡga]. By completely separating the two syllables she will evoke the required stop. It may then be elicited repeatedly through use of the same prompt, and finally generalized as specified in the subskills above. Visual strategies that may be used to demonstrate tongue placement are those described for the plosives [g, k].

Tactile strategies involving placement of the child's finger in his mouth are usually effective because the position of the tongue as contact is made, the force and the speed of closure, and the absence of plosive burst can all be felt. Other tactile strategies such as those suggested for [g, k] can also be used.

The Nasal [ŋ]

Targets and Subskills

The [ŋ] is a linguavelar nasal. There are no specific lip and jaw targets for the [ŋ], although the lips should be parted and the teeth spaced as required for the preceding vowel. The tongue target for [ŋ] is contact of the dorsum with some part of the velum. The point of tongue contact normally varies according to vowel context as with the linguavelar plosives and stops. The velum is lowered in order to direct the breath stream through the nose.

The sound does not occur in word-initial position in English. In medial position it is usually followed by a consonant (as in the word *finger*), and in final position it should be produced without an intrusive /g/. Pronunciation of the word *bring* as /brɪŋgə/ instead of /brɪŋ/ is considered to be an example of substandard speech. The sound does not occur in all vowel contexts. It is most commonly encountered with the vowels /a/ as in *song*, /ʌ/ as in *lung*, /æ/ as in *hang*, and /ɪ/ as in *sing*. Its most frequent use is as the morpheme *ing* in such words as *hearing, seeing, feeling*, and *talking*. In certain dialects the /n/ is regularly substituted for the /ŋ/ in morphemic usage (so that /θɪŋkin/ is said for *thinking*). The presence of the sound in other contexts indicates that such usage is not due to the speaker's incompetence. Rehearsal of the following subskills ensures generalization of the sound to phonetic and phonologic contexts:

Subskill 1: Production of [ŋ] in isolation.

Subskill 2: Use of [ŋ] to arrest syllables constructed with the vowels [a], [ʌ], [æ], and [ɪ] (i.e., [aŋ], [ʌŋ], [æŋ], and [ɪŋ]).

Subskill 3: Repetition of a series of syllables arrested with [ŋ] (i.e., [aŋaŋaŋ], [ʌŋʌŋʌŋ], [æŋæŋæŋ], and [ɪŋɪŋɪŋ]).

Subskill 4: Alternation of syllables ending in [ŋ] and syllables beginning with [k] and [g] (e.g., [æŋkɛægkɛ], [ʌŋgoʌŋgo]).

Subskill 5: Alternation of syllables ending in [ŋ] and syllables ending in other consonants (e.g., [ɪŋɪfɪŋɪf], [æŋæp̄æŋæp̄]).

Subskill 6: Production of syllables ending in [ŋ] which vary in pitch over a range of at least eight semitones.

Production of the [ŋ] in isolation (Subskill 1) is unnecessary if the sound can already be evoked. The sound is relatively easy to evoke in isolation; hence, this subskill provides a point of entry to the generalization program. Subskill 2 demands the use of only the four vowels with which the sound most commonly occurs. Rehearsal with these vowels as in Subskills 2 and 3 yields the orosensory-motor patterns which are required to differentiate the sound from all others. Speed in the repetition task establishes the most appropriate point of linguavelar contact.

Subskill 4 is required to teach the child how to arrest the sound with the plosives [k, g], which most frequently follow the [ŋ] in medial position. Rehearsal of this subskill provides excellent training in the rapid elevation of the velum, and its mastery can substantially reduce faults due to nasalization (see Chapter 13).

Alternation of syllables ending in [ŋ] and syllables ending in other consonants is required to specify the continuant characteristic of the sound and to ensure that the sound can be released correctly into vowels. Such skill is necessary to avoid a hiatus in running speech when the /ŋ/ is followed by a vowel, as in the phrase *hang on*.

Subskill 6 for [ŋ], like Subskill 4 for [k̄, ḡ], is an ideal exercise to establish independent control of vocal pitch and tongue movement. It also serves to focus the child's attention on pitch and thus fosters the production of [ŋ] in the absence of conscious attention to its articulation.

Teaching Strategies

The context which best facilitates the production of [ŋ] is that provided by the other nasals [m] and [n]. Although these sounds usually have a duration of 100 msec. or less in normal speech, their phonetic quality is not affected by duration. The teacher therefore has ample time to produce the three sounds on one breath, thus demonstrating that they share nasal manner of production and are differentiated only by the place dimension.

Auditory strategies are applicable for all but totally deaf children because, as with [m] and [n], the sound is characterized by a low-frequency murmur at about 250 to 300 Hz. The [ŋ] is additionally characterized by both variant and invariant energy above 2,000 Hz (see Chapter 14). If the sound cannot be evoked through auditory imitation alone, then auditory/visual imitation should be used. Sufficient information for this purpose is usually provided if the child is asked to listen for continuity of the low-frequency murmur and to watch the articulatory adjustments as the teacher slowly intones [m-n-ŋ]. For the [ŋ] in this sequence the teacher should drop the jaw to about the extent required for production of [a]. This is sufficient to allow the child to see' the tongue tip drop from the [n] position.

The child's ability to hear the [ŋ] sounded in isolation should be tested as specified in the introduction to the previous chapter. The sound should, of course, be taught within the distance over which it is audible. If, within this distance, the sound cannot be evoked by auditory imitation or by auditory/visual imitation, then tactile strategies should be used in conjunction with audition and vision. For the totally deaf child, tactile strategies supplemented by audition will suffice.

Visual strategies such as those described for [g, k] may be used to illustrate tongue posture and point of linguavelar contact, but on their own they are ineffective.

Tactile strategies may be used to demonstrate the continuity of nasality, tongue posture, and the point of linguavelar contact. Continuity of nasality may be felt by placing the finger on the bridge of the nose. Tongue posture and the point of linguavelar contact may be felt by inserting the finger in the mouth. The sound may also be evoked by asking the child to say [n] while holding down the tip of the tongue. If [n] has been adequately rehearsed, the child should have no trouble in first producing a palatal [ŋ]. Once this can be readily elicited, the finger should be placed not on the tongue tip but over the alveolar ridge. An attempt to produce [n] should then evoke [ŋ]. As soon as the sound can be reliably elicited with the finger in the mouth, the finger should be withdrawn as the sound is being produced. Rehearsal of the sound in isolation then provides a point of entry to the generalization program (Subskills 2 through 6).

The tongue can also be raised to approximate the velum by pushing the tongue root upward through exerting pressure under the chin with a finger on each side of the trachea. We have used the strategy experimentally to verify its effectiveness but have never needed to employ it in teaching the [ŋ]. It is less direct than the alternatives described above; and although it may evoke the sound, it may leave the child unable to effect linguavelar contact in the absence of imposed force.

The Liquid [r]

Targets and Subskills

There are many allophones of [r], and one speaker may use several of them. The [r] is frequently mispronounced by normally hearing children or pronounced in a restricted range of phonetic contexts. The clinical literature therefore contains a considerable body of research and opinion relative to the teaching of [r]. Much of this literature has been briefly reviewed by Shriberg (1975). Quite often, [w] is substituted for [r] by normally hearing children even when they are able to differentiate the two sounds as spoken by an adult (Locke and Kutz, 1975). This substitution is common among hearing-impaired children because the [r] is often produced with lip-rounding. The greatest problem, how-ever, is the difficulty in generalizing the [r] from one context to another, which even normally hearing children experience. We suggest that this problem arises because the various allophones of [r] are usually pro-duced with quite different tongue placements. Our solution to this problem is to evoke a consonantal [r] that can be used in most phonetic contexts and that can also provide the required coloring for [ɝ] and [ɚ] without substantial modification of tongue position.

The targets for the [r] we teach are principally those affecting the tongue. The lips are very slightly rounded during the initial phase of the consonant, and the jaw is lowered to the extent required for the adja-cent vowel but is not otherwise involved in the glide. The velum is raised. In word-initial position, the glide is begun with the tip and blade of the tongue curved slightly upward and pointing toward the back of the alveolar ridge. The lateral margins of the tongue are in con-tact with the upper molars so that a channel over the top and around the edges of the tip of the tongue is formed. The back of the tongue is ele-vated toward the velum. From this position, which is approximated for 30 to 40 msec. in running speech, the tongue moves rapidly (in about 50 msec.) to assume its position for the following vowel. Subskills that should be rehearsed to generalize production of the consonant to vari-ous phonetic contexts and to give [r]-coloring to various vowels are list-ed below:

Subskill 1: The use of [r] to release the central vowels in single syllables (e.g., [ra], [rʌ]).

Subskill 2: Production of initial [r] in single syllables with all vowels (e.g., [ru], [ræ], [ri]).

Subskill 3: Repetition of syllables released with [r] in all vowel contexts (e.g., [ririri],[rururu], [rɔɪrɔɪrɔɪ]).

Subskill 4: Production of [r] in medial position with various vowels (e.g., [aru], [ɛri], [ura], [əræ]).

Subskill 5: Same procedure as in Subskill 4, but with one vowel stressed, the other not.

Subskill 6: Same procedure as in Subskill 4, but with syllables spoken in a whisper, a quiet voice, and a loud voice.

Subskill 7: Production of [r] in final position in single syllables with vow-els commonly colored with [r] (i.e., [ar], [ɔr], [ɝ]).

Subskill 8: Alternation of syllables released with [r] and syllables released with other consonants (e.g., [rɛlɛrɛlɛ], [runurunu], [rawa-rawa], [rusurusu]).

Subskill 9: Production of syllables constructed with [r] and various vowels varying in pitch over a range of at least eight semitones.

The purpose in first rehearsing [r] with central vowels (Subskill 1) is to ensure that the tongue moves maximally, thus to create the strongest possible orosensory-motor patterns. Tongue tip rather than tongue body movement would be stronger with back vowels, but the danger in rehearsing the sound first with back vowels is that the marked lip-rounding which characterizes these vowels might appear to be a desired lip target behavior. If the child associates marked lip-rounding with the sound, then it is harder for him to differentiate it from [w], which may be substituted. The tongue movement is visible only in the context of central vowels.

Once the sound can be reliably elicited in the context of central vowels, its production should be generalized to all other vowels (Subskills 2 and 3). The procedure illustrated in Figure 16.1 is useful in this regard. The motor-kinesthetic patterns associated with this sound are probably stronger than those associated with any other consonant if the sound is taught, as we suggest, with tongue tip retroflexion. However, the pattern of tongue movement changes drastically with vowel context. Because the dorsum of the tongue is raised during production of [r], it may be easier to generalize first from the central to the back vowels in which the dorsum is also raised, and finally to front vowels, in which coarticulation is most difficult. This procedure is also recommended for another reason: namely, that F_3, which differentiates the [r] from the [l], is lower in frequency in the context of back vowels and hence more audible to those whose upper limit of hearing lies under 2,000 Hz.

Subskills 4, 5, and 6 are designed to develop the rapid assumption of the tongue target for the glide regardless of the tongue's prior position. By stressing one vowel or the other, the glide to and from the target position is modified. If the first vowel is stressed, the vowel takes on [r]-coloring; hence, the exercise prepares the child for Subskill 7. If the last vowel is modified, the rate of glide is increased. When the sequence is whispered, the acoustic characteristics of the F_3 are enhanced and breath flow is increased. It is important for breath flow to be relatively high during [r] production since this ensures a degree of turbulence which also helps to distinguish the [r] from the [l] in front vowel contexts and in blends in which, following unvoiced consonants, the [r] is unvoiced.

The purpose of Subskill 7 is to establish production of the [r]-colored vowels. If this does not occur without problem after systematic rehearsal of previous subskills, the child should return to Subskill 4. As he repeats the first vowel, the teacher should raise her finger; and as he repeats the second vowel, she should lower it. When the child has associated the finger movement with the sound production so that it can be used as a prompt to indicate the desired rate of production, the teacher can control the onset and duration of the [r]-coloring by moving quickly to the [r] position (high point of the finger movement). The second vowel can then be omitted and Subskill 7 accomplished.

Subskill 8 is to provide the child with the opportunity to contrast the production of [r] with the production of other consonants. Of particular importance here are the contrasts with [w], [l], [n], and [s]. The first two of these sounds are the most difficult to differentiate from [r], and alternation of [r] with [n] and with [s] demands considerable skill in controlling the front portion of the tongue.

Rehearsal of Subskill 9 ensures that the child can produce the [r] without undue conscious attention and prepares the child to use the sound within any intonation contour.

Teaching Strategies

The strategy for evoking any sound must be decided by consideration of (a) what prerequisite skills for production are present, (b) what prerequisite behaviors remain to be acquired, and (c) how the necessary behaviors can best be demonstrated and coordinated. In this case, the child who has followed the program suggested in this text will have all of the behaviors needed except one: namely, that of tongue retroflexion. Several sounds already in his repertoire ensure the other necessary behavior patterns. The elevation of the back of the tongue toward the velum is present in production of the back vowels. The rapid raising or lowering the tongue tip to or from the palato-alveolar region has been learned in the development of other voiced continuants, namely, [l] and [ʒ]. These vowels and consonants therefore offer contexts that facilitate evocation of the sound. Tongue retroflexion can be promoted by eliciting either [l] or [ʒ] and, during production, having the child retract the tongue tip toward the palate. An [r]-like sound, once evoked and reliably elicited in this manner, provides the necessary point of entry to the generalization program.

This program differs in several ways from most that have been used with normally hearing children. First, it seeks to reduce the diversity of the articulatory patterns that are commonly met in producing the [r] initially (as in *rat*), intervocalically (as in *around*), in stressed vocalic position (as in *bird*), in unstressed vocalic position (as in *another*), and in blends (as in *try*). Second, it begins with the consonantal [r] rather than its vocalic allophone, the reverse of the usual practice (Shriberg, 1975). Such an approach is essential if one considers the reduction of articulatory variation to be important. Furthermore, Elbert and McReynolds (1975) have shown better transfer across contexts from consonantal [r] than from vocalic [r]. Third, generalization training is primarily carried out with syllables rather than with words. While some programs develop the sound at the phonetic level using syllables as we do (see Elbert and McReynolds, 1975), clinicians have traditionally worked at a phonologic level using words (Slipakoff, 1967).

Auditory strategies may be effectively used with children whose hearing extends up to about 2,000 Hz because the first three formants of [r] all fall below this frequency. Children with hearing up to 1,000 Hz can be expected to hear the F_1 and F_2 glides but not the F_3 glide, which differentiates the sound from [l]. The first two formants, however, specify the durational aspects of the sound and are helpful in evoking it.

Visual strategies for evoking [r] include showing the child how to retroflex the tongue tip by pushing it up and back from an [l] or [ʒ] position, providing hand analogies, etc. Such strategies are best used in conjunction with audition or touch.

Tactile strategies—which should be used by the child, not the teacher—include (a) evoking the [r] by pressing the tongue tip up and back from the [l] or back from the [ʒ] position; (b) reducing lip-rounding by holding the lower lip down during production, a strategy that makes the child focus his attention on tongue movement; and (c) feeling the tongue movement in central vowel contexts by placing the finger over the alveolar ridge.

The Affricates [tʃ] and [dʒ]

Targets and Subskills

The [tʃ] and [dʒ] are linguapalatal affricates, the one unvoiced and the other voiced. The digraphs used to represent these sounds indicate their nature. Each is a blend of a stop (not plosive) and a fricative element. There are no essential lip targets, although lip-rounding is permissible. The jaw is neutrally raised and may assist in effecting linguapalatal closure in the context of central vowels. There are two tongue targets, one for each phase of the sound. In the stop phase, the lateral margins of the tongue are placed firmly against the upper teeth and gums, and the tip and blade are placed equally firmly against the front of the palate at the edge of the alveolar ridge, further back than for the normal [t]. In the second phase, which begins after about 30 to 50 msec., the intraoral pressure is released by lowering the tongue tip so that an aperture somewhat similar to that required for the [ʃ] is created. Both tongue targets vary somewhat according to the demands of vowel context, much as they do for [t̄] and [ʃ]. The velum should be raised to produce complete or nearly complete velopharyngeal closure.

From the description of the [tʃ, dʒ] targets given above, it is clear that a similar, two-phase articulatory sequence occurs when [t] is followed by [j]. As mentioned earlier, many words in which this sequence originally occurred are currently produced with a [tʃ]. An example is the word *question*, which most people now pronounce as /kwɛstʃən/ rather than /kwɛstjən/. That such assimilation occurs in normal speech suggests that one way to evoke the sound is to have the child produce syllables that contain the [t̄-j] sequence. Subskills which ensure the generalization of [tʃ, dʒ] to various contexts are as follows:

Subskill 1: Production of [tʃ, dʒ] in initial position in single syllables constructed with all vowels, including [a], [u], and [i].

Subskill 2: Repetition of a series of syllables in which [tʃ, dʒ] releases one vowel or another (e.g., [tʃatʃatʃa], [dʒidʒidʒi]).

Subskill 3: Production of [tʃ, dʒ] in medial position in various vowel contexts (e.g., [atʃa], [udʒ u], [ædʒɚ]).

Subskill 4: Same procedure as for Subskill 3, except that one vowel or the other is stressed.

Subskill 5: Production of [ʃ, dʒ] in final position in single syllables constructed with one vowel or another (e.g., [ɛtʃ], [ɛdʒ], [utʃ], [ʌdʒ]).

Subskill 6: Alternation of syllables released with [tʃ, dʒ] and syllables arrested with other consonants (e.g., [tʃi ti tʃi ti], [tʃo ʃo tʃo ʃo], [dʒenedʒene]).

Subskill 7: Production of syllables released with [tʃ, dʒ] which vary in pitch over a range of at least eight semitones.

The rationale underlying the inclusion and ordering of the subskills proposed for the generalization of [tʃ, dʒ] is similar to that proposed for other consonants discussed in this chapter. In essence, the subskills involve production of the sound in all vowel contexts by the procedure illustrated in Figure 16.1; the repetition of the consonants in all vowel contexts; their production in initial, medial, and final position; their alternation with other consonants; and their coordination with suprasegmentals, particularly stress and pitch.

Teaching Strategies

All the prerequisite behaviors for the [tʃ, dʒ] have been mastered if the program advocated in this text has been followed. To coordinate them is to evoke the sound. This can best be achieved in four steps.

First, the fricative [ʃ] is used to release the whispered back vowel [u]. The result is [ʃu] as in the word *shoe*. Second, the stop [t̄] is used to arrest the vowel. The result is the whispered [ʃut̄] as in the word *shoot*. Third, a series of the syllables is whispered: i.e., [ʃut̄ʃut̄ʃut̄]. Fourth, the teacher indicates that this series is equivalent to [tʃutʃutʃu]. To do this, she has only to ask the child to whisper the syllable each time she moves her finger. Hesitation in the middle of a rhythmic series will yield the desired result. After it has been evoked, the syllable [tʃu] should be repeated until it can be elicited reliably.

A whisper is initially employed in the above strategy to emphasize oral breath flow. It may be repeated with voiced vowels once the [tʃ] has been evoked. Back vowels are used so that tongue placement is palato-alveolar rather than alveolar and so that low-frequency components of the [ʃ] are emphasized.

A second and similar strategy involves the alternation of two syllables, one arrested with the stop [t̄] and the other initiated with the fricative [ʃ]: e.g., [ot̄ʃuot̄ʃuot̄ʃu]. When the second of the two syllables in such a series is stressed, the sound usually emerges. The initial vowel can then be dropped and the syllable beginning with [tʃ] elicited reliably. If this strategy is initially attempted in the context of front vowels, the tongue contact for the stop [t̄] tends to be gingival rather than palatal—too far forward for the sounds to blend easily. Of course, the sound has to be made in the context of front vowels, but its generalization to such a context should not be attempted until the stop is habitually made with the tongue in a palato-alveolar position during production of syllables such as [tʃu], [tʃo], and [tʃa].

A third possible strategy—the use of a [t̄-j] sequence—has already been mentioned. As in the strategy described immediately above, the [t̄] is best used to arrest, and the [j] to release, a back vowel.

Great care must be taken when evoking [tʃ, d̠ʒ] to ensure that the child associates the first phase of these consonants with stop rather than plosive production. There is confusion on this point in many texts. It must be evident to the thoughtful reader that plosive release prior to initiation of the second phase of the consonant leads to (a) premature release of the intraoral pressure that is required for the sharp onset of the fricative component and (b) completely inappropriate motor patterns. Whereas stops and fricatives can be blended, plosives and fricatives cannot. *Auditory strategies* for evoking [tʃ, d̠ʒ] are feasible if the child has hearing up to and beyond 1,000 Hz since the rapid F_1 transitions which characterize stops are audible below this frequency, as are some of the components of the fricative noise.

Visual strategies may be of use (a) to prompt the component behaviors and (b) to provide speechreading cues. Since the jaw is raised so that the teeth contribute to the sibilant feature, the sound can be visually differentiated from other lingua-alveolar sounds.

Tactile strategies may be of some help (a) to indicate tongue placement for the stop phase of these consonants and (b) to demonstrate the sharp onset of the fricative breath stream. If the child advances his tongue too far in the first phase of production, placement of his finger on the alveolar ridge will help to evoke the desired palato-alveolar stop.

Summary

This chapter describes target behaviors and subskills relating to the production of consonants in Teaching Steps 2 and 3: namely, those principally involving the tongue. These consonants, differentiated by both manner and place of production, may not be easy to evoke by auditory or visual imitation since many of their acoustic features lie mainly in the frequency range above 2,000 Hz, and the critical articulatory gestures of the tongue may not be readily visualized. We describe a range of strategies by means of which each consonant can be evoked and elicited reliably from children with different degrees of hearing impairment. A program to facilitate generalization of each sound to a variety of phonetic contexts is also proposed.

REFERENCES

Brown, W. S. Jr., McGlone, R. E., & Profitt, W. R.   Relationship of lingual and intraoral air pressures during syllable production. *J. Speech Hear. Res.*, 16, 141–151, 1973.

Elbert, M., & McReynolds, L. V.   Transfer of /r/ across contexts. *J. Speech Hear. Disord.*, 40, 380–387, 1975.

Houde, R. A.   A study of tongue body motion during selected speech sounds. *Santa Barbara—SCRL Monogr.* #2, 1967.

Leeper, H. A. Jr., & Noll, J. D.   Pressure measurements of articulatory behavior during alterations of vocal effort. *J. Acoust. Soc. Am.*, 51, 1291–1295, 1972.

Locke, J. L., & Kutz, K. J.   Memory for speech and speech for memory. *J. Speech Hear. Res.*, 18, 176–191, 1975.

Shriberg, L. D.   A response evocation program for /ɜ˞/. *J. Speech Hear. Disord.*, 40, 92–105, 1975.

Slipakoff, E. L.   An approach to the correction of the defective /r/. *J. Speech Hear. Disord.*, 32, 71–75, 1967.

=/17/=

Voiced-Voiceless Distinctions and the Treatment of Deviant Consonant Patterns

In Chapters 15 and 16 we were concerned with the differentiation of consonants first according to manner and, second, according to manner and place. We indicated whether the sounds we discussed were usually voiced or unvoiced but proposed no strategies by means of which individual members of the voiced-voiceless pairs such as [b, p] or [s, z] could be differentiated. We were, nevertheless, concerned with laying the foundations for acquisition of the voiced-voiceless distinction. We suggested that, from the earliest stages of consonant development, the child should be able to whisper vowels as well as to voice them; that voiced plosives should be evoked and generalized before their unvoiced counterparts; and that unvoiced stops and unvoiced fricatives should be taught before their voiced cognates. The contrasts afforded and the voice control developed by teaching sounds in the order proposed usually lead to the child's learning to distinguish and to produce voiced and unvoiced members of a cognate pair without specific training if he has substantial residual hearing. They also provide a frame of reference for teaching the voiced-voiceless distinction to children with little or no residual hearing.

In this chapter we shall discuss voiced-voiceless distinctions between consonant pairs and suggest ways in which they may be developed. Teachers who feel strongly that it is important for the child to make manner and voicing distinctions in parallel may use the proposed strategies in teaching plosives from the earliest stage (Consonant Teaching, Step 1). However, the introduction of the additional dimension would increase the time required to complete Teaching Step 1 and thus delay

354

the introduction of Teaching Steps 2 and 3. Further, early concern with teaching the child to produce the voiced-voiceless distinction, especially between stops and fricatives, may serve no practical purpose (see Chapter 8) and may actually impede progress (see below).

TEACHING STEP 4:
Target Behaviors, Subskills, and Teaching Strategies
Relating to Voiced-Voiceless Distinctions

The Plosives [b, d, g] versus [p, t, k]

Targets and Subskills

The voiced-voiceless distinction between the plosives [b, p], [d, t], and [k, g] is more complex than that between consonants having other manners of production. The nature of the distinction depends, in part, on the position of the plosive in a word. In word-initial position, the closure phase of these consonants is normally unvoiced. Thus, whether one says *bat* or *pat*, *down* or *town*, or *goat* or *coat*, the interval before the release of the initial constriction is usually silent. It is possible to produce voice during the initial closure phase, but the practice is somewhat irregular. In intervocalic position voicing continues through the closure phase for [b, d, g] but not for [p, t, k], except in substandard speech in which words such as *butter* may be pronounced /bʌdɚ/ instead of /bʌtɚ/. Additionally, the intervocalic voiced-voiceless distinction may be signaled by rate of closure and by shortening of the preceding vowel (see the section on stops, below). The voiced and unvoiced plosives are differentiated more strongly by their release characteristics than by differences in the closure phase. In [b] the voice onset time (VOT) is about 0 msec., which means that the release of the articulatory constriction and the onset of vocal cord vibration are more or less synchronous. In [d], VOT may be delayed by a few milliseconds, and in [g] a delay of 20 to 30 msec. is not uncommon. In [p, t, k], VOT is usually some 20 to 40 msec. later than in the voiced cognate. If an abnormally early VOT develops in a hearing-impaired child's production of [b] (a fault that is likely to occur if one attempts to teach the voiced-voiceless distinction between [b] and [p] at the outset), then rehearsal of short syllables initiated with [g, k] often remedies the problem by helping to establish coordination of articulators and larynx. Since there is less space between the larynx and the [g, k] occlusion than between the larynx and the [b, p] occlusion, there is less possibility for the prevoicing of the plosive to occur.

Whereas the burst characteristics of the voiced plosives are weak, brief (10-30 msec.), and usually unaspirated, the burst characteristics of the unvoiced plosives are strong, long (30-50 msec.), and usually aspirated. The relative strength of the burst is determined by the vocal cords. If they are brought together for voicing, they interrupt the breath flow and hence reduce the intraoral pressure and weaken the burst. If they remain parted, then intraoral pressure is increased and the burst on its release is strengthened. During the burst portion of the unvoiced plosives the vocal cords are not fully abducted. They are brought sufficiently close together to produce aspiration, a turbulent breath flow at the glottis, which augments the burst and increases its duration. Aspiration-assisted bursts are almost always present in word-initial and intervocalic plosives but not in blends releasing words like *spot*, *stop*, or *skip*. In such blends, the unvoiced plosives [p, t, k] have short VOTs, weak bursts of brief duration, and no aspiration. If the initial consonants of these blends are removed—erased from a tape recording, for example—these plosives are heard as being voiced.

Articulatory mechanisms throughout the vocal tract differ according to whether a plosive is voiced or unvoiced. The distinction is not simply one of vocal cord vibration. In voiced plosives the whole larynx is lowered, whereas in unvoiced plosives it is held fairly rigidly in place. In voiced plosives the pharynx is relaxed, whereas in unvoiced plosives it is tense. The tongue contact in the voiced plosives [d, g] and the lip contact in [b] are less forceful during the closure phase than with [t, k] and [p]. Such differences extend to most voiced and unvoiced sounds. Linguists have therefore come to term English voiced sounds "lax" or "lenis" and unvoiced sounds "tense" or "fortis."

We shall assume that the voiced plosives [b, d, g] have been taught through the use of strategies described in Chapters 15 and 16. To produce their unvoiced counterparts, the child must learn four new target behaviors: namely, non-voicing during the closure phase of these plosives in intervocalic position, VOT delay in word-initial position, aspiration-aided burst release, and greater force of articulation. All four behaviors are closely correlated with the production of one feature: namely, aspiration immediately following release of constriction. Aspiration poses no problem for the child who has rehearsed the subskills for [h] (see Chapter 15). The child who has followed the sequence suggested in this text can also produce the stops [p̄, t̄, k̄]. He has, therefore, only to coordinate behaviors over which he has acquired considerable control. Such coordination can be fostered through sequential development of subskills as follows:

Subskill 1: Production of [ʌp̄] and [ha].
Subskill 2: Alternation of [ʌp̄] and [ha] (i.e., [ʌp̄haʌp̄ha].
Subskill 3: Production of [pʰa] (i.e., bilabial release of [ha]).
Subskill 4: Repetition of [pʰa] (i.e., [papapa]).
Subskill 5: Production of [p] with all vowels.
Subskill 6: Alternation of syllables released with [p] and syllables released with other consonants including [b] (e.g., [pumupumu], [pɔbɔpɔbɔ].
Subskills 7–12: Production of [t] in six steps as above, beginning with [ʌt̄] and [ha].
Subskills 13–18: Production of [k] in six steps as above, beginning with [ʌk̄] and [ha].
Subskill 19: Repetition of sequences including [p, t, k] and [b, d, g] (e.g., [pʌtʌkʌpʌtʌkʌ], [budugubudugu]).
Subskill 20: Comparison of intervocalic [b, d, g] and intervocalic [p, t, k] (e.g., [ipi-ibi], [itu-idu]).

The plosives [p, t, k] may, of course, be written [pʰ, tʰ, kʰ], but duration of the aspiration following plosive release is not so great as that associated with the consonant [h]. Subskills 1 to 3 establish aspirated release of the plosive. The durational characteristics of the plosive burst can be established through rehearsal of Subskill 4: namely, repetition of a series of syllables released with the unvoiced plosive. If a series of syllables released with [p, t, k] is practiced at an optimal rate, the orosensory-motor patterns associated with the sounds' correct production rapidly become familiar to the child. Non-voicing of these consonants in intervocalic position is taught through Subskills 2, 4, 6, 19, and 20. Delay in VOT relative to the VOT of the voiced cognates is developed in Subskills 3, 4, 5, 6, and 19. Aspiration-aided burst release is called for in every subskill. The greater force of articulation associated with unvoiced plosives is encouraged from Subskill 3 onward. The tense-lax contrast is called for in Subskills 6, 12, 18, 19, and 20.

Teaching Strategies

Auditory strategies should be successful with most hearing-impaired children since some acoustic cues on the voiced-voiceless distinction are present below 500 Hz. These signal the presence or absence of voice during the closure phase, relative VOT, aspiration, and plosive burst associated with [b, p] and [g, k] in the context of back vowels. The child should, if possible, be trained to discriminate between [po-bo], [to-do], and [ko-go] before, during, and after his being taught to produce the distinction.

Visual strategies for teaching the voiced-voiceless distinction are limited to prompting activities or the use of electronic devices that provide a visual display. The presence or absence of voice cannot be seen through speechreading.

Tactile strategies include feeling the vibrations produced by voice by touching the chest, neck, or face. They are a useful adjunct to vision, as place cues can be seen, and manner and voicing features can be felt.

The Stops [p̄, t̄, k̄] versus [b̄, d̄, ḡ]

Targets and Subskills

The distinction between voiced and voiceless stops is signaled by three types of cues. First, there is usually vocal cord vibration during closure in the voiced but not in the unvoiced stops. Second, vowels tend to be longer when they precede the voiced sounds. Third, closure is usually effected less rapidly for voiced stops than for their unvoiced counterparts. The three types of cues tend to be correlated. Thus, as a rule, long-duration vowels are associated with stops having slower closure and more extensive vocal cord vibration.

There are, then, three targets in making the voiced-voiceless distinction. These are:

1. Shorter vowels preceding [p̄, t̄, k̄] than preceding [b̄, d̄, ḡ].
2. Faster closure for [p̄, t̄, k̄] than for [b̄, d̄, ḡ].
3. Vocal cord vibration during [b̄, d̄, ḡ] but not during [p̄, t̄, k̄]

If the program suggested in this text has been followed, then the prerequisite behaviors for this distinction will have been developed during rehearsal of various subskills. For example, short vowels and rapid closure will have been developed in teaching the unvoiced stops. Longer vowels and less rapid closure will have been developed in teaching the voiced plosives in an intervocalic position. Continuity of voicing during closure will have been developed by production of the voiced plosives in an intervocalic position and in a series of repeated syllables such as [bababa], [dididi], and [gogogo]; and discontinuity of voicing will have been developed by repetition of syllables containing unvoiced fricatives such as [sesese], [ʃuʃuʃu], and [θaθaθa]. It remains, then, to coordinate and contrast these behaviors in order to achieve the targets.

The development of the voiced-voiceless distinction in stops at a relatively earlier stage in consonant development appears to be unacceptable. In Teaching Step 1 the child has not acquired the laryngeal control that he will develop through training in the various subskills in later teaching steps. As closure for [b̄]—the first stop to be taught—is effected at the lips, vocal cord vibration can continue for much longer than is required to signal voicing. Indeed, vocal cord vibration can continue as long as subglottal pressure is greater than intraoral pressure. Thus, long-duration transglottal breath flow can occur because the intraoral space for [b̄] is relatively large. The risk, then, in attempting to evoke and develop [b̄] in the first teaching step is in having the child produce too much voice during stop closure and build up too much intraoral pressure in doing so. There is a further risk: namely, that the child will come to associate all vocal tract closure with voicing. If such an association is made, then all plosives and stops will be adversely affected: initial plosives will tend to be prevoiced, all medial plosives and stops will tend to be voiced, and [p̄, t̄, k̄] will not be differentiated from [b̄, d̄, ḡ] in word-final position. If, on the other hand, only the unvoiced stops are taught in Teaching Steps 1, 2, and 3, then at this stage (Teaching Step 4) one has simply to contrast the differential duration of vowels, the relative rates of vocal tract closure, and continuity versus discontinuity of voicing.

Teaching Strategies

The voiced-voiceless distinction in stops may be evoked only within the context of previously acquired speech behaviors. If speech has been systematically developed and abundant vocal play encouraged, the child with substantial residual hearing will probably develop the distinction without specific training. The child with little or no hearing, however, may need prompting before the voiced stops can be evoked and contrasted with their previously developed unvoiced counterparts.

The obvious starting point in teaching voiced stops is the closure phase of the plosives [b, d, g]; to prevent habitually excessive duration of voicing, the [g] is preferred. The teacher should have the child repeat a string of syllables containing [g] (e.g., [gogogo]) with each syllable being released as she lowers her finger. Once a rate of two or three syllables per second has been established and voicing is continuous throughout the series, she has simply to hesitate before lowering her finger and the voiced stop will be evoked. It should then be contrasted with the previously acquired unvoiced [k̄] through comparison of syllables such as [ʌk̄-ʌḡ], [ɛk̄-ɛḡ]. The vowel durations should differ substantially so that the [ḡ] is habitually produced in the context of lengthened vowels and the [k̄] in the context of shortened vowels. The lengthening or shortening of the vowel—indeed, of the whole syllable— should lead to desired differences in the relative rates of closure. Previous training on the unvoiced stops should ensure that voicing is not generalized to closure for [k̄]. The subskills listed for the development of stops in Teaching Steps 1, 2, and 3 should then be repeated to ensure that production of the [p̄, t̄, k̄] and [b̄, d̄, ḡ] is stabilized and that these sounds can be used in all phonetic contexts.

The unvoiced stop may, of course, also be developed from the unvoiced plosive. The closure phase of unvoiced plosives and the production of unvoiced stops share forceful, rapid articulatory gestures and shorter durations of the preceding vowel, probably because the breath flow is unimpeded by laryngeal valving. If the teacher prefers to teach both the voiced and unvoiced plosives from the first stage of consonant development, she may, therefore, employ a strategy similar to that described above in evoking the [p̄, t̄, k̄]. In this case she should first ensure the habitually correct production of the unvoiced plosives through rehearsal of the subskills described in previous chapters.

Auditory and tactile strategies are superior to visual strategies since the voiced-voiceless dimension cannot be seen in speechreading. The acoustic cues associated with voicing are mainly durational and can be made available either through audition (if hearing is present beyond 500 Hz) or through tactile reception of vibratory patterns.

The Semivowels and Liquids [w, j, l, r]

Targets, Subskills, and Teaching Strategies

As mentioned in previous chapters, the semivowels and liquids may occur in both voiced and unvoiced form. Before, between, or following voiced vowels and voiced consonants they are invariably voiced. Following unvoiced plosives and fricatives they are frequently unvoiced, as in the word-initial blends [tw], [sw], [hj], [fl], [fr], [sl], etc. It is suggested that these blends should be practiced in whispered syllables much as rehearsal of the component sounds has been advocated in the subskills described in previous chapters. However, their appropriate voicelessness in blends will be assured without specific training providing that the blend is articulated at a normal rate and that the unvoiced plosives and fricatives which precede them are correctly produced. This is because the mechanical forces involved oppose rapid onset of vocal cord vibration in such blends. Such delay in voicing following unvoiced plosives and fricatives is occasioned by the relatively sluggish action of the larynx. Voicing cannot be initiated immediately when the vocal cords are appropriately adjusted to produce aspiration for the plosive or to permit sufficient transglottal flow for fricative turbulence.

The Fricatives [f, θ , ʃ, s] versus [v, ð, ʒ, z]

Targets and Subskills

Turbulent breath flow is a critical dimension in the production of fricatives. It must be present whether they are voiced or unvoiced. The turbulence normally present in unvoiced fricatives may disappear when the hearing-impaired child attempts to produce their voiced cognates. This is because turbulence is created only when the breath stream passing through a small aperture is sufficiently strong to induce it. When a sound is voiced, the intraoral pressure—and hence the airflow through the vocal tract constriction—is reduced because the vocal cords, adducted for voicing, interrupt it. If manner and place of production and the degree of constriction have been established, and the voiceless fricatives can be produced automatically, then the production of their voiced cognates calls for two additional behaviors. These are (1) vocal cord vibration and (2) increase in subglottal pressure to sustain sufficient breath flow to support turbulence during voicing.

Teaching Strategies

To evoke the voiced fricatives one does not have to teach new behaviors. Rather, one's task is to coordinate behaviors that are already within the child's repertoire. The easiest way to evoke the voiced fricative is to have the child produce a series of repeated syllables in which the [f, θ, ʃ, s] occur (e.g., [ɪʃɪʃɪʃ], [ʌsʌsʌs] and then have him repeat the series with continuous voicing (e.g., [ɪvɪvɪv] and [ʌzʌzʌz]). To isolate the voiced fricative, one may then ask the child to repeat and contrast, first, syllables such as [ʌfʌ] and [ʌvʌ] in which the fricatives are in an intervocalic position; next, syllables in which the fricatives are in word-final position (e.g., [ʌs] and [ʌz]); and finally, the fricatives on their own.

Practice in sustaining the fricative in syllables such as [ʌf, ʌv], [ɪθ, ɪð], [æʃ, æʒ], and [us, uz] provides the child with the orosensory-motor patterns by means of which he must learn to differentiate the voiced and voiceless counterparts. Games are useful in this regard. For example, an object may be moved one step further toward a goal for every second the desired sound is sustained accurately. Once the voiced and voiceless fricatives have been evoked and contrasted and can be elicited reliably, they should be rehearsed within a program of subskills that ensure their automaticity and their generalization to all phonetic contexts. The subskills suggested in Teaching Steps 1 and 2 are adequate for this purpose.

Auditory strategies are useful to indicate the presence of voicing if hearing extends beyond 500 Hz. However, presence of turbulent breath flow can be detected through conventionally aided audition only if hearing extends over 1,000 Hz (for mid-frequency fricatives in the context of back vowels) or to over 3,000 Hz (for the [s, z]). The turbulence of [s, z] can, of course, be heard by children with less residual hearing if frequency transposing hearing aids are used. It is in the teaching of the fricatives that frequency transposition has its greatest advantage. It does not follow that once these sounds have been developed by means of frequency transposing aids the child should continue to use the aids. They may be disadvantageous in other contexts.

Visual strategies that may be helpful in evoking, contrasting, and developing the voiced-voiceless distinction in fricatives are best limited to those involving prompting activities and visual aids. All fricatives have turbulent energy at about 4,500 to 5,500 Hz. An instrument containing a filter which passes energy only in this frequency band can therefore be used to detect and display the presence of such turbulence. The output of the instrument may be via a light meter or (if tactile cues are preferred) a vibrator. Similar instruments may be used to detect and display the low-frequency energy associated with voicing.

Tactile strategies include the child's use of direct touch to detect the presence of voicing and the strength of breath flow required to produce turbulence. The use of an instrument which provides a tactile cue (vibration or electrical stimulation) indicating voicing and high-frequency turbulence may be helpful for children with little or no hearing. Aids providing cues on high-frequency turbulence may be a useful adjunct for those who can detect only the voicing feature through low-frequency residual audition.

The Affricates [tʃ] versus [dʒ]

Since these sounds are blends consisting of stop and fricative components, the targets, subskills, and teaching strategies associated with evoking, contrasting, and developing them are implicit in the text above. They will not be treated separately since the thoughtful reader should have no problem in generalizing from notions already presented.

The Treatment of Deviant Consonant Patterns

It is, without doubt, better to prevent the development of deviant consonant patterns than to allow them to occur. In this text, we have suggested various ways in which deviant patterns may be prevented. Foremost among these is the orderly teaching of the various aspects of speech. We also stress rehearsal of consonant patterns first at the phonetic level to lay adequate foundations for automaticity, for the development of feedforward capability, and for the deliberate generalization of consonants to a variety of phonetic contexts. It is made clear in previous chapters that to evoke the sound and then seek its immediate transfer to the child's phonology is unrealistic. We emphasize the need for the repetition of sounds in syllables and the alternation of sound patterns with others so that they become clearly differentiated within the child's phonetic repertoire. Additionally, we call for consonants to be rehearsed in syllables within the framework of suprasegmental patterns to ensure that they can be produced with appropriate rhythm, stress, and intonation in phonologic speech.

Adherence to the program advocated in this text generally results in patterns that are accurate and adequate. Accordingly, treatment of deviant patterns that are present in the speech of children who have followed less effective programs is best carried out through redevelopment along the lines suggested in this text rather than through correction by means of isolated remedial techniques. Correction may enable one to obtain a particular pronunciation on a given occasion; but it is virtually useless as a means of ensuring habitually correct usage of sound patterns—usage that will endure beyond the moment. Consideration of the various faults that frequently occur in the production of consonants by hearing-impaired children gives strong support to this view.

Faults Due to Inadequate Breath Control

Faults in the production of consonants that may be caused by inadequate breath control include those that affect voicing, aspiration, manner distinction, and the interaction of these qualities with the suprasegmental structure of phonologic speech. The general nature of speech breathing and voicing was considered in Chapter 11. We shall therefore discuss only specific problems in this section.

Adequate breath control for appropriate voicing can only be achieved through the use of speech. Thus, if consonants are weakly voiced, the first step is to question whether the child uses speech sufficiently often. Inadequate breath control usually affects consonants and vowels equally, for it is difficult for the child to use different adjustments in breath control to produce voice for the two types of sounds. Remediation should therefore begin with training in the production of intensity differences in vowels and diphthongs and proceed through the repetition of strings of syllables constructed with voiced consonants. Particular care should be taken to ensure that voicing in series of syllables such as [bibibi] and [nonono] is continuous and sustained for at least five seconds. Many faults in speech breathing are due to teaching consonants mainly or only in isolation or in single syllables. Of course, the limited use of specific consonants in isolation or in single syllables may be justified or, for certain continuants, even recommended. Requisite breath control can only be developed, however, if consonants are primarily viewed as elements superimposed on the flow of breath and voice. A duration of five seconds is a relatively light requirement in the production of a series of syllables and represents the minimum requirement if sentences are to be adequately phrased in communicative speech.

Breath faults affecting aspiration are singled out because aspirated sounds such as [h] and the burst release of unvoiced plosives are usually pulsed through momentarily increasing subglottal pressure during their production. The mechanism by which this is achieved differs from that involved in the production of most other sounds for which relatively constant subglottal pressure is exerted. Faults affecting aspiration are best dealt with by repetition of the subskills described for [h] in Chapter 15 and by rehearsal of unvoiced plosives to the point of automaticity. Faults in aspiration may, of course, be due to inadequate adjustment of the vocal cords, which should impede—but not interrupt—the flow of breath. Work with [h] must yield sufficient turbulence generated at the larynx, not simply in the oral tract.

Without a sufficient and continuous breath stream, manner distinctions can be wrongly learned or can become less salient than they should be. Thus, the [b], instead of being a voiced plosive, can in conditions of extremely limited breath flow become a suction stop ['b]. The sound, like lip-smacking during bilabial closure, indicates that [b] has been evoked and rehearsed in isolation. It does not appear when one teaches bilabial closure as a way to interrupt a continuous stream of breath and voice. The only sure path for remediation of such a fault is development of the sound as suggested in Teaching Step 1. Of the manner distinctions that become less salient as a result of inadequate breath flow, that of fricative turbulence is the most notable. The liquids [l] and [r] may also be seriously affected. We know of no strategies for the development of these sounds, other than those described in previous chapters, that can lead to habitually adequate breath supply for the production of manner distinctions.

Some hearing-impaired children may make certain sounds with an excess of breath, but this is not to say that their breath supply is too great. Rather, what breath they use is expended inappropriately. If speech is breathy, then it is usually because there is poor control of the larynx, poor adjustment of the articulators, or both. The fault is usually best treated by strengthening the voice (see Chapter 11) and by ensuring appropriate constriction of the vocal tract by the articulators. If articulation is too slow, then too great an intraoral pressure tends to be built up during closure so that, on release, the burst energy is too strong. The fault here stems from the duration of closure, not from the breath stream. Similarly, fricatives can sound breathy simply because the constriction formed is so large that more than the usual amount of breath is required to induce turbulence. Teaching the child to form a smaller aperture for the fricatives may be sufficient to cure the problem. If such measures are not successful, then the best strategy is not to demand less breath but to require that the breath is expended over a longer period of time—for example, in saying syllables, repeating words, or producing sentences that call for breath release over several seconds. This strategy demands development of negative (restraining) muscle activity that will prevent the lungs-thorax system from returning too quickly to its resting level (see Chapter 11).

Nasalization and Denasalization

The faults that arise in consonant production through nasalization and denasalization are, at root, caused through inadequate development of velar target behaviors. They may therefore be treated as a single problem. The problem may be organic or functional in origin. Organic problems such as cleft palate may have been diagnosed in the course of the oral-peripheral examination (see Chapter 9). If so, they should have been treated, and the teacher should know (or learn) through consultation with the surgeon concerned how far velopharyngeal function has been or is expected to be restored. Removal of adenoids may adversely, but rarely permanently, affect velopharyngeal closure. Specific training or retraining strategies may be required to restore effective velopharyngeal function following adenoidectomy. These involve the types of exercises that have been described toward the end of Chapter 13.

The most common reason for nasalization's affecting non-nasal consonants is that the nasal/non-nasal distinction has not been adequately taught. The solution is to develop or redevelop the consonants by means of the strategies described in Chapters 15 and 16.

Tension

Problems in consonant production may arise because the articulators are too tense or too lax. Tension, which may be generalized throughout the body or focused in the head and neck region, is usually associated with apprehension, insecurity, or inexperience in speech production. Problems caused by overall flaccidity are usually due to low drive to achieve and too little use of speech. Problems of either type may stem from a physical condition which requires medical attention or from psychological conditions which call for counseling for the child and his parents. Frequently such problems can be overcome simply by making speech training in class and speech experience out of school interesting. If tension or flaccidity is specifically related to the production of a particular consonant or group of consonants (for example, only with the [l] or with all lingua-alveolar consonants), then the problem calls for systematic speech training procedures rather than medical or psychological assistance. Those described in previous chapters are sufficient. Nonspeech exercises for the remediation of specific speech problems are to be avoided.

Exaggeration and Prolongation

Exaggerated lip, jaw, or tongue movements are behaviors that have been taught and reinforced. The hallmark of poor teaching, they result from the use of inappropriate strategies to evoke and elicit the desired consonant patterns (strategies often applied before the child has acquired the prerequisite behaviors for the sound's production) and from failure to carry out a systematic program to refine and generalize the use of the sound in a variety of phonetic and phonologic contexts. Above all, habitual exaggeration indicates that insufficient attention has been given to rehearsal of the sound in sequences which require rapid rates of production. Rapid rates of production demand and hence lead to the economy of movement that typifies normal speech. Exaggeration and prolongation can thus be seen as twin deficiencies, each feeding the other at the expense of precision and intelligibility.

To prevent exaggeration and prolongation the teacher should speak to the child normally during conversations and lessons, avoid the presentation of exaggerated models in the speech teaching process, accept and reinforce only those patterns produced by the child that conform closely with the desired target behaviors, and provide specific training to develop adequate rates of production.

The remediation of habitual exaggeration and prolongation requires the redevelopment of the sounds along the lines specified in Chapters 15 and 16. Exaggerated lip patterns are often used by the child as a substitute for appropriate tongue gestures. For example, in the production of [r], lip-rounding rather than tongue adjustment may be used to lower

F_3. In this case, one may have the child place his finger on the lower lip to prevent movement until the appropriate tongue movement is established in the rehearsal of the sound. Similarly, lip-rounding rather than tongue velarization may be used to produce the low formant values for [w]. Having the child place a finger at each side of the mouth to prevent lip-rounding during production of syllables such as [we], [wi], and [wo] will focus attention on and develop appropriate tongue motion.

Exaggerated jaw movement is often encouraged in teaching the lingua-alveolar sounds such as [d], [t], and [l] through allowing the child to use the jaw to assist in closure. This leads to weakening of all consonants in this group because the more the jaw does, the less the tongue needs to do. It also leads to prolongation because the jaw cannot be moved as rapidly as the tongue. The best remedial strategy to adopt is rehearsal of the subskills underlying these consonants (see Chapter 16) while a pencil is held firmly, but gently, between the teeth. This provides the child with orosensory-motor patterns associated with the tongue movement that are congruent with the rapid, unexaggerated production of these sounds.

Exaggerated tongue movement—if present—is usually limited to the extrusion of the tongue, in imitation of the teacher's model, during production of sounds such as [l] and [θ , δ]. Use of such an exaggerated model is usually based on the teacher's false assumption that it aids speechreading. It demonstrates a lack of concern for the possible unintelligibility of the child's speech to those unfamiliar with hearing-impaired children taught in this way. The remedy is for the teacher to reorient her own and the child's attention to the acoustic patterns of spoken language. Tongue movements made by the child may frequently be inexact, but they are rarely exaggerated. The way to correct inexact tongue placement is to develop the consonants in the variety of phonetic contexts specified in Chapter 16 while paying particular attention to the transitional features produced by effective coarticulation.

Intrusive Consonants and Voicing Errors

Most intrusive voicing occurs because the child substitutes plosives for stops in medial and word-final positions. It may also occur if the child has not learned to make voiced-voiceless distinctions or if he is unaware of a word's correct pronunciation. The most common reason for substitution of plosives for stops is that the child has not been taught to produce stops or that he can produce them but has been led to confuse them through the practice of teaching plosives and stops in association with their common orthographic symbols, ''b,'' ''d,'' and ''g.''

The prevention of such faults has been discussed in previous chapters. Their remediation calls for diagnosis of their cause and subsequent training at both the phonetic and phonologic levels to familiarize the child with correct models of production. The type of training advocated in Chapters 15 and 16 is applicable.

Substitution, Omission, and Distortion

Faults of substitution, omission, and distortion are of concern only if they occur in phonologic speech—speech that is used meaningfully for communication. There are numerous reasons why such faults may occur; hence, it is important to diagnose the cause before attempting to initiate treatment. Substitution errors, for example, may occur because the child (1) does not know the word's correct pronunciation, (2) has learned and habitually come to use an approximation to the word before he has mastered production of the sound for which another has been substituted, (3) cannot produce this sound in the context afforded by adjacent sounds in the word, (4) can produce the sound only in single syllables and not with all vowels, (5) has not learned to differentiate the sound from the one substituted, or (6) has never produced the sound in the first place. A similar range of possible reasons may be invoked to explain why sounds may be omitted or distorted in running speech.

If the reason for the child's error (substitution, omission, or distortion) is that he does not know the correct pronunciation although he is capable of producing the word correctly when told how to do so, the problem can be solved simply by providing him with the correct pattern. On the other hand, if the child has acquired an approximation to a word and has come to use this approximation habitually because he could not produce all the component sounds when the word was first acquired, the problem is more complex. The old, inadequate pattern must be replaced with the new, correct form. This will require considerable rehearsal of the appropriate pattern in sentence structures that relate to meaningful activity and thus provide strong syntactic and semantic associations with the correct form. If the problem is due to the other possible causes listed above, then remedial treatment should feature the development of the sound at a phonetic level as described in this and previous chapters. There is a constant danger that the child will not readily use sounds phonologically even when they lie within his phonetic repertoire. For this reason, regular evaluation to identify discrepancies between phonologic and phonetic level skills is essential. One factor that frequently contributes to a child's failure to use the full range of speech patterns at his disposal is the readiness of adults (particularly parents) to accept approximations beyond the stage when such acceptance is helpful. Initially they must try hard to understand the child's every effort at speech in order to encourage the habitual use of speech in communication. In doing this they often learn to "tune in" to the child's intended meaning but, at the same time, "tune out" awareness of abnormality. Parents should be encouraged to observe phonetic and phonologic evaluation (see Chapter 9) to help with the rehearsal of subskills and to assist in teaching the child to use sounds thus developed in his everyday speech. Such concern with the child's progress helps them to develop a keen ear for substitutions, omissions, and distortions. This is essential if they are to foster the type of speech in their child that can be understood without placing an undue burden on the outside listener.

Summary

In this chapter we discuss both the differentiation of consonants through the development of the voiced-voiceless distinction and the prevention and treatment of deviant consonant patterns.

We indicate that the voiced-voiceless distinction is produced in a variety of ways—not solely by the presence or absence of vocal cord vibration—and that the form of the distinction varies somewhat in relation to manner and place of production as well as to position of the consonant in the word. We relate the distinction to its acoustic correlates, treated in Chapter 14.

In our examination of deviant patterns of consonant production we emphasize that there are no shortcuts to remediation. Indeed, in our discussion we support the view that effective remediation is synonymous with development or redevelopment of sounds through a systematic program involving a variety of phonetic and phonologic contexts.

/18/

Consonant
Blends

Consonants often occur in clusters in initial, medial, and final position within words and in abutting position between words. When they do so, the characteristics of one, both, or all of the clustered sounds are usually modified. Consonant clusters are frequently blended to the extent that they are produced and perceived by normally hearing speakers as quite distinct units (Pickett, 1958; Claxton, 1974). Indeed, the patterns resulting from the blending process may bear little resemblance to their original elements. The [tr] blend is a good example. In the normally rapid pronunciation of the words *rat race* the abutting [t] and [r] yield a single sound rather like the affricate [tʃ]. About two-thirds of consonant blends involve a change in manner of production (e.g., [st], [nz]) and about one-third demand a change in manner and place of production (e.g., [sm], [ps]) (Denes, 1963). The voicing feature tends to be modified considerably in the blending process. Thus, if the first element is unvoiced the second element will also tend to be so, even if the second element is normally voiced in a vowel context.

Articulatory constraints in the production of consonants in blends clearly differ from those in the production of single consonants in vowel contexts. While the articulatory targets for the various consonant sounds in blends may be the same regardless of context, the trajectory of the tongue to and from these targets will differ vastly according to whether the adjacent sound is another consonant or a vowel (Saporta, 1955; Koutstaal and Smith, 1972; Gallagher and Shriner, 1975). It therefore seems logical that specific training in blend production should be provided if the consonant elements themselves have had to be taught. It also seems logical to attempt to arrange such training so that ability to blend consonants is systematically developed through a series of steps,

370

each of which provides a foundation for acquisition of the next. Such an attempt has been made in this chapter. The need for such structured training is indicated by Nober's (1967) findings that few of the older, and none of the younger, of his 46 hearing-impaired subjects could produce consonant blends (see Chapter 2).

Blends pose many problems for hearing-impaired children. Not only do they call for the development of new forms of articulatory behavior, but they also are difficult for hearing-impaired children to hear, see, and feel. The articulatory duration of the elements is not the same in consonant clusters as in vowel contexts (MacNeilage, 1963; Hawkins, 1973; O'Shaughnessy, 1974). Indeed, duration of elements tends to vary from one consonant cluster to another. Thus, the [s] before [p] in [sp] is usually shorter than the [s] before [t] or [k] (Schwartz, 1970), probably because the [sp] involves sequential tongue and lip targets and is hence easier to produce than either the [st] or [sk], which involves sequential tongue targets. Since the blending of consonants may produce a distinctly different sound pattern from that associated with each of the two or more elements of which the blend is comprised, the child must—if his hearing is sufficient for the task—learn a further range of auditory discriminations. Invariant acoustic cues previously associated with the elements may be changed and variant acoustic cues either changed or eliminated (see Malécot, 1960). Clusters are also extremely difficult to speechread. If presented in nonsense syllables, they tend to be seen as single elements or confused with other clusters about 90% of the time (Franks and Kimble, 1972). They are also more complex and hence more difficult to identify through touch than are simple elements. Vision and touch together can, however, lead to the unambiguous identification of elements in a cluster for purposes of teaching speech to children who cannot discriminate between them through audition.

As in previous chapters on teaching consonants (Chapters 15, 16, and 17), our first concern will be with evoking the required sound patterns. Since the elements which form each blend are in the child's repertoire, the prerequisite behaviors for blend production are already available to us. They remain to be coordinated. Beyond evoking the sound patterns, one's task is to work systematically toward the child's production of blends in the variety of phonetic and phonologic contexts in which they occur. We do not propose to list the essential subskills as in previous chapters, but advise the reader to develop the blends discussed below as systematically and with as much care as that called for in the production of simple consonants. In short, the teacher should set out to:

1. Evoke each blend through reference to its elements.

2. Elicit it reliably in a given context, using prompting strategies if they are required.
3. Generalize the child's production of each blend to all vowel contexts.
4. Repeat the blend in a wide variety of phonetic level contexts at reasonably rapid rates.
5. Alternate syllables containing the blend with syllables containing other blends or single consonants at reasonably rapid rates.
6. Rehearse syllables containing the blend in conjunction with suprasegmental features by varying stress and voice pitch.
7. Use each blend in various phonologic contexts as soon as it can be produced in similar contexts at the phonetic level.

In this chapter we shall examine three types of consonant blends: word-initial blends, word-final blends, and medial-lexical blends. Our classification of these blends and our ordering of their teaching are both theoretical and pragmatic. They have been supported by experimental work that we have carried out over the past 15 years but have not previously reported and by a factor-analytic study (Edwards and Anderson, 1972) which indicates that blends can, indeed, be grouped much as we have proposed they should be.

Word-Initial Blends

We specify five types of word-initial blends. Our specifications are based on whether the blend calls for mainly successive (sequential) or simultaneous (coformulated) adjustments and whether one or two organs—the tongue, or the tongue and the lips—are principally involved. The various types of blends are discussed in the order in which we have found them to be most readily acquired by hearing-impaired children.

The Two-Organ Sequential Blends
[sm], [sp], [sw]

These are the simplest of blends because the second element cannot be initiated before the first has been produced. All three blends are nevertheless influenced by assimilation: the [m] in [sm] is partially devoiced when the blend is produced at normal rates; the [p] in [sp] is produced without aspiration; and the [w] glide in [sw] may be partially or completely devoiced in rapid speech.

These blends can be evoked simply by associating the [s] with touching one knee and associating a syllable initiated with the second element—say [mæ]—with touching the other knee. Touching the two knees sequentially will then yield [smæ]. A similar strategy can be used to evoke, say, [spa] and [swi]. If the production of the blend is then generalized to other vowel contexts and repeated in a series of syllables (e.g., [swiswiswi]) at a sufficiently rapid rate, the required assimilation (blending) should take place without teaching that the [m] and [w] should be partially devoiced or that the [p] should be unaspirated.

Children taught elementary consonants in association with orthographic symbols often have problems with assimilation because their inclination is to attempt to make every sound an invariant entity. Before orthography is introduced, they are much more at ease in imitating whatever sound is actually yielded by the blend. The [p,t,k] following fricatives in initial blends might as logically be written [b,d,g] since the sounds are unaspirated. This was demonstrated by Lotz, Abramson, Gerstman, Ingemann, and Nemser (1960), who found that when the [s] was edited out of recordings by means of tape cutting, the voiced plosives were heard. Before the common orthographic spellings of clusters are known to them, young children often transcribe such blends as [sb], [sd], and [sg] rather than as [sp], [st], and [sk] (Fink, 1974). Indeed, if a child insists on wrongly producing the syllable [spa] as [spʰa] because he has previously associated sound and orthography, he may be corrected by substituting the [sb] for the [sp] blend. After all, there is no good reason why it is written as [sp] in the first place.

The voicelessness in blends of consonants that have previously been taught as voiced may be encouraged, if necessary, by having the child first whisper the whole syllable; next, voice only the vowel; and finally, practice the syllable in the desired form. Such steps are, however, rarely necessary except when orthography has led to rigidity of production. To avoid such rigidity one should evoke, elicit, repeat, alternate, and have the child use consonants and consonant blends in phonologic speech before referring sound patterns to a written form.

The Single-Organ Sequential Blends
[sk], [sl], [sn], [st], [θr]

These blends are slightly more difficult than those discussed above because production of both elements principally involves adjustments of the tongue. The second element in each of these blends also differs somewhat from its form in vowel contexts. Thus, the [k] and the [t] are both produced without aspiration, more like [g] and [d]. The [l] in the [sl] blend and the [r] in the [θr] blend are both produced partially or completely without voice. The [n] is also partially devoiced.

These blends can be evoked and developed by strategies similar to those described for [sm], [sw], and [sp]. Similar caveats relating to orthography also apply. Because these sounds are mainly lingua-alveolar, their acoustic patterns will be audible only to those children with substantial residual audition above 1,000 Hz. Children with less hearing have to rely only on vision and touch to differentiate among these blends in speech reception and only on orosensory-motor patterns to differentiate among them in speech production.

The Two-Organ Coformulated Blends

[bl], [br], [fl], [fr], [kw] [pl], [pr], [tw]

These blends differ from those treated immediately above in two important ways. First, the elements in each blend may be produced sequentially but are prepared simultaneously. The tongue target for the [l] in the [bl] blend, for example, is reached during the [b] closure so that there can be no intervening sound between the two elements. In effect, one seeks a bilabial release of the syllable initiated with [l]. Second, most of these blends contain some low-frequency energy. Children with hearing that does not extend beyond 1,000 Hz may therefore learn to produce some of these blends through auditory imitation. Those blends learned in this way may then serve as examples of the type of articulation required in blends that cannot be heard.

Coformulation cannot be fostered by the same type of strategy suggested for teaching earlier blends. If one attempts to associate the first sound with lifting one hand and the second with lifting the other, one is likely to obtain an intrusive neutral vowel between the two elements. This is particularly true if one attempts to use the same procedure to teach the blends released with stops (the [bl], [br], [pl], [pr], and [tw]), for the strategy virtually demands plosive release. Hence, it yields /bəlu/ instead of *blue*, /bəraun/ instead of *brown*, and so on. Two quite different strategies are therefore recommended.

The strategy of choice is to have the child repeat a series of syllables in which the second consonant of the blend releases a vowel and the first arrests it: e.g., [lʌb̄,lʌb̄,lʌb̄], [rʌb̄,rʌb̄,rʌb̄]. If the teacher uses the motion of dropping one finger as the signal for the child to start each syllable, insisting that the child does not release the articulatory constriction for the final sound in the previous syllable until the signal is given, then she immediately evokes the series [lʌb̄,blʌb̄,blʌb̄ or [rʌb̄,brʌb̄,brʌb̄], as the case may be. The strategy is applicable to each of the blends in this teaching step—indeed, to all blends. It is, of course, essential that the child be able to produce all stops accurately and that he not confuse them with their plosive counterparts. After the blend has been evoked in this way, it should be elicited as an initial blend releasing all vowels and then generalized to a variety of phonetic and phonologic contexts.

The second strategy of choice is to have the child make the appropriate articulatory constriction for the second consonant in the blend before making the first: i.e., [l] before [b] for [bl], [r] before [f] for [fr], and so on. When the constriction for the second sound has been made, the child can be asked to make the constriction for the first and to release the sounds in synchrony when the teacher signals either by dropping her finger or by providing a pattern for speechreading.

There are several adjacency (coarticulation and assimilation) effects in this group of blends. For example, the plosives that occur as the first sound in the blend are released through the following consonant. There is no invariant acoustic energy in the stop phase of these sounds, and the variant acoustic energy associated with them when they are coarticulated with a consonant is quite different from that associated with them when they are coarticulated with a vowel. In short, they are different sounds with superficially similar articulatory characteristics. Additionally, the [l], [r], and [w] tend to be partially or wholly devoiced when they are released by [f], [k], [p], or [t], and their durations are shorter than when they are produced in a simple CV context. There also tends to be a fricative component in the release energy of the [k] as the tongue moves not to a vowel but to a semivowel target. The teacher who is aware of adjacency effects and listens for them is likely to develop the type of listening behaviors that will allow her to help the child develop normal speech. It is not enough for her to perceive a wide range of allophonic variations categorically as a single sound.

The Single-Organ Coformulated Blends
[dr], [gl], [gr], [kr], [ʃr], [tr]

These are among the most difficult of blends to produce since the tongue must be shaped for or be moving toward two targets simultaneously. For example, the back of the tongue is elevated and the tongue-tip contact modified to facilitate the [r] as the [d] or [t] is formed in [dr] and [tr] blends. The tongue similarly prepares for the [l] and [r] during the closure phase of the [g] in [gl] and [gr] blends. These are also among the most difficult blends for the teacher to describe to the child because the tongue targets are much more complex than they are in simple CV contexts. On this account, the range of strategies which can be used to evoke these blends is limited. One cannot, for example, evoke these blends by description, manipulation, or visual imitation; and since the majority of sounds in this group are differentiated principally through their high-frequency acoustic characteristics, few of them can be learned through audition alone except by children whose hearing extends well above 1,000 Hz.

If the child has mastered the previous types of blends, he will come to those in this step with a clear notion of the blending process and, of course, with the abundance of articulatory skills prerequisite to their satisfactory production. The sounds, although complex, can be evoked by reference to previously acquired speech patterns.

In teaching these blends, the strategy of choice is to have the child release syllables with the second element of the blends and arrest them with the first. Thus, [dr] may be evoked by producing [rɛd̄rɛd̄rɛd̄] in synchrony with the teacher's signal to initiate each syllable. Hand signals or speechread patterns will suffice. If the child is required to maintain closure of the [d̄] until the signal is given, the [drɛ] pattern will quickly emerge. If there is difficulty, the child's success with the same strategy in acquiring the [br] blend should be recalled by having him rehearse this blend immediately prior to his attempting the [dr] blend. Once a series of syllables beginning with [dr] can be elicited, the use of the blend should be generalized to a wide range of phonetic and phonologic contexts. All blends in this step can be evoked by means of this strategy.

Some children can produce these blends if they are first asked to repeat syllables initiated with the second element of the blend and then asked to release those syllables with the first element: e.g., [lilili-gligli-gli]. There is a tendency, however, for the plosive to be released into a vowel if this strategy is adopted, so that [gli] becomes [gəli]. It is best to evoke these blends first by the strategy previously described so that one does not run the risk of encouraging intrusive voicing. The objective should always be to foster error-free learning. It provides much more opportunity for reinforcement. Nothing succeeds like success, particularly if success is both immediate and consistent.

The adjacency effects are marked in this group of blends and are of the same types as in other groups of blends previously described. The variant acoustic energy associated with release of the stop/plosive is modified by the contiguity of the consonants: the [r] tends to be devoiced in [kr] and [ʃr] and its characteristics are substantially changed in [tr]. The duration of all sounds is reduced in blend production, which partly explains why speechreaders tend to confuse blends with single elements.

Complex Word-Initial Blends
[skr], [skw], [spr], [str]

These blends are combinations of various blends discussed above. The [s] portion of the blend can, of course, only be heard by children whose hearing extends to about 3,000 Hz. The [kw] and [pr] portions of the [skw] and [spr] blends, however, contain substantial energy below 1,000 Hz, particularly if produced in the context of back vowels. Auditory imitation is thus facilitated in such contexts.

The most effective strategy for evoking these blends, if they cannot be obtained through auditory-vocal imitation, is to associate the [s] portion of the blend with touching one hand and a syllable released with the remaining portion of the blend with touching the other. The two portions can then be produced sequentially since [s] + [kwi] = [skwi]. These blends lend themselves to this approach since the two elements in the second portion of each blend are coformulated. Development of automaticity in the production of these blends is essential. It can only be fostered by their rehearsal (repetition and alternation) in a variety of phonetic contexts and, following acquisition, by the encouragement of their use in the child's phonology.

Word-Final Blends

Among the word-final blends, those with final [s] and [z] are the most common; they are also perhaps the most important because they are used to indicate inflected forms. Knowledge and use of these sounds as morphemes are impeded if these blends cannot be produced. The [s] morpheme typically follows unvoiced consonants and the [z] morpheme voiced consonants. The [z] morpheme is not invariably produced with vocal cord vibration, and much valuable time can be wasted by the teacher who insists that it should be. Providing that the duration of the fricative is short relative to the duration of the previous voiced consonant, the [z] is adequately signaled. In other words, an [s] or unvoiced [z̥] may be substituted for the [z] following voiced sounds if it is of sufficiently brief duration. Such production is not substandard speech, whereas invariant production of the voiced [z] would be. The unvoiced [z̥] is a perfectly normal pronunciation and is disputed only by those who have developed rigid and simplistic notions about voicing through overmuch attention to the written form.

As with word-initial blending, word-final blending leads to several adjacency effects. Consonants produced in word-final blends may be radically different in their durational, voicing, and transitional characteristics than consonants produced in other contexts. They must therefore be rehearsed carefully to ensure that they can be habitually and correctly coarticulated in word-final position. Consonants in word-final blends, of course, involve either sequential production or coformulation; but since these articulatory behaviors have been mastered through rehearsal of word-initial blends, it is now convenient to focus attention on other features: namely, whether the sounds used to arrest words are stops or continuants. Five categories of word-final blends may thus be delineated. They are treated below in the order in which we have found that hearing-impaired children can most readily acquire them.

Continuant-Continuant Blends

[fs], [lm], [ln], [lz], [mz], [ns], [nz], [ŋ z],
[sḷ], [θ s], [sṇ], [vz]

Continuant consonants are characterized by relatively strong invariant acoustic energy. Techniques such as those used in play audiometry can therefore be employed to test whether the child is able to hear these sounds and, if so, over what distance. One may thus determine empirically whether it is feasible to teach word-final blends constructed with these consonants entirely through hearing or whether other sense modalities should be used as a supplement or as an alternative to audition. Those blends that the child can hear should be taught first. There are two strategies by means of which these blends may be taught if they cannot be directly evoked through imitation. The simpler one is to have the child repeat syllables which are released with the second member of the blend and arrested with the first. Thus, the [fs] pattern will be produced if the series [sʌfsʌfsʌf] is repeated rapidly and the child is then asked to say [ʌfsʌfsʌfs] and finally [ʌfs]. If the blends ending in [z] are evoked in this way, the [s] may be substituted. If the [z] rather than the [z̥] is taught, care must be taken to keep the sound brief; otherwise the blend will always sound stressed in phonologic speech. The [sḷ] as in *whistle* and the [sṇ] as in *listen* cannot be evoked by this strategy because the final sounds are syllabic. They may be evoked by the alternative strategy described below.

Because all blends in this group are continuants and their elements are sequential rather than coformulated, they may be evoked by producing a syllable which ends in the first sound and then adding the second sound initially produced in isolation: e.g., [ɛl] + [m] = [ɛlm]. Blending can be effected by decreasing the interval between the first and second consonants in the blend in successive trials. A tactile prompt such as touching one hand to elicit the syllable and touching the other to elicit the final element may be helpful. Increasing the speed with which the hands are touched will then lead to the reduction of the interval between the sounds and to their blending.

Continuant-Stop Blends

[ft], [ld], [lp], [lt], [mp], [nd], [nt], [ŋk],
[sk], [sp], [vd], [zd]

Word-final blends that are formed with a continuant followed by a stop cannot be evoked by either of the strategies described immediately above. If such strategies are used, then the child will acquire the notion that the final stop is always released—i.e., that it is a plosive. This is not the case. If the words in which these blends occur fall at the end of a sentence, normal speakers may—but do not usually—release the sound with a burst. Only if they occur before words that are initiated with vowels or glides should they be released in sentences. They are, therefore, best learned as blends ending in stops.

The stop arrest of vowels will already have been learned by the child, and his analogous experience with stops in vowel contexts therefore provides the most logical point of departure. It is frequently possible to evoke the stop arrest of continuant consonants by first having the child stop vowels and, thus having established what manner of production is required, simply asking for imitation of the blend. The strategy works best with the stop arrest of fricative blends such as [ft], [sk], [sp], and [vd] in which both manner and place of production change as the blend is produced. Once the manner of consonant arrest is learned in such contexts, it is more readily generalized to others.

An alternative strategy is to teach the blend first in the context of vowels, under which condition it is normally released—e.g., [æftu]. (This sequence occurs in phonologic speech when words such as *have to* are adjacent to each other.) To evoke the stop arrest of the consonant the child should alternate the two syllables [æf, tu] as the teacher prompts him to begin each by dropping a finger. By stopping the prompt when the finger is raised, prior to production of the second syllable, the teacher will evoke [æft]. This procedure should then be repeated until [æft, æft, æft] can be elicited reliably. The blend should then be used to arrest a variety of vowels. Each of the blends in this (continuant-stop) group can, if necessary, be evoked in this way. It is particularly important to alternate syllables containing these blends with syllables initiated with other consonants (e.g., [ænd-mi], [ɪsk̄-fɔ]) so that the stop (without intrusive burst) comes into habitual use before plosives, nasals, fricatives, and affricates.

Stop-Continuant Blends

[bḷ], [bz], [dḷ], [dz], [gḷ], [gz], [kḷ], [ks],

[pḷ], [ps], [tḷ], [tm̩], [tn̩], [ts]

There are two types of word-final blends that may be classed as stop-continuants. In one, the stop is followed by the fricative [s] or [z], usually an inflected form in phonologic speech; and in the other, it is followed by a syllabic consonant. Those in which the stop is followed by a fricative can be evoked by first repeating syllables released with the fricative and arrested with the stop (e.g., [zad̄zad̄zad̄]) and then deriving [adzadzadz] and finally [adz]; or by eliciting [ad] + [z] and then, through reduction of the interval between the two sounds, deriving [adz]. In such blends, the [s] may be substituted for the [z]. Similar strategies were described for evoking continuant-continuant consonant blends. The stop characteristics of the first sound must be emphasized, and no intrusive burst between the stop and fricative should be allowed to occur.

Blends in which syllabic [ḷ], [m̩], or [n̩] follow the stop can simply be taught as two-syllable clusters: e.g., [æb̄] + [ḷ]. If pronounced slowly in normal speech the stop is often released so that the [bl] may, in fact, become [bəl]. Thus the two types of blends should be taught separately.

Stop-Stop Blends

[kt], [pt], [gd], [bd]

If these blends occur at the end of a sentence or prior to words within a sentence that are released with a vowel or glide, the final stop may be released with an unvoiced burst. The [kt] and [gd] blends and the [pt] and [bd] blends are differentiated primarily by the duration of the vowel preceding the blend (longer for voiced than unvoiced) and secondarily by brief vocal cord vibration during the closure phase of the [b] and [g]. In other words, the [d] stops are normally unvoiced in these blends. On this account, if the blends are evoked by the strategy of repeating syllables released with the second stop and arrested by the first (e.g., [tʌk̄tʌk̄tʌk̄], then [ʌk̄tʌk̄tʌkt]), and, finally, [ʌktʰ]), the [t] should be used in all cases. Thus, rather than using [daḡdaḡdaḡ] to evoke the [gd] blend, one should use [taḡtaḡtaḡ].

The blends can also be evoked by alternating syllables such as [ɪktu] [æp̄tu] and then arresting the child's production of the second syllable after the stop has been formed. If this strategy is adopted, then, again, the [t] rather than the [d] should be used to release the second syllable of the [gd] and [bd] blends. The strategy not only yields the appropriate blend but also avoids risk of intrusive voicing.

Complex Word-Final Blends
[fts], [kts], [mbḷz], [ndz], [skt], etc.

There are several dozens of these blends. We define them as complex because they combine many of the word-final blends treated above. Most are the inflected forms of words ending with consonant clusters and, hence, are blends already learned to which either the [s,z] or [t,d] must be added. Inflected forms are best taught by adding the [s] or the [t] rather than the [z] or the [d] to the previously learned blend. The strategies by means of which these blends can be taught may be derived from those described for teaching other blends, above.

At the end of sentences, blends such as [skt], [tn̩d], and [spt] are usually produced with the final sound released. Thus, *asked*, *buttoned*, and *lisped* might be pronounced /æskt^h/, /bʌtn̩d^h/, and /lɪsp̄t^h/. When they precede words released with a vowel or glide, as in *asked where*, *buttoned up*, or *lisped as*, the final sounds in these blends are also released with a burst. However, if they precede other consonants, the last sound is usually omitted entirely. It is, indeed, rare to find a speaker who would release the final [t] in the word *asked* in such a phrase as, *I asked Peter*. Normal speakers who omit the final stop of the complex blend signal the presence of two stops by doubling the duration of the silent period of the closure. The speaker may, indeed, make the articulatory closure for the final [t].

The main reason that certain stops are unreleased in particular contexts in running speech is that their release would impede the natural rhythm of a phrase, i.e., the stress-timing of syllables. Further, all consonants cannot be produced at the same rate. Speed of production depends on the extent of neural innervation of the articulators, their mass, and the range and type of movement demanded by the context of the articulation. Accordingly, most blends cannot be made as fast as single elements. It is for this reason that we specify rates of repetition and alternation of at least three syllables per second for CV or VC sequences but "reasonable rates," i.e., rates the teacher judges to be well within normal limits, for blends.

Medial and Interlexical Blends

Speech is not typically produced with breaks between syllables and words. Hence, sounds are blended both within words as one syllable joins another and between words as they are produced in a phrase. Many of the blends that arise in and between words do not occur in either word-initial or word-final position. The blends [ŋtʃ] in the word *juncture* and [lr] between the words *individual reaction* serve as examples.

The combinations of consonants that can occur in word-initial and word-final blends are restricted to those discussed earlier in this chapter. However, the combinations of consonants that can occur in medial blends (those between syllables in a word) and in interlexical blends (those between words in a phrase) are limited only by the number of consonant sounds and consonant blends in a language. Any consonant can become adjacent to any other, and any word-final blend can be followed by any consonant, except /ʒ/ or /ŋ/, or by any word-initial blend. Fortunately, all possible combinations of sounds are covered by relatively few rules of production. As we cover these rules (below), the reader will see that the majority will already have been learned by the child who has followed the program advocated in this text. They will have been derived through the *alternation of syllables* containing one consonant or another or the alternation of syllables containing blends. In much the same way, the child will have learned, through *repetition of syllables*, that the arresting consonant in one syllable becomes the releasing consonant for the next when the following syllable begins with a vowel and when repetition rates approximate the syllabic rate of normal speech.

We propose that few of the rules underlying the production of word-medial and interlexical blends remain to be taught. Further, few rules remain to be applied if skills acquired at the phonetic level have been consistently encouraged in speech communication. Since medial and interlexical blends occur in and between words, they should be acquired through phonologic level experience rather than phonetic level practice.

Adjacency Rules

Homorganic Blends: Blends which share place and manner of production are termed "homorganic." Thus, if the words *ham mutton, top pile, kiss Susan,* and *big kick* were to appear together in a sentence, homorganic blending would normally occur in that the two adjacent sounds would not usually be differentiated. No disjuncture would be called for unless a break between the sounds were needed to avoid possible ambiguity. Such ambiguity is illustrated in the phrases *he was stabbed* and *he was tabbed*. Disjuncture between homorganic blends may often be avoided by using change in the pitch of voice to signal word boundaries. Word boundaries may also be signaled without disjuncture by lengthening the duration of articulatory constriction. Thus, the general rule is that in homorganic blends the arresting and releasing consonants are made as one.

Sounds Following Stops: If *fricatives* follow stops, intraoral pressure is released through the fricative with the result that sounds resembling affricates are produced. If both the stops and fricatives are lingua-alveolar sounds, the affricates [tʃ] and [dʒ] tend to occur. Fricatives following unvoiced stops tend to be partially or wholly devoiced. If the *nasals* [m] and [n] follow stops, disjuncture occurs. Voicing is not continued throughout closure, even if the voiced stop and the nasal share place of production. When the *glides* [w,j,r,l] follow unvoiced stops, they usually become unvoiced and sounds rather like affricates tend to emerge. When the stops are voiced, disjuncture rather than blending tends to occur and vocal cord vibration may be interrupted unless speech is relatively rapid.

If *affricates* follow stops, the two sounds are produced as separate sounds except when the stops are lingua-alveolar, in which case they are homorganic with the affricates and the two sounds become one. Voicing is, however, interrupted if [tʃ] follows [d̄]. If *plosives* follow stops, the stop and the plosive are produced as separate sounds unless they are homorganic. If *vowels* follow stops, the stop is released as if it were a plosive initiating the subsequent syllable.

Sounds Following Nasals: When *voiced fricatives* follow nasals, breath and voicing are continuous. Voicing is never carried over from the nasals to the unvoiced fricatives. When *unvoiced fricatives* showing place of production follow the nasals, an intrusive unvoiced plosive may be heard as the tongue or lips releases the constriction: e.g., in *comfort* an intrusive /p/ may be heard as the lips part, and in *conservation* a low-intensity, intrusive /t/ may be heard between the first and second syllables so that the second syllable is released with [ts] rather than [s].

When *nasals* follow nasals, voicing and nasality are continued from one sound through the other: e.g., there is no break in voicing or nasality between the words *come now* and *bang my*. Homorganic nasals are produced as one sound. If the *glides* follow nasals, voicing is continuous, but there is no other interaction between the sounds. If *voiced plosives* follow nasals, voicing is continuous. There is a tendency for the nasal consonant to shift place to conform to that of the plosive. Thus, *conform* may often be said as /kəmfɔrm/ rather than /kənfɔrm/ and *open* may be pronounced as /opm̩/ rather than /opən/, particularly in contexts such as *open mine* or *open pop bottles*. When *affricates* follow nasals, voicing is continuous if the affricate is [dʒ], but not if it is [tʃ].

Sounds Following [r,l]: If *voiced fricatives* follow these sounds, voicing is continuous. If unvoiced fricatives follow [l], a low-energy [t]-like sound may be produced as the /l/ is released. This intrusive sound occurs mainly when the following syllable is [ʃi] as in *all she*. If *nasals* or *glides* follow [r,l], voicing is continuous; but if either *voiced* or *unvoiced* *plosives* or *affricates* follow [r,l], voicing is usually interrupted during the closure phase.

Sounds Following the Fricatives: *Unvoiced plosives* following fricatives are produced without aspiration unless they initiate stressed syllables. *Voiced plosives* following voiced fricatives are normally voiced during the closure phase. Following unvoiced fricatives, plosives that are voiced in vowel contexts usually become partially or wholly devoiced. If a *nasal* follows a voiced fricative, voicing is continuous throughout the two sounds. If a nasal follows an unvoiced fricative, it may be partially devoiced. If a *glide* follows a voiced fricative, voicing is continuous. If a glide follows an unvoiced fricative, it is usually produced without voice.

If a *fricative* follows another fricative, turbulence is continuous. If the second fricative is unvoiced, the first—even if usually voiced—may be produced without vocal cord vibration. If both fricatives are voiced, voicing is continuous. Duration is doubled if the sounds are homorganic. If the *affricate* [dʒ] follows a voiced fricative, voicing is usually continuous. If it follows an unvoiced fricative, it tends to be produced as [tʃ]. When the affricate [tʃ] follows any fricative, its duration may be reduced, but its production is otherwise unchanged.

Sounds Following the Affricates: The interactions between affricates and the sounds that follow them are in every way similar to those described for fricatives, above.

Dissimilation and Omission: Dissimilation is the process by which sounds that are awkward to produce in a particular sequence are changed or omitted. The pronunciation of the words *government* and *candidate* as /gʌvɚ mənt/ and /kænədet/ are examples. One should never insist that a hearing-impaired child use pronunciations of words that are more precise than those commonly used by normally speaking adults in his community. If it is usual for people to say *his'n ours* for *his and ours* or *out o' change* for *out of change* and the child speaks similarly, then he has acquired the vernacular. If one's goal is communication, one should be delighted with such speech.

Imitation

The role of imitation in normal speech and language development is not yet well understood (Rees, 1975). It is evident that speech patterns are, in some way, acquired through imitation since regional dialects and languages differ with respect to the range and variety of speech sounds they contain. Apparently words, too, are acquired through some form of imitation; otherwise language would have no common core vocabulary. In the earliest stages, certain language structures are also imitated; but as soon as the normal child has acquired a core vocabulary and has been provided with sufficient examples of how it may be used, he generates his own (often faulty) syntactic patterns. Indeed, generation of language is evidenced by his use of patterns that do not conform to the syntactic rules employed by the adult (see Brown, 1973).

We suggest that the hearing-impaired children should develop speech, as far as possible, in the same way as normally hearing children. One should not teach motor speech and vocabulary through imitation if they can be acquired through exposure to the clear, meaningful models of communication that can be made available in a stimulating environment where verbal interaction is the rule, where the child uses residual hearing to the full, and where he has adults and peers who talk to him and expect him to talk to them. It is when the child cannot develop spoken language skills without specific training that imitation has to be used. If its use is restricted to the development of motor speech and vocabulary, imitation is probably no more harmful than it is necessary. If it is used extensively at phrase and sentence levels, however, it may stifle the child's generation of his own language patterns. A child cannot learn to generate language through imitation. This is a process that must be learned through interactive communication.

Most hearing-impaired children who have to have specific training in speech at the phonetic level can generate their own speech patterns phonologically if the training has been adequate and if the environment is appropriate. Furthermore, one should not have to drill extensively at phrase and sentence levels in order to establish speech rhythm, stress, and intonation patterns if sufficient training at the phonetic level has been provided and if the child is given enough experience of normal speech in everyday life. Of course there are exceptions. Some intervention at the phonologic level may be necessary, particularly with those children who are totally deaf and with those who have developed habitually deviant patterns. However, the phonologic use of speech and the development of spoken language are creative processes with which imitation should not be allowed to interfere.

We shall be pleased if this text leads readers to adopt the notions we have put forward, in a sense, to imitate. We shall be delighted if, beyond this, it leads them—through creative teaching and research—to generate further knowledge that can be of benefit to hearing-impaired children. In short, we invite the reader to regard the application, refinement, and extension of the material presented in this text as an ongoing challenge.

Summary

A systematic approach to the teaching of word-initial and word-final consonant blends is described and strategies for evoking these blends through reference to previously acquired behaviors are suggested. The nature of word-medial and interlexical blends is also examined, and rules for pronunciation of adjacent consonants are specified. It is suggested that imitation of speech sounds and words is probably no more harmful than it is necessary for children who cannot acquire spoken language skills without specific training but that imitation at the phrase and sentence levels might stifle the child's ability to generate his own spoken language structures. Such ability can, we feel, only be developed through interactive communication.

REFERENCES

Brown, R. *A First Language.* Cambridge, Mass.: Harvard University Press, 1973.

Claxton, G. L. Initial consonant groups function as units in word production. *Lang. Speech*, 17, 271–277, 1974.

Denes, P. B. On the statistics of spoken English. *J. Acoust. Soc. Am.*, 35, 892–904, 1963.

Edwards, K. J., & Anderson, J. G. A factor-analytic study of the articulation of selected English consonants. *J. Speech Hear. Res.*, 15, 720–728, 1972.

Fink, R. Orthography and the perception of stops after s. *Lang. Speech*, 17, 152–159, 1974.

Franks, J. R., & Kimble, J. The confusion of English consonant clusters in lipreading. *J. Speech Hear. Res.*, 15, 474–482, 1972.

Gallagher, T. M., & Shriner, T. H. Articulatory inconsistencies in the speech of normal children. *J. Speech Hear. Res.*, 18, 168–175, 1975.

Hawkins, S. Temporal coordination of consonants in the speech of children: Preliminary data. *J. Phonet.*, 1, 181–217, 1973.

Koutstaal, C. W., & Smith, O. W. Relation of effort ratings of CCVCS by congenitally deaf to Greenberg and Jenkins' S scale. *Percept. Mot. Skills*, 34, 643–646, 1972.

Lotz, J., Abramson, A. S., Gerstman, L. J., Ingemann, F., & Nemser, W. J. The perception of English stops by speakers of English, Spanish, Hungarian and Thai: A tape-cutting experiment. *Lang. Speech*, 3, 71–77, 1960.

MacNeilage, P. F. Electromyographic and acoustic study of the production of certain final clusters. *J. Acoust. Soc. Am.*, 35, 461–463, 1963.

Malécot, A. Nasal syllabics in American English. *J. Speech Hear. Res.*, 3, 268–274, 1960.

Nober, E. H. Articulation of the deaf. *Except. Child.*, 33, 611–621, 1967.

O'Shaughnessy, D. Consonant durations in clusters. *IEEE Trans. Acoust., Speech & Signal Processing*, ASSP-22, 282–295, 1974.

Pickett, J. M. Perception of compound consonants. *Lang. Speech*, 1, 288–304, 1958.

Rees, N. S. Imitation and language development: Issues and clinical implications. *J. Speech Hear. Disord.*, 40, 339–350, 1975.

Saporta, S. Frequency of consonant clusters. *Language*, 31, 25–30, 1955.

Schwartz, M. F. Duration of /s/ in s-plosive blends. *J. Acoust. Soc. Am.*, 47, 1143–1144, 1970.

Index of Subjects

A

Accuracy of production
  judgments of, 154
  levels of, 179–180, 294
  and rate, 90–91
Acoustic cues
  on manner, 261–265
  on place, 267–273
  in speech, 27–30
  in vocalization, 196–197
  in voice patterns, 199–200
  on voicing, 277–279
  in vowels, 226–228
Acquisition
  levels of, 86–102
Affricates
  acoustic properties of, 265, 279
  [tʃ, dʒ], targets and subskills, 350–351
  teaching strategies, 351–353
  voiced-voiceless differentiation of, 362
Alternation in syllabic context
  of consonants, 154–155, passim
  to produce consonant blends, 374, 382
  of vowels, 152–153, 238–239, 245
Alveolar consonants, 319–331
Amplification
  checks on the adequacy of, 157
  with conventional hearing aids, 30–31
  with frequency transposing aids, 31–32
  and manner distinctions, 265–266
  and place distinctions, 274–276
  and vocalization, 196–198

and voice control, 190, 207
and voicing distinctions, 279–280
and vowel production, 232–233
and whispering, 205
Analogy as a teaching strategy, 109, 288
Analysis of speech samples, 146, 151–156
Antecedent (prerequisite) skills, 105–107, 113, 287
Articulation tests, 136
Articulators
  coordination of, 13, 124, 184, 252, 287
Articulatory targets, 69–71, 114–129, 173–176
  for alveolar and palatal sounds, 316–339
  for front consonants, 286–315
  for palatal and velar sounds, 339–353
  for vowels and diphthongs, 220–226
Assimilation, 126–129, 370–384
  in adjacent consonants, 382–384
Audiogram, 23–26
Audiological status, 157
Audition
  and distance, 291
  in speech production, 77–78
  in speech reception, 22–32, 50–54, 95–96
  in teaching consonants, 265–266, 273–276, 279, passim
  in teaching vowels, 231–233
Automaticity, 68, 89–91, 122, 148, 180
  and latency, 90

B

Babble, 92–93
Blends, 113, 370–372
  classification of, 126–129
  evaluation of, 155–156
  in medial and interlexical position,
  128–129, 381–382
  rules of adjacency, 128–129, 382–386
  teaching of, 370–386
  in word-final position, 377–381
  in word-initial position, 372–377
Breathing
  common errors related to, 13
  mechanisms of, 185–186
  target behaviors, 186–188, 293
  treatment of deviance in, 211–212,
  363–365

C

Clusters *see* Blends
Coarticulation, 14, 26, 70, 77, 100–101,
109, 113, 118, 249, 258–259, 293, 317–
319, 370–372, 375
Conscious control, 76–77
Consonants
  classification of, 258–260
  common articulatory errors in, 15–
  16
  evaluation of, 153–155
  in isolation, 80
  manner distinctions among, 261–
  267
  order of development for, 120–125
  place distinctions among, 267–277
  production of, 30
  teaching of, 286–362
  treatment of deviance in, 362–369
  voicing distinctions among, 277–
  281
Corollary discharge theory, 68
Correction strategies, 89, 99–101
Criterion measures, 135–137, 179–180,
294
Cued speech, 34–35, 97
Cultural variables, 158–159

D

Demonstration as a teaching strategy,
288

Diadochokinesis, 90, 141–142, 151
Diphthongization of vowels, 14–15,
237
  remedial treatment for, 244–246
Diphthongs, 119, 152, 223–224,
passim
Dissimilation, 384
Distinctive features, 120
Distortion of consonants, 368–369
Duration
  in phonologic level speech, 215–217
  as a voicing cue, 123–124, 277–279
  see also Vocal duration

E

Emotional status, 158
Evaluation, 135–169
  to determine goals, 179–181
  of oral-peripheral structures, 137–
  143
  of phonetic level speech, 147–157
  of phonologic speech, 144–147
Exaggeration
  treatment of, 80, 86–87, 246–248,
  366–367
Exertion, 198
Explanation as a strategy, 287
Exteroception, 77, 80, 228

F

Facial structures, 137–141
Falsetto voice, 37, 204, 214–215
Faults in speech production
  common errors, 12–17
  remediation of, 241–254, 362–369
Feedback, 66–68, 74–83, 93–98
Feedforward, 69–70, passim
Fingerspelling, 1, 56
Formant values, 28–30, 107–108, 220–
  228, passim
  and transitions, 258–281, passim
Frequency of phoneme occurrence,
110–111
Fricatives
  acoustic properties of, 264–265, 271–
  273, 278–279
  [f, v, θ, ð], targets and subskills,
  311–313

teaching strategies, 313–314
[h], targets and subskills, 309–310
teaching strategies, 310–311
[s, z], targets and subskills, 334–336
teaching strategies, 336–339
[ʃ, ʒ], targets and subskills, 331–333
teaching strategies, 333–334
turbulence in, 80, 292
voiced-voiceless differentiation of, 361–362

G

Generalization
across vowel contexts, 107–108, 316–319
of fricatives, 80
of manner, 34
to various phonetic contexts, 286, 354, 370

H

Hard palate, 142
Harmonic structure, 28
Health
state of, and speech, 158
Hearing *see* Audition
Hearing Aids *see* Amplification
Hearing levels and speech, 16–17, 88–89, 94, passim
Hierarchical development, 112–114
Hypernasality *see* Nasalization

I

Imitation, 148–149, 232, 287, 385
Intelligence, 158
Intelligibility
studies of, 11–12
tests of, 137
Intensity *see* Vocal intensity
International Phonetic Alphabet, 6–7
Intervention
guidelines for, 181–182
Intonation patterns
in phonologic speech, 216–217
production of, 190–191
see also Vocal pitch
Intrusive voicing, 16, 107, 125, 296, 299, 367–368

J

Jaw, 33–34, 70, 118, 139–141, 220–222, 246–247, 320, 331–332, 335, 367

K

Kinesthesis, 22, 74–76, 228–230
see also Orosensory patterns

L

Language, 3, 101, 144, 199
see also Phonologic speech
Larynx, 143, 208–209, 213–215, 239, 252
see also Vocal cords
Lipreading *see* Speechreading
Lips, 32–33, 74, 116–117, 122, 127, 139, 220–221
sounds involving the, 295–315, 355–362, 372–376
Liquids
acoustic properties of 264, 270
[l], targets and subskills, 329–331
teaching strategies, 331
[r], targets and subskills, 346–349
teaching strategies, 349–350

M

Manipulation, 36–37, 208, 233–235, 288–289, 341–342, 346
Manner distinctions
acoustic cues relating to, 261–265
choice of strategy in teaching, 292–293
in developing consonants, 286–315
importance of, 122–123, 261
sensory correlates of, 265–267
Manual communication, 5–6
Meaning, 98–99
Mirror
use of, 79, 292
Model of speech acquisition, 173–183
general applicability of, 181–182
Motor codes, 76
Motor-kinesthetic patterns, 228–230
Motor theory of speech reception, 5, 26–27
Multiple faults, 252–254
Multisensory speech reception, 45–62

N

Nasal consonants
acoustic properties of, 262–263, 269
[m], targets and subskills, 176–179,
301–302
teaching strategies, 302–306
[n], targets and subskills, 326–327
teaching strategies, 327–328
[ŋ], targets and subskills, 344–345
teaching strategies, 345–346
Nasalization
faults due to, 14, 176, 248–252, 365
Neural response time, 67
Neutralization
faults due to, 116, 242–243
Nonsegmental aspects, 115–116, 155
Nonspeech behaviors, 106
Nonverbal sounds, 95–96
Normalization of vowels, 28, 222–223
Northampton Charts, 58–59

O

Omission of sounds, 368–369
Operant conditioning, 81, passim
Oral anesthesia, 75–76
Oral-peripheral examination, 137–143
Oral stereognosis, 75
Order of teaching
history relating to, 107–110
and normal development, 111–114
and phoneme frequency, 110–111
rationale for, 115–130
structure in, 105–107
traditional approach to, 107–110
in vowel development, 239
Order of testing, 153
Orosensory patterns, 74–75, 86, 118,
228–230
Orthography, 56–58, 373
see also Writing

P

Palate, 74, 142
sounds involving the, 328–329, 331–
333, 350–351
Pharynx, 77, 212–213, 248–249, 301
Phonation, 13
see also Vocalization, Voice, Voiced-
voiceless distinction, etc.
Phonetic level development, 86–92,
173, 239, passim
evaluation of, 147–157
Phonetic-to-phonologic transfer, 88–
89, 95, 148, 240
Phonologic level development, 87, 98–
99, 173, 319
derivation of meaning from speech,
97–99
evaluation of, 144–147
mechanisms underlying, 87–88
in relation to model of acquisition,
173–176
as a systematic process, 319
voice patterns in, 215–217
Pitch see Vocal (voice) pitch
Place distinctions
acoustic cues relating to, 267–273
in developing consonants, 316–353
importance of, 123
sensory correlates of, 273–277
Planning teaching procedures, 156,
180–181, 287
Plosives
acoustic properties of, 261–262, 267–
268, 277–278
[b, p], targets and subskills, 295–296
teaching strategies, 296–298
[d, t], targets and subskills, 319–321
teaching strategies, 321–323
[g, k], targets and subskills, 339–340
teaching strategies, 340–342
voiced-voiceless differentiation of,
355–358
Prerequisite behaviors, 105–106, 113,
287
Prolongation, 243–244, 366–367
Prompting techniques, 289
see also Visual cue systems
Proprioception, 74, 77, 86, 91, 93–94,
228

R

Rate
of alternation, 152, 154–155, 237–
238, 243–244, 295, 381
diadochokinetic, 90, 141–142, 151

and diphthongization, 244–245
and exaggeration, 246
of repetition, 154, 294, 319, 381
typical of deaf speakers, 13
Reaction time, 67–68
Remedial treatment
of deviant consonants, 362–369
of deviant voice patterns, 211–215
of deviant vowels, 241–254
Repetition in syllabic context
of blends, 372, passim
of consonants, 295, passim
of vowel targets, 237–238
see also Rate
Research
model as framework for, 182
Residual hearing, 16–17, 22–32,
passim
see also Audition, Amplification
Respiration, 13, 185
see also Breathing
Rhythm, 13–14, 124

S

Sampling procedures
phonetic level, 149–151
phonologic level, 145–146
Schwa [ə], 223
Semivowels
acoustic properties of, 263–264, 269–
270
[j], targets and subskills, 328
teaching strategies, 329
unvoiced allophones of, 360
[w, ʍ], targets and subskills,
306–307
teaching strategies, 307–309
Sense modalities
in speech production, 74–83
in speech reception, 22–40
Sensory salience
of consonants, 122, passim
Signs
and speech, 60–62
Social conditioning, 198–199
Soft palate, 142
Spectrograms, 28–30, 116–117, 220–
221, 226–227, 252–254

Speech
acquisition, stages of, 112–114, 173–
179
and communication, 101–102
drills, 92–93
in early infancy, 91
importance of, 1
intelligibility, studies of, 11–12
and memory, 5, 54
physical requirements for, 137–139
prevailing standards of, 6–9
readiness, 114
teaching model, 173–183
Speechreading
of consonants, 33–34
and listening, 50–51, 204
of manner cues, 266
of place cues, 276
skills involved in, 35
and speech awareness, 96–98
of suprasegmental features, 32
in teaching vowels, 235–236
and touch, 52–53
and visual capacity, 157–158
and visual problems, 32
of voicing cues, 280
of vowels, 32–33
Stops
acoustic properties of, 262, 268–269,
278
as distinct from plosives, 120–122,
262, 296
[k̄, ḡ], targets and subskills, 342–343
teaching strategies, 343
[p̄, b̄], targets and subskills, 298–
299
teaching strategies, 299–301
[t̄, d̄], targets and subskills, 323–324
teaching strategies, 325–326
voiced-voiceless differentiation of,
358–359
Substitution
of consonants, 368–369
of vowels, 241
Suprasegmental aspects, 28, passim
see also Nonsegmental aspects
Syllables as minimal units, 26–27, 70,
109, 122, 317–319

Symbolization systems, 54–60

T

Tactile cues
  and speech awareness, 96
  in speech production, 74–77
  in speech reception, 36–39, 45–49,
    51–54
  in teaching consonants, 266–267,
    277, 280, passim
  in teaching vowels, 233–235
Tadoma method, 36–37
Tape recording samples, 145–146
Targets
  see Articulatory targets
Teachers' skills, 8–9, 135, 181
Teaching speech in words, 91–92
Teeth, 139–141
  role of, in sibilants, 332, 334–335
Tense-lax distinction in vowels, 222
Tension
  problems due to, 365–366
Tongue, 70, 118, 127, 141, 220–222,
  224–226, 236–238, 316–317, 367, 372
Total communication, 6, 60–62
Touch
  see Tactile cues

V

Velar targets
  and coarticulation, 70
  and feedback, 77
  and hypernasality, 248–252, 365
  for nasal consonants, 301–302, 326,
    344
  for vowels, 248–249
Velopharyngeal function, 248–252
Verbal instructions, 288
Visible speech, 59
Visual aids, 79–83
Visual cue systems, 34–35, 96–98
Visual feedback, 79–81, 292
Visual reinforcement, 81–83
Vocal abuse, 213
Vocal cords, 191–192, 198, 211–215
Vocal duration, 115
  evaluation of, 151
  subskills, 200–201

teaching strategies, 201–203
Vocal intensity, 115
  evaluation of, 151–152
  subskills, 203–204
  teaching strategies, 204–206
Vocal (voice) pitch, 81, 115
  context dependent, 252
  evaluation of, 152
  mechanisms underlying, 189–190
  and obtaining chest register, 213
  subskills and teaching strategies,
    206–211
Vocal play, 287
Vocal tract
  differential shaping of, 231–236
  maintaining configuration of, 236–
    237
  organs comprising, 220–221
Vocalization, 111, 114–115, 195–199
  acoustic properties of, 200
  on demand, 199
  in infants, 111–112, 114–116
  target behaviors, 196
  teaching strategies, 197–199
Voice onset time, 124–125, 192, 277–
  279, 355, passim
Voice target behaviors, 192–193
Voiced-voiceless distinction, 123–125,
  277–280, 354–362
Voicing, mechanisms of, 188–189
Vowel sounds
  acoustic properties of, 226–228
  common defects in, 14–15
  evaluation of, 152–153
  and formant values, 28–30, 107–108,
    220–228, passim
  formation of, 28–30
  order of teaching, 116–120
  production of, 28, 220–223
  subskills relating to, 230
  target behaviors, 223–224
  teaching strategies, 231–240
  visual correlates of, 228–229

W

Whispering, 204, 205, 233, passim
Writing, 56–57, 143
  see also Orthography

Index of Authors

A

Abbs, J.H.	25, 77
Abercrombie, D.	3, 109, 126, 215
Abramson, A.S.	123, 124, 278, 373
Abravanel, E.	53
Adams, M.	288
Adams, R.E.	80
Adamson, J.E.	141
Ainsworth, S.	149
Ainsworth, W.A.	268, 270
Alcorn, K.	36
Alcorn, S.	36
Algefors, E.	290
Ambler, S.	278
Anderson, F.	191, 207
Anderson, J.G.	372
Andrésen, B.S.	122, 268
Angelocci, A.A.	12, 14, 15, 223
Annett, J.	66
Ansberry, M.	140
Archambault, P.	80
Arndt, W.B.	141, 154
Arnold, T.	107
Arrowsmith, J.P.	36, 75
Ashbell, T.S.	141
Aston, C.H.	51, 280
Avondino, J.	92

B

Baer, D.M.	115, 148, 202
Bankson, N.W.	140
Barber, C.G.	33, 108
Barney, H.L.	224
Barnwell, T.P.	216
Barrett, R.G.	136
Beiter, R.C.	262
Bell, A.G.	13, 17, 59, 77, 79, 116
Bell, A.M.	187
Bell-Berti, F.	222

Bellefleur, P.A.	31
Bellerose, B.	149
Bender, R.E.	2
Bennett, C.W.	33, 36, 51, 82, 234, 280
Berg, F.S.	8
Berger, K.W.	30, 32, 33
Berko, J.	145
Dever, T.G.	216
Binnie, C.A.	51
Birtles, G.J.	51
Bishop, M.E.	75, 247
Bjork, L.	67, 263
Bjuggren, G.	136
Black, J.W.	12, 13
Blasdell, R.	217
Blomquist, B.L.	90
Blott, J.P.	136
Blumstein, S.E.	25
Boberg, G.	290
Bobrow, D.G.	53
Bolinger, D.L.	216
Bonet, J.P.	56, 236
Boomer, D.S.	69
Boone, D.R.	189
Boothroyd, A.	14, 23, 25, 39, 51, 52, 80
Borden, G.J.	234
Borst, J.M.	264
Brackbill, Y.	199
Bradshaw, J.L.	78
Brannon, J.	11, 14, 81
Braverman, J.H.	12
Brebner, J.	53
Brehm, F.E.	116
Bright, M.	13
Broad, D.J.	268
Broadbent, D.E.	28, 53, 222
Brown, R.	385
Brown, W.S. Jr.	321
Brutten, M.	53

Buck, M.   92, 149
Buell, E.M.   92
Buffardi, L.   53
Burroughs, G.E.R.   110
Butterworth, B.   69
Byrne, M.C.   140

C

Callow, M.   278
Calvert, D.R.   13, 17
Carhart, R.   9, 52
Carney, P.J.   70, 249
Carlin, T.W.   189
Carr, A.   140
Carr, J.   91, 111, 114, 186
Carrell, J.   226
Carter, E.T.   92, 149
Castle, D.   56
Cawkwell, S.   25
Chen, H.P.   111, 112
Chen, M.   124
Chistovich, L.A.   67
Chomsky, N.   120
Chovan, W.I.   58
Christiansen, R.L.   77, 251
Christmas, J.J.   296
Ciocco, A.   17
Clarke, B.R.   14, 34, 35
Clarke School for the Deaf   58, 137
Claxton, G.L.   126, 370
Cole, R.A.   260, 271
Coleman, R.O.   248
Colton, R.H.   248
Compton, A.J.   88
Comroe, J.H. Jr.   185
Conkey, H.   149
Connery, J.M.   190
Connor, L.E.   17
Conrad, R.   58
Constam, A.   236
Cooker, H.S.   248
Cooper, F.S.   15, 26, 30, 67, 81,
                                   122, 226, 260, 262,
                                   264, 267, 268, 269
Cooper, W.E.   25
Corbett, L.S.   268
Cornett, R.O.   34, 97
Cox, B.P.   268, 280

Cramer, K.D.   39
Crawford, G.H.   207
Crawford, H.H.   141

D

Dale, D.M.C.   9, 17
Dalston, R.M.   270
Daniel, B.   67
Daniel, Z.   269
Daniloff, R.G.   22, 70, 75, 249, 287, 288
Darley, F.L.   11, 136, 138
Davis, H.   17
Day, R.S.   294
DeLand, F.   9
Delattre, P.   30, 122, 226, 262,
                                   263, 264, 267, 268, 279
de l'Epée, C.M.   1, 36, 116
Denes, P.B.   111, 123, 261, 279, 370
DiCarlo, L.M.   2, 78, 101, 114
Dickey, S.   136
DiSimoni, F.G.   149, 216
Dixon, R.F.   14
Dodd, B.J.   82
Doehring, D.G.   51, 233
Dorman, M.F.   124
Doudna, M.   116
Downs, M.P.   157
Draper, M.H.   185
Dudley, H.   113
Dyer, H.L.   92
Dytell, R.S.   37

E

Eccleston, M.M.   92
Edwards, K.J.   372
Eimas, P.   25
Elbert, M.   77, 250, 350
Elliott, L.L.   23, 68
Englemann, S.   52
Erber, N.P.   25, 33, 39, 50, 51
Evarts, E.V.   67, 68
Ewanowski, S.J.   74
Ewing, A.W.G.   17, 91, 97, 101,
                                        114, 136, 236
Ewing, E.C.   17, 91, 97, 101,
                                        114, 136, 236
Ewing, I.R.   34, 50

F

Fairbanks, G.	66, 123, 124, 265, 294
Fant, G.	27, 80, 120, 260, 262, 264, 272
Farman, J.J.	136, 137
Farrar, A.	114
Fellendorf, G.W.	12
Fertig, R.H.	268
Fillmore, C.J.	261, 268
Fink, R.	373
Fisher, C.G.	33
Fisher, H.B.	136
Fisher-Jorgensen, E.	268
FitzSimons, R.	158
Fletcher, H.	264
Fletcher, S.G.	8
Fodor, J.A.	216
Foust, K.O.	24
Franks, J.R.	371
Franzén, O.	15, 94
Freeman, F.	124
Frisina, D.R.	12
Fristoe, M.	136
Fritzell, B.	77
Fromkin, V.A.	69, 126
Fry, D.B.	16, 57, 86, 88, 204
Fucci, D.	141
Fujimura, O.	262

G

Galanter, E.	68
Gallagher, T.M.	153, 370
Gammon, S.A.	22, 75
Garner, W.R.	26
Garrett, M.S.	57
Gates, A.	78
Gault, R.H.	39, 52
Gay, T.	108, 117, 224, 262, 263, 267
Geldard, F.A.	22
Gelder, L. van	249
Gengel, R.W.	24
Gerankina, A.G.	56
Gerber, A.	286
Gerstman, L.J.	30, 122, 216, 226, 262, 264, 265, 267, 373
Gerweck, S.	158
Gewirtz, J.L.	198
Gibson, E.J.	88
Gibson, J.J.	27, 75, 87

Girardeau, F.L.	136
Glaser, R.	135
Goda, S.	12
Goff, G.D.	37, 94
Goldman, M.D.	186
Goldman, R.	136
Goldman-Eisler, F.	69
Goldstein, M.A.	17, 37, 92
Goodenough, C.	216
Gordon, B.	159
Goss, R.N.	159
Gottsleben, R.	145
Gray, G.W.	191, 198
Green, D.S.	13, 189, 191
Green, F.	36, 116
Greene, D.	187
Greene, M.C.L.	142, 143, 189, 217
Griffiths, C.	16
Grimm, W.A.	123
Grossman, R.C.	74
Gruver, M.H.	37
Guilford, J.P.	146
Guttman, N.	31

H

Haggard, M.P.	69, 126, 278
Hall, E.T.	37
Halle, M.	120, 122, 261, 264, 268, 272, 278
Hamilton, P.	53
Hamlet, S.L.	69, 71
Hampton, J.	288
Handel, S.	53
Hanson, R.J.	261
Hardick, E.J.	32
Hardy, W.G.	68
Harms, R.T.	128
Harris, F.R.	136
Harris, K.S.	33, 70, 76, 116, 117, 122, 261, 267, 271, 272
Hart, B.O.	57
Harvold, E.P.	140
Hattis, B.F.	74
Hawkins, S.	113, 371
Haycock, G.S.	9, 17, 36, 76, 79, 107, 108, 136, 138, 187, 207
Hecker, M.H.	269
Heffner, R.M.S.	126

Heider, F.   33
Heider, G.M.   33
Heidinger, V.A.   9, 12, 14, 16
Heinz, J.M.   271
Heise, G.A.   25
Henderson, J.M.   187
Herriman, E.   268
Hirsh, I.J.   26
Hixon, T.J.   186, 188, 229, 264
Hodgson, K.W.   2
Hoffman, H.S.   267, 268
Holbrook, A.   14, 207, 223
Holder, W.   92
Hood, R.B.   12, 14, 189, 191
Hoops, R.A.   189
Horton, C.E.   141
Houde, R.A.   317
House, A.S.   27, 29, 37, 75, 123, 124,
               226, 262, 265, 268, 269, 294
Howarth, J.N.   9, 12, 14
Hudgins, C.V.   12, 13, 14, 15, 16,
                     17, 107, 114, 187, 188
Huffman, E.   141
Hughes, G.W.   122, 261, 264, 272
Hughson, W.   17
Huizing, H.C.   16
Huntington, D.A.   33
Hutchinson, J.M.   75, 293
Hutton, C.   50

I

Ingemann, F.   373
Irion, P.E.   32
Irvin, B.E.   280
Irwin, J.   78
Irwin, O.C.   111, 112

J

Jackson, P.L.   51
Jakobovits, L.A.   159
Jakobson, R.   120
Jassem, W.   260, 272
Jeffers, J.   233
Jensen, P.   217
Johansson, B.   31
John, J.E.J.   9, 12, 14
John, V.P.   159
Johnson, A.   154

Johnson, D.   269
Johnson, S.   247
Johnson, T.S.   77, 250
Johnson, W.   138, 139
Johnston, M.   136
Joiner, E.   36, 107
Jones, E.P.   57
Judson, L.S.V.   190

K

Kagami, R.   52
Kaplan, E.L.   112, 216
Kaplan, G.   112
Katz, J.   25, 31
Keele, S.W.   90
Kelly, C.A.   147
Kelsey, C.A.   229
Kent, R.D.   34, 70, 249
Kerridge, P.M.T.   12
Kim, C.W.   22, 75
Kimble, J.   371
Kinsey, A.   92, 186
Kirman, J.H.   39, 235
Kirshner, A.J.   158
Klatt, D.   216
Klopping, H.W.E.   6
Knox, A.W.   77, 250
Koenigsknecht, R.A.   270
Kopp, G.A.   14, 223
Konno, K.   185
Koutstaal, C.W.   370
Kozhevnikov, V.A.   67
Kresheck, J.D.   149
Kreuger, A.L.   141
Kringlebotn, M.   39
Kutz, K.J.   346

L

LaBenz, P.J.   280
LaBerge, D.   90
Lach, R.   91, 198
Ladefoged, P.   26, 28, 67, 185, 222
Lahey, B.B.   136
Lambert, W.E.   159
Lane, H.L.   115
Lane, H.S.   56
Lang, J.K.   279
LaRiviere, C.   268

Larr, A.L. 136
Lashley, K.S. 69
Laver, J.D.M. 69
Lawrence, P.S. 17
Leckie, D. 232
Lee, F.F. 39
Lee, L.L. 145
Leeper, H.A. Jr. 321
Lehiste, I. 216, 252
Lenneberg, E.H. 91, 112, 185
Levine, E.S. 158
Levitt, H. 31, 80, 279
Lewin, L.M. 93
Lewis, M.M. 88
Liberman, A.M. 15, 26, 27, 30, 35,
67, 81, 122, 226, 260,
262, 263, 264, 267, 268
Lichten, W. 25
Lieberman, P. 28, 116, 117, 120,
188, 192, 199, 217, 222
Lindblom, B.E.F. 69, 70, 118, 216, 223
Lindner, G. 13
Ling, A.H. 5, 51, 91, 96, 98, 159, 198
Ling, D. 17, 23, 28, 31, 33, 34, 35,
36, 39, 51, 53, 91, 92, 94, 98, 108,
110, 111, 120, 157, 159, 190, 198,
232, 233, 234, 263, 273, 276, 280
Lintz, L.B. 265
Lisker, L. 122, 123, 124, 270, 278
Locke, J.L. 346
Logemann, J.A. 136
Lotz, J. 373
Love, J.K. 107
Loveless, N.E. 53
Lysaught, G.F. 122, 261

M

MacAulay, B.D. 82
MacDonald, J.D. 136
MacKay, D.G. 69
MacKay, D.M. 68
MacNeilage, P.F. 66, 70, 117, 261, 371
Mager, R.F. 136
Magner, M.E. 56, 93
Malécot, A. 268, 269, 371
Mangan, K.R. 223
Manolson, A. 91
Maretic, H. 31, 108, 120

Markides, A. 8, 9, 12, 15, 16, 237
Martin, E.S. 269, 276
Martin, J.G. 215
Mártony, J. 13, 15, 35
Mase, D.J. 139
Mason, M.K. 13
Massaro, D.W. 27, 67
Massengill, R. 251
Matsuya, T. 248
Matthews, P.B.C. 76, 188
Mattingly, I.G. 69
Mavilya, M.P. 91
McCall, G.N. 251
McCarthy, D. 88
McClean, M. 249
McClumpha, S. 249
McCroskey, R.L. 75
McDonald, E.T. 113, 136, 138, 286
McGettigan, J.F. 58
McGlone, R.E. 189, 321
McNeil, J.D. 294
McNeill, D. 67
McReynolds, L.V. 350
Mead, J. 185, 186
Meadow, K.P. 158
Menyuk, P. 88
Mermelstein, P. 113, 223
Meyer, M.F. 56
Milisen, R.L. 92, 149
Miller, G.A. 25, 68, 123, 263, 267
Miller, J. 101
Millward, R. 90
Mindel, E.D. 1, 5
Minifie, F.D. 229, 264
Miyazaki, T. 248
Moll, K.L. 34, 70, 118, 248, 249
Moller, K.T. 77, 251
Molter, M. 265
Monro, S.J. 58
Monsen, R.B. 13, 265
Montagu, A. 22
Montgomery, A.A. 51, 287
Montgomery, G.W.G. 6, 12
Moray, N. 53
Morley, D.E. 16, 280
Mowrer, D.E. 82, 136
Murai, J.I. 112
Muyskens, J.H. 114

Myklebust, H.R. 35, 53, 83, 158

N

Naish, S.J. 23, 157
Nakata, K. 262, 269
Nakazima, S. 112
Neate, D.M. 39, 52
Negus, V.E. 189
Nemser, W.J. 373
Netsall, R. 67
New, M.C. 34
Nicely, P.E. 123, 263, 267
Nickerson, R.S. 14
Niemoeller, A.F. 89
Nitchie, E.B. 33
Nober, E.H. 11, 15, 16, 25, 371
Noll, J.D. 321
Nooteboom, S.G. 69
Nordmark, J. 94
Norman, D.A. 53
Northcott, W.H. 6
Northern, J.L. 157
Novikoff, D.P. 234
Numbers, F.C. 12, 14, 15, 16, 17
Numbers, M.E. 59, 109, 186
Nye, P.W. 80

O

O'Connor, J.D. 264, 270
Ohala, J.J. 69
Öhman, S.E.G. 113
Oller, D.K. 147
O'Neill, J.J. 32, 50
Osgood, C.E. 69
O'Shaughnessy, D. 371
Otis, W. 269
Owens, E. 23, 264
Owrid, H.L. 145
Oyer, H.J. 32, 116

P

Paget, R. 119
Palmer, B. 199
Path, M. 77, 251
Pendergast, K. 136
Percifield, P. 288
Perkell, J.S. 238
Peters, R.W. 123
Peterson, G.E. 29, 223, 224, 252
Peterson, S.J. 142
Piaget, J. 53, 79
Pick, H.L. 78
Pickett, J.M. 39, 52, 80, 207, 236, 269, 276, 278, 280, 370
Pike, K.L. 215
Pitman, J. 57
Pleasonton, A.K. 75
Pollack, D. 51, 95
Pollack, I. 50
Posner, M.I. 76
Postman, L. 25
Powers, M.H. 23
Presto, M. 217
Pribram, K.H. 68
Proffit, W.R. 321
Pruting, C.A. 149
Ptacek, P.H. 187
Putnam, A.H.B. 75

Q

Quigley, S.P. 12
Quinn, G. 251

R

Radley, J-P.A. 122, 261
Ramey, C.T. 199
Raphael, L.J. 123, 124, 222, 278, 279
Rawlings, C.G. 13, 296
Reddy, D.R. 260
Reeds, J.A. 268
Rees, N.S. 385
Reeves, J.K. 8
Repp, B. 67
Rheingold, H.L. 198
Rhodes, R.C. 268, 280
Ringel, R.L. 74, 75
Risberg, A. 290
Risley, T.R. 115
Rockey, D. 156
Roe, W.C. 296
Rooney, A.G. 217
Rosen, J. 227, 268, 280
Rosenberg, D. 199
Rosenthal, R.D. 279
Rosenstein, J. 37
Rosenzweig, M.R. 25

Rosov, R. 52
Ross, H.W. 198
Rozanska, E.v.D. 213
Russell, L.H. 116

S

Samuels, S.J. 90
Sander, E.K. 187
Sanders, D.A. 5, 34, 95
Saporta, S. 370
Scharf, D.J. 123
Scheib, M.E. 268
Schein, J.D. 8
Schiff, W. 37
Schlesinger, H.S. 158
Schubert, E.D. 264
Schulte, K. 51, 97
Schultz, M.C. 227
Schvey, M.M. 122, 261
Schwartz, A. 199
Schwartz, M.F. 371
Scott, B. 260, 271
Scott, D.A. 92
Scott, E. 296
Scripture, E.W. 13
Scuri, D. 13, 77
Selmar, J. 136
Severeid, L.R. 70, 249
Shaffer, C.M. 93
Shankweiler, D.P. 15, 26, 33, 67, 81, 260
Sharf, D.J. 262, 270
Sheets, B.V. 88
Shelton, R.L. 77, 141, 154, 250
Sheppard, W.C. 115
Sher, A.E. 23
Sherman, D. 139, 265
Sherman, J.A. 148, 202
Ship, N. 91, 198
Shipp, T. 189
Sholes, G.N. 33, 117
Shprintzen, R.J. 251
Shriberg, L.D. 346, 349
Shriner, T.H. 153, 370
Sicard, R.A.C. 57
Siegel, G.M. 78, 149
Siegenthaler, B.M. 268, 280
Silverman, S.R. 17, 56

Singh, K. S. 226
Singh, S. 226, 279
Skinner, B.F. 82, 115
Skolnick, M.L. 251
Slipakoff, E.L. 350
Slis, I.H. 278
Sloane, H.N. 82
Smith, A.D. 262
Smith, C.R. 12, 15, 16, 33
Smith, F. 46, 216
Smith, L.L. 293
Smith, M.W. 149
Smith, O.W. 370
Smith, P.J. 22, 75
Smith, S.B. 269, 279
Snow, K. 149
Socolofsky, G. 149
Soder, A. 136
Soderberg, G.A. 78
Sofin, B. 39, 53
Sonderman, J.C. 251
Sonesson, B. 189
Soron, H.I. 192
Spradlin, J.E. 136
Spriestersbach, D.C. 138, 139
Stark, R.E. 17, 80, 125, 280
Steinberg, J.C. 110, 111
Stetson, R.H. 69
Stevens, K.N. 14, 27, 28, 226, 262, 264, 268, 271
Stewart, R.B. 17, 237
Stockwell, E. 32
Stockwell, R.P. 136
Stone, J. 294
Storm, R.D. 80
Storrs, R.S. 1
Story, A.J. 36, 57, 91, 107, 108
Strevens, P. 272
Studdert-Kennedy, M. 15, 26, 67, 81, 223, 260
Subcommittee on Human Communication and Its Disorders 23
Suchman, R.G. 32
Sumby, W.H. 50
Sundberg, J.E.F. 70, 118
Sussmann, H.M. 25, 261
Suzuki, H. 52

Sykes, J.L.   91

T

Taine, M.   92
Tait, C.A.   264
Takahashi, T.   52
Taylor, H.   136
Telage, K.   141
Templin, M.C.   11, 88, 136
Thomas, W.G.   12
Tiffany, W.R.   226
Toback, C.   12
Tobin, C.   124
Todd, G.A.   199
Turton, L.J.   136
Tyack, D.   145

U

Umeda, N.   265
Upton, H.W.   35
Utley, J.   58

V

Van Praagh, W.   59
Van Riper, C.   78
Van Uden, A.   12
Vegely, C.   66
Vernon, M.   1, 5
Voelker, C.H.   13, 14, 110,
                    111, 137, 189, 191
Vorce, E.   9, 17, 101, 137

W

Wakita, H.   236
Walden, B.E.   120, 261
Waldon, E.F.   17
Walker, N.F.   58
Wallis, J.   56, 57
Walsh, H.   120
Wang, W.S-Y.   261, 268
Ward, P.H.   251
Warren, D.W.   140, 142
Wathen-Dunn, W.   27
Watson, J.   114
Watson, J.S.   199
Watson, T.J.   23

Weaver, A.T.   190
Weber, J.L.   147
Wedenberg, E.   17, 38, 233
Weir, R.   146
Weksel, W.   216
Werth, L.J.   77, 251
West, J.J.   147
West, R.   140
Whetnall, E.   16, 57
White, H.W.   107
Whitteridge, D.   185
Wickelgren, W.A.   58, 69, 120
Wiener, N.   66
Willemain, T.R.   39
Willis, D.   269
Wilson, L.S.   280
Winitz, H.   88, 91, 115, 120,
                  149, 158, 159, 268
Wise, C.M.   191, 198
Witting, E.G.   17
Woldring, S.   39
Wolf, M.M.   115
Wolff, P.   116
Wood, C.C.   294
Woodhouse, R.J.   229
Woodward, H.M.E.   144
Woodward, M.F.   33, 108
Worcester, A.E.   58
Worster-Drought, C.   142
Wright, J.D.   109
Wyke, B.   76

Y

Yale, C.A.   92, 107, 108
Yamaoka, M.   248
Ysseldyke, J.E.   158

Z

Zaliouk, A.   36, 37, 59, 96, 97, 116, 213
Zeiser, M.L.   51
Zilstorff, K.   189
Zink, G.D.   157
Zlatin, M.A.   124
Zola, I.K.   159
Zwitman, D.H.   251